Duke Sla

Duke Slater

Pioneering Black NFL Player and Judge

NEAL ROZENDAAL

Foreword by SHERMAN HOWARD

McFarland & Company, Inc., Publishers
Jefferson, North Carolina, and London

LIBRARY OF CONGRESS CATALOGUING-IN-PUBLICATION DATA

Rozendaal, Neal.
Duke Slater : pioneering black NFL player and judge /
Neal Rozendaal ; foreword by Sherman Howard.
 p.   cm.
Includes bibliographical references and index.

ISBN 978-0-7864-6957-4
softcover : 50# alkaline paper ∞

1. Slater, Duke, 1898–1966.
2. African American football players—Biography.
3. Football players—United States—Biography.
4. African American judges—Illinois—Chicago—Biography.
I. Title.
GV939.S49R69 2012   796.332092—dc23   [B]   2012023082

British Library cataloguing data are available

©2012 Neal Rozendaal. All rights reserved

*No part of this book may be reproduced or transmitted in any form
or by any means, electronic or mechanical, including photocopying
or recording, or by any information storage and retrieval system,
without permission in writing from the publisher.*

On the cover: Iowa tackle Duke Slater, 1919
(Center for Media Production, University of Iowa)

Manufactured in the United States of America

*McFarland & Company, Inc., Publishers
Box 611, Jefferson, North Carolina 28640
www.mcfarlandpub.com*

For my parents, Bill and Norma,
and my family
and to the memory of
Judge Frederick Wayman "Duke" Slater

Table of Contents

Acknowledgments	vi
Foreword — The Gentle Giant, by Sherman Howard	1
Preface	3
Introduction	5
1 — George Slater's Influence (1898–1912)	9
2 — A Football Journey Begins (1912–1913)	13
3 — The Pride of Clinton High (1914–1916)	20
4 — Spanish Flu and a World War (1916–1918)	31
5 — From Unknown to All-American (1919)	42
6 — Overcoming Adversity (1920–1921)	51
7 — A Championship for the Hawkeyes (1921–1922)	60
8 — Coloring the Line (1922–1923)	76
9 — The Greatest Independent (1924–1925)	89
10 — Sweet Home Chicago (1926–1927)	102
11 — Last Man Standing (1928–1929)	115
12 — A Brilliant Finish (1930–1931)	125
13 — Fighting Against Exclusion (1931–1940)	138
14 — From the Field to the Bench (1941–1951)	150
15 — Truly Superior (1951–1959)	158
16 — Death of a Pioneer (1959–1966)	168
17 — A Legend in His Lifetime (1966–1972)	176
18 — Fading from Memory (1973–2012)	184
Appendices	191
A. Records and Point Totals	191
B. The Games	192
C. Coaching Career	194
D. All-Pro Selections	195
E. African Americans in the NFL	196
F. Pre-World War II All-Pro Selections	196
Chapter Notes	198
Bibliography	209
Index	211

Acknowledgments

On a personal level, I would like to thank God for having the opportunity to present this story to you. My parents Bill and Norma, to whom this book is dedicated, have been wonderfully supportive of my dreams. I sincerely could not have wished for better parents—I love you two. To my fiancée, Ashley Ackerley, I don't know how I would have finished this book without your love and enthusiasm. You mean the world to me! I also need to thank my siblings Seth, Jolie, and Jill for their supportiveness of my books and my career. My sincere gratitude is given to Mark Bond, Rob and Annabelle Tanzer, Michael McGinley, Matt Fall, and Andy Ver Woert for their friendship and support. To all my family and friends I failed to mention, you know how much I appreciate you, and I promise I'll list you by name next time.

Professionally, I begin by thanking everyone who helped make this book a reality. I am indebted to Seth Rozendaal and Ashley Ackerley for their research assistance. Thanks to Sherman Howard for his recollections and for providing the foreword. Bill Misiewicz should be applauded for his efforts on Duke Slater's behalf at Clinton High School. Also, many thanks to Kathryn Hodson for helping me navigate the University of Iowa Special Collections and the university's vertical files.

I am indebted to the many, many people who have assisted me in reaching readers. My utmost thanks to Gary Dolphin, Kirk Ferentz, Tom Kakert, Ron Gonder, Frosty Mitchell, Bob Brooks, Mike Hlas (who works at the *Cedar Rapids Gazette* with Marc Morehouse and Scott Dochterman, which seems like a journalistic embarrassment of riches to me), Keith Murphy, Brice Miller, Pat Williams, Chuck Morris and Don Hansen, Tim Lary, Larry Renaud, Scott Nolte, and J.O. Parker, among others. I couldn't reach my audience effectively without you taking the time to honestly evaluate and discuss my books, so I thank you. I want to mention Lyle Hammes and Michael Maxwell, who I have had the privilege of working with in the past. The players, coaches, administrators, and fans of the University of Iowa have been very inspirational to me through the years, and I applaud your devotion and loyalty.

Finally, to anyone reading this right now, no book would exist without the support of you, the reader. For that, you have my sincerest gratitude.

Foreword: The Gentle Giant
by SHERMAN HOWARD

Sherman Howard grew up on the South Side of Chicago in the 1930s. There he met Duke Slater, who helped convince the standout high school football star to attend the University of Iowa. Howard spent one year with the Hawkeyes before transferring to the University of Nevada. He later played five years of professional football, finishing his career with the Cleveland Browns under legendary coach Paul Brown. After his playing days, Sherman Howard returned to Chicago as a high school teacher and football coach, and he remained close friends with Duke Slater for the rest of his life. When Slater passed away in 1966, Howard served as one of his pallbearers. Here are Sherman Howard's recollections of his mentor and friend, Duke Slater.

Integrity, commitment, honesty, dependability—these are all things that Paul Brown used to call the "eternal verities" that separate one man from another. Duke Slater had all those qualities—every one. You immediately noticed something different about him and the way he conducted himself. I can't think of anyone I would say measured up to him, period, as a man.

Even going back to when he was at Iowa, he was the embodiment of manhood. Knute Rockne and all his players at Notre Dame remembered Duke at Iowa. They remembered that he played without a helmet and that picture of him blocking the whole side of the Notre Dame line. When Duke was playing, he was one of the only blacks in college football. To make an All-American team in those days, a black player had to be special.

Duke played ten years in the NFL and withstood all that physical play. A black player couldn't play in those days unless he had superior ability, so he must have been great to play ten years. Duke stayed in there even when they had a ban on blacks in the late 1920s. He was the only one in the league, and every year he'd be right back out there. He was the epitome of the black player in the NFL. You wished every player was like Duke, but they just weren't.

Duke played with some great guys, and all of them said Duke was one of the greatest. Back then, when people mentioned the greatest football players of all time, he was always listed as one of them. Everybody who played in the NFL knew who he was, from George Halas on down. Paul Robeson, Hunk Anderson, Fritz Pollard, Ernie Nevers, Sol Butler—everybody knew Duke and thought he was one of the greatest. I knew some guys who were very, very prejudiced, but when you mentioned Duke Slater, they just wouldn't say anything, because he was such a force at that time as the only black in the league.

The University of Iowa always used Duke as the guy who would talk to the blacks about going to Iowa City, and the way he talked to you was like God telling you where to go. In Iowa, you just had to mention Duke Slater's name and everybody knew who he was. If any of the coaches had a problem in any particular area, especially with blacks, they'd call on Duke. He was the greatest recruiter for blacks they had. Most of those guys that came to Iowa went through Duke.

When I was a youngster, there was an Old Timers Club where great athletes in the Chicago area would mentor young kids. Every one of them — Jesse Owens, Ralph Metcalfe, everybody — knew and respected Judge Slater. They always referred to Duke as an example of someone to look up to, and he carried himself that way. If you had a problem, you'd go to Judge Slater, and the way he'd talk to you was like a father to his child. He spoke to people in his courtroom the same way. Whenever a criminal went before Judge Slater, he had a parental tone of voice while telling them what they'd done. He might say, "I guess I got to give you twenty years, son." But he'd talk to them like a father.

In our Chicago community, we looked to him for everything, really. If you asked him to do something, he was always willing and would do it with such finesse and greatness. It seemed to come naturally to him. He was a guy where you didn't have to worry about whether he was telling you the truth or not. Without rambunctiousness or boasting, Duke said what he believed in, and that was it. He was like a minister without being one.

One time, an alderman refused to give me a job, so I called Duke and told him what happened. He said, "That's all right; I'll take care of it. Go back over there on Monday." That's all he said. When I went back, the alderman said, "I didn't know you knew Duke! Why didn't you tell me you know Duke Slater?" After that, I never had any trouble with anybody. Whenever I'd look for a job, people would say, "He's a good friend of Duke Slater's; don't worry about him." That's the way it was in Chicago. When you tell people about it today, they don't believe somebody like that existed. But he did.

I remember another time we needed a speaker for a school banquet. Duke said, "Well, how about Whizzer White? I'll call him." And whenever Duke would call, people would say, "Whatever you want, Duke." Sure enough, Whizzer White was our speaker, and he was a Supreme Court justice at the time. We just couldn't get over that. When you talked to Duke, he knew everybody and it seemed like everybody knew him.

What was truly amazing about Duke was his personality. Duke was very mild in conversation, a quiet guy who never boasted. You couldn't believe how he was so humble and down-to-earth. When people mentioned his accolades to him, he would just smile and say, "I was just doing my best." That's the way he was until the day he died. I saw him right before he passed, and he was still upbeat. I thought by the way he talked to me he was doing all right. Nobody even knew he was dying. He didn't want us to do anything special; he was just grateful for everything.

There will never be another one like him, to tell you the truth. He's one of those unique personalities you come across in life. I call him "the gentle giant," and he was a giant in everything, really — conduct, reliability, compassion for others, dependability. Duke did a tremendous job while here on Earth. We all used to quote Matthew 25:23 and say God's going to say, "Well done, good and faithful servant." All in all, someone would need to be very great to even reach up to Duke Slater. He was just an ideal person.

Preface

As a student at the University of Iowa, I must have passed Slater Hall hundreds of times and never given it much thought. When you live on campus, walking past Slater is the fastest way to get to Melrose Avenue, the road in front of the stadium which turns into the state's biggest street party on Iowa football game days. I was raised as a Hawkeye fan pretty much by default. I grew up in Iowa and loved sports, and in a state with no major professional sports teams, nothing compares to the tradition, success, and fan support of the Iowa Hawkeyes. I've been an Iowa fan as long as I can remember, and I was thrilled to earn my degree from there as well.

Years later, after I learned more about Duke Slater I came to the opinion that in terms of contributions to the athletic program on the field and off, Slater was the greatest Hawkeye football player ever. That's purely my opinion, and it's met with shock, and sometimes even outrage, by fellow Hawkeye fans. Many Iowans have been indoctrinated into the belief that no Iowa football player has or ever will surpass 1939 Heisman Trophy winner Nile Kinnick, and they assume any statement otherwise must be uninformed. On the contrary, I have the utmost respect for Kinnick and everything he stood for as an athlete and a man. But in the discussion of the greatest Hawkeye football player of all time, far too many people pass over Duke Slater with the same nonchalance with which I breezed past Slater Hall for so many years.

It's time to take a closer look. Kinnick is well-remembered by Hawkeye fans. Four nonfiction books have been written about him and the 1939 Ironmen. In addition, there are multiple magazine articles, television specials, two fictional accounts, and a screenplay about Nile's life. Yet for all the retrospection Nile Kinnick has inspired, no one has ever once told the full story of Duke Slater's life. I hope by reading this book, people will have a better understanding of why I regard Slater as the greatest Hawkeye football player who ever lived. The more I learned about Slater, the more simultaneously fascinated I became at his incredible accomplishments and outraged I found myself over how completely neglected he is today.

I was even more shocked at his achievements in pro football and the blatant disregard for those achievements. Duke Slater was the first black lineman in NFL history, and he was the greatest African American player in the league before World War II. But more than that, he was one of the best pro football players of the 1920s—of any race. Slater was a perennial all-pro and feared but respected by opponents. Amazingly, he accomplished all this despite being the only black player in the entire NFL for most of the late 1920s.

Yet Duke's remarkable role in sports history seems to have been glossed over and forgotten. Over the past decade, there has been a resurgence of interest in early African Americans of pro football, culminating with the election of Fritz Pollard to the Pro Football Hall of Fame in 2005. In much the same way Slater has been overshadowed in Iowa City by Kinnick, he has been overlooked in pro football history in favor of Pollard. As with Kinnick, I mean Pollard no ill will. I have a tremendous appreciation for his accomplishments, and his induction to Canton was well-deserved. But Duke Slater's career was longer, more decorated, and frankly, more Hall of Fame worthy than Pollard's, and I write that with absolutely no disrespect intended toward Pollard.

I spent nearly five years researching Slater in the hope of compiling his definitive biography, and numerous sources were consulted in writing this book. *Slater of Iowa*, by James Peterson, has the most complete biography of Duke's early years. The *Clinton Herald* and *Clinton Daily Advertiser* provided many of the Clinton High School game accounts. Duke Slater's years with the Hawkeyes were covered thoroughly by the *Iowa City Press-Citizen*, the *Cedar Rapids Gazette*, the *Mason City Globe-Gazette*, the *Waterloo Courier* and *Waterloo Times-Tribune*, and the *Daily Iowan*, among others. The University of Iowa Special Collections and the university's vertical files were also very helpful in finding information about Slater's time in Iowa City.

The *Rock Island Argus* and the *Davenport Democrat & Leader* were the principal sources of information on Duke's career with the Independents. *When Football Was Football*, by Joe Ziemba, is a masterwork that outlines the history of the Chicago Cardinals organization wonderfully. The *Chicago Tribune* and the *Chicago Herald-Examiner* covered Slater's years with the Chicago Cardinals nicely as well. The Pro Football Researchers Association has tremendous, invaluable details about the early era of professional football and should be commended for the great work they do keeping pro football history alive. The *Chicago Defender* provided in-depth information on Duke Slater's professional career after football that was indispensable when trying to give a well-rounded account of his life. I would also like to thank everyone who graciously shared their thoughts and memories of Duke Slater, including Sherman Howard, Gary Herrity, and Bob Brooks.

I have been inspired by the great Hawkeye material I've read over the years, much of it written by talented storytellers like Al Grady, Tait Cummins, George Wine, Mike Chapman, Gus Schrader, Buck Turnbull, Bert McGrane, Ron Maly, Mike Finn, and Maury White. I can only hope that this work has as much impact on others as their work has had on me. Many of the photos in this book were kindly provided courtesy of the personal collections of Gary Herrity and Matt Fall. Every effort has been made by the author to cite and/or contact copyright holders for the use of copyrighted material; the author extends sincere apologies for any inadvertent omissions, which are the sole responsibility of the author.

One editorial note — newspaper articles and sources from his time often refer to Slater as a Negro, colored, or using various other labels. Those references remain intact as a matter of historical accuracy. When I refer to him in the current context, I will use the modern adjectives black and African American interchangeably.

There is still much, much work to be done to restore Slater's legacy to its rightful place in sports history. If you would like to help, please visit www.dukeslater.com for more information on Duke Slater and projects we are undertaking on his behalf. As always, I thank you sincerely for taking the time to read my book; that's something I never take for granted. I hope you enjoy this true story of an exemplary man. Oh, and go Hawks!

Introduction

Duke Slater is the most underrated athlete of the twentieth century. On the surface, that seems like a bold statement. But when all of Slater's accomplishments and the esteem in which he was held during his life are considered, it seems impossible to believe he has been all but forgotten today, banished to the history books. His life story reads like the script of a Hollywood movie, something too unbelievable to be non-fiction. As Sherman Howard rightly observed in the foreword, when you tell people about Slater today, they can't even believe someone like him existed. It is the forgotten story of a true legend, a man who made an incredible, indelible impact on football before quietly fading into history.

Born in December 1898, Fred "Duke" Slater was instantly attracted to the sport of football while playing pickup games in the rough streets of the South Side of Chicago. His father, George, was an articulate, college-educated, opinionated African American minister. Like most African American families around the turn of the twentieth century, however, the Slaters were extremely poor. This fact was illustrated in 1913, when Duke first went out for organized football at Clinton High School in eastern Iowa. At that time, students had to pay for their own helmets and shoes. George couldn't afford both, so Duke played his entire high school career and most of his college career without a helmet.

Slater enrolled at the University of Iowa in 1916, where he achieved his greatest fame as a tackle for the Hawkeye football team from 1918 to 1921. Duke was a three-time all–Big Ten selection and a two-time All-American in football at Iowa. He was a second team All-American as a sophomore in 1919, becoming Iowa's first black All-American and just the sixth black All-American ever in college football. Two years later, he notched his name in Hawkeye lore as a senior by helping the football team to one of the greatest seasons in school history. Slater's line play propelled the 1921 Hawkeyes to an undefeated season, their first outright Big Ten title, and in the eyes of many, a mythical national championship.

If you wanted to construct the perfect 1920s football lineman, Duke Slater would have been the end result. He was a giant of a man, weighing over 200 pounds. That doesn't seem heavy by modern standards, but he was one of the largest, most massive players of his time. Slater was quite literally regarded as "the man mountain of football."[1] Moreover, that size and weight was wrapped up in a chiseled frame, forged by years of manual labor and a relentless work ethic. Slater was strong, not pudgy, and one of the most powerful men to ever play football.[2] George Trevor, sports expert of the *New York Sun*, claimed that "Iowa's ebony giant [possessed] the sinuous strength of a python" when he named Slater one of the greatest tackles in football history.[3]

Everything about Duke was big — his feet, his hands, and his wingspan. Duke had a good foundation on his big feet, and it was almost impossible to topple him.[4] Ball carriers would underestimate Slater's tremendous reach and pay dearly when his strong hands latched onto them and threw them helplessly to the ground. "He had phenomenal brawn, with such strength in his hands that he tossed blockers aside like toys," former Big Ten commissioner Tug Wilson wrote. "When his hands fastened on a ball carrier, there was no way out and nowhere to go."[5]

As if these advantages weren't enough, Duke was also extremely fast for his size. Slater could run down the field when his team punted the ball and be on top of the punt returner with the speed of a typical end. Even when the opposition ran a running play away from Slater's side of the field, he was often fast enough to chase the ball carrier down from behind and drag him to the ground for a loss. Slater's tackling was one of the dreaded terrors for opposing ball carriers when Duke was on the field.[6]

Physically, Duke Slater had every gift a great lineman might need. But what separated him from so many of his contemporaries was his mind. Duke was extremely intelligent and clever on the football field. He would overpower opponents on the line with sheer strength and "use that strength to intelligent advantage," as Coach Knute Rockne once said.[7] Coach Howard Jones declared that Slater was "simply never out of position, never fooled by a fake, [and] never mistaken on where the opposing ball carrier was going."[8] Duke's ability to break down a play and get into the proper position every time contributed to his success, and his mental abilities perfectly complimented his physical ones.

All of these skills helped Duke Slater become a gridiron legend and one of the first African American football stars in history.[9] Slater was dynamite on offense and could hold up one side of the line on defense. His exceptional leg drive and quick-charging style were unstoppable, and he played with the power and the tenaciousness of a tiger.[10] Prominent rival coaches helplessly assigned two or three men on the line to the task of neutralizing Duke, but he merely shucked them off with his brute strength.[11]

In 1921, Duke Slater earned first team All-American honors from several sources, 25 years before Jackie Robinson broke the color barrier in Major League Baseball. When the College Football Hall of Fame opened in 1951, they elected 54 members into their inaugural class. Duke was the only African American among the inductees. He also had a less-publicized track career for the Hawkeyes, placing nationally in the hammer throw and discus events at the 1921 NCAA Track and Field Championships.

The fame he gained through his exploits at Iowa enabled him to sign with the Rock Island Independents in 1922 and become the first African American lineman in NFL history. He played five seasons with Rock Island, earning all-pro honors in his final four seasons. He was extremely durable, never missing a single game due to injury over his long career and typically playing all sixty minutes of each contest. In 1926, the Independents disbanded, and Slater's contract was quickly scooped up by the Chicago Cardinals. By signing with the Chicago (now Arizona) Cardinals, Slater became the first black player to play for a current NFL franchise. Joining the Cardinals meant a return to the South Side of Chicago and the neighborhood where Slater was raised as a young boy.

By the late 1920s, some influential NFL owners were attempting to institute a color ban and exclude black athletes from professional football in the same way they were excluded from professional baseball. Ownership was able to effectively chase African Americans out of the league entirely—with the exception of Slater. In 1927 and 1929, Duke Slater was the only black player in the National Football League, and he was an all-pro selection both seasons. His outstanding play single-handedly kept the door open for a select few African Americans to continue to join the NFL and delayed a color ban from taking effect in professional football for seven years.

Duke Slater played in the NFL for ten seasons, from 1922 to 1931. He was able to accomplish this remarkable feat, unduplicated by another African American until after World War II, because of his peerless talent and temperament. No matter how rough the going, Duke never lost his temper and diffused tense racial situations with humor and understanding.[12] Despite being a black man in an era of racial barriers in sports, he was accepted as an equal in both college and pro football by his teammates, who found it easy to forget in the heat of battle that there was a difference in skin color.[13] Duke Slater was described by friends and foes alike as a gentleman on and off the field, and that gentlemanly nature caused Slater to be held in the highest regard by his peers.[14]

After a full decade and seven all-pro selections in professional football, Slater called it a career in 1931 and retired as one of the greatest linemen in league history. However, he was quickly drawn back into the game he loved. Two short years after Slater retired, the NFL enacted their ban on black athletes, and the door he had worked so hard to hold open was slammed shut. He fought against this injustice by organizing and coaching several African American all-star teams, using his fame to attract attention for these athletes and leading them against opposing teams of white players. These games illustrated that African Americans had NFL–caliber talent and could compete against white players without racial incidents.

But there was more to Slater than merely football. During several of his NFL offseasons, he returned to the University of Iowa to take classes at the university's law school. He earned his law degree from Iowa in 1928 and passed the Illinois bar the following year. He promptly opened a legal practice on Chicago's South Side, and Slater's example served as an inspiration for young African Americans. As a famous former football player and a wealthy attorney, he gained the admiration of black and white audiences alike. With the articulate, intelligent speaking style he inherited from his father, Slater worked with several charities and gave numerous speeches to young people.

Duke also changed the face of the University of Iowa's athletic department forever. He played a prominent role in recruiting athletes—including a large number of notable black athletes—to Iowa City. The school developed a reputation as a "safe haven" for African American players, and more than any other individual, Slater was responsible for fostering that reputation. Both through personal recruiting efforts as well as sheer name recognition, Duke guided black athletes to the University of Iowa and left an indelible mark on the university's athletic department.[15]

African American athletes at that time carried a stigma as being athletically gifted but mentally inferior, a wicked stereotype that persisted even decades later as black quarterbacks fought for opportunities and acceptance in pro football. This stereotype was even more prevalent in the 1930s and 1940s, yet Slater defied this prejudice by making a name for himself intellectually. He spent years as a popular Chicago lawyer until he was voted to the Cook County Municipal Court in 1948. He was just the second African American elected as a judge in the city of Chicago. Judge Slater served as a distinguished jurist for nearly two decades, eventually becoming the first African American to ascend to Chicago's Superior Court in 1960. In doing so, he served a living refutation to the shameful claims of intellectual inferiority made against black athletes.

Judge Duke Slater passed away from cancer in 1966 at the age of 67. His life was a true rags-to-riches tale of perseverance and achievement. He was raised in humble beginnings as a poor child in Chicago, but six decades later, he died there as a famous former athlete, a revered judge, and an inspiration for thousands. On the field or on the bench, Duke Slater was a standout in every possible way. As Dan Daly aptly wrote, "From his first year to his last, Duke Slater was a star."[16]

At the time of his death, Duke Slater was one of the most famous and admired athletes in America. He was certainly a star when he lived, but he is a relative unknown today. Meanwhile, his peers—men like Jackie Robinson, Larry Doby, Jesse Owens, Joe Louis, Bill Russell, Willie Mays, Ernie Banks, and others—have gone on to become some of the most honored men in sports. What makes all of them remarkable is that they were both trailblazing and elite at the same time. Each was one of the first African Americans in their respective sport. They suffered the taunts, jeers, and bigotry that accompanied a black athlete challenging the white sports establishment. Despite that treatment, each one was talented enough to earn recognition as one of the greatest athletes of any race within their sport. That rare combination of being a racial trailblazer and an elite athlete made Slater's peers some of the most acclaimed men in American sports history, but Duke himself—a legend in his lifetime—remains a largely forgotten part of our nation's athletic past. And of every injustice Duke Slater gracefully endured in his life, that just might be the worst one of all.

Because he died in 1966 before the completion of the civil rights movement, Slater never fully discussed the persecution and bigotry he faced during his playing career and throughout his lifetime. He passed away over 45 years ago, and without his input or that of his contemporaries, this book paints an incomplete picture of an admirable man and a spectacular athlete. What it hopefully provides, however, is a long overdue opportunity to document his accomplishments and remember him. The story of Fred "Duke" Slater, a legendary lineman and judge, is one that should never be forgotten. The triumphs he was able to achieve, in spite of the times in which he achieved them, make him one of the most extraordinary men of the twentieth century.

Chapter 1

George Slater's Influence (1898–1912)

The man the world came to know as Duke Slater was born into a remarkable family. His grandfather, George Washington Slater, and grandmother, the former Sarah Venable, were Missouri natives who lived through the Civil War as young teens. George and Sarah Slater witnessed the emancipation of their race firsthand. "On January 1, 1863, Lincoln, of blessed memory, issued the Emancipation Proclamation which made them freedmen—free from chattel slavery, for they had been abject slaves," their son later wrote. "Their ecstasy knew no bounds. [My parents] have told me of how the colored people shouted, sang, praised God, rolled and tumbled. It meant so much to them."[1]

They were now free from slavery, but with no formal education, the Slaters still faced a life of hardship. "Big George," as George Sr. was called, found work as a butcher and traveled the Midwest in search of a meager living. George and Sarah eventually had seven children; their oldest, George Washington Slater, Jr., was born in Missouri in 1873. The Slater family spent George Jr.'s formative years during the 1880s in the town of Leon in southern Iowa.

By the 1890s, Big George and his large family had relocated to the Hyde Park Township of Chicago's rough South Side. They lived near 62nd and Ada Streets in a growing, poor, and completely autonomous "Black Metropolis" in the Windy City. Big George became a popular masseur and developed a loyal following for his services at the Palmer House.[2]

Even at an early age, George W. Slater, Jr. was articulate and intelligent. He earned a high school diploma, a significant academic accomplishment at the time, and even took two years of college courses at the University of Chicago and Illinois Wesleyan University. However, George found his true calling in the ministry. Reverend Slater married Letha C. Jones, a Missouri native, in 1893, and the two of them began their life together at 3009 La Salle Street in Chicago. On December 19, 1898, George and Letha were blessed with their first child, a son they christened Frederick Wayman Slater.

Though his place of birth is officially listed as Normal, Illinois, Fred Slater was a Chicago native from the time he was a few months old. As a very young boy, he learned the game of football by playing pickup games on the streets and in abandoned lots with the other neighborhood boys. Fred later recalled that when he went to visit his grandparents, he frequently played prairie football in one particular vacant lot at Racine Avenue and 61st Street. Normal Park, the home field of the NFL's Chicago Cardinals, would be constructed over that site years later.[3]

None of the neighborhood children had any formal football instruction, but they learned the rules of the game by watching older boys. Most boys who enjoyed playing football wanted to carry the ball, but young Fred was a natural lineman whose favorite part of the sport was tackling. This preference meant he was welcome whenever a game was being played. Even if there was a pickup game in mixed racial company, all these neighborhood games were short a few extra linemen to do the blocking and tackling. Since linemen were always needed, Fred could find a game almost every afternoon after school.

During this time, Fred Slater obtained his popular nickname. "As a boy, I had a dog named Duke, and somehow or other the boys started calling me Duke," he explained.[4] Duke Slater is the name he proudly carried with him for the rest of his life.

Duke's father George, meanwhile, scraped out a modest living as the minister of Zion Tabernacle Church.[5] Reverend Slater conducted a mission for the domestic servants who worked in the mansions in the area. Despite the visible presence of gambling in the neighborhood, Rev. Slater preached brimstone sermons against its evils, and he earned admiration and respect from the people of his community.[6]

Even though his given name was Fred Slater, he embraced the nickname Duke his whole life, signing autographs as "Duke" Slater.

Life on the South Side was tough under the best circumstances, but a crippling recession and rising unemployment caused by the Panic of 1907 made conditions even more difficult. Several members of Reverend Slater's church were starving, so that winter he attempted to buy food for his congregation at a large discount from a wholesaler. However, since Slater was a minister and not a retailer, the wholesaler ultimately refused to sell him the food. He reported back to his congregation, calling the situation "positively wicked," and he vowed to find a solution.[7]

That solution arrived in the form of Reverend George Woodbey, a self-educated former slave and a leading advocate of black Christian Socialism. "I bought several books on the subject of socialism and read them eagerly," Rev. Slater wrote. "The more I read, the more I was entranced with the purity, simplicity, and justices of the principles, purposes, and methods of socialism. I saw that tenets of socialism were the solution of our problem, the ethics of Jesus in economic action, the solution of the poverty question with its attendant evils, the making possible of a practical brotherhood, and the solution of the more serious phases of the so-called race problem."[8]

George Slater converted to and quickly became one of the nation's foremost leaders of the black Christian Socialist movement.[9] An intelligent thinker and a powerful speaker, Rev. Slater argued to his black congregation that any upheaval of the current economic system would be beneficial to the African American community. He believed that allowing the government to control economic activity in the United States was the best and most efficient way to grant blacks their rightful share of the nation's economic prosperity. "This competitive system must give way to the socialistic or collective system, whereby the government guarantees to every man — white, black, yellow, brown, or red — equal justice and opportunity," Slater declared.[10]

Reverend Slater was largely attracted to Marxism because he saw the ideology as, first and foremost, a means of solving racial problems. "If every Negro voter in the United States would vote for the socialist ticket ... the worst phases of the race problem would be practically settled in less than six months," Slater wrote.[11] Furthermore, he felt that capitalism was the enslavement of the poor in the service of the rich, terminology that surely resonated among his followers. "You are their slaves—to work only when they want you to and to receive only that pay which they are pleased to give and to make you pay for the necessities of life what they choose," he proclaimed. "I know you proud Americans in 'the land of the free and the home of the brave' don't like the word 'slave,' but that's what you are."[12]

If capitalism was the enslavement of the poor by the rich, then promoting socialism was like advocating emancipation. "As I see it, the Socialist Party today is, in spirit, the old abolitionist party of chattel slavery days and is destined to free all wage-slaves—white, black, yellow, and brown," Slater wrote. "Just as the old system of chattel slavery had to be destroyed before the colored man became freedmen, just so must wage slavery and industrial competition be destroyed before the race problem will ever approximate an appreciable solution."[13]

Reverend Slater became a distinguished orator, pamphleteer, and contributor to the socialist press. From September 8, 1908, through March 27, 1909, he wrote a regular column for the *Chicago Daily Socialist* entitled, "Negroes Becoming Socialists." Slater's articles marked the first time in American history a socialist organization carried writings by a black writer on a regular basis.[14] His commentaries attracted widespread attention from both black and white socialist organizations. Eugene Debs, the Socialist Party's presidential candidate in 1908, praised Slater by writing, "Rev. George W. Slater, Jr., is doing an excellent work in educating the black men and women of the country and showing them that their proper place is in the socialist movement. Comrade Slater is himself a fine example of the educated, wide-awake teacher of his race, whose whole heart is in the work and who ought to be encouraged in every possible way to spread the light among the masses."[15]

George Slater's political messages opened doors for him. He began to travel the Midwest, spreading the revolutionary message. Rev. Slater moved with his pregnant wife and five children to Aurora, Nebraska, where he performed odd jobs as a teamster. In 1910, Letha gave birth to the couple's sixth child, but the event was marked with tragedy. Soon after, Letha Slater, Duke's mother, died at the age of 36. "This was a great blow to the lad at an age when mothers are so important to boys," biographer James Peterson observed regarding the eleven-year-old Duke. "The family pitched in and carried on as best they could."[16]

With the untimely death of Letha, Reverend Slater was the single father of six children. George enlisted the help of his two younger sisters, Jennie and Pauline, to help raise his family. When the two sisters planned a move to the West Coast, Rev. Slater made a difficult decision. Duke's two youngest sisters, three-year-old Annabelle and one-year-old Aurora, were sent to Los Angeles to live with Jennie and Pauline. Bidding farewell to his sisters was just one of the sacrifices Duke faced during a difficult childhood.

George could now plan his future around the four older children, and that future included a move from Nebraska to Iowa. While traveling around the Midwest, Reverend Slater gave a speech at the Second Baptist Church in Ottumwa, Iowa, which made him well-known in black churches across eastern Iowa.[17] Rev. Slater's outspoken socialist activity eventually tapered off, especially when the Russian Revolution of 1917 precipitated the First Red Scare shortly after World War I. But in 1912, his popularity as a socialist speaker led to an opportunity to assume the pastorate at Bethel African Methodist Episcopal (A.M.E.) Church in Clinton, Iowa, for a sum of $600 a year.

Serving as the pastor of Bethel A.M.E. Church was a great financial opportunity for Reverend Slater and his family, and he accepted it with enthusiasm. Although no one knew it at the time, George's move to Clinton also marked the formal beginning of a football odyssey for his 13-year-old son, Duke, who would develop into one of the greatest athletes of all time.

Chapter 2

A Football Journey Begins (1912–1913)

Clinton is a Mississippi River town in eastern Iowa, less than 150 miles west of Chicago. At the time, Clinton had a small community of African Americans that had lived there since the days of the Underground Railroad. These residents welcomed the Slaters with open arms, and Duke enrolled as a freshman at Clinton High School in 1912. Clinton's Red and Black had one of the state's most successful football programs, claiming a mythical state championship in 1910. After honing his game on the neighborhood streets of Chicago, Slater embraced the possibility of playing football for such an accomplished high school program.

However, Duke faced one major obstacle to beginning his athletic career — his father. Although Duke played football informally as a child, George wanted to discourage his son's love of the sport. Rev. Slater felt football was too dangerous, and his concern was not unfounded. Eighteen deaths in American football in 1905 prompted the intervention of President Theodore Roosevelt and famously triggered the formation of a college athletics oversight organization now known as the NCAA. But even by the 1909 season, college football alone still claimed eleven fatalities.[1] Clearly, it was a vicious sport for any athlete, and the paucity of African Americans would make organized football even more hazardous for Duke. Rev. Slater's safety concerns were so great that he forbade his son from playing on the football team in his freshman year at Clinton High School. In fact, George didn't even allow his son to attend games as a fan that year.[2]

In the absence of football, Duke struggled to remain motivated about school. Early in 1913, Duke told his father he wanted to quit high school and get a job. This news was very troubling to George Slater, but he knew he couldn't order his son back to school unless Duke's heart was in it. With an ulterior motive in mind, George allowed Duke to quit school and helped him get a job with a Clinton commercial ice company. Duke's job consisted of cutting ice on the Mississippi River and working in freezing subzero temperatures. The bitter cold he experienced working outside in an Iowa winter illustrated clearly for Duke what the future held for a young black man who didn't possess a high school education.

Just as his dad had hoped, Duke decided to return to school. "Except for that bit of strategy by the astute Reverend Slater, Iowa and the Big Ten might never have gotten to see one of the greatest tackles of all time," author Mervin Hyman later wrote.[3] Slater continued to perform his job cutting ice throughout high school to raise money for the family, but he could now see the importance of an education to his future.

Duke finished his freshman year, and as the fall of 1913 approached, he again wanted to try his hand at football. He missed a great season for Clinton High School in 1912; for the second time in three years, Clinton claimed a mythical state championship. Young Duke had grown from 122 pounds as a freshman to 144 pounds as a sophomore and didn't want to miss out on yet another season.[4]

But George Slater refused to relent. He still believed football was a game played by roughnecks and steadfastly refused to allow his son to join the team. Although Duke reluctantly obeyed his father the previous year, he was willing to take a risk in 1913. He tried out for the football team without his father's knowledge and joined Clinton High's practices.

Football equipment available to high schools in those days varied widely. It wasn't uncommon to see players on the same high school team with various colored sweaters and odd mixtures of football uniforms. Unlike some schools at that time, Clinton supplied a jersey to its players. But Slater was a lowly sophomore, a new player on the team, and the jersey issued to him was tattered from years of rough play.

Duke needed the help of his stepmother. In 1912, Reverend Slater married a woman named Missouri. Biographer James Peterson described Duke's stepmother as "a kind, understanding woman [who] came to mean a great deal to young Fred."[5] Missouri Slater saw how much football meant to Duke, and she supported his dream. Duke took the jersey home to have her patch it up. As she worked on his jersey one evening, however, George Slater arrived home. He asked her what she was doing, and Duke's secret football playing was discovered.

Reverend Slater was greatly displeased. He issued an ultimatum to his son and told him to give up his hopes of ever playing football. Duke was devastated, and his football career could have very well ended right there. Instead, he decided to go on a hunger strike to protest his father's commands. Several days passed, and Duke wasn't eating. He later said he went into a mental tailspin around the house. "I wasn't any good for anything when he told me I'd have to quit football," Duke recalled.[6] Missouri, who continued to support her son, pleaded with George to reconsider.

George Slater did. Surely, he saw how much playing football meant to his son, and even though he had concerns about his son's safety, he allowed Duke to rejoin the team on one condition. He made it very clear that football was highly dangerous, and he made Duke promise he would take great care to not get hurt. George wanted Duke to take every precaution he could to avoid injury on the field.

These words of warning from his father had a profound effect on Duke Slater's football career. Frequently after high school games, Duke returned home with bumps, bruises, and other injuries, but he was careful to conceal them out of fear of alarming his father. That habit of shrugging off and hiding injuries would be very useful as his football career progressed and spectators scrutinized him for any sign of weakness. African American football players of that era were frequently attacked as being mentally weak when they showed any pain or reaction to the vicious treatment they were given. Slater's habit of concealing injuries, combined with the great size he developed as he matured, created an aura of physical invincibility that became his trademark.

Financial realities, however, forced Rev. Slater to compromise on his son's safety. While Clinton High School supplied jerseys for their players, they didn't provide shoes or helmets. A helmet was priced at six dollars, and shoes cost four.[7] When Duke asked his father for ten dollars, George couldn't afford it. "We were too poor to buy both headgear and shoes. My father said I could take my choice," Duke said later.[8] "Shoes were more essential than

2. A Football Journey Begins (1912–1913)

This 1913 Clinton High School team photograph shows the "Osborne shift" in action. Burt Ingwersen is on the far left with the football, while the linemen and backs are lined up several yards to the right. Duke Slater is third from left in the front row (courtesy Gary Herrity).

a helmet. Since I couldn't quite see playing barefooted, I went without a headgear. I never could get used to wearing one after that."[9]

Without a helmet, avoiding injury as his father instructed was a much more difficult task. Still, Slater played his entire high school career and most of his college career without a football helmet. "No parent should permit his children to participate in any sport without proper equipment," Slater later said.[10] But he never lost his sense of humor about the situation. "In thinking back, I'm sure Dad made a mistake. I wear size 14 shoes, and he would have saved money if he had bought the helmet," Duke joked.[11] Indeed, his father needed to put in a special order to Chicago for his son's shoes because Duke's feet were so big. Duke Slater's enormous feet attracted constant attention from onlookers through the years.

The football coach at Clinton High School was Clinton M. Osborne. He possessed a terrific football mind and established a winning program at Clinton. Coach Osborne invented a special trick formation he called the "Osborne shift." Aubrey Devine, Slater's future teammate at Iowa, described the shift as "an unusual spread formation in which the center would pass the ball sideways 20 or 30 yards to a halfback lined up behind several linemen and blocking backs."[12] It was a very difficult formation to defend, and it helped lead Clinton High School to several strong seasons.

The 1913 team looked ready to continue that fine tradition. In addition to Slater, another newcomer to the squad that year was center Burt Ingwersen from Fulton, Illinois. Fulton didn't have a football team, and Clinton, the town right across the Mississippi River, was the nearest city where football was played. As a result, Ingwersen decided to attend school at Clinton High.

The strength of Clinton's team was at the tackle positions in the line. Cyril J. Mooney, the team's captain, served as the regular left tackle, while the right tackle position was manned by Merv Kline. Kline was an incredible basketball player who led Clinton High School to the state basketball tournament in 1914 and 1915 and was the tournament's leading scorer both seasons. He had developed into an excellent football tackle as well, earning first team all-state honors in 1912. Slater was a natural tackle, but a spot in the starting lineup wasn't guaranteed with excellent players like Kline and Mooney on the roster.

Ringwood Park, Clinton's home field, was little more than a pasture near the school. Duke's first organized football game took place on that field on September 20, 1913, against Rochelle (IL) High School. Slater had the opportunity to start at left tackle, because Captain Mooney missed the game with a shoulder injury. The game with Rochelle was expected to be an easy one for Clinton, and it was. The Red and Black won, 94–0, scoring 14 touchdowns, including six by quarterback "Nanny" Berrien.[13] The *Clinton Herald* was impressed with several of the new starters, including Slater. "Many of the men had never mixed in a real game before and showed very creditably. The colored boy, Slater, showed up well in Captain Mooney's place at left tackle," the *Herald* stated. "Slater was green but was in the game from start to finish."[14] Playing the game from start to finish would become a hallmark of Slater's career.

Although Duke played well, the following week he went from playing a complete game to never leaving the bench. Mooney returned from injury, and Slater was benched for the entire contest against Englewood (IL) High School. Clinton cruised to a 47–6 victory in a game marred by rough play.[15] However, Captain Mooney decided to rest his injured shoulder again for the team's third game versus DeKalb (IL) High School, giving Slater another chance to start at left tackle. The game with DeKalb High was another mismatch. The visitors failed to make a first down all day, and the contest was stopped after only three quarters of play to allow DeKalb to catch the 5 P.M. train home. That saved DeKalb from further embarrassment in Clinton's 108–0 victory.[16] For the second time, Slater played the entire game.

The fourth contest of the 1913 season for Clinton High School was against Rock Island (IL) High School. Unlike Clinton's first three games, this one was expected to be a real test. Only forty miles south of Clinton down the Mississippi River were the "Tri-Cities" of Moline and Rock Island, Illinois, and Davenport, Iowa. Clinton High had heated rivalries with the high schools in those towns, and Clinton's long football rivalry with Rock Island added to the anticipation of what was expected to be a close contest. Cyril Mooney returned to the lineup for Clinton at left tackle, but Duke Slater's play in his first two games earned him a starting spot at left guard.

Football fans from around the area packed the stands for the game of the year. Clinton quickly scored a touchdown in the first four minutes to take a 7–0 lead, but the Red and Black were outplayed the rest of the half by the visiting team. "When Rock Island had the ball, holes would be ripped through Clinton's line big enough to drive a team through," the *Herald* observed. Coach Osborne even benched Slater in an effort to bolster the line, but it didn't help.[17]

In retrospect, Slater confessed that he deserved the benching and admitted he had attempted to avoid contact with two of Rock Island's best players in the first half. "They knocked me around a lot and I started to quit once or twice," Duke later recalled.[18] Although Clinton led, 7–0, Osborne razzed Slater in the halftime locker room for permitting end runs to go around him.

Duke was surprised when Osborne re-inserted him into the lineup to start the second half. On the second half kickoff, a Rock Island halfback named Whisler received the ball and came downfield behind a big guard named Philbrook. "I was the only man left between them and the goal, so I had to stay there," Slater recalled.[19] Duke avoided Philbrook's block and came up upon Whisler. Unfortunately for Whisler, he dodged the same direction Slater did. "Somehow I got his head in the crook of my arm and the halfback didn't play the rest of the game," he laughed.[20] Duke would list that play as the turning point in his football career. "Just one split second makes all the difference," he said in telling of his changed mental attitude that followed that tackle.[21]

Duke's tackle also snapped Clinton out of its lethargic play against Rock Island. Clinton dominated the second half and eventually won, 42–0.[22] "They went into the game in the second half with a determination, which soon made Rock Island look like a bunch of infants. Every man on Clinton's team outplayed his man from then on," the Herald declared. "Mooney, Kline, Slater, Fredericksen, and Ingwersen took turns in breaking through and spilling the play before Rock Island could start."[23]

After four straight home wins, Clinton prepared for their first test away from Ringwood Park. The opponent was Oak Park High School from suburban Chicago. Coach Robert Zuppke built Oak Park's football program into a powerhouse before leaving for the head coaching position at the University of Illinois prior to the 1913 season. The Chicago school was led by star halfback Johnny Barrett, who would go on to play for the NFL's Chicago Tigers in 1920.

Coach Osborne was warned before the game that Oak Park was a rough team, and this was proven in the second quarter. Clinton was driving when Kline gained ten yards on a forward pass. Oak Park's giant center, Templeton, took a running jump and planted both of his feet in the middle of Kline's back. He was ejected from the game for that play, and the penalty set up a Clinton touchdown, but the contest was bound to be rough.

Clinton held a 14–13 lead after three quarters when the officiating began to frustrate the visitors. One official in particular, referee Heneage, drew the ire of the Clinton organization. Earlier in the game, Heneage negated a Clinton touchdown with an offside penalty and took away a long Kline reception to the Oak Park one-yard line by declaring Kline an ineligible receiver. After Barrett rushed for a touchdown to give Oak Park their first lead, 19–14, Clinton tried to make a comeback. Kline made a huge play for the Red and Black, catching a deep pass at the Oak Park 10-yard line, but referee Heneage again flagged Kline as an ineligible receiver and negated the gain. An interception by Barrett soon ended Clinton's best chance to retake the lead.

On Oak Park's first play after the interception, Glatts, a Clinton player, broke through and drilled Barrett for a loss. Barrett was shaken up on the play, and Heneage promptly penalized Clinton and ejected Glatts, ruling that he had used "dirty" football. Glatts' ejection seemed to take the heart out of Clinton's squad, and Barrett rushed for two more touchdowns late in the game to help Oak Park win going away, 32–14.[24] Slater played all sixty minutes at left guard in the loss.

The squad returned to Ringwood Park and prepped for Bowen High School, another Chicago team. Bowen was the reigning champion of the small school division of Chicago high schools, but they were no match for the Red and Black. Slater recovered a fumble early in the game to give Clinton its first good scoring chance, and the home team rolled to a redemptive 67–0 triumph.[25]

"Clinton opponents learned early to stay away from Fred's side of the line," Peterson wrote.[26] More importantly, he was beginning to develop a fan base, starting with one fan in particular. Duke's father heard neighbors saying complimentary things about Slater's play, so he went out to watch him play in a game. He enjoyed it immensely and became one of his son's biggest fans, attending every game he could.[27] With his father George now supporting his athletic career, Duke was poised to unlock his full potential.

Despite their loss to Oak Park, Clinton was in the discussion for the mythical Iowa high school state championship. Clinton's only scheduled game versus an Iowa high school opponent in 1913 was a road tilt with the Bunnies of Cedar Rapids High School, coached by former Hawkeye center Willis "Fat" O'Brien. Given Clinton's relative lack of instate games, Coach Osborne knew how important the Cedar Rapids contest would be in making Clinton's case for state championship honors. Cedar Rapids sent scouts to Clinton's game against Bowen, and as a result, Osborne instructed his quarterback, Edward "Nips" Murphy, not to use any new plays in that game.[28]

Clinton High took the field in front of the largest crowd to ever attend a football game in Cedar Rapids, and that field quickly deteriorated into a sloppy, muddy mess. This didn't slow the Red and Black machine, however, which dominated play from start to finish. Clinton scored a touchdown within the first two minutes of the game and tacked on a touchdown in each of the four quarters to cruise to a convincing 26–0 victory.[29] The *Cedar Rapids Gazette* admitted, "The visitors lived up to their record as one of the speediest and cleverest high school football teams in the state."[30]

Much of the credit for Clinton's excellent record was due to the team's rigorous physical conditioning. Their practice field was about three miles away from the school gym, and the boys on the team were not provided transportation; instead, Coach Osborne made the team run to and from the field for practice. As the boys made one of their three mile sprints before practice, Slater told Ingwersen, "I can think of a lot easier things in life than running back and forth!"[31]

Clinton's next opponent was the freshman team of Cornell College. In those days, college freshmen were ineligible to play varsity football, so many colleges had junior varsity squads or teams exclusively for freshmen. These teams often scrimmaged against equivalent college squads or local high school teams. After their big win over Cedar Rapids, Osborne was so confident of a victory over the Cornell freshmen that he decided to sit several starters, including Captain Mooney, and Slater started at Mooney's tackle spot.

Cornell's freshmen were stronger than Osborne expected. Clinton scored a touchdown four minutes into the game, but Cornell quickly responded with a game-tying touchdown. Mooney, Murphy, and the other resting starters were rushed into the game, and Slater shifted back to left guard to make room for Mooney. From that point, the Red and Black seized control of the game, taking a 27–6 lead at halftime on their way to a 41–18 win.[32]

Since Clinton had no game scheduled the following week, local merchants arranged for the entire football team to travel to Iowa City and watch the University of Iowa take on Ames College in their 1913 homecoming game. The Hawkeyes featured Clinton alums Ernest Willis and Bill Donnelly in their lineup, so many Clinton residents were particularly interested in the instate battle.[33] Duke Slater made his first trip to the Hawkeye campus with his Clinton teammates and saw Iowa annihilate the Aggies, 45–7, the largest margin of victory in the history of the series. Clinton's team was welcomed with open arms by the Hawkeye squad, with several Clinton players joining Iowa's team for dinner Saturday evening before returning home Sunday morning. Slater and his teammates were also shown around the city and through all the university buildings that weekend.[34]

"We all had a great time," Coach Osborne said, calling it a "splendid" trip. "I want to say that Iowa has the fastest football team I ever saw in action. Ames played a gritty game but stood no chance against such a backfield as Iowa possesses." The *Herald* added, "Every man on the team had nothing but big words to describe their trip with and all were of the opinion that they had learned a lot of football."[35] The entire experience and the hospitality received by the Clinton team must have made quite an impression on young Slater, and his first trip to Iowa City is something he would remember a few years later.

Many teams scheduled a special game on Thanksgiving Day, and Clinton High was no different. Their final opponent of the 1913 season was Keewatin Academy of Prairie du Chien, Wisconsin, an amateur outfit that was more of a prep school than a true high school. Keewatin provided little resistance to the Red and Black. Clinton ended the year in style, scoring an astonishing seventeen touchdowns in a 116–0 victory. Duke was benched toward the end of the blowout for his first break after playing four straight complete games.[36]

Three Iowa schools—Clinton, Davenport, and West Des Moines—all claimed the mythical state championship at the end of the 1913 season. Davenport had a 5–0 record against instate schools, which gave their supporters a claim on the state title.[37] West Des Moines was also undefeated, and their principal stated Davenport was "running a bluff for the title" because Davenport allegedly refused to schedule West Des Moines.[38] Both schools agreed on one thing, however; Davenport and West Des Moines felt Clinton's title claims were invalid because the Red and Black played only one instate school.

The explanation for that was simple. The Iowa Athletic Association briefly suspended Clinton for not filling out a report in 1912 listing their players, their ages, and their number of years in athletics. The school was quickly reinstated after sending their list and paying a late fee, but it disrupted their scheduling of instate football games for the 1913 season, and Clinton was forced to fill out the schedule with several Illinois schools instead.[39]

Still, Clinton alleged West Des Moines and Davenport were at fault for not making an effort to arrange games with them. "It is certain that if any high school team in the state wants to scrap it out with Clinton for the title, they will find the home battlers only too ready and willing to go a little mess with them. Certain it is that this city has the prize team of Iowa among the schools," the *Daily Advertiser* reported. "Having lost but one game during the season and that with the champs of the high schools in the nation, Oak Park, Clinton can readily lay claim to all state title glory."[40]

Clinton finished the 1913 season with an 8–1 record, outscoring their opponents 555–56. The *Clinton Herald* called the 1913 squad Clinton's best all-time football team, declaring, "Never has Clinton had such an all-star aggregation as during the past season." The *Herald* lauded Slater's progress and named him one of the key stars on Clinton's championship squad. "Slater at left guard has developed into a bulwark of strength and should develop next year into the strongest lineman on the team," it noted.[41]

Much of the praise for their season went to Coach Clinton M. Osborne. Osborne was Slater's first coach and hugely influential in teaching young Duke line play. "Coach Osborne has been a demon all season in teaching the boys the art of interference," the *Herald* observed. "College men have said that they never have seen the like on any high school team."[42]

Coach Osborne, for his part, gave the credit for the team's success right back to Slater. "Fred Slater, from the time he reported for practice on the Clinton High School football team in September of 1913, showed that he had possibilities," Osborne later reminisced. "He was big, learned fast, and soon developed into one of the best high school linemen I ever coached. He played guard, where he took care of all plays directed through the center of the line. He was hard to move out of the way on defense and opened holes for the ball carriers on offense."[43]

Duke Slater's first football season was an unqualified success. Clinton's 1913 squad turned out to be one of their best in history, and the 1914 team was expected to be even better. For Slater, his long journey in football had only begun.

Chapter 3

The Pride of Clinton High (1914–1916)

Clinton fans immediately began looking forward ambitiously to the 1914 football season. Clinton High would return nine of their eleven starters from the mythical state championship team of 1913; the only graduation losses were at fullback and Captain Cyril Mooney's left tackle spot. With Kline holding down the right tackle position, Duke Slater took over for Mooney at left tackle. Slater was happy to leave his old left guard position behind. "I was glad when I later moved over to tackle," he admitted. "Burt Ingwersen was such a fiery leader at center and he pounded his guards on the back so hard, they suffered more punishment from him than from the opposing players."[1]

The biggest loss for the 1914 Clinton football squad wasn't the graduation of any player. Coach Osborne left to take over the head coaching position at Northwestern College in Naperville, Illinois, and Clinton hired Coach Petersen as his replacement. Petersen had played college football for Highland Park College in Des Moines and had been a reserve player at Ames College.[2] He was determined to make the coaching transition as seamless as possible for the current Clinton players, keeping plays like the Osborne shift in the playbook.

Slater got the start at left tackle for the first game of the year against Englewood (IL) High School of Chicago. Englewood garnered only two first downs in the game and never threatened to score. Meanwhile, Clinton notched four touchdowns in a season-opening 27–0 victory. Duke set up one of those scores in the second quarter by recovering a fumble on Englewood's ten-yard line.[3]

Clinton's next game took them to Prairie du Chien, Wisconsin, to face Keewatin Academy. Clinton demolished Keewatin to end the 1913 season, but the 1914 squad was an entirely different group. Headmaster Kendsigdon of Keewatin declared, "We intend to show the United States that Keewatin Academy can support an athletic team which is equal to any school, short of the universities."[4] Kendsigdon backed up the claim by enrolling several star football players with extensive high school and college football experience.

Keewatin's halfbacks were Johnny Barrett and Joe Guyon. Barrett was the Oak Park star largely responsible for handing Clinton their only loss in 1913. Captain Joe Guyon, on the other hand, had been named a college All-American in 1913 as a teammate of the legendary Jim Thorpe at Carlisle Indian School. Guyon was earning additional credits at Keewatin to regain college eligibility, and two years later he would again make the college All-American team playing for Coach John Heisman at Georgia Tech.

Duke Slater was rapidly developing physically. After weighing 160 pounds at the conclusion of his sophomore season, Slater was the heaviest player on the 1914 Clinton team at 176 pounds. However, Barrett weighed 195 pounds and Guyon weighed 190, and that was just Keewatin's backfield. Slater squared off against Jordan of Keewatin, a massive tackle who carried 230 pounds and had played several seasons at Carlisle Indian School. Jordan's claim to fame was outplaying Harvard captain Robert Fisher, a two-time consensus All-American, in an 18–15 Carlisle victory over the Crimson in 1911.

Keewatin immediately assumed command of their game with Clinton with a long scoring drive, capped off by a Barrett ten-yard touchdown run. But the smaller, younger Clinton players did not back down. Midway through the second quarter, Slater shifted into the backfield at the snap on a few plays and served as a fullback carrying the ball. Duke made several nice gains on the drive, which ended on a one-yard touchdown run by Nips Murphy. Keewatin and Clinton ended the half with the score tied, 7–7.

Keewatin's experience began to show in the third period. Guyon scored a 15-yard touchdown using a "criss-cross" play made famous by Carlisle Indian School. Early in the fourth quarter, Guyon ran for a ten-yard touchdown on the exact same play. Trailing 21–7, the Clinton players began to wear down before their heavier opponents. With minutes remaining in the game, Murphy was drilled by Guyon and fumbled the ball at the Clinton two-yard line. Keewatin scored on a two-yard run for the final points in a 27–7 victory.[5]

The local newspapers felt the competitive loss was as good as a victory for the high school squad. "It is very doubtful if a high school in the Mississippi valley has ever met a team in the same class in the guise of an academy school," the *Herald* wrote.[6] "They made a showing that few other secondary schools in the country can equal," *Daily Advertiser* agreed.[7] Even Kendsigdon was impressed by Clinton's performance. "You may consider that you have a truly wonderful team, and it is a certainty that no high school team of the west can play as clean, hard, or skillful a game as the Clinton team," he declared.[8]

Clinton's next opponent was nearly as formidable. The Red and Black had to travel to West Aurora, Illinois, to battle their local high school, which had not lost a football game in three years. West Aurora won the Illinois state championship the previous season, and their fans were extremely confident of victory. As Coach Petersen stepped off the train car in Aurora, a gambler immediately approached him and offered a $100 bet on West Aurora, an offer Petersen declined.

Clinton's captain, Nips Murphy, suffered a knee injury against Keewatin and was sidelined for the West Aurora game. He served as the team's official water boy, carefully looking over Clinton's water supply. There had been a typhoid epidemic in Aurora, and the coaches of both teams had to monitor what their players drank. Instead of their usual routine of drinking out of pails or sucking a sponge, Clinton players drank only boiled water from jugs.

Clinton Osborne, who coached ten miles from Aurora in Naperville, visited the Clinton team and delivered the pregame pep talk. It worked. Ray Blinkinsop, who was manning the quarterback spot in Murphy's absence, carried the ball 15 yards for the game's first touchdown. Just before halftime, halfback Nanny Berrien added another score on a five-yard touchdown run. The Red and Black took a surprising 14-point advantage to the locker room.

Heavy rains on Saturday morning turned the field into a wet, muddy crater by the second half. With Murphy out of the game and in possession of a two touchdown lead, Clinton was content to run the clock in Aurora's territory for much of the second half, while both teams' ball carriers slipped and skidded on the turf. Slater and his fellow linemen repeatedly broke through and mussed up the home team's plays before they began. West

Aurora penetrated Clinton territory only twice during the entire game and never threatened to score, as Clinton cruised to a 14–0 upset victory.[9]

West Aurora's fans lost a lot of money on the game and were not pleased with the Clinton squad. Burt Ingwersen said, "After the game, the crowd headed for Duke Slater. They were going to be rough. I guess they weren't accustomed to seeing a great Negro athlete." Slater found himself in a very dangerous situation, backed against a large tree. However, Duke had a way of diffusing such confrontations with incredible charm. He got down in a lineman's stance and invited his hecklers to come at him one at a time. Duke then playfully repelled and tackled each one to the delight of the spectators. Ingwersen marveled, "You should have heard the crowd change from howlers to cheerers. Duke sure could win friends."[10] The incident illustrated both the dangers for an African American athlete at that time and Duke's remarkable ability to overcome such prejudice.

With a defeat of the defending Illinois state champions in the books, Clinton's players turned their attention to defending their own mythical state championship. The first step toward that goal came the following week as they traveled to Iowa City to take on Iowa City High. City High's head coach, Ralph McGinnis, was the captain of the University of Iowa football squad in 1913. McGinnis rushed for four touchdowns in the Iowa-Ames game Clinton's squad attended the previous season. The winner of the Clinton-Iowa City game would be considered a leading contender for the eastern Iowa championship.

McGinnis' Iowa City squad found one offensive play that worked against the Clinton defense early in the game. The home team exploited it repeatedly and spent most of the first half in Clinton territory, but City High squandered several scoring chances. With a few minutes remaining in the first half, the Red and Black offense roared to life. Halfback Billy Vorwick rushed for a five-yard touchdown just before halftime to give Clinton the lead, and the visitors carried that momentum out of the halftime locker room. The Red and Black used sweeping end runs and their famous Osborne shift to score two more touchdowns in the second half, and Clinton cruised to a 20–0 victory.[11]

Much of Clinton's improved second-half performance was credited to the "great work" of young Slater. The *Clinton Daily Advertiser* reported, "[Slater] finally broke up the one play that Iowa City made gains with consistently. He did it by tearing his way through the line and breaking up the formation in its incipiency. Clinton's ends had trouble during the first half from this same formation, but when Slater and Kline solved it and came to their aid in the second session, they stopped it in a hurry. Clinton's line was impregnable."[12] Clinton's physical conditioning was again paying dividends in 1914. Although Iowa City sent in several substitutes, the Red and Black played the entire game with the same eleven men.

Duke and his teammates were treated royally by the locals in Iowa City. Following the game, the great McGinnis admitted the better team won.[13] Clinton's team members were then given a big reception at the high school building after supper, with five hundred Iowa City students in attendance. "Both the team and officials of the Clinton team were loud in their praise for the treatment that was given the Clinton team while it was in the city," the *Herald* added. "The Clinton boys will have a warm spot in their hearts for the Iowa City team and management."[14] This was Duke Slater's second positive experience in Iowa City, and the team brought an important victory back to Clinton.

Clinton's next contest was a "practice game" against Mount Morris (IL) College. Clinton wanted a relatively easy game, because a showdown with their archrivals from Davenport loomed. Mount Morris was a perfect opponent, as this was their first football team in twelve years. Clinton officials booked the game two weeks earlier when the Mount Morris squad happened to be on the same train that took Clinton to West Aurora.[15]

The Red and Black got the easy game they sought, obliterating Mount Morris College, 109–0, on 16 touchdowns and a safety.[16] Slater and Kline switched tackle positions in this game; Slater started at right tackle, the position where he would become famous, for the first time in his career. Duke also rushed for 83 yards on seven carries and scored his first career touchdown on a two-yard run midway through the third quarter. "Kline and Slater were used to a great extent in carrying the ball and each responded well. These two human plows galloped through or shook off the opposition for gains of ten and fifteen yards repeatedly," the *Daily Advertiser* observed.[17]

Clinton played without Murphy, who attended the Davenport-Dubuque matchup to scout their upcoming opponent. Davenport downed Dubuque, 55–0, and had previously defeated Cedar Rapids. With Clinton's victory over Iowa City High, the Clinton-Davenport game was seen as the championship of eastern Iowa. Both schools claimed the mythical state championship of 1913 and dismissed the title claims of the other, so this game between two rivals was hugely anticipated across the state.

Slater traveled with his teammates to Three League Park in Davenport for the eastern Iowa championship of 1914. Duke was a crucial factor for Clinton, because Davenport's linemen were the strength of their team. In particular, Davenport's left guard Lawrence Block and left tackle Robert Kaufmann, Slater's future teammates at Iowa, were considered excellent linemen. The crowd that gathered for the game numbered over 3,000, one of the largest football crowds in Davenport history. Jerry Mack of the *Davenport Democrat & Leader* described, "The bleachers and west section of the grandstand were jammed full of howling humanity. On the east side of the field stretched a long row of automobiles behind a crowd that stood almost five deep during the game."[18]

Clinton High got off to a hot start, scoring a touchdown four minutes into the game. Halfway through the second quarter, Clinton still led by seven points when Kline padded the lead. With the wind at his back just beyond midfield, Kline booted a beautiful 52-yard drop kick through the uprights to give Clinton a 10–0 halftime advantage.

Even the officials couldn't slow the Red and Black offense in the second half. Billy Vorwick had four apparent second-half touchdowns all taken away by penalty. Despite the officiating, Murphy was able to throw a touchdown pass to Harry Morrison and give Clinton a 17–0 lead. Davenport rushed for a touchdown early in the fourth quarter to cut their deficit to ten points, but it wasn't nearly enough. Clinton claimed an important 17–7 victory to clinch the mythical eastern Iowa high school championship.[19]

The Clinton team won over skeptics in Davenport with their terrific play. Coach Nixon of Davenport conceded Clinton had the best team for their size he had ever seen.[20] Mack noted, "The Clinton team was fast and shifty, and it was almost impossible to stop them. They had a system of interference that few high schools in the country could have equaled."[21]

Now established as the top team in eastern Iowa, the Red and Black turned their sights back toward bragging rights over the state of Illinois. They had already defeated Englewood and West Aurora, two of the three strongest schools in Chicago. The third, Lane Tech, was Clinton's next opponent. With a victory, Clinton would have a claim over all the top teams in Cook County. Lane Tech had a long history of stellar African American athletes. Fritz Pollard graduated from there in 1912, and Lane was led in 1914 by halfback Virgil Blueitt, one of three brothers who would star for the Chicago school.[22]

Lane Tech and Clinton kicked off what was billed as the high school championship of the middle west. The Clinton squad roared out of the gates, scoring a touchdown less than three minutes into the game. What fear the local fans had of Lane's strength dissipated, and Clinton High notched big play after big play. Even though the game was cut short minutes into the fourth quarter to allow Lane's players to catch their train home, the Red and Black steamrolled their Chicago visitors to the tune of a 73–7 win.[23]

"Kline and Slater at tackles had no difficulty with their opponents," the *Daily Advertiser* beamed. The paper gave Slater recognition for his ground gaining ability and praised his fine defensive work.[24] West Aurora defeated Champaign (IL) High School, the strongest downstate team, that same week. Because of Clinton's victories over West Aurora, Lane Tech, and Englewood, the Red and Black now claimed supremacy over Illinois high school football. Coach Payne of Lane Tech remarked, "I will hand it to Clinton. They have a fast team. Cook County cannot produce anything like them. Their shift plays and formations are certainly good, the style of play and interference being more like college ball than high school. We are not ashamed to be beaten by a team like this."[25]

After two highly anticipated games, Clinton High relaxed with a "warm up" game against Dubuque High School. Coach Petersen felt Dubuque would pose little challenge, so he used several substitutes in the first half to give them more experience. Slater and Ingwersen started the game and led the Clinton reserves to a 21–0 halftime advantage. Nevertheless, Petersen criticized the team at halftime for their lethargic play.

A Clinton booster found a creative way to lift the Red and Black team out of their funk. He offered Duke Slater a five-pound box of candy if he stopped everything that came in his direction in the second half. The clever inducement paid off. Duke dominated on defense in the second half, racking up multiple tackles for losses and forcing a fumble that set up a Clinton touchdown. He also gained 19 yards on six carries and scored on a five-yard touchdown run. Slater's play helped Clinton roll to a 73–0 victory.[26]

"Ingwersen and Slater were the two bright spots of the team," the *Herald* declared.[27] "By offering a box of candy to Slater, one of the fans had the big colored lad fighting like a demon the last half of the game. He did not miss a tackle the entire half and time and again threw his man for a loss of from one to ten yards."[28] Needless to say, after the game, Slater got his box of candy.[29]

In early November, Clinton accepted an offer to play West Des Moines on Thanksgiving Day. When it was scheduled, the game was hyped as the state championship of 1914, since Clinton and West Des Moines shared the mythical state championship the previous year. Once the game was scheduled, however, West Des Moines was upset by their crosstown rivals from East Des Moines. This upset left Sioux City as the state's only undefeated team, while Clinton clearly possessed the eastern Iowa championship. Clinton wanted to replace West Des Moines with Sioux City to decisively determine the state title, but West Des Moines insisted the game go forward as planned, and Clinton was forced to abide by the contract.

West Des Moines High was a formidable foe. Their quarterback was Aubrey Devine, a future College Football Hall of Fame player and teammate of Slater's at Iowa. Aubrey's brother, Glenn Devine, played the left guard spot for West Des Moines. West's left halfback, Sid Nichols, would later play two years for the Rock Island Independents of the NFL. This very talented roster was coached by Walter "Stub" Stewart, who had been a legendary football, basketball, and baseball player and coach for the University of Iowa.

The Clinton administration had such respect for West High that they brought back

Coach Osborne the Monday before the game to school Clinton's team on a few new plays. In a highly unusual move, Osborne had full control of the team, with Coach Petersen's blessing, for three days before the big Thanksgiving match. The clash was the most anticipated high school game in the state in 1914. But even as Clinton prepared for a shot at the state championship, Duke Slater still faced prejudice.

Clinton's team arrived in Des Moines the day before the big game, and they gathered for a meal in the hotel dining room. Duke Slater was a big reason why Clinton was contending for their second straight state championship, but that didn't sway hotel management, who informed Duke that he needed to eat in the kitchen because he was black. Coach Osborne asked the team to decide whether they wanted to stay or leave, and the entire team got up and walked out. "We wanted to eat with Duke. He was one great man," right guard Charles Dunn explained. Teammate Harry Morrison agreed, "We were behind him to a man." Despite such reprehensible treatment, Morrison said the incident never bothered Duke. He described Slater's reaction to the entire encounter by saying, "He could rise above anything."[30]

Although West Des Moines had lost any claim to the state title with their loss to East High, the Clinton–West Des Moines battle still had a championship atmosphere. The game was played on Thanksgiving Day, November 26, 1914. The venue was Drake Stadium in Des Moines, and it was the first Thanksgiving game staged at that stadium in seven years. The three officials chosen for the game signaled the magnitude of the event—they were Walter Eckersall, a former All-American quarterback at the University of Chicago, a sportswriter for the *Chicago Tribune*, and the leading football authority in the country outside of the East Coast; Jesse Hawley, the head coach of the Iowa Hawkeyes; and Clyde Williams, a former All-American quarterback at Iowa and the athletic director at Ames.

Before an impressive crowd of 10,000 spectators on a perfect day for football, West Des Moines and Clinton kicked off their highly publicized game. West High recovered a fumble at the Clinton four-yard line as the first quarter ended, but Clinton responded four plays later by stopping West Des Moines six inches short of the goal line to get the ball back on downs. The Red and Black then began a very impressive 99-yard drive for the game's first touchdown, capped by a 17-yard scoring run by Billy Vorwick. Clinton led, 6–0, at halftime.

Nichols came out in the second half with a vengeance. First, he recovered a fumble at Clinton's 12-yard line. Next, he used a shift play to run for a touchdown and keep his streak intact; Nichols had scored a touchdown in every West High game in 1914. West now had momentum, and a few minutes later, Aubrey Devine threw a 30-yard touchdown pass to give West Des Moines their first lead of the game, 13–6. But Clinton responded to the challenge. Ingwersen recovered a Nichols fumble at West's 15-yard line, and Nanny Berrien soon broke free on a run for the game-tying touchdown. Kline's extra point attempt officially knotted the score, 13–13.

The fans had seen a spectacular show, and tension rose as the score remained tied and time wound down in the final period. With less than two minutes remaining in the game, West High took the ball and began one last drive toward Clinton's goal. They had the ball within ten yards of the goal line when Devine called for a passing play. He later recalled, "I tried to forward pass but never was able to get rid of the ball as a big boy wrapped his arms around me and smothered me to the ground. That was my first taste, so to speak, of Duke Slater. In later years he was on my side, which made the going much easier."[31] Slater's sack of Devine drove West Des Moines back 12 yards and forced a much more difficult field

The 1914 Clinton football team claimed the school's third consecutive state championship. Duke Slater is sixth from left in the second row; fourth from left in the second row is Burt Ingwersen (courtesy Gary Herrity).

goal attempt by Nichols, which sailed wide of the goalposts. The game ended seconds later in a 13–13 draw.[32] It was the only tie game of Duke's high school career.

West High outgained Clinton, 318 yards to 221, with Sid Nichols alone accounting for an incredible 224 yards. What really hurt Clinton were six turnovers, including four lost fumbles and two interceptions; West High, conversely, had only one turnover, the fumble by Nichols in the third quarter. Both local newspapers praised the "magnificent contest" and hailed the talented players on both sides. "There were probably more stars of the first magnitude together than have taken part in any one high school football game in the state this season," the *Clinton Herald* reported.[33]

That statement was validated when the *Des Moines Register* selected their first all-state team in 1914. Five Clinton players were honored—Nips Murphy and Merv Kline on the first team, Nanny Berrien and Billy Vorwick on the second team, and Burt Ingwersen as a third team all-state selection. Sid Nichols was selected as the captain of the first official Iowa all-state team, while Glenn Devine was a third team pick.[34] Two players who were not named, Duke Slater of Clinton and Aubrey Devine of West Des Moines, would later be inducted in the College Football Hall of Fame, so the talent on the field that day was quite extraordinary.

At the time, the tie game was seen as an enormously disappointing result for Clinton. Sioux City High, meanwhile, lost their first game of the season to Englewood High of Chicago, 21–13. Therefore, both Sioux City and Clinton claimed the mythical Iowa high school championship of 1914. Sioux City made their claim as the only major undefeated and untied team against other Iowa high schools. Clinton, conversely, also claimed the state title. Since Sioux City and Clinton were the only two undefeated schools against instate opponents, and because Sioux City lost to an Englewood school that Clinton defeated earlier in the year, 27–0, Clinton overlooked the tie against West High and claimed the mythical state championship as well. Neither school wanted to jeopardize their claim with a game against the other, so Sioux City and Clinton shared the Iowa state championship of 1914.

With that, Clinton's 1914 season came to an abrupt end, but it was another very successful year. Clinton High claimed their third straight mythical state championship and their fourth in five seasons. They had a 7–1–1 record and outscored their opponents 353–54. Duke Slater played every single minute of every game for Clinton in 1914; he and Kline were the only Clinton players to accomplish that feat. Slater showed flashes of brilliance and was a dependable starter on two straight state championship squads, but he later said he and Burt Ingwersen were "just a couple of punks" on Clinton's title-winning teams.[35] In his senior season in 1915, however, Duke Slater would finally begin to blossom into a star.

The 1913 and 1914 Clinton High School football teams were expected to be contenders for the mythical state championship, but the 1915 squad faced very low expectations. Due to graduation losses, transfers, and boys quitting school, Clinton needed to replace nine of their eleven starters, plus three reserves who had played significant minutes. Only seniors Duke Slater and Burt Ingwersen returned from the previous season's starting lineup; Ingwersen was elected 1915 team captain. Duke would also need to adjust to his third coach in three seasons, because Coach Petersen left the squad in the hands of Coach Craig.

Clinton's opening opponent in 1915 was Englewood High School. Englewood returned nearly their entire lineup from the team that defeated Sioux City the previous season, and they were pegged as the favorite to win the Cook County championship. Even the *Clinton Herald* predicted an Englewood victory over Clinton. "With luck breaking even, it is the honest opinion of the followers of the game that Saturday's game should be a victory for the visitors," the *Herald* reported. "Not by a large score but a decisive one."[36]

However, Slater and his teammates had a surprise for the hometown fans. After a succession of carries, Duke planted the ball inside Englewood's two-yard line as the first quarter expired. He then determinedly plowed over the goal line on the first play of the second quarter for Clinton's first touchdown of the year. Clinton High took a surprising 6–0 advantage into halftime.

Clinton added another touchdown run in the third period to increase their lead to 12–0, and the Red and Black soon forced Englewood to punt. Clinton's two senior leaders, Slater and Ingwersen, broke through the line and blocked the kick. That gave Clinton the ball deep in Englewood territory and set up a third rushing touchdown. In the fourth quarter, Slater nearly had a second score when he appeared to intercept a low pass and run it back for a Clinton touchdown; however, the officials conferred, ruled the ball had hit the ground, and called the pass incomplete. Regardless, one touchdown from Slater was enough to stake Clinton to a 19–6 upset victory.[37]

The Clinton team was better than even their fans expected, but the next challenge was their first trip to Rock Island in four years. The Islanders still remembered Slater's hit and the second half performance that sent them down to a decisive defeat two years earlier, and they were looking to even the score. Rock Island had just opened a new municipal field, and over 1,000 fans arrived to see the upriver boys tangle with their Tri-City challengers. It was the first game of many that Duke Slater would play in Rock Island, Illinois.

Pregame reports indicated Rock Island didn't have one of their strongest teams in 1915, and those reports proved to be correct. Clinton controlled the game from the opening kickoff, scoring on touchdown runs in each of the first three periods. The visitors defeated Rock

Island handily, 20–0.³⁸ Quarterback "Whitey" Knight looked like a worthy successor to Murphy with two of those touchdown runs. Meanwhile, the *Clinton Herald* said Slater was proving to be a star on both offense and defense. "Slater was always ready with a gain when called upon and was in front of every onrush the Islanders made at his side of the line," the *Herald* reported.³⁹

After a 2–0 start against high school teams, Clinton returned home to square off against the junior varsity squad of Dubuque German College. The game turned into a fierce defensive struggle. The key play came early in the third quarter after Clinton gained good field position on a poor Dubuque punt. The Red and Black drove to Dubuque's 18-yard line when Slater took a handoff, ran through the right side of the line, and rumbled 18 yards into the end zone. It was the only score in an otherwise defensive game, and Clinton captured a grueling 7–0 victory.⁴⁰

Despite improbable odds, the undefeated 1915 Clinton squad was in contention for another mythical state championship. Iowa City High School made a visit to Clinton, and a victory would again establish Clinton High as one of the top contenders for the championship of eastern Iowa. Iowa City High was now coached by Van Meter, a former football coach at Clinton High, so the visitors were even more motivated to come away with a victory.

The home fans were treated to a thrilling fourth quarter of play. Clinton was driving for a go-ahead score when Eglan of Iowa City intercepted a pass and ran seventy yards for a touchdown. Just like that, Iowa City silenced the Clinton rooters by seizing a 14–7 lead. But Clinton fought back, and with five minutes left in the game, end Bud Welsh caught a 25-yard pass, broke two Iowa City tackles, and ran into the end zone for the game-tying score.

A 14–14 draw now loomed as the most likely outcome, a result that would knock Clinton High out of state title contention. Clinton regained possession with a few seconds left on the clock, however, and they quickly drove down the field. The home team got close enough to give Coe a shot at a 32-yard field goal. Many Clinton fans feared the distance was beyond his range, but Coe's kick sailed true as time expired, punctuating a thrilling 17–14 victory. Duke, who "again proved a terror on defense," received substantial credit for the big win.⁴¹

The victory kept Clinton in the race for the mythical state championship of 1915. Davenport High was scheduled to arrive in two weeks, and for the second straight season, the Davenport-Clinton game would determine the eastern Iowa championship. Coach Craig wanted a "practice" game for his team the week before the Davenport match, so he arranged for Sterling (IL) High to come to Clinton on October 23. Sterling was playing its first season of football in four years, but the *Herald* observed, "While a victory is expected, the Sterling team has been in some stiff battles this year and will give Clinton a battle."⁴²

Coach Craig benched a number of his usual starters for the Sterling game, but Slater was in for the opening kickoff. Bill Donnelly's younger brother started for Whitey Knight at quarterback to gain some experience running that position. Clinton held a 14–0 lead after one period, and the second quarter belonged to Duke Slater. He rushed for a four-yard touchdown and added a 20-yard touchdown carry later in the period to give Clinton a 27–0 lead at halftime.

Craig shifted his lineup at halftime. Several players that started the game were normally reserves and didn't have the physical stamina to play all sixty minutes. Due to the small number of players on the roster, Craig had to insert some of his usual starters into the lineup when the reserves became exhausted. Slater, however, continued to dominate the game. He raced 15 yards for a touchdown, his third of the contest, shortly into the second half.

By the fourth quarter, Donnelly finally needed a rest, so Knight went into the game. The Red and Black were comfortably ahead, 43–0. Knight rushed for twenty yards to near Sterling's goal line, but he was tackled hard and left the game. Clinton added another touchdown and a safety before time was called and earned a 52–0 win.[43]

It was a pyrrhic victory. Slater's three touchdown game was ignored when news spread that Knight had suffered a broken collarbone and would miss the important battle with Davenport. His injury solidified Davenport as a strong favorite in the game, as they were seeking to wrest the title of eastern Iowa champions away from their rivals. Coach Nixon bluntly stated, "Of all the games we play this season, there is none that I would rather see won than this one."[44]

A tremendous crowd gathered at Ringwood Park on October 30, 1915, to witness two undefeated teams battle for the eastern Iowa championship. Play moved along very slowly; Davenport took their time running plays, while Donnelly lacked the experience at quarterback to call plays efficiently on offense for Clinton. However, Clinton's defense put up a strong fight at every turn. In the third quarter, Slater made the best defensive play of the game. On one play in Clinton territory, Davenport gave the ball to their best halfback, Carl Makeever. Makeever took the handoff on a running play when he met up with Slater. "Slater, bursting through, grabbed one hand of Makeever as he went by with the ball, and, with but one hand, literally swung him off his feet and back for a loss of several yards," the *Herald* described.[45]

Davenport and Clinton entered the final quarter locked in a scoreless tie. With only a minute remaining in the game, the scoreboard still read 0–0. Davenport was forced to punt, but the Clinton return man bobbled the kick and Shuler, Davenport's quarterback, recovered the ball at Clinton's 30-yard line. There were only seconds left, so Davenport took to the air. Shuler threw two incomplete passes. On third down, Shuler passed to Makeever, who slipped behind the defense and ran in for a touchdown just as the final gun sounded. Davenport didn't even try the extra point, and the team swarmed the field to celebrate a dramatic 6–0 victory.[46]

The touchdown as time expired was Davenport's only completed pass of the game. It was the only home loss in Duke Slater's three years at Clinton, but he and his fellow linemen were praised for their great defensive work. "That green line met and threw back the rushes of the heavy veteran Davenport forwards and backs and proved impregnable," the *Herald* noted. "With Slater leading, the Clinton forwards broke through and stopped them before they got started."[47]

Still, Davenport High had won revenge for their loss in 1914. Now the Red and Black were seeking revenge of their own. Clinton's next opponent was Keewatin Academy, the school that handed Clinton High their only loss the previous season. Guyon and Barrett, Keewatin's backfield stars in 1914, had left the school for other opportunities, so the two teams were more evenly matched than they had been in their last meeting.

The match with Keewatin turned into a low-scoring affair. For most of the game, Clinton held a surprisingly comfortable 2–0 lead thanks to an early safety. The Red and Black defense dominated, and Keewatin only made three first downs the entire game. Coe tacked on an insurance field goal with seconds remaining in the contest to cap off a 5–0 Clinton victory.[48] The *Herald* praised "the wonderful defensive work of Slater," reporting that "the big tackle ripped his way through the Keewatin line time and again to down men behind their line."[49]

After two weeks off, Clinton High prepared for their final game of the season on Thanksgiving Day. The opponent was Crane High of Chicago, which had won the Cook County championship. The matchup with Crane would be Slater's last game as a member of the Red and Black. Nearly 1,000 spectators showed up at Ringwood Park to say farewell to their seniors, including Duke Slater and Captain Burt Ingwersen.

Clinton's team came out sluggish in the first quarter, on account of their long layoff. Their offense came to life soon after, however, with two rushing touchdowns in both the second and third quarters. Duke Slater gave his home fans one last play to remember. In the final period, Slater took the ball and capped his high school career by rushing 15 yards for the last touchdown of the season. Clinton's 1915 season ended with an easy 35–0 victory over the reigning Cook County champions.[50]

"Slater, in addition to shattering the opposition's interference time and again, was highly successful in carrying the ball when yards were a necessity," the *Herald* said in recapping Duke's final game in the Red and Black.[51] Duke played the entire game against Crane, just as he had all season long. Slater, Coe, and Ingwersen were the only three Clinton players who played every minute of every game in the 1915 season. Duke played 17 straight high school games without a helmet and without a break.

Considering their preseason expectations and inexperience at the start of the season, the 1915 Clinton team performed admirably. Clinton High finished with a 7–1 record and outscored their opponents 155–26. Slater was just one of several outstanding players on Clinton's two mythical state championship teams, but as a senior, he became a star and guided the Red and Black to an excellent record. He led the 1915 Clinton squad in scoring with six touchdowns on the season, a terrific feat for a lineman, and his defensive play helped the Red and Black post five shutout victories.

In addition, Duke's athletic exploits and soft-spoken nature earned him the admiration of his fellow Clinton natives. "He was well-respected by all his classmates and all the people of the community," local historian Gary Herrity said. "In those days, everybody—whites and blacks included—revered him as a top-notch individual."[52]

Duke Slater's high school football career was a remarkable success. More importantly, his love of football and his father's emphasis on education led to a renewed effort in the classroom. Perhaps Reverend Slater's proudest moment came on June 8, 1916, when his oldest son graduated from Clinton High School. That was only the start of Duke's educational journey, and his next stop took him to Iowa City and the Big Ten.

Chapter 4

Spanish Flu and a World War (1916–1918)

Reverend Slater always emphasized the value of an education. George had taken a few college classes while in Chicago, and he wanted his son to attend college as well. Duke's options were extremely limited, however. Few universities admitted African Americans, and since George couldn't afford to send his son to a school out-of-state, Duke could only consider Iowa universities.

Slater initially turned his attention to Lenox College, a small college in Hopkinson, Iowa.[1] Duke was entertained at the home of the school's president, and his plan was to study pre-law there before going to Harvard on a law scholarship.[2] However, Duke's meeting with the president of Lenox College caught the attention of Judge Ralph P. Howell. Howell graduated from of the University of Iowa's College of Law and was later elected judge of the Eighth Judicial District of Iowa. He also became president of the University of Iowa Alumni Association in 1917, and as a loyal Hawkeye, Howell wasn't about to let Slater head to another school without a fight. Howell enlisted the help of two fellow judges and Iowa law school graduates. Slater stated that Judge L.F. Sutton, an 1877 graduate of Clinton High School, was influential in his decision to go to Iowa.[3] Sutton and Howell had both been captains in the Iowa National Guard, and Sutton became a notable Clinton attorney with the law firm of Chase, Seaman, and Sutton.

The third man who sold Duke on the University of Iowa was Judge Mike McKinley. McKinley starred for the Hawkeye football team in 1893 and 1894 and was elected as a judge to the Cook County Superior Court in 1911. As a former Hawkeye football star and Chicago Superior Court judge, Mike McKinley provided young Slater a glimpse into his own future. With the coaxing of these three judges, Duke made the ninety mile trek west from Clinton to Iowa City and enrolled at the University of Iowa in 1916.[4]

Still, a college football career was by no means a certainty for Slater. African American athletes were extremely unusual in college football at that time. Almost all southern colleges banned blacks from competition altogether. While northern colleges were much more receptive than their southern counterparts, black college football players were rare. By 1917, there had only been about two dozen African American players in the history of major college football. Two of those few African American football players—Frank "Kinney" Holbrook and Archie Alexander—once competed for the Hawkeyes. Kinney Holbrook, the first black athlete to play at the University of Iowa, lettered in football in 1895 and 1896 and in track in 1896 and 1897. He was a talented halfback who guided the Hawkeye football team to its first conference title in 1896. Holbrook led Iowa in scoring that season, rushed for 12 touchdowns, and led the way for black athletes at the University of Iowa.

If Slater had any doubts about his ability to excel on the Hawkeye football squad, Archie Alexander could serve as a shining example for him. Like Slater, he came from humble beginnings. The son of a janitor, Alexander enrolled at the University of Iowa in 1908 to pursue an engineering degree. He became a three-time letter winner for the Hawkeye football team at the tackle position from 1909–1911. Archie performed admirably, winning the respect of fans and teammates alike and later becoming the first black graduate of the University of Iowa's College of Engineering. The memory of Alexander at Iowa was still fresh in the minds of Hawkeye fans in 1917, so Slater could be comforted by the fact that an African American lineman starring for the Hawkeye football team wasn't unprecedented.

Of course, that didn't mean the journey would be easy. Both Holbrook and Alexander encountered racial controversy during their time in the Hawkeye lineup. An ugly, vicious game broke out against the University of Missouri in 1896, because Missouri's fans and players detested Holbrook's presence on the team. Archie Alexander was benched for all three of the Hawkeyes' football contests against Missouri schools from 1909–1911. African Americans were also forced to make alternate travel arrangements for road games, and they were not allowed to stay in the dorms on campus. But while Slater's dream to join the Hawkeye football team wouldn't be achieved easily, Holbrook and Alexander proved it was possible. By the time Duke Slater was finished at Iowa, his career is the one that would be used as an example for future African American athletes to follow.

Slater was familiar with Iowa City from his trips there in 1913 and 1914. However, the Hawkeye coach at that time, Jesse Hawley, was replaced in 1916 by Howard Jones. Jones starred at end for Yale from 1905–1907; Yale never lost a game in his three years there. He then took the head coaching job at his alma mater, and the 1909 Yale club established itself as one of the greatest teams college football had ever seen. Yale was unbeaten, untied, and unscored upon that season. A record nine of the eleven players chosen for the 1909 All-American first team were from Yale. Jones spent several years after that in private business, but he was lured out of football retirement by the largest coaching contract in Iowa's history—five years at an average of $5,000 annually.[5]

The 32-year-old Jones was a hands-on coach. He was only a decade removed from his playing days, so his best teaching method involved showing players the proper techniques himself. One observer who witnessed Jones' practices recalled, "His assistants tried to get him to organize the practices and let them do most of the heavy work. He'd promise to do it, but after fifteen minutes on the field, he'd be down on the ground showing them personally how to block, following every play on the dead run, and acting as though he were still playing end at Yale. He just couldn't relax and let others do the heavy work."[6]

Duke Slater made an immediate impact on his new coach, in every sense of the word. During one of Duke's first practices in the fall of 1917, Jones was teaching offensive line play. The coach was showing his players that a smaller, faster, aggressive offensive lineman could attack and repel a bigger, slower defensive lineman. Coach Jones toppled several Hawkeye players at the line of scrimmage and continued to ask for opposition.[7] Slater, a newcomer who Jones had never seen in action, volunteered.

The practice players took their positions, and the whistle blew. Jones charged quickly at Slater and drove into him aggressively, hoping to knock him off balance. Instead, Duke neutralized the charge and pushed his coach backwards. Within seconds, Howard Jones was lying on the ground on his back with Duke Slater on top of him. From that point forward, Jones never demonstrated a technique on a player unless he had first sized up the player's abilities by watching him in practice, and Jones never again demonstrated any move on Duke Slater.[8] The incident earned Slater the respect of his varsity coach, which would put him on the fast track to athletic stardom.

Meanwhile, Duke supported himself financially by taking every odd job he could find. He peeled a bushel and a half of potatoes every day in the basement of the Jefferson Hotel during the school year.[9] He also performed hard manual labor during the summer; on his World War I registration form, Duke listed himself as a "Coal Shoveller" when asked for his occupation. He handled the towel concession in the locker room of the old Armory and hauled bricks for a local construction company. "You got a little help, but you also worked for it," Slater recalled.[10]

Since freshmen were ineligible for varsity competition, Slater spent the 1917 season playing with Iowa's freshman team. His coach was Irving "Stub" Barron, the captain of the 1915 Hawkeyes. Duke's freshman team played a few scrimmages and practiced against the varsity. Slater continued to display his athletic ability after the season as well, as he was the main entertainment during the 1917 football team's awards banquet. He took part in a boxing match with Pat Wright, a member of Iowa's athletic faculty.[11] Duke quickly progressed from sideshow entertainment to the main event in 1918, however, as his first year of varsity college football began.

World War I threw the college football season of 1918 into a state of upheaval. Players who had starred in college football just years before were involved in military service overseas. On account of the war, several major universities canceled their football seasons altogether, and many other schools played very limited schedules.

Control of conference football schedules in the Big Ten was given to the War Department in 1918. Eligibility rules were suspended, and anyone who reported for football was allowed to compete. Freshmen were temporarily eligible for varsity play, and the season would not be charged against the future eligibility of any player in the conference. This meant that Duke could play the 1918 season and retain three more years of eligibility.

Although Slater played left tackle for most of his high school career, Jones shifted him to the right tackle position. In the week leading up to Iowa's first game of the season versus the Great Lakes Naval Station Blue Jackets, Duke made headlines for his versatility. The team's biggest weakness was at punter, and Jones sought to fill the void by holding tryouts with Slater competing for the job. Slater also impressed spectators with his powerful running. During a midweek scrimmage against the Iowa reserves, the *Capital Times* reported, "The plunges of Slater, Negro tackle, could not be stopped by the second team's line."[12] The *Waterloo Courier* said he was "expected to prove a whirlwind at tackle" and that he had "developed here as one of the finest tackles ever to set foot on Iowa Field."[13]

Colleges provided helmets for their players, but players were not technically required to wear them. Iowa offered Slater a helmet, but he was so accustomed to playing without one in high school he wanted to continue playing helmetless. However, Coach Jones had a team rule that no player could start a game without proper equipment, including a helmet, so Duke developed a habit over his career at Iowa. He would wear his helmet for the opening kickoff, but after the play ended following the kickoff, he would fling his helmet in the air toward the Iowa bench.[14] This helmet toss became a game-opening ritual Iowa fans routinely looked for as a Hawkeye game began.

Great Lakes Naval Station stood as a formidable challenge for the young Hawkeyes. The Blue Jackets were strong favorites over the Hawks, because most of the sailors previously played collegiately at other major programs. The Blue Jackets featured Paddy Driscoll, a former Northwestern All-American, at the quarterback position and the legendary George Halas at end. Slater was physically well-developed; at over 200 pounds, he was already, as a freshman, one of the largest players in the Big Ten Conference. He was still inexperienced, however, and matched up against the Blue Jackets' best lineman, Charlie Bachman, an All-American at Notre Dame from 1914 to 1916. This game pit grown men against relative youths, as the 19-year-old Duke clashed with the 25-year-old Bachman.

In Slater's first college contest, Great Lakes jumped out of the gates early. The Blue Jackets ran the Hawkeyes right down the field in the first quarter and scored on an 18-yard touchdown run by reserve halfback McClellan. In the second quarter, the young Hawks struck back, marching down to field to the Blue Jackets' two-yard line. Slater shifted to the backfield and took the ball on a running play. "I saw a big hole in the Great Lakes' line," Slater humorously recalled. "I threw all my weight and strength into the play and I went over [the goal line]." He soon clarified his statement. "*I* went over all right, but when I crossed the goal line, I didn't have the ball. God only knows where *it* went."[15]

Great Lakes recovered Slater's fumble and ran out the clock, clinging to a 7–0 halftime lead. Early in the second half, Driscoll dropkicked a 37-yard field goal to extend Great Lakes' advantage to 10–0. The Hawkeyes drove into Blue Jackets territory several times in the second half, but they could never punch through a score, and Great Lakes triumphed, 10–0.[16]

Despite the fumble, Duke played admirably in his first collegiate game. The *Iowa City Press* noted, "Slater, Iowa's wonderful giant Negro tackle, carried the ball repeatedly. Throughout the day, Slater starred as a line-bucker."[17] The *Courier* added, "Slater, the Iowa tackle, distinguished himself by making many star plays."[18]

Walter Eckersall concurred. In his recap in the *Chicago Tribune*, the legendary football critic wrote, "Slater, Negro right tackle, is about the best lineman any football follower will see in the conference this year. He held his own against Bachman of the Great Lakes last Saturday and made a lot of ground in carrying the ball after being called back five yards or more from the scrimmage line. He is heavy, weighing over 200 pounds, and is fairly active for a man of his size."[19]

Many were calling Iowa a promising team despite the loss, but there were questions about whether or not the Hawkeyes would even play a full schedule. As October began, the War Department forbade schools from scheduling overnight trips for the rest of the month. In the days before air travel or interstates, this declaration shook up the sports world. Schedules were thrown into chaos, and an emergency meeting was called in Chicago for Big Ten schools to discuss the matter.

In light of this announcement, Iowa requested and received clearance from the War Department to play their next game against Nebraska. The Cornhuskers had won eight straight Missouri Valley Conference titles and were dominating the series with Iowa in 1918. Nebraska had notched eight wins and a tie in the last nine meetings between the schools, and Iowa had lost their last three games in the series by a combined score of 133–24.

The matchup in Lincoln was met with excitement across the Midwest. As many teams around the country took to the field for the first time that year, Eckersall labeled the Iowa-Nebraska contest as the feature game of the official opening of the 1918 season. Slater had his hands full against a Nebraska line that boasted a fantastic lineman, Link Lyman.

The game was a physical, defensive battle from the start, but Iowa's offense snapped to life in the third period. The Hawkeyes made steady gains behind the running of fullback Fred Lohman to advance the ball to Nebraska's 12-yard line. Then Lohman surprised the

Nebraska defense by pulling back and firing a 12-yard touchdown pass to Captain Ronald Reed for Iowa's first score of the season and a 6–0 lead.

On Iowa's next possession, Slater lined up at fullback on a key third down play and barreled ahead for four yards and a first down to keep the drive alive. Slater's powerful runs drove Iowa into scoring position, and he then went back to work on Nebraska's weakening defensive wall. Lohman soon slammed ahead for Iowa's second touchdown. The Cornhuskers by this time were worn out from Iowa's physical charge, and they never challenged the Iowa end zone for the rest of the game. Duke Slater had his first collegiate victory with Iowa's 12–0 decision over Nebraska.[20]

Before Duke Slater had even played a single game in a Hawkeye uniform, he was hyped as one of the finest tackles to set foot on Iowa Field (© University of Iowa-CMP Photograph Service).

The Hawkeyes were lauded by critics. Eckersall declared, "The Hawkeyes' victory showed beyond all questions of doubt that their strong game against the Great Lakes a week before was no fluke and that they are entitled to consideration as a championship possibility."[21] Comparisons were being made to Iowa's 1900 team, an undefeated crew that claimed Iowa's only Big Ten title and widely considered the greatest team in school history. The Hawkeyes clearly had their best team in years, but the entire 1918 college football season was on the brink of cancellation.

Spanish flu may sound innocuous today, but in 1918, this terrifying disease spread across the globe like wildfire. The Spanish influenza pandemic of 1918 killed more people in a single year than the entire conflict of World War I. Spanish flu claimed 50 million to 100 million lives worldwide in just 18 months. That was more than the number of deaths attributed to the Black Death Bubonic Plague outbreak from 1347 to 1351, making the Spanish flu outbreak of 1918 the deadliest pandemic in human history.

What made the disease even more deadly is that, contrary to a normal flu, Spanish flu was disproportionately dangerous to people from ages 20 to 40. Since turned a victim's immune system against its host, the virus was most fatal to otherwise healthy young people with strong immune systems. Of course, football players and many spectators fell into this group. Spanish flu was also easily transmitted, and large crowds could be dangerous. It was a recipe for disaster for a public sporting event.[22]

Coach Jones returned from the emergency Big Ten meeting in Chicago with his schedule in disarray. The Northwestern contest scheduled for the coming Saturday and the Chicago game the following week had both been indefinitely postponed. Since Jones didn't want to wait three weeks for Iowa's next scheduled game, he sent word up to Moray Eby at nearby Coe College that he needed an opponent quickly. Eby, Coe's head coach, had been a star end on the aforementioned 1900 Hawkeye team, and he was happy to accommodate his alma mater.

The Hawkeye team sustained several injuries in the Nebraska contest, and both Lohman and Reed were sidelined for the Coe game. Lineman Glen Greenwood was also hampered, so John Synhorst, a transfer from Central College in Pella, received his first start at tackle opposite Slater. Iowa's talent advantage over Coe was lessened by the loss of these stars. Even Slater himself sat out a practice in the middle of the week to heal various bumps and bruises.

There were reports the day before the Coe game that the contest would be canceled as flu conditions in Iowa City worsened. However, the game was saved by the presence of Iowa's Student Army Training Corps. The University of Iowa had a large group of young men participating in the S.A.T.C., which was designed to prepare officers for the army by combining military and academic instruction. Almost 1,500 "citizen soldiers" participated in the program, including Slater, who underwent training at Fort Sheridan.[23] Dutch Louis trained with Duke in the S.A.T.C. and shared a double bunk with him, and Slater's feet were now extremely big. Louis remarked that when they lined up their shoes at the foot of the bed for inspection, Louis' 8C shoes looked funny next to Duke's 15½-EEEE's.[24]

This unusually large S.A.T.C. presence made the University of Iowa an excellent place to stage a football game. Since Iowa's campus doubled as an army training ground, security could be more easily maintained to guard against the deadly Spanish influenza. The Coe game was only authorized after the university banned everyone from the stands in the interest of public safety, with members of the S.A.T.C. enforcing the measure.

In the absence of any fans, Iowa kicked off to Coe. The Crimson and Gold put up a valiant fight in the first half, keeping Iowa off the scoreboard until minutes before halftime when Hawkeye halfback Joe Sykes sprinted for a ten-yard touchdown. On their following possession, Coe was forced to punt. The punter fumbled the snap, and quarterback Bill Kelly recovered the loose ball in the end zone for a Hawkeye touchdown. Within minutes, the Hawkeyes tallied two quick scores to take a 14–0 advantage to halftime.

Fourteen quick points at the end of the half allowed Coach Jones to make a few substitutions, but Slater remained in the game. Iowa needed just one more score to put the pesky visiting squad away for good. Late in the third quarter, Coe was setting up to punt in their own territory. Duke broke through the line, blocked the punt, scooped up the ball, and nearly scored with it, powering down to the Coe five-yard line. Iowa soon notched their third touchdown to put the game out of reach.

A rare occurrence took place in the final period. Slater was hit by a Coe player and had to call timeout for an injury. Fortunately for Iowa, the game was such a blowout Jones was able to pull Slater from the game early in the fourth quarter. Freshman Lester Belding added the final score of the game on a long punt return for a touchdown that surely would have electrified the crowd, had there been a crowd. That play provided the final score in Iowa's 27–0 victory.[25] Iowa did most of their offensive work against Coe over Slater's right side of the line. The *Iowa City Press* noted one of Iowa's feature performances was "the great line work of Slater, the colored wonder."[26]

For Iowa's next opponent, Howard Jones secured a game with another small local school, Cornell College in Mount Vernon, Iowa. The Hawkeyes led the overall series with Cornell, 11 games to one. The lone Cornell victory occurred in 1911. Cornell's captain and star quarterback that year was Emerson "Pony" West, an all-state performer. West kicked a field goal with under three minutes left to break a scoreless tie and secure a 3–0 victory for Cornell. West's leadership on the field that day made him a campus hero as the man who beat the Hawkeyes.

On Wednesday, October 16, 1918, as Cornell and Iowa prepared for their game, newspapers reported that Pony West had suddenly passed away from Spanish influenza. His death underscored the very real devastation the pandemic was causing as it swept across the American Midwest. For the second straight week, the general public was barred from Iowa Field. As was the case against Coe, Iowa's second straight "Quarantine Game" was witnessed only by members of the university's S.A.T.C.

The weather also jeopardized the game. Five minutes after the opening kickoff, a heavy downpour soaked the field. Due to the rain and the quarantine, accounts of this game were vague, but it was a mismatch from the start. Iowa jumped out to a 13–0 lead after one quarter, and they added another touchdown in the second period. Officials considered calling the game at halftime, but the rain let up enough that the teams finished out the contest. Two more second half touchdowns made it a 34–0 Iowa victory.[27]

The school announced that, on account of Spanish flu, no more football would be played for the foreseeable future. Iowa's homecoming game with Grinnell College was canceled because the entire state was under quarantine. No one knew if or when the season would resume, but Coach Jones kept his team busy with scrimmages and experimented with different plays and formations. The *Iowa City Press* reported, "Jones has a series of new plays that revolve around Slater, the giant Negro tackle, and he is using these open formation attacks with disastrous effect on the scrubs."[28]

The Hawkeyes received some welcome scheduling relief as the calendar moved into November. The War Department lifted their ban on overnight trips and allowed Big Ten teams to take trips of no more than 48 hours. This made Big Ten play possible, and Iowa scheduled a matchup at neighboring Illinois. The game was jeopardized when Illinois officials wired midweek that Spanish flu conditions in Urbana had worsened. However, the flu outbreak in Iowa relented enough to lift the statewide quarantine, so the site of the game just shifted to Iowa City.

Iowa had won their last three games by a combined 73–0 score and were heavily favored over the Illini. The game had special significance to Slater, who saw a familiar face across the line. His old teammate, Burt Ingwersen, was serving as Illinois' team captain. Ingwersen and Slater were matched directly up against each other in Slater's first conference game.

Early in the contest, the Illini drove down to the Iowa's 20-yard line, where their drive stalled. Illinois halfback Jesse Kirkpatrick dropped back to attempt a field goal. Duke Slater crashed through the line and blocked the kick, and Iowa recovered the ball and returned it 35 yards. But the deflection came at a price, because Slater had blocked the field goal attempt with his face. "That was a tough day for Slater," Ingwersen recalled. "The ball struck Duke on the nose. For the rest of the game, Slater bled like a stuck Iowa pig. There wasn't much he could do."[29]

As the second quarter opened, it was clear that Illinois coach Robert Zuppke had his game plan for attacking Iowa's defense. The Illini began a methodical march down the field, calling plays away from Slater's side of the field, and the drive culminated in a Kirkpatrick ten-yard touchdown run. Nevertheless, Slater continued to stand strong on defense. The Illini were stifled for the rest of the half because Duke tackled Laurie Walquist, Illinois' terrific halfback, for big losses on two consecutive possessions.

However, Iowa's offense never got in gear, and Illinois dominated the second half.

Fullback John Sabo ran for two touchdowns, while Iowa didn't threaten the Illinois goal the entire game. The Illini left town with a convincing 19–0 victory.[30] Ingwersen's team got the win, but he acknowledged Slater's performance. "Slater played with a fury," Ingwersen recalled. "He pushed us around."[31] The *Iowa City Press* agreed, writing, "Slater, the big Negro tackle, performed brilliantly," while Slater was listed as someone who "starred" for Iowa by the *Cedar Rapids Gazette*.[32]

Iowa's next game was against Minnesota, and the Gophers, not the Illini, were expected to be the Hawkeyes' biggest challenge. After their performance against Illinois, Iowa was now a heavy underdog to the visiting Gophers. Not only was Iowa coming off a blowout loss, but the Hawks had never defeated their northern rivals in 12 tries. The combined score in those losses was 463–30 in favor of the Gophers. In their last meeting, Minnesota had defeated the Hawkeyes, 67–0.

Much of the week's practice focused on trying to counter the "Minnesota shift," a clever offensive shift invented by Minnesota's head coach, Doc Williams. The two guards and the center lined up on the line of scrimmage and the quarterback moved under center. The other seven players would "shift" forward into a power running formation just before the quarterback took the center snap. This late forward movement often confounded opposing defenses and left them on their heels at the snap. Current rules make such shifts illegal today, but at that time, it was a very effective offensive design.

The threat of Spanish flu was slowly waning, and 7,000 fans came out for rescheduled homecoming festivities culminating with the Iowa-Minnesota contest. The 1918 Hawkeye squad was excellent defensively, but all year, they had been desperately searching for offense. Early in the third quarter, the team turned to Fred Lohman. Behind Iowa's strong line, the powerful fullback plowed ahead for 17 yards on three consecutive carries. With the ball at the Minnesota 23-yard line, Lohman fired a pass to Bill Donnelly, who was tackled a foot short of the goal line. On first and goal, Lohman plunged over the line for the Iowa touchdown, giving Iowa a 6–0 lead over the Gophers.

The Minnesota shift wasn't working against the stout Iowa defense, and as the fourth quarter began, the Gophers tried to pass the ball for gains instead. But that strategy didn't work either, and six points was enough for Iowa on this day. When the final gun sounded, the Hawkeyes had their first win ever over Minnesota with a 6–0 upset.[33]

The Hawkeye line was instrumental in providing openings for Lohman's powerful charges, and defensively, they completely shut down the feared Gopher running attack. Minnesota never penetrated Iowa's 30-yard line during the game, and the Hawkeye defense handed the previously undefeated Gophers their first shutout loss in five years. Iowa's durability was also put to the test, since the Hawks made no substitutions during the game. All eleven men, including Slater, went the distance in the win.

Pandemonium reigned in Iowa City. The loss to Illinois was all but forgotten in the wake of this upset win. Revelers were still celebrating the victory when they received a much larger piece of good news: German Kaiser Wilhelm II had abdicated the throne. Two days later, on November 11, 1918, Allied powers and Germany signed an Armistice ending World War I.

The final game on Iowa's schedule was at Ames, but Coach Jones knew he had a strong team on his hands and decided to look for more opponents after the Ames game. Though the state of Iowa was no longer under a Spanish flu quarantine, the city of Ames was. Iowa's S.A.T.C. presence again made Iowa City a more secure venue, so school officials agreed to move the contest from Ames to Iowa Field. The game with the Aggies was billed as the state championship, and the Hawkeyes were overwhelming favorites.

Ames received the ball first, and Duke was ready from the opening snap. Slater tore through the Aggie line on Ames' first offensive play and drilled the ball carrier for a loss. As usual, Iowa's defense played terrifically, while their offense struggled to gain momentum. Like the week before, the Hawkeye offense didn't kick in until the third period; quarterback Bill Kelly scored on a run from a yard away for a 7–0 Iowa lead.

The Aggies responded with a nice drive to midfield, but they were then forced to punt. The kick was fielded by Lohman at the ten-yard line, and he broke free for a spectacular 85-yard return. That set up a five-yard touchdown run on the next play and finally took the fight out of the visitors. Coach Jones pulled Slater near the end of the game, and Lester Belding added a touchdown run with minutes remaining to give Iowa the undisputed state championship and a 21–0 victory.[34]

"Slater, the giant Negro tackle, figured prominently in the Ames defeat," reported the *Des Moines Daily News*. "He opened up great holes for his backs on the offense and on the defense stopped the Ames backs dead as they reached the line of scrimmage, piling up the entire left side of the Cyclone line in one heap."[35] The *Gazette* agreed, "Slater, the giant Negro tackle, starred in the line."[36]

Iowa sported a 5–2 record, one of their best seasons in years. Jones wanted a few more games to show the strength of his Hawkeye team, and Northwestern agreed to play in Iowa City the following Saturday. The Wildcats were near the top of the Big Ten standings, and they hoped a convincing win over Iowa would give them a claim on the conference title. The Iowa-Northwestern contest was the sixth consecutive game for the Hawks at Iowa Field; the Spanish flu conditions and Iowa's S.A.T.C. presence provided the Hawkeyes with six straight home games for the first and only time in school history.

A train delay pushed back the starting kickoff six hours, and the delay seemed to have a more detrimental effect on the Hawkeyes than the Wildcats. The Hawks fumbled the return of the opening kickoff, and Northwestern recovered at the Iowa 35-yard line. Four minutes into the game, Northwestern's quarterback, Marshall Underhill, ran up the middle on a draw play and plunged into the end zone. Lohman evened the score in the second quarter with a one-yard touchdown run, but after four first half turnovers—including three lost fumbles and an interception—the Hawkeyes were fortunate to be locked in a 7–7 tie at halftime.

Iowa cut down on their mistakes in the second half. A Northwestern fumble led to Iowa's first field goal of the year, a 27-yard boot by Kelly that gave the Hawkeyes a 10–7 lead. The conditioning of the Hawkeye squad paid off in the fourth quarter. The Wildcats faded down the stretch, and Iowa's backs ripped off long gains at will. Lohman notched two more touchdowns for the Hawks, and Iowa handed Northwestern their only conference defeat of the year by a 23–7 score.[37]

Duke Slater and his linemen were praised for their terrific play. The *Iowa City Press* reported that "after the game, referee Burch said that Iowa's giant tackles, Slater and Synhorst, were the greatest pair he had seen this year. In Saturday's game they simply tore the Northwestern line to pieces and opened up huge holes, big enough for three men to get through."[38]

Howard Jones scheduled one last game for his Hawkeyes against a military team from Camp Dodge. Slater, one of three Hawkeyes to start every game for Iowa in 1918, was penciled in the starting lineup across from Camp Dodge's tackle, an army major named Bradley.

The 1918 Iowa football team finished with six wins, the most of any Hawkeye squad since 1905. Duke Slater is sixth from left in the second row. Leaning against the concrete in the far right of the photograph is Coach Howard Jones.

Bradley had sporadic playing experience with the Army football team years earlier. Everyone expected the Hawkeyes to rout the Dodgers, but it wound up being a miserable season finale for the Hawks. The game was played on November 30 in Des Moines, and the weather conditions were poor. It snowed the night before the game, and the snow melted to cover the field with water and mud.

Iowa's defense continued to dominate, holding the Dodgers to just 56 yards all game, but the Hawkeye offense sputtered in the lousy field conditions. Major Bradley displayed remarkable toughness battling Slater on the line. The Hawkeyes turned the ball over on downs at the Camp Dodge two-yard line in the first quarter, and later, Kelly missed a 15-yard field goal. Iowa ended the year with an unsatisfying tie against Camp Dodge, the only draw of Duke's college career. Both the *Iowa City Press* and the *Iowa City Citizen* mentioned that Slater "stood out" during play.[39]

Walter Eckersall was an official in the game and later reported he was watching Duke Slater closely, though not as a result of his play. In an article titled, "Color Line Is Forgotten," Eckersall noted that games were often called off because athletes from the south refused to play against African Americans. "Last Saturday at Des Moines, Iowa and Camp Dodge struggled to a scoreless tie," he wrote. "The Dodge team had Major Bradley of the regular army playing right tackle, while opposed to him was Slater, the giant Negro tackle of the Hawkeye team. Major Bradley hails from a town in the southern part of Missouri. He had been born and raised along the strict southern lines of relationship between southerners and Negroes. Before the game started, Major Bradley was asked if he cared to play against Slater, and the major replied in the affirmative."

Eckersall was warned to be on the alert for any rough tactics during the game. "A few plays was enough to convince anyone that the best of feeling existed between the pair," Eckersall continued. "On several occasions, Major Bradley helped Slater to his feet when the latter was handled roughly. The conduct of these players brought forth much favorable comment from high officials in the army and those closely identified with the university."[40]

Duke Slater would be recognized years later as one of the most famous athletes in America, but his opponent that day became even more well-known. His full name was Omar Nelson Bradley, and he developed into one of the greatest military men in United

4. Spanish Flu and a World War (1916–1918)

States history. He was stationed in Camp Dodge while waiting to be sent to Europe, but his deployment was scuttled on account of the Spanish flu outbreak. By the time conditions eased, the armistice had been signed, ending the war. Omar Bradley saw his fair share of combat in the next world war, however; he eventually rose to the rank of General of the Army, which is often referred to as a five-star general. Bradley was the fifth and last man in U.S. Army history to attain that rank in 1950.

A few days after the game with Camp Dodge, Eckersall made the official all–Big Ten selections. Slater earned an honorable mention all-conference selection "for his consistent play throughout the year."[41] The *Iowa City Citizen* expressed surprise that Slater was relegated to only an honorable mention. "Slater, the giant Negro tackle for the Hawkeyes, was entirely ignored although his playing has been a feature in nearly every Iowa game this season," the *Citizen* stated.[42]

The *Des Moines Daily News* called Slater a star as they named him to the all-state team as a freshman. "Slater, who is placed at right tackle, is perhaps one of the greatest tackles the state has produced in many years. He proved a whale on the offensive this season, opening up great holes in opposing lines and standing like a stone wall on the defense," the *Daily News* wrote.[43] The *Iowa City Citizen* added, "Slater of Iowa is a giant in size and knows how to use his great strength to advantage. His side of the line was practically invincible this last season and many opponents' plays were spilled at the start by the muscular darky."[44]

The 1918 Hawkeye team was cheered as one of the greatest in school history and arguably the school's best since 1900. Iowa's 6–2–1 record was a source of pride. The six victories were the most by a Hawkeye club since 1905. The team's defense was so dominating that only three of Iowa's nine opponents— Great Lakes, Illinois, and Northwestern — managed to score against them. The losses to Great Lakes and Illinois were no great embarrassments. Illinois won the Big Ten title, and Great Lakes, which defeated Illinois earlier in the year, went on to win the Rose Bowl game, 17–0.

1918 was an anomalous year in American history and college football. Thirty-eight men and women at the University of Iowa died that year from Spanish influenza, a small sample of the destruction brought about by the pandemic. As World War I came to a conclusion, the nation quickly returned to normalcy. For Duke Slater, the 1918 football season was merely the first step in a collegiate career that would bring him widespread fame. The following season gave Slater his first true glimpse of the national spotlight.

Chapter 5

From Unknown to All-American (1919)

Duke Slater spent the spring of 1919 trying his hand at other sports. Jones urged Slater to try out for basketball to develop agility, so Duke spent hours shooting baskets in the gym.[1] However, few of Duke's shots were swishing the net, and he actually considered basketball a rougher sport than football. "I never was treated so roughly in my life," Duke said years later. "After three or four days of it, I was looking around for a headgear and shoulder pads. As soon as I could find an excuse, I quit."[2]

Jones realized Duke would never make a decent basketball player, so he banned Slater from the gym for the rest of the semester and suggested he spend his free time studying so he could remain academically eligible to play football.[3] Duke stayed in shape by working out with the track team instead. He represented the Hawkeyes in the shot put event at the Big Ten conference indoor track meet on March 22 and made the finals of the event. "Slater, giant Negro football star on Jones' great 1918 grid eleven, is a shot putter of no mean ability," the *Iowa City Citizen* marveled.[4]

Slater continued to display those abilities during outdoor track season. He won the shot put event and placed second in the discus throw at the Hawks' dual meet with Minnesota on May 12. In Duke's first trip to Minneapolis, reporters were impressed by the "remarkably well-built Negro."[5] At the state meet in Des Moines two weeks later, Slater threw the discus 120 feet, 8 inches to claim the state title in the event. He finished the season as one of nine Hawkeyes who qualified for the Big Ten outdoor championship meet on June 7. Duke received an athletic letter after a promising rookie track season.

Iowa received good news that summer when the Big Ten Conference ruled that tackle John Synhorst was eligible to play for the 1919 Hawkeye football team. "With Synhorst and Slater, the Hawkeye line will be in possession of the best pair of tackles in the conference, and Coach Jones will have at least two positions on the team over which he will have no cause for worry," the *Des Moines Daily News* wrote.[6] The *Cedar Rapids Gazette* added, "When [Synhorst] appeared late last week, he brought joy to more than one player and friend of the team, especially big Slater, the colored lad who holds down the opposite tackle. With an enthusiastic grin and an arm about his shoulder, he trailed Synhorst all over the university the first day he was there. 'Now, we'se goin' to do some'n for sure,' he exclaimed. And it looks like they will, too."[7]

The 1919 college football season featured stiff competition at every turn, since rosters nationwide were filled with former servicemen returning from overseas. With seven returning starters, the Hawkeyes were an experienced football team in 1919. Iowa's biggest flaw the previous season was a lack of offense, but the Hawkeyes were hoping two new backfield men, Aubrey and Glenn Devine, would help rectify that. The two sophomores immediately started at the right and left halfback positions for Iowa.

Nebraska was Iowa's first opponent of the 1919 season, and the Cornhuskers were still angry over the loss the Hawks gave them the previous year. Nebraska was again led by Link Lyman, who was confident he could neutralize Slater in their rematch. In fact, he privately assured his coach, Henry Schulte, that Slater would be hogtied and handled by the time Lyman got through with him.[8]

Iowa wasted no time illustrating that their offensive woes the previous season were fully behind them. The Hawkeyes promptly drove down the field and scored on a 20-yard touchdown pass from Captain Fred Lohman to Glenn Devine. Later in the quarter, Slater made his presence felt. Nebraska's halfback and captain, Paul Dobson, dropped back into punt formation. Duke tore through the line and blocked the punt, which the Hawkeyes recovered on the Nebraska 20-yard line. That great field position led to a one-yard touchdown run by Aubrey Devine, and Iowa extended its lead to 13–0 after one quarter.

Slater "smeared the Huskers for losses time and again," throwing a Cornhusker ball carrier for a 13-yard loss as the second quarter opened.[9] Nebraska end Clarence Swanson, a future College Football Hall of Famer, recalled how Duke won his individual tussle with Lyman. "The game hadn't progressed far until out came a couple of subs with a stretcher," said Swanson. "They rolled Lyman onto it, and as they carried him past where I was standing, Link said, 'Any message you want delivered to your folks?'"[10]

Iowa dominated the first half of play, but on a cloudy, overcast day, the weather emerged victorious in the second half. Shortly after the kickoff, rain began pouring down in sheets over the players. The second half devolved into a punting match, with neither team able to successfully move the ball. Iowa ultimately triumphed over Nebraska for the second straight year by an 18–0 score.[11]

"Slater was in on every play Saturday, playing a whale of a game for a starter. He is Iowa's original kick-blocking expert," the *Iowa City Citizen* gushed.[12] "Slater played the game of his life.... One expert critic from out of town declared that he had seen a good many classy tackles perform in his day but never one like Slater, who consistently nipped plays on the opposite side of the line from his position. Although he blocked but one kick from Nebraska, the enemy booter was always escaping by narrow margins from the fast charging Hawkeye lineman."[13]

Slater emerged victorious from his battle with Lyman, but now an even bigger challenge was on the horizon — a rematch with Ingwersen and Illinois. The Hawkeyes traveled to Urbana confident in their ability to dethrone the defending conference champions. Iowa was scheduled to go with the same starters they used against Nebraska, but the Big Ten Conference had other ideas. The morning of the game, the conference sent word to Coach Jones that they had reversed their previous ruling on John Synhorst, who was now ineligible for play, effective immediately. Synhorst's dismissal on such short notice wasn't the biggest controversy that surrounded this game, however.

With Iowa holding a 7–0 advantage in the second quarter, an Illini drive stalled at Iowa's 33-yard line. Albert Mohr of Illinois punted the ball, which hit the ground at the one-yard line. Kelly, the Iowa return man, backed away from the ball, because touching it would create a live ball that either team could recover. Kelly assumed that since no Hawkeye touched the punt, it couldn't be recovered by Illinois. But Walquist sprinted down the field, scooped up the ball, and dove over the goal line.

Referee Walter Eckersall granted Illinois a touchdown. The Illini allegedly took advantage of a loophole in the rule book at the time, which stated that if a kicking team's player was behind the punter at the time of a punt, that player was eligible to recover the football as an "onside punt" for the kicking team. Eckersall ruled Walquist had been behind Mohr at the time of the punt and was therefore eligible to recover the ball and carry it over the goal line for a touchdown. The unusual play cut Iowa's lead to 7–6 and proved to be a critical play in the defensive struggle that followed. It drew Illinois close enough that halfback Ralph Fletcher was able to give the Illini the lead with a 35-yard field goal in the third quarter, and that made the difference as the Hawkeyes fell, 9–7.[14]

After a failed foray into college basketball, Duke Slater embraced the field events for the Hawkeye track team. In his first season, he won the state title in the discus throw.

Synhorst's eligibility issues were overshadowed by Illinois' controversial "onside punt." Since it was such an uncommon play, spectators weren't watching where Walquist lined up on the punt. The *Iowa City Citizen* reported skeptically, "Of course it was not absolutely impossible for Walquist to have raced approximately forty yards and recover the pigskin before it rolled across the goal, but it is a peculiar thing that so spectacular a stunt should have passed unnoticed by scores of football experts, newspaper men and Big Ten scouts who were watching every move of the two teams. No one of fifty different spectators, Illinois fans, conference coaches on scouting duty, or newspaper men, interviewed by the writer, saw Walquist behind his punter when the alleged on-side kick was made. Great surprise was expressed when the play was credited a touchdown."[15]

Despite the very controversial loss, Slater was seen as Iowa's biggest star, and every source agreed Duke outplayed Ingwersen between the lines.[16] "Slater played the greatest game of his life and was clearly beyond anything on the field," the *Citizen* declared.[17] "Slater licked his old high school teammate, Ingwersen, to a standstill and removed once and for all whatever doubt existed as to his ability to do the job."[18] In the *Chicago Tribune*, Eckersall also had praise for Duke. "Slater, the giant tackle, was strong throughout. He broke up Illinois' plays time after time and frequently followed around behind the line and caught the runners from behind," he wrote.[19]

It was impressive for a sophomore tackle to trump Ingwersen, the captain of the 1918 all-conference team. Even Ingwersen himself acknowledged Slater played a terrific game and that he had improved tremendously from the previous year. He said it was impossible to gain a yard through Slater in their 1919 meeting.[20] Although Duke put a physical pounding on his old Clinton teammate, Ingwersen helped deliver a victory for Illinois. His hardheadedness often frustrated Zuppke, and his coach later related an incident from that game to illustrate Ingwersen's stubborn temperament. "I told Ingwersen that I hoped that big Duke Slater would hit him so hard it would knock some sense into his head," Zuppke laughed. "Duke hit him once, and as Burt staggered to the bench, he came up to me and said, 'That whole team can't knock any sense into my head!'"[21]

Iowa needed to put the controversial loss behind them quickly, because their next opponent was the Minnesota Golden Gophers. The Hawkeyes defeated Minnesota for the first time ever in Iowa City in 1918, but the Hawks had never claimed a victory in Minneapolis. Slater and his teammates stepped onto a slightly soggy field in front of one of the largest crowds to ever see a football game at Northrop Field. Unofficial attendance topped 12,000 as the Gophers battled the Hawks.

A poor Minnesota punt and a nice return by Aubrey Devine set up a Devine touchdown on the first play of the second quarter, but the Gophers quickly responded. Minnesota advanced the ball to the Iowa 35-yard line before Slater tackled Minnesota halfback Pete Regnier for a loss, forcing a punt. On their next drive, the Gophers showed they had learned their lesson. They ran the ball exclusively at the left side of the Iowa line and away from Slater. This worked, and the Gophers converted a fourth down from the one-yard line to score a touchdown and tie the score, 6–6, at halftime.

With one minute left in the game, the contest appeared certain to end in a draw. However, Aubrey Devine, who took over the quarterback position in the second half, made a dazzling 30-yard run to spark a Hawkeye drive. Iowa's advance stalled in Minnesota territory, but Devine's 27-yard field goal attempt split the uprights with seconds remaining. The Hawkeyes celebrated their first victory in Minneapolis over the Gophers, 9–6.[22]

Iowa's defense greatly contributed to the win over their northern rivals, and Duke was credited as one of the key cogs in that machine. The *Waterloo Times-Tribune* lauded Slater's "powerful game on defense."[23] The *Iowa City Citizen* added, "The big Clinton Negro ... put up the same fighting game against Minnesota that featured the Illinois-Iowa contest."[24]

Iowa was expected to win their next contest against South Dakota handily, and the Hawkeyes lived up to expectations. The Hawks built a comfortable 20–0 lead in the first half on the strength of two Devine touchdown passes to Belding and a touchdown run by Fred Lohman. Late in the third period, Lohman threw a 40-yard pass for Iowa's fourth touchdown. Jones began freely substituting his linemen at that point, pulling Slater after three quarters of action. South Dakota was able to put two touchdowns on the board against the Iowa reserves in the final quarter to make it a respectable 26–13 final.[25]

Slater's magnificent line play in the first half of the season brought speculation of conference honors or perhaps even the highest recognition of all. "Slater is the Old Gold man who is expected to land on the All-American [team]," the *Waterloo Courier* declared. "That he can be kept off the all-conference and all-western mythical elevens is not to be thought of, for the Iowa tackle has been playing a line game far above any other individual performer at his position this year."[26]

The only team in two years to defeat Slater's Hawkeyes, other than Illinois, was Paddy Driscoll's Great Lakes squad. Iowa traveled to Evanston, where Driscoll was serving as an assistant coach for his alma mater. The Northwestern assistant previewed the Hawks before the game. "In Slater they have one of the best tackles in the west. He weighs over 200 pounds and is fast and powerful," Driscoll observed. "He takes care of one whole side of the line on defense."[27]

Aubrey Devine was the early star for the Hawks, pinning Northwestern deep in their own territory on punts and running 15 yards for the game's opening touchdown. The Wildcats responded, however, as two long passes netted 55 yards and led to a game-tying touchdown run by Captain Robert Kohler. A very competitive first half ended in a 7–7 tie.

The Hawkeyes established control of the game in the third quarter with some powerful running. Strong runs by Fred Lohman and Aubrey Devine started an Iowa drive that ended with a Devine one-yard touchdown run. The Hawkeye defense slammed the door on the Wildcats from that point forward, containing Northwestern on their own side of the field late in the game to prevent any chance of a game-tying score. Iowa held on for a hard-fought 14–7 victory.[28]

Duke Slater was a second team All-American in 1919. He was just the sixth African American in college football history to earn All-American honors and the fourth Hawkeye All-American following Clyde Williams, Jim Trickey, and Fred Becker (© University of Iowa–CMP Photograph Service).

In particular, Duke Slater emerged victorious. Willis Brightmire, Northwestern's quarterback who was calling their plays on the field, repeatedly challenged Duke's side of the line, but Slater halted multiple Wildcat drives with strong tackles. "Slater played a wonderful game," the *Times-Tribune* reported. "Brightmire must have believed the big Negro's prowess a myth, for he directed several plays against the right side of Iowa's line with disastrous results before he learned the futility of such an attack. Reports showed that Northwestern gained one yard through Slater and lost about seven in three or four other tries at his position."[29]

Walter Eckersall, the *Chicago Tribune* sportswriter, was so impressed with Slater's performance that he delivered a frequently-repeated analysis of Slater's play. Under the heading "Slater is a Wonder," he wrote, "In Slater, giant colored tackle, Iowa has one of the best forwards in the country. This man is one of the most powerful players seen since the days of Joe Curtis of Michigan, Walker of Minnesota, and Buck of Wisconsin. He is so powerful that one man cannot handle him and opposing elevens have found it necessary to send two men against him every time a play was sent off his side of the line."[30] Paddy Driscoll also marveled at Slater's outstanding play. Driscoll declared, "Slater at one tackle is powerful and fast. He charges hard and made many holes for the backs. On defense he takes care of one whole side of the line in great shape. He is the first one down the field under punts and tackled many Northwestern men in their tracks."[31] The *Times-Tribune* concluded, "Slater at tackle attracted the usual amount of attention by nailing plays for losses and by handling his opponent in the same easy manner that has forced officials to consider him for an all-conference berth."[32]

Iowa's third consecutive victory set up a pivotal matchup with the University of Chicago. Chicago and Iowa were two of the strongest teams in the conference. Each squad had only one loss on the season; both losses were delivered by Illinois. Duke Slater was playing his first college game on the South Side of Chicago, where he grew up. In his homecoming, he faced an enormous challenge in Chicago's lineup, which featured Charles McGuire at guard, Charles Higgins at tackle, and Fritz Crisler at end.

Iowa took the field in Chicago in front of 18,000 Maroon fans for one of the most anticipated games of the year. The Hawkeye offense took a risk early in the game. Iowa faced fourth and goal from the Chicago two-yard line, and the team decided to forgo the field goal. The gamble paid off when Aubrey Devine connected with his brother Glenn on a pass for the Hawkeye touchdown to give Iowa a 6–0 lead.

In the second quarter, Chicago's offense got aggressive as well. The Maroons faced a fourth and one situation at the Hawkeyes' six-yard line, and Chicago elected to go for it. They rushed for two yards to gain a first down, and Chicago's quarterback, Percy "Red" Graham, rushed for a two-yard touchdown two plays later. The game was deadlocked, 6–6, going into intermission.

Slater kept the Maroon line extremely busy. Chicago's defensive strategy was to split their ends wide and have them roll in and dive at the opposing tackle. Paul Hinkle was the Chicago end on Slater's side of the line. "I missed him the first two times," Hinkle related later. "The third time he hit me so hard, we gave it up."[33] Their new strategy left Higgins with no end help in his matchup against Duke. Higgins was struggling with the assignment, so Duke patted him on the back and gave him a few pointers. Slater's on-field coaching brought a rousing cheer from the Chicago fans.[34]

The second half settled into a battle between two evenly matched teams. With five minutes to play in the game, Graham kicked a 20-yard field goal to give Chicago a 9–6 lead. Time was running short for the Hawkeyes, but several carries by Devine moved the ball down the field. Finally, Lohman powered forward for a first down on the Chicago two-yard line with under a minute remaining on the clock.

Despite struggling earlier in the game, Charles Higgins had caught his second wind. Duke later confessed that Higgins was about the strongest lineman he ever tried to block and called him as fine a tackle as ever played football. Higgins was playing wide of Duke down at the goal line, and Duke wanted Aubrey Devine to call an inside run so he could block Higgins out rather than trying to move him in. A play called "Number 45" was just such an inside run. As the teams approached the line, Slater stood up and yelled to Devine, "Call number 45, Aub!"

Devine ignored Slater's advice and called a run to the outside. Slater couldn't budge Higgins, and the Chicago tackle stopped the play at the one-yard line. It was now second down, and Slater, exasperated, again stood up and yelled, "Call number 45, Aub!" But once again, he called for an outside run, and this time the ball carrier was dropped six inches shy of the goal line. The players lined up for third down, and Slater, almost with tears in his eyes, screamed, "Call number 45, Aub!!" But before the Hawkeyes could snap the ball, the final gun sounded, and Iowa absorbed a 9–6 defeat.[35]

Duke later called Higgins and McGuire two of the greatest linemen he had ever seen. The Maroons returned the compliments. McGuire called the victory his greatest thrill in football.[36] Fritz Crisler, who went on to become a legendary coach and athletic director at the University of Michigan, mentioned that after playing sixty minutes against the helmetless Slater, his ears were still ringing the following Thursday. Slater, playing well within the rules, continually pounded Crisler with blows to the side of his head and open hands to his face.[37] Crisler famously remarked, "Duke Slater was the best tackle I ever played against. I tried to block him throughout my college career but never once did I impede his progress to the ball carrier."[38]

"Dusky Duke Slater accomplished all that the advance notices credited him with," Albon Holden of the *Chicago Tribune* reported. "No man in the west can make the big dark boy from Iowa look bad, but McGuire held him even every step."[39] The *Iowa City Citizen* noted that Slater "performed true to prediction. He kept two Maroon linesmen extremely busy all the while and very few plays were tried through his position." It added that he and Devine had "again proved that they have no equals in the conference in their respective positions."[40]

Iowa's final game of the year versus the Ames Aggies was an emotional affair. Iowa Field was filled to capacity for the homecoming match. Before the game, Iowa held a ceremony on the field honoring Fred Becker and Frank Grubbs, two former Hawkeye players that died fighting in World War I. The ceremony was complete with a firing squad and the band playing Taps.

The Hawkeyes played appropriately inspired football at the start of the game. Iowa put together a long drive that consumed 16 plays and 70 yards and ended with Devine completing an 11-yard touchdown pass. On the other side of the ball, Slater was a defensive force for the Hawkeyes. The *Iowa City Citizen* reported, "Duke Slater, the giant Negro, played a whale of a game in the first half and worried the Aggie backs by continually breaking through the line."[41]

Duke Slater continued his defensive domination of the visitors in the second half. Ames attempted a 37-yard field goal in the third quarter to try to reduce their 7–0 deficit, but Duke powered through the line and blocked the kick, which Iowa recovered. The Hawkeye defense, led by Slater, completely stifled the Ames attack. On one Ames drive, Slater tackled an Aggie for a five-yard loss. On another, Duke sacked their quarterback for a loss of 13 yards. Time and again, Slater's defense prevented Ames from gaining momentum. With just a few minutes remaining, Devine added a 25-yard drop kick to put the game away for the Hawks, and they claimed a 10–0 victory over their instate rivals.[42]

Several newspapers praised "the dusky Hawkeye tackle of wide repute."[43] The *Des Moines Capital* noted, "Slater's play was … conspicuous; he broke through to down White and Boyd for heavy losses on several occasions."[44] The *Cedar Rapids Gazette* declared Slater "never played a better game," rushing in and bringing the Ames ball carriers to earth from behind when plays were run to the other side. "The work of Slater was especially deserving of credit as he was through the line on every punt or forward pass, and several times not only broke up the play but threw the man who received the ball for material loss."[45]

"Slater was responsible for many of the Aggie losses by continually breaking through the line and spilling runners for losses," the *Daily Iowan* agreed.[46] "His speed in view of his poundage has surprised those fans who have seen the big fellow in action. No line is proof against his charge on defense, and on offense, Iowa backs always relied upon making a gain through Duke's tackle when other plays failed."[47]

However, the Iowa-Ames game of 1919 was marred by one of the worst racial incidents of Slater's college career. Captain Gilbert Denfield, the Aggies' opposing tackle, had been physically overpowered by Slater all day long. As the teams were leaving the field after the game, Denfield went 15 feet out of his way to physically confront Slater.[48] Duke tried at first

5. From Unknown to All-American (1919)

The 1919 Iowa football team finished five points shy of an undefeated season. Duke Slater is in the middle of the photograph, fifth from left in the second row. The first four players in the front row are, from left, Lester Belding, Glenn Devine, Captain Fred Lohman (holding the football), and Aubrey Devine (courtesy Matt Fall).

to avoid a collision and told Denfield, "Go away and leave me alone." But the Ames captain persisted in shoving Slater and eventually threw a punch at him, striking Slater with a glancing blow. Duke responded by dealing Denfield an uppercut that knocked him to the ground.[49] For a few moments, it looked as though the melee would spread, as both teams were ready to fight on behalf of their respective teammates. But the two were soon separated, and the teams parted ways.[50]

The 1919 football season was over, and it was a very successful one for the Hawkeyes. Iowa finished with a 5–2 record and lost just two games by a combined five points. Their losses were a two-point loss to Illinois on a controversial "onside punt" and a three-point defeat by Chicago where the game ended with Iowa six inches from the game-winning score. Illinois, the 1919 Big Ten champions with a 6–1 record, claims a mythical national championship for that season, despite the fact they not only lost a game but won a second on a disputed call.

With the season concluded, post-season honors rolled in for Duke Slater. He was one of five players the *United Press* unanimously selected all–Big Ten.[51.] The *International News Service* explained, "Duke Slater, the gigantic black man from Iowa, usually found that opposing teams had put two or three men to watch him in every game, yet he almost always took care of virtually all of his side of the line. He is a terrific charger on offense and a regular buttress on defense."[52]

Leon Brigham of the *Iowa City Citizen* made Slater's All-American case by arguing, "Slater has stood out on the line as the most powerful forward in the country. He has been the terror of all conference coaches and the nemesis of opposing players. Extremely fast for a man of his poundage, the giant Negro is the first man down on punts. He opens gaping holes for his backs on offense and tears through the best lines in the conference on defense."[53]

On December 13, Walter Camp announced his All-America teams in *Collier's Magazine*. Although other experts also selected All-Americans, Camp's selections were by far the most respected and creditable. His teams were heavily biased toward eastern players, but he did select a few Big Ten players for All-American honors. Duke Slater joined Clyde Williams and Jim Trickey as only the third Hawkeye ever named an All-American by Camp when he was chosen as a third team All-American in 1919.

It was a tremendous honor for Slater, but two days later, Walter Eckersall went even further. Eckersall, considered the foremost expert on college football outside the East Coast, selected Slater as a second team All-American. The *Iowa City Citizen* marveled at his accolades. "Fred Slater, giant Hawkeye tackle, is being showered with honors of a mythical nature which, if they could be cashed, would bring the big Negro a handsome fortune," the *Citizen* declared. "Now, Slater's many friends are waiting for some dopester to raise Camp and Eckersall and place the great Negro athlete on the first All-American team. That the wait may not be too long, the *Citizen* will officially proclaim Slater for this honor. Iowans will have to be shown that there is possibly a better man in the United States for a tackle position than Coach Jones' wonder before they can accept either Camp or Eckersall as an authority on the matter."[54]

Despite the *Citizen*'s plea, no recognized expert did step up and select Slater as a first team All-American in 1919. Those honors would need to wait—for now. Nevertheless, even as a second team All-American, Duke made history. He was just the sixth African American to earn All-American honors in college football, joining William Henry Lewis, Bobby Marshall, Edward Gray, Fritz Pollard, and Paul Robeson.[55] Duke Slater had gone from unheralded freshman to All-American in just two short years, but the peak of his college career was still to come.

Chapter 6

Overcoming Adversity (1920–1921)

Duke Slater became known all throughout the Midwest in 1919. 1920 was a year of great adversity for Slater, however. Problems began to surface in January. A mild case of Spanish flu rippled through Iowa City, and Duke was one of eight students hospitalized.[1] Still, he soon recovered and joined Coach Jack Watson for a second season with the Hawkeye track team.

Following a short, disappointing indoor track season, the outdoor season was much more successful for Slater and the Hawks. On May 8, 1920, the Hawkeyes trailed early in a dual meet against Minnesota before coming from behind to upset the Gophers, largely due to the performance of Slater. He won the individual field championship by earning Iowa 11 points, winning the discus toss and finishing second in the shot put and the hammer throw.[2] One week later, Duke helped the Hawks squeak out a close victory in a dual meet against Ames by shattering the state record for the discus throw. Slater's toss topped the previous record by five feet.[3]

The Hawkeye outdoor track squad then traveled to Des Moines for the state meet. Iowa rolled to the state championship, thanks in part to two record-breaking tosses by Duke Slater. Slater's shot put throw broke the previous meet record that had stood for 13 years. But even more impressively, his discus toss shattered the previous record at the state meet by nearly 14 feet. "Duke Slater will very likely get a bid to enter the Olympic Games because of his record breaking heave," the *Iowa City Press* predicted.[4]

In Iowa's final dual meet of the season against Northwestern, Slater participated in four events—javelin, hammer throw, discus, and shot put. He was again the field champion, scoring 15 points and winning the hammer throw, discus, and shot put events. That meet was Iowa's final tune-up before the conference meet in Chicago, but the Hawkeyes finished with a lackluster performance there to end the track season on a sour note.

Nevertheless, Slater sought to live up to the *Press*' Olympic prediction. The preliminaries for the 1920 Olympic Games were held at Stagg Field in Chicago on June 26. Top finishers at the Midwest regional would advance to Cambridge, Massachusetts, where the national trials would be held. The *Times-Tribune* reported, "When in form, Slater is almost unbeatable, and Hawkeye fans are confident he will place if entered at Chicago."[5]

Duke wanted to compete in the discus and shot put events, but he needed money to travel to Chicago. The university board of education failed to meet in time to provide Slater with financial backing, so a number of Duke's friends stepped up to provide funds for him to get his tryout. Iowa agreed to reimburse Slater at a later date if he placed at the meet at Stagg Field. But it was all for naught, as his application to compete at the Midwest preliminaries was received after the deadline and his Olympic dream came to an abrupt halt. Hawkeye fans lamented his technical disqualification, as many felt "he would almost have been certain of going east for the final trials."[6]

Duke Slater spent the school break performing his usual summer jobs. He shoveled coal, laid bricks, and hauled gravel. One classmate, Jim Mavrias, recalled, "Duke had the biggest hands I've ever seen. I remember when they were putting in the brick street by the Field House. Duke worked on it, putting bricks down. He kept four men busy handing them the bricks."[7]

In addition to the brick street by the Iowa Field House, he also helped construct the Burlington Street Bridge in 1920. B.J. Lambert, the head engineer of the project, encountered a problem one day that summer. The railroad delivered a gondola car full of gravel, and they wanted the gravel unloaded and the car returned that day. Unfortunately for Lambert, it was noon on Saturday and all the men except Duke had already left the job.

Duke offered to help. He grabbed a huge #12 grain scoop and climbed into the rail car. According to Lambert, a steady stream of gravel came over the side of that car all afternoon and by dark, the gondola car was empty.[8] These off-season jobs allowed Slater to stay in shape and earn money for tuition, but they also created tales of his work ethic and strength that made him a campus legend.

Slater, who was called "the kingpin of colored tackles," reported for his third season on the football team September 16.[9] "The husky Negro is in wonderful shape and expects to have the best year of his career, which is saying something," the *Gazette* reported.[10] The *Courier* added, "He was generally recognized as the most clever tackle in the west and ... will indeed be a terror."[11]

Duke Slater's fantastic performance for the football squad in 1919 had an enormous cultural impact on the Hawkeye community and created opportunities for other African American athletes almost immediately. The first man to follow in Duke's footsteps was a strong black tackle from South Dakota named Leroy Kinney. Kinney wanted to be a football player and a field athlete, just like Slater. Slater took Kinney in as his roommate, and Duke promised to do everything he could to make him a star.[12] Kinney was ineligible for varsity football in 1920, but he had all the physical gifts to be a projected starting lineman for the Hawkeyes in his sophomore year in 1921.

The media claimed the 1920 Hawkeyes were "expected to be the strongest in history [and] a strong contender for the Conference championship."[13] Iowa returned most of their starters from a team that finished five points shy of an undefeated season, and they also added a talented crop of sophomores to the team, the most notable of which was Gordon Locke, a big, bruising backfield man.

Predictions about Iowa's individual players were flying around as well. "Duke Slater will be the best lineman in the west this season," the *Waterloo Times-Tribune* suggested.[14] "How any football team in the west will be able to gain through the Iowa line this year is apparently impossible — on paper," the *Iowa City Press* concurred. "The giant Slater, if he carries the same avoirdupois as in 1919, will tip the scales around 205. Slater and Belding are all-Western men. How anybody can gain ground around Iowa's right end or on the right side of the Hawkeye line is a puzzle."[15]

The 1920 Hawkeye squad gathered to select a team captain, and the *Iowa City Citizen* listed four players under consideration for the honor. They included Fred Lohman, the previous team captain; William Kelly, the team's starting quarterback in 1919; Lawrence Block, a senior lineman; and Duke Slater. Kelly eventually earned the honor, but the mere mention of Slater as a candidate for the captaincy was indicative of the respect he had earned from his teammates.

Iowa's first opponent was the Indiana Hoosiers in Bloomington. The Hoosiers opened the season with a 47–0 drubbing of Franklin College, and Iowa was actually Indiana's homecoming game. But the *Waterloo Courier* confidently reported, "The Hawkeyes retain Slater, Belding, and Aubrey and Glenn Devine. Indiana cannot match this quartet of stars and upon them rests much of Iowa's hopes for victory."[16]

Gordon Locke and Aubrey Devine proved to be a powerful combination in their first game as teammates. The two backs alternated runs in a long drive near the end of the first period. As the second quarter opened, Devine charged over from a yard away to score the season's first touchdown. Later in the period, Indiana tried to fool the Hawks with the same "onside punt" play that cost Iowa against Illinois the previous season. This time, however, the Hawkeyes were ready for it and recovered in Indiana territory. Two plays later, Aubrey Devine passed to his brother Glenn for a 25-yard touchdown and a 14–0 margin at halftime.

The Hawkeyes were still ahead by 14 points and seemingly in control with two minutes left in the game when a 28-yard desperation pass was followed by a 35-yard touchdown throw by Indiana quarterback Russell Williams. Iowa was then forced to punt with mere seconds remaining. Charlie Mathys, Indiana's marvelous halfback, made a terrific return of the punt down to the Iowa 30-yard line. On the final play of the game, Williams was sacked as he prepared for a game-tying touchdown pass, and the Hawkeyes held on for a 14–7 victory.[17]

It was an extremely rough, physical game. Four of Iowa's starters were knocked out of the game due to injury. The strong, helmetless Slater was not one of them, but it wasn't due to a lack of attention on Indiana's part. "The Hoosiers persisted in trying to knock the big tackle out of action by kicking him in the head as the opportunities presented themselves," the *Iowa City Press-Citizen* reported.[18] However, Slater "was invincible in the Old Gold line," the *Waterloo Courier* declared.[19]

Duke would later call the Indiana game of 1920 the roughest tussle of his career.[20] "We were really battered and bruised, all of us," Slater confessed.[21] An easy game against Cornell College of Mount Vernon, Iowa, was just what Iowa needed. The Hawkeyes coasted to a 48–0 lead at halftime, and Duke and the rest of the starting lineup rested in the second half of Iowa's 63–0 victory.[22]

The Hawkeyes quickly turned their attention to the Illini and their old nemesis, Coach Bob Zuppke, who was up to his usual mind tricks. A reporter asked Zuppke about All-Americans, and he replied, "I cannot very well talk in terms of All-American teams, because I do not believe in that institution. To me the All-American team is a ludicrous conception. I would use a more strenuous word, but the word 'ludicrous' is about as ridiculous as I can think of." But then moments later, when asked about Aubrey Devine and Duke Slater of the Hawkeyes, Coach Zuppke stated they had "All-American material."[23] Despite Zuppke's flattery, Iowa remembered the controversial "onside punt" from the previous season, and the 1920 game had the makings of a great struggle. Ingwersen had left Illinois to join pro football, but the Illini still had Laurie Walquist and brothers Robert and Ralph Fletcher in their backfield.

The Illini spent the entire first half threatening the Hawkeye goal, only to be turned back repeatedly by Slater and the Iowa defense. On one series, Walquist ran the ball three straight times at Slater and only gained four total yards, leading to a missed field goal by Ralph Fletcher. Slater sacked Walquist for a loss on third down on Illinois' next possession, which resulted in another missed field goal attempt. In the second quarter, Duke sacked Robert Fletcher and forced a fumble, resulting in a big yardage loss that ended one of their drives. But Illinois eventually got close enough for Ralph Fletcher to connect on a 16-yard field goal, and the Hawkeyes trailed at halftime, 3–0.

The defense was playing well for Iowa, but offensively, the Hawks could barely scratch out first downs. The decisive play came in the third quarter when Captain Kelly fumbled a punt. Charley Carney scooped up the ball, broke several tackles, and sprinted into the end zone for an Illinois touchdown. The Illini tacked on another field goal later in the period and used a fake field goal play to set up another touchdown and a dominating twenty-point lead. Aubrey Devine kicked a 40-yard field goal in the fourth quarter to prevent a shutout, but the Hawks suffered a devastating 20–3 defeat.[24]

The postgame analysis of the loss blamed the Hawkeye linemen for the team's poor performance with one notable exception. "Slater Starred," the *Des Moines Capital* announced. "Slater, Iowa's tackle, was always in the game, figuring in every play. Slater's strong defensive work undoubtedly kept the score from being any larger. Illinois could not gain through Iowa's right side of the line."[25] "Slater Plays Star Game," the *Courier* agreed. "The bronze giant Slater was prominent in the Iowa defense."[26] The *Times-Tribune* observed, "Slater was the only Hawkeye lineman who really played up to expectations."[27]

Coach Zuppke was not as complementary. Although Zuppke was extravagant in his praise of Slater prior to the game, he brashly stated after the victory that Iowa was easy to beat as he sent plays around Slater.[28] Illinois had now claimed three victories over Slater's Hawkeye clubs, and even with Ingwersen no longer around, Duke hadn't been able to counter Zuppke's magic.

Several Hawks were bruised and battered in the meeting with Illinois, and the squad still hadn't fully recovered from the punishing Indiana game. To make matters worse, the Hawkeyes next had to travel to the Windy City to take on the University of Chicago, the other team that defeated Iowa in 1919. The Iowa-Chicago game of 1920 started inauspiciously for the Hawkeyes. Aubrey Devine fumbled the opening kickoff, and although the Hawks recovered, it was a sign of things to come.

Locke fumbled on Iowa's first possession to give Chicago the ball in Iowa territory. Duke Slater tried to pick the Hawks up, nailing a Chicago ball carrier in his tracks and forcing a long field goal attempt. Slater then broke through the line and blocked the kick, with Iowa recovering on their own 35-yard line. But the Hawks weren't in sync. A fumble by Aubrey Devine set up Maroon quarterback Lou Tatge's short touchdown run which put Chicago ahead, 7–0.

The errors continued to pile up for Iowa in the second half. Aubrey completed a long pass to his brother at the Chicago 25-yard line, but another fumble destroyed Iowa's scoring chance. Late in the third quarter, Aubrey came up short on a 48-yard field goal attempt, which was Iowa's best opportunity to crack the scoreboard. The physical battles against Indiana and Illinois had taken their toll on this Iowa squad. The weary Hawkeyes never threatened in the fourth period, and Chicago tacked on a late field goal for insurance to seal their 10–0 victory.[29]

After the game, the *Courier* was somewhat critical of Slater, saying that he "was a prominent figure all through the game, but in the second half, Chicago battered him into submission and he could hardly lift his size 14 feet at the finish."[30] This was likely due to the fact that Slater was playing through pain in the final quarter after colliding with his own lineman, Lawrence Block. In typical fashion, Duke refused to leave the game, but he developed two large bruises on his forehead.[31] His injuries were more apparent when he sat out a couple of practices in the ensuing week, a rare occurrence for Slater.

A helmetless Duke Slater trails an unidentified Hawkeye ball carrier down the field in this undated photograph.

Fortunately, Duke and his teammates had a bye week to rest up and heal their injuries before their next game versus Northwestern. The Hawkeyes readied themselves for just their second home game of the season. A steady rain was falling when Iowa and Northwestern kicked off at a muddy Iowa Field. Locke sprinted ahead for a 35-yard touchdown in the first quarter to give the Hawks a 7–0 margin. At one point in the second quarter, the Wildcats tried the same "onside punt" that Illinois had used in 1919, but as was the case against Indiana earlier in the year, the Hawks were ready for it and fielded the kick cleanly. The half ended with Iowa still holding a seven point lead.

In the third quarter, Iowa sustained a long drive down the field by making long runs behind Slater's blocks. With the ball at Northwestern's four-yard line, Slater decided to take on some of the coaching as well. Devine called for an end run, but Slater turned back and whispered to Aubrey to follow him into the end zone. Perhaps recalling the 1919 game against Chicago, Devine changed the play to an inside run. Slater created a massive hole for Aubrey to walk into the end zone, giving the Hawks a 13–0 edge. The rest of the game was dictated by the sloppy, muddy field. Players slipped and slid and failed to generate much offense in the foul conditions, but Iowa added a late touchdown to pad a 20–0 win.[32]

An amusing occurrence took place after Iowa's decisive victory. As Slater was passing by the stands, a visiting Northwestern fan tried to bait Slater. In a possible reference to Leroy Kinney, the Wildcat fan yelled, "Say, Duke, I understand Iowa will have an all-colored team next year."[33] Slater responded in his powerful bass voice, "Don't let them worry you, white boy. They are only trying to scare you."[34] That exchange became one of boxing great Joe Louis' favorite stories.[35]

With Iowa back on the winning track, the Hawkeyes braced for a homecoming battle against Minnesota, a team they had defeated two years straight. It was the final home game of the year for the Hawkeyes. Iowa hoped to become the first team to defeat the Gophers in three straight seasons since 1899. In contrast to Coach Zuppke, Minnesota coach Doc Williams was vocal about his plans to stay away from Slater's side of the field.

Coach Williams stayed true to his word. The Gophers made extensive use of their "Minnesota shift" and ran away from Slater on nearly every play on a 65-yard drive, which ended

The 1920 Iowa team had a somewhat disappointing year but still managed to compile a fine 5–2 record. Duke Slater is second from left in the second row; seated next to Slater, third from left in the second row, is Gordon Locke.

in a Gopher touchdown. Minnesota held their 7–0 lead until right before halftime, when Iowa's running game got on track. Devine and Locke repeatedly ran behind Slater down the field, and with the ball on the one-yard line, Slater cleared a hole for Locke to score a touchdown and tie the game at intermission.

Sophomore Gordon Locke took the starring role in the second half, adding a second rushing touchdown to give Iowa a 14–7 lead. Early in the fourth quarter, Minnesota had possession of the ball on their own 12-yard line. Captain Neal Arnston, the Gophers' quarterback, dropped the ball, and Slater dove on it to give Iowa possession. From there, Locke plowed in for a touchdown to give the Hawks a 14-point lead and put the game out of reach. He later tacked on a fourth rushing touchdown to guide Iowa to a 28–7 victory.[36]

"Fred Slater smeared plays right and left," the *Press-Citizen* beamed. "The tackles—especially the 'Duke'—opened holes for trucks to go through, especially Slater, who played a stellar tackle game."[37] The *Daily Iowan* observed, "Slater allowed no Gopher tackler through the line while on the offensive."[38] The *Gazette* reported, "That Doc Williams, the Minnesota mentor, feared Duke Slater was evident from the way two men played him throughout the fray. However, when the ball was carried to within shadow of the goal, it was through the dusky giant that Locke found the hole in which to carry the ball over."[39]

The *Waterloo Times-Tribune* gave a dissenting view, publishing a scathing article questioning Slater's play in the 1920 season. "What's the matter with Duke Slater?" the *Times-Tribune* asked. "Football followers seem to agree that Slater is not putting up the same brand of football this year that made him famous in the west last fall. The Duke hasn't blocked any punts yet this year! Opposing quarterbacks do not hesitate this season to direct play at the right side of the Iowa line; last year they kept away from the Hawkeye right tackle, who seemed to mix in every play. Against Minnesota it was noticed that Slater would come through the Gopher line to jam up a play but that he was apt to miss the man with the ball."

The article did compliment Slater's play offensively. "To give credit where credit is due, Slater has been a power in the Iowa line on offense this season. Saturday he opened up the holes through which Locke plowed to four touchdowns. More than once, Slater has been called to send the play his way and he has been right there with the road paved and level for the Iowa backs to carry the ball for good gains."

The *Times-Tribune* also conceded that most schools were using two men to try to neutralize Slater defensively. "But last year it took more than two men to handle Fred," the article taunted. "Anyhow, coaches and followers of the team alike agree that Slater isn't playing the football of which he is capable. Duke's friends are saying he will redeem himself against Ames by playing the game for the whole Iowa line like he did some times last year. Duke is fast, active, and good at diagnosing the play of his opponents and he has the same little friendly regard for Ames that all sons of Iowa profess. If he has been saving up for the Cyclones, he has a lot of defensive performances stored away to unloosen against Paine's athletes."[40]

The *Iowa City Press-Citizen* rushed to Slater's defense. "Some disgruntled fans aver that Fred Slater has not been playing [great] football," the *Press-Citizen* observed. "Who else on the Iowa team has done more than Duke in helping to put the Old Gold in the win column? What about the Indiana, Chicago, Northwestern, and Minnesota games? Was his play not satisfactory in these tilts? It must be remembered that two or three men are often placed on him, and how many men is one man expected to play and get away with it? Watch him Saturday."[41]

This rare criticism put the spotlight on Slater for the 1920 season finale against Ames. He had an unpleasant incident with the Aggie team the previous season, and now he had to visit Ames and face their hostile crowd. The Aggies immediately delighted that crowd by recovering an onside kick on the opening kickoff, and they maintained their momentum when Bill Byers connected on a field goal to give Ames a 3–0 lead. But the Aggies then attempted another onside kick, and Slater pounced on this one for the Hawks. That returned the momentum and field position to the Hawkeyes, and near the end of the first half, Iowa's offense methodically put together a 16-play drive that ended with a two-yard touchdown run by Aubrey Devine.

The third quarter featured the biggest play of the game. On fourth and three from the Ames 23-yard line, Iowa decided to forgo the field goal try. Aubrey Devine dropped back and connected with Belding for a 23-yard touchdown pass. This score gave Iowa a 14–3 advantage and a little breathing room in a previously close game. Although Ames scored a touchdown late in the fourth quarter, the Hawkeyes earned a workmanlike 14–10 victory.[42]

Duke quieted the verbal epithets of the partisan Ames crowd. The fans targeted Slater and hurled jeers and insults at him, but Duke performed admirably.[43] Slater even won over a few former critics with his play. "Fred Slater convinced some dubious fans that he is a tackle of the first water by his all-around play that was brilliant against the Farmers," the *Press-Citizen* declared. "[Lafe] Young, the giant Aggie who opposed the 'Duke,' was hardly able to hobble off the field after the milling Fred had put him through, while the husky Iowa tackle could have gone through another game. Fred was down on the punts; he broke through and tossed the halves for losses, while smashes through the line were dead the moment he was chosen to stop them."[44] The *Daily Iowan* complimented Slater's "brilliant defensive game," declaring, "Slater came out in old time form, messing up several Ames plays and opening avenues for the Iowa backs."[45]

Slater was named first team all–Big Ten for the second straight season. "Some think that Slater has not played the football he should this year," sportswriter Bill Evans wrote. "It is doubtful if the big fellow has ever opened up and played his limit, but he has displayed enough to land him on most of the teams that are being chosen. He will stand an equal chance with the west's stars in landing among the All-American men that are picked. He is big, weighing more than 200 pounds, goes through fast and has that uncanny ability of knowing where the play is going. His tackling is deadly, while he gets down on punts nicely. He is not content in stopping line plays at him, and more than once has been seen to go around ends and break through and stop the backs before they found the line of scrimmage. Teams have played two and three men against him all year, but with little success."[46]

Sportswriter Harry Page agreed. "While Slater may have not shown up at his best the entire season, there is little doubt that he leads the conference as a tackle," Page wrote.[47] The *Capital Times* added, "Slater was a tower of strength in the Iowa line and almost single-handed bolstered up the [Iowa] defense into a formidable affair."[48]

Eckersall officially placed Slater on the all–Big Ten team. "Slater of Iowa is placed at right tackle because of his consistent play all year," he wrote. "While a marked man in every contest, the colored warrior seldom permitted gains through him. On several occasions, offensive teams delegated as many as two men to keep him out of the plays. Being strong and powerful, he is the proper man for the position."[49]

Duke Slater led Iowa to a third place finish at the 1921 NCAA Track and Field Championship Meet by placing in the hammer throw and discus events. He earned seven athletic letters at Iowa, four in football and three in track.

With the 1920 football season concluded, the University of Iowa asked the Big Ten Conference for an official ruling on the subject of Slater's athletic eligibility. Some newspapers had been operating under the assumption that Slater's college career was finished, since 1920 was his third varsity football season. In fact, the *Times-Tribune* reported, "It is doubtful whether he will be ruled eligible for next season."[50]

According to Big Ten rules at the time, if Slater earned a degree in the spring of 1921, he would not be eligible for athletic competition. However, Duke was motivated to pursue a career in the legal field after being influenced by his mentor, Judge Mike McKinley. Slater had transferred from the College of Liberal Arts and was a freshman in the College of Law in 1920, so he would not be graduating in 1921.

On December 6, the Big Ten ruled that Duke was, in fact, eligible for a fourth season of varsity football in 1921. The waiver only applied to football, though, so Slater was ineligible for track in 1922. His football eligibility was met with great applause from Hawkeye fans. "Duke is eligible to star again in 1921 on Iowa Field, and on the fields where Iowa meets its gridiron foemen — every one of whom fears this giant tackle even as his Satanic Majesty shrinks from holy water," the *Press-Citizen* said.[51]

While waiting for his final track season, Slater tried his hand at boxing by sparring in three five-round fights against his roommate, Leroy Kinney. "The boxing bout between the two S.U.I. tar babies ... had the fans on edge every minute of the five rounds," the *Press-Citizen* reported at their first fight. "There wasn't an idle second in this match and though the South Dakotan seemed to have a little more science than the pugnacious Duke, the latter hung on doggedly and gave blow for blow throughout. The clash took like wildfire with the fans."[52] Their second match was equally well-received by the local sports fans. "Applause galore greeted these dusky knights of the fistic art and they amused the throng delightfully," the *Press-Citizen* observed.[53]

As the calendar turned to 1921, Duke prepared for his final year on the Hawkeye track team. One day at practice, Tom Martin, an Iowa law student and assistant professor of military tactics, watched Slater and the rest of the field athletes throw. He told the coach that the athletes' form was incorrect. "Let me show you," Martin said, picking up the 35-pound weight. He then heaved the hammer a couple of inches short of the school record. Impressed by his teaching and skill, the university hired Martin to be the weight coach for the track team.[54]

With Martin's coaching, Slater had a terrific final track season. In April, Duke qualified for the shot put event at the 1921 Drake Relays in Des Moines. He also set a school record in the discus throw that stood for six years.[55] Slater won the discus and shot put events at a dual meet event the following month against Chicago at Stagg Field, and his performances in the shot put, discus, and hammer throw events earned him an invitation to the first ever national collegiate championship meet on the weekend of June 16, 1921.

Duke and his qualifying Hawkeye teammates gathered in Chicago for Slater's last track meet in an Iowa uniform. At the inaugural NCAA national championship meet, the Hawkeye track team placed a surprising third in the country. The majority of the Iowa's points were racked up by sprinter Eric Wilson and Duke Slater. Slater individually placed third in the nation in the hammer throw and fourth in the country in the discus throw.[56]

Much of the credit for Slater's tremendous finish to his track career was owed to Coach Thomas Ellsworth Martin. Martin earned his law degree from Iowa in 1927 and eight years later, he was elected mayor of Iowa City. He moved from that post to Washington, D.C., as he was elected for eight consecutive terms in the U.S. House of Representatives from 1939 to 1955 and the U.S. Senate for a term from 1955 to 1961. Senator Martin later called Duke Slater the favorite athlete he coached. "Duke was one of the best coordinated athletes I ever saw," Martin proclaimed.[57]

The 1920 football season brought Duke fewer accolades and some rare criticism, but he overcame it to earn his second all-conference selection and place highly at the 1921 NCAA track championships. Moreover, Duke Slater had one more season in a Hawkeye football uniform, and it was the 1921 Iowa team that would bring him everlasting fame.

Chapter 7

A Championship for the Hawkeyes (1921–1922)

The first order of business for the 1921 Hawkeye football team was choosing a team captain. Aubrey Devine was elected to the position by his teammates, while Slater finished second in the voting. Duke won a gleaming silver cup as a tribute for placing second in the balloting.[1] By finishing second, he narrowly missed out on being the first African American to captain a Big Ten football team, but his second-place finish illustrated how revered he was by the other members of the squad.

Duke Slater was in terrific physical shape as the season drew near. He and several of his teammates, including Leroy Kinney, spent the summer hauling wheelbarrows full of concrete for 50 cents an hour. That concrete was used to build additional bleachers and walls at Iowa Field.[2] Slater appeared for his first football practice in the fall of 1921 and "was greeted with a handsome welcome," the *Iowa City Press-Citizen* noted.[3]

Slater's arrival, however, highlighted the segregation he continued to face. The *Press-Citizen* continued, "He came up to the armory in a racing car with one of his colored brothers, immediately got a suit, shoes, and locker, and made his appearance in a very few minutes on the field."[4] As an African American, Duke was not allowed to live in the dormitories. Instead, he lived with four of his Kappa Alpha Psi brothers at the Kappa House. Unlike his teammates, who could walk to practice from the dorms, Slater was forced to hitch a ride to practices from his fraternity brothers.

Duke wasn't the only African American projected to start for the Hawkeyes. Fans expected Leroy Kinney to get the nod opposite Duke at left tackle, which would make Slater and Kinney the first black teammates to start for a Big Ten school.[5] However, the opportunity for this ground-breaking racial event was lost the week of the opening game, because Leroy Kinney was declared academically ineligible for the season.[6] Kinney's case served as a reminder that playing in the Big Ten as an African American meant overcoming not only obstacles related to race and talent but academic hurdles as well.

In the opening game of the 1921 season, Iowa scored three touchdowns in the first five minutes of play against Knox College and poured it on to win easily, 52–14.[7] Slater's opponent was woefully outclassed, so he "took pity on his light Knox opponent" and supplied a few coaching tips.[8] Slater was affable and friendly and just as he had done against Chicago in 1919, he gave his opponent verbal instructions on tackle play during the progress of the contest.

Slater's opponent said afterward, "He was a real fellow. He gave me a lot of pointers about playing my position, how to block an opponent, and even how to stop him, which I had not been able to do up to that time. In thinking it over afterward, however, I realized that the times I had succeeded in blocking Slater were when the play was on the other side of the line. At that, I learned more football playing one game against him than in all the other games I have played."⁹ After the game, Knox head coach Sam Barry and his players called Duke "the cleanest player they had been up against."¹⁰

The Knox game was just a preview for the biggest college game of Duke Slater's life. Iowa and Notre Dame prepared to meet for the first time in their schools' histories. The Irish, coached by the legendary Knute Rockne, had won 20 consecutive games and were unbeaten in their last 22. In fact, Coach Rockne had only lost one game since becoming Notre Dame's head coach in 1918. The 1921 Irish ran only the most basic plays against their first two opponents and still defeated them by a combined score of 113–10. Notre Dame was unsurprisingly favored by two touchdowns over the Hawkeyes.¹¹

This team pin commemorates Iowa's 1921 season with the faces of every player on the roster. Duke Slater can be seen at the bottom of the pin, above the letter A in the word Iowa.

Arguably Rockne's greatest halfback, George Gipp, had just passed away after an excellent college career, but Notre Dame was still loaded with stars. Hunk Anderson, a tough lineman Gipp recruited to South Bend, would be lined up across from Slater. The newspapers began to speculate about what would happen when Hunk Anderson and Slater met. Bets were made about which one would be forced to leave the game first.¹²

Rockne coached his team at length on Slater, and when the Irish players arrived at Iowa Field's locker rooms before the game, they got a glimpse of Duke's size. Somehow — quite possibly in a psychological move by Coach Jones — an old pair of Slater's sneakers was left in one of the visiting lockers. The Notre Dame team gathered around and marveled at the shoes. "What the devil? Who are we playing, giants?" one of the players gasped.¹³

The favored Irish made quite an impression on the Hawkeyes as well. Duke recalled, "I'll never forget when we first came onto the field. We actually were frightened. We had only two or three footballs to warm up with. Notre Dame had twenty. Notre Dame was suited up neat and sharp. We had baggy pants — looked like a bunch of hicks. We just kept staring at the Notre Dame players."¹⁴

Coach Jones made sure his star tackle wasn't getting too comfortable. In the locker room before the game, Jones went up to Slater and said, "I am going to start you, but don't get too cocky. If you don't go too well, I'll snatch you out. You haven't made this team yet."¹⁵ But he took the pressure off of the rest of the team before they took the field. "Jones told us merely that we were going to learn a great deal of football that day and that the conference season started next week," Slater recalled. "Then he sent us out."¹⁶

The Hawkeyes charged out of the locker room loose, while Notre Dame started overconfident. "They came down for a lark," Duke observed.[17] The Hawkeyes surprised the Irish by easily driving down the field. Iowa's success came primarily on a play where Locke carried the ball through holes in the Notre Dame line created by Slater. "As I remember, Locke made several good gains on the play," Aubrey Devine reminisced.[18] "The gains that accounted for the greatest yardage were all plays where Locke plunged behind Slater."[19]

Hunk Anderson was ready for a physical game. Slater said, "Right from the start, Hunk Anderson lined up across from me and snarled, 'Look at all this raw meat here.'"[20] All the pregame talk about whether or not he was tougher than Slater clearly got under his skin. "Hunk wasn't playing with us or against Iowa. He had him a big one-man game with Duke Slater," one of Anderson's teammates said later. "But while Hunk was playing Slater, Slater was playing with Iowa and against Notre Dame.... We tried to get Hunk to settle down, but he was hell-bent on proving he was the best lineman."[21]

Slater recalled, "[Hunk] was going after me hard and not paying any attention to Locke pounding by. Finally I said to him, 'Why don't you go after Locke instead of me? He has the ball!' And Hunk replied, 'Rock told me to pour it on you.'"[22] Later, Hunk said Coach Rockne instructed him to "beat a tattoo on Slater's head" in the game.[23] But while Hunk was fixated on pounding Duke, Iowa used Slater's blocking to drive down inside of Notre Dame's one-yard line. On fourth down, Duke made a rare miss in blocking off Anderson, but Gordon Locke powered ahead anyway for the game's first touchdown.

The Hawkeyes regained possession a few minutes later and began advancing down the field again. Slater made a practice of grabbing Anderson by the back of his jersey, lifting him off the ground with one arm, pushing him out of the play, and then going after the men in the secondary to pave the way for Locke and Devine.[24] Hunk's physical play was taking a toll, but Duke was using Hunk's aggression against him. One Notre Dame lineman said, "Hunk was mauling him, but this big Slater would turn around, real quiet like, to Aubrey Devine, the quarterback, and say, 'Right through here, Aub.' And here they'd come.... That Slater never batted an eye. He would move Hunk in or out. And he'd say, when they needed a yard or so, 'Right through here, Aub.'"[25]

Notre Dame end Roger Kiley remembered the same dialogue from Duke. "On offense, [Slater] blocked Hunk Anderson in or Hector Garvey out," he said. "Before each play, he'd stand up and say to Aubrey Devine, 'Big day today, Aub. Right through here.'"[26] Slater created massive openings in Notre Dame's line between tackle Hunk Anderson and guard Hector Garvey. Duke recalled, "Hunk kept trying to talk Garvey ... into coming in closer to help stop the Iowa gains, but Garvey wouldn't do it. They had been coached to stop Aubrey Devine and were watching him all right but forgot about Locke—and how that Locke did run and plunge."[27]

F.W. Kent, the University of Iowa's official photographer, snapped an unforgettable picture of one of Locke's plunges. It showed Duke Slater, gigantically active and low to the ground, taking on three Notre Dame men while opening up a hole "big enough for an automobile to drive through."[28] Gordon Locke was shown driving ahead for several yards through the hole created by the helmetless Slater. The photograph would be shown in the Sunday edition of the *Chicago Tribune* and go down as one of the most famous pictures in the history of Hawkeye football.

Iowa made it down to the Notre Dame 30-yard line, and Devine drilled a long field goal to give the Hawkeyes a 10–0 lead. Notre Dame was shocked by Iowa's offensive start, yet Rockne's troops were not rattled. Johnny Mohardt completed a long pass in the second quarter to Kiley for a touchdown that cut their deficit to 10–7. "We still couldn't shut off

This iconic photograph by University of Iowa photographer F.W. Kent captures Duke Slater on the ground blocking the entire left side of the Notre Dame line in Iowa's 10–7 victory over Notre Dame in 1921. Fullback Gordon Locke is carrying the ball through the hole, while Slater's right arm is at an angle to shield his head from incoming tacklers. Standing on the far left in the photograph is Lester Belding, and watching from the backfield is Aubrey Devine, second from left (© University of Iowa–CMP Photograph Service).

their offensive power and were lucky to have held Iowa to only ten points," Hunk Anderson conceded.[29]

The teams retreated to their locker rooms at halftime, and Hunk explained to Rockne what was happening. "Duke Slater was having a field day ... Duke was a hell of a body blocker and you couldn't play him outside nor inside because he was big and quick and could easily sideswipe you out of the play with his body block," said Hunk.[30] "Duke repeatedly swept me out of the way by body-blocking me from the side. When I shifted outside Slater, it enabled Belding to take a crack at me from the other side while Slater hit me with his body-block. Frequently, I found myself sitting on the grass."[31]

Anderson decided to change tactics in the locker room at halftime. "In the second half, I played directly in front of Slater and in this way was able to keep my feet and also see and avoid the side block by Belding," Hunk recalled. "This maneuver proved a fairly successful defense. Slater was a deadly blocker when he could hit a man with a body-block from the side."[32] Duke continued to take a physical pounding in the third quarter. "Hunk kept giving me the business. My ears were ringing," Slater remembered.[33] Hunk wasn't the only Anderson Slater had to worry about. Notre Dame end Eddie Anderson admitted that he wore a special thumb guard to gouge rival linemen.[34] Finally, Duke trotted over to the bench and retrieved the helmet he discarded after the opening kickoff. "It doesn't fit," Slater remarked, "but it sure feels good."[35] Slater later joked he never knew what a helmet was for until he played against Hunk Anderson. "I noticed Duke go to the bench and put on a helmet," mentioned Hunk. "He sure had a hard head because after banging him on the head a few times, my elbow moved back about two inches."[36] Indeed, Hunk actually hurt his hands pounding them on Duke's head all day.

By the fourth quarter, the game had turned into a defensive stalemate, and Iowa still held a three-point advantage. Notre Dame gained yards, but the Hawkeye defense made key stops in their own territory. Aubrey Devine's long punts kicked Iowa out of trouble, and Slater was often the first man down the field to drill the Notre Dame return man for no gain. Kiley said, "On defense, Slater's long arms kept his big hands in my face all day. I was unable to get by his hands with a blocking headroll Rockne had taught us. He was really tough to block."[37]

As time ticked away, the frustrated Notre Dame players began sniping at one another. During a timeout, the Irish captain, Eddie Anderson, started to criticize Hunk for letting Slater outplay him. Hunk snapped back, "How about changing jobs with me?"[38] Slater's great offensive play allowed him to repeatedly get into the secondary and deliver crushing blocks against Notre Dame linebacker Chester Wynne. Wynne recalled being battered by Duke on almost every play, and he finally screamed at Kiley, "Come in here where the game is being played." For years following the game, Wynne was kidded by his teammates about spending the whole afternoon in Slater's arms.[39]

One story suggests that at one point late in the game, Slater stood up in the Iowa defensive line and dared the Irish to send the ball his way. In an interview years later, Rockne allegedly finished the story by saying, "And this crazy Irishman threw four straight plays at Slater, so we lost the ball."[40] While that particular exchange is unconfirmed, those are the types of legends that sprung up about Duke Slater after the Hawkeye defense held on for a dramatic 10–7 victory over Notre Dame.[41]

The *Daily Iowan* raved, "The giant Slater at right tackle was a joy killer for the Notre Dame backs on many occasions and although he carried no ball over for a touchdown, he was largely responsible for the Iowa victory."[42] The *Press-Citizen* added, "Duke Slater played the greatest game of his career, making huge holes in the left side of the Notre Dame [line], through which Aubrey Devine and Locke sifted through for big gains. The 'Duke' also was all over the field, tackling receivers of punts, stopping the man to whom the ball was snapped, and even running down the runner [from] behind when Notre Dame essayed one of its great interference end runs. He also recovered a fumble at a timely time."[43]

Slater said the battle with Rockne's machine was the toughest game he ever played.[44] "Duke Slater did the work of three men in the line," beamed Coach Jones afterwards. The coach called the game the biggest moment of his coaching career.[45] Near the time of his death, Jones listed the 1921 Iowa-Notre Dame contest along with the USC-Notre Dame game of 1931 as his two greatest victories in coaching.[46]

Francis Wallace, a sportswriter for the *New York Daily News* and an author of several books on Notre Dame, wrote, "Duke Slater, still there at the finish, had no doubt been responsible for considerable of the final frustration. Duke, incidentally, played the full sixty minutes that day and was in there after most of our tough guys had come out — perhaps because he played it like a gentleman. He had done one of the fine things in my football memories. Chet Grant, our quarterback weighing all of 138 pounds, recklessly caught a punt with big Slater bearing down on him. Grant could have been annihilated in his defenseless position, but Duke just sat him down gently. Slater won Notre Dame's lasting respect that day."[47]

The celebratory mood in Iowa City didn't last long. The Hawkeyes were physically battered after the Notre Dame game; Locke was hospitalized with a bad back, while Aubrey Devine had a brace in his jaw. To make matters worse, Illinois was next on the schedule, and Slater held a 0–3 record against the border school. Duke had only lost six games in a Hawkeye uniform, and half of those defeats came at the hands of Zuppke's Illini.

On a personal level, fans remembered Zuppke's bragging words about how he sent plays at Slater the previous year. "Additional wonderment is in whether or not Zuppke will direct much of his attack at Duke Slater, who played so stellarly last Saturday," reported the *Gazette*. "Zuppke, it is known, has boasted considerably about the success of his men in gaining over the giant Negro tackle and he has in other years shown no worry over the presence of Slater in Iowa's line."[48]

Iowa met Illinois for their homecoming game of 1921, with a sellout crowd of over 15,000 spectators in attendance. Behind closed doors, Coach Zuppke spent the week preparing his squad for Duke. "All week long, Zup [was] harping on Slater," Illinois lineman Jim McMillen recalled. "It was Slater this and Slater that, and by the time we took the field that bright October afternoon, we expected to see a right tackle about nine feet tall. We were wrong. He looked to be all of ten feet and about as wide as a three holer. The only comforting thing about the whole situation was, the Duke was smiling."[49]

Despite his use of a helmet against Notre Dame, Slater went back to his routine of tossing it to the sideline as the Illinois game began. It was a defensive game for most of the first half, but with minutes remaining before halftime, the Hawkeyes took command. Devine intercepted an Illinois pass at the Iowa 25-yard line and returned it 22 yards. Then Locke, who was questionable to even play before the game, carried the ball eight times for 42 yards, including a four-yard touchdown run that gave Iowa a 7–0 margin at intermission.

Locke continued to produce in the second half. He ripped off a 37-yard gain on Iowa's first offensive play of the third quarter, and several plays later, the Hawkeyes faced fourth and goal three yards from the Illinois goal line. Iowa decided to go for it, and Locke charged through a huge hole created by Slater into the end zone to give Iowa a 14–0 edge.

McMillen was normally a guard, but he played center in this game. He laughed that the position change "incidentally probably saved my life that day, because it is common knowledge that left guard plays opposite an opposing right tackle." He continued, "As we lined up, the Duke started on a line of chatter that only ended with the final whistle. The theme was mostly what dire things might happen to anyone so bold as to try and get through his side of the line. By quitting time, he not only had us brainwashed but also physically convinced."[50]

Zuppke defiantly directed his running attack, led by fullback Jack Crangle, right at Slater. But all afternoon, Slater spread his huge arms, planted his feet, and stopped Crangle in his tracks. Near the end of the game, the fullback came straight at Slater on a run and crashed into him with everything he had. Slater didn't move an inch and took him down in a heap. As they untangled, Slater lifted the battered Crangle to his feet, flashed a wide grin, and whispered, "Ain't we havin' fun, Mr. Crangle?"[51]

The Illini offense sputtered helplessly all game long against the solid Hawkeye defense. McMillen recalled, "As the game progressed, it became apparent that the Duke was feeling sorry for our awkward and futile efforts. He began picking the Illinois boys up and sending them back with a friendly pat on the back and words of encouragement. This was my introduction to Duke Slater, All-American gentleman."[52] At long last, Slater's Hawkeyes prevailed over Illinois, 14–2.[53]

Duke Slater opens a hole in the Illinois defense in Iowa's 14–2 triumph over the Illini. Fullback Gordon Locke rushed for an astonishing 202 yards in the victory (courtesy Gary Herrity).

"Hawkeyes Win Biggest Game of the Season," the *Daily Iowan* declared. "Much of the praise for [Locke's] sensational gains belongs to the giant Slater who time and again opened the hole in the Illinois line which enabled Locke to advance. Slater was also a star at defense and prohibited the Indians from making any noticeable gains through his position."[54]

The *Cedar Rapids Republican* exclaimed, "Locke through Slater — that was the cause of the downfall of the Illini. The dusky Duke opened up narrow holes in the right side of the line, which the driving and diving Old Gold fullback slid through with an amazing amount of force and speed."[55] The *Gazette* concurred. "Slater was a stonewall for the orange and blue backs to pound against. He stopped plays that were started in his direction, crossed the line to assist his comrades defending the other side, while on the offense it was through holes opened by the giant Negro that Locke often shot for gains upwards of ten yards."[56]

All eleven starters for the Hawkeyes played the full game, while Zuppke tried several substitutes in a failing effort to slow down Duke. "All efforts were made by the Illini mentor to stop the Duke Slater hole-making and the Locke rushes, but all in vain. Fresh men were not better than the others and it was a very much chagrined and disappointed coach that left the field," the *Press-Citizen* reported. "On defense, Duke Slater and Belding were stopping everything that came their way ... when one speaks of offense, he must include the mighty 'Duke,' who was opening up holes big enough to drive a team through ... most of the Iowa gains were through Slater's side of the line."[57]

Iowa's next game was their first road test of the year at Purdue, and Slater's performances were gaining praise. "For the past two seasons, Duke Slater's side of the Iowa line has been a stone wall, and mighty few gains have come through it," reported the *Waterloo Courier*. "On the offensive, the giant Negro tackle has smashed opposition and torn holes for his backs to dash through. A play-by-play report of the games this season shows fully half of the gains were made by Captain Devine or fullback Locke 'through Slater' or 'over Slater.'"[58]

Even the *Chicago Tribune* took notice of Duke's play. "Giant Slater Good As Ever," their subheading said. "Duke Slater, the colored tackle, is playing his usual steady game. Slater is a giant in stature and has been an almost unanimous choice of critics for their all-conference and all-western teams the last two years. Slater improves as the games wear on. He seldom tires and is in the thick of battle at all times."[59]

When the Hawkeyes arrived in West Lafayette, there were standing pools of water on the field. The condition of the field was so bad that workmen attempted to bail out places in the field with buckets and a drainage ditch was dug from the center of the field to run off some of the water. Although Aubrey Devine passed to Belding for a seven-yard touchdown in the second quarter, the field conditions made it difficult to add more points to the score. Devine attempted to drop kick a 23-yard field goal, but the ball sank in the mud which caused the kick to sail just under the crossbar as time expired in the first half.

Gordon Locke had started the game, but he was benched after only a few minutes when it became apparent he was too hurt to continue. His absence from the lineup became apparent in the third quarter. On two occasions, the Hawkeyes had fourth and goal from the Purdue one-yard line but couldn't power it over the goal line. But Purdue's offense had done little in the game, and their second goal line stand pinned them deep in their own territory. The Boilermakers tried to punt out of trouble, but Devine caught the punt at the Purdue 30-yard line and swerved through the entire Purdue team for an Iowa touchdown.

A 13–0 advantage was more than enough for the Hawkeyes in these field conditions, so Iowa ran down the clock. The Hawk defense and the horrible field conditions stifled Purdue's offense the whole game. The Boilers punched over a one-yard touchdown run on fourth down as the final gun sounded, but Iowa easily claimed a 13–6 victory.[60] Although the lousy field and Locke's absence suppressed Iowa's offense, the *Cedar Rapids Republican* still accused the Hawkeye team of overconfidence. "Aubrey Devine and Slater were the only two Iowa players who were in the game with all they had," the *Republican* alleged.[61]

The Hawkeye football squad's next opportunity to disprove that allegation came in Minnesota versus the Gophers. Slater had never lost to Iowa's northern rivals, and Iowa was trying to join the Wisconsin Badgers of 1896–1899 as the only schools to defeat the Gophers in four consecutive seasons. Minnesota prepared a secret weapon, a gigantic 295-pound guard named Babe Roos, to counter Slater. "The Gophers say that the Duke will not tear any holes through this baby elephant," the *Press-Citizen* warned.[62] "The left side of the [Minnesota] line is being primed to meet the ripping play of Slater, Iowa's Negro tackle," the *Courier* reported.[63]

Over 22,000 fans, including 6,000 Hawkeye fans, made the trip to Minneapolis to watch Iowa and Minnesota square off. The Hawks dominated the game from the start. Devine scored on an eight-yard touchdown run after an Iowa interception, and Iowa's defense didn't allow the Gophers to get any momentum on offense. With three minutes to go in the first half, Belding reeled in a long pass from Aubrey and carried a Minnesota defender into the end zone to give the Hawkeyes a 14–0 cushion at halftime.

The Hawkeyes were playing a spectacular defensive game. One fan at the game reminisced, "I remember how Slater's huge frame would come crashing through and one of his powerful hands reach out and spill many a runner. In the Minnesota game, a Gopher back seemed yards out of Slater's reach. Suddenly from somewhere, one of Slater's long arms shot out and at the limit of his reach, he gripped the halfback and slammed him down as if he were a child."[64]

Iowa's defense was overshadowed by an offensive onslaught in the second half. First, Aubrey Devine rammed behind Slater for a one-yard touchdown run early in the third quarter. Devine shook off several tacklers on another touchdown scamper later in the period, which gave Iowa a commanding lead going into the fourth quarter. But Aubrey Devine wasn't finished; he helped the Hawkeyes to two more touchdowns in the final period with a 38-yard scoring pass to Belding and yet another touchdown run, his fourth of the game. In one of the greatest performances in Iowa football history, Aubrey Devine scored all 41 of the Hawkeyes' points by running, passing, or kicking in Iowa's 41–7 win over Minnesota.⁶⁵

While there was effusive praise for Devine's performance, Slater also got his due. "Everything went against the Gophers in the last two periods, and they cracked under the ferocious charging of Slater and other Iowa linemen," the *Courier* observed.⁶⁶ Duke ran circles around Roos, who was too slow and had to be taken out of the game. The *Daily Iowan* exclaimed, "Slater, of course, played like he always does. He should have the Minnesota writer who said he was slow converted by this time to the belief that he is the fastest big man playing football."⁶⁷

The victory was particularly sweet for Slater and Belding, who joined Wisconsin's Pat O'Dea as the only players to defeat Minnesota four straight seasons. Duke's tremendous performances were raising speculation of the highest possible honors. "Slater, the giant Negro tackle, has outplayed every man he has met this year and has already been suggested as an All-American possibility," the *Times-Tribune* noted. "It is certain that he will have to be taken into consideration if he continues to play the same brand of football throughout the year."⁶⁸

On Nov. 11, Slater appeared at a track and field ceremony and accepted a medal for breaking several school records. Meanwhile, the 5–0 Hawkeye football squad prepared for Indiana in Slater's final college game at Iowa Field. The team was motivated by their extremely physical contest against the Hoosiers the year before, a game that left Iowa vulnerable to two subsequent losses.

The temperature at kickoff was ten degrees, and a light snow fell during the game. Fans waited for Slater's helmet toss after the opening kickoff, but it never came. Citing the cold weather, the Indiana contest was the first time Duke wore his helmet from start to finish.⁶⁹

Indiana stood little chance against the Hawkeye seniors in their final home game. Aubrey Devine followed behind Slater for three touchdowns in the first quarter alone, including a four-yard run as time expired on the period. The *Cedar Rapids Republican* reported, "Every second or third play the flock of sportswriters jotted down, 'Aubrey Devine through Slater for 15 yards.' When the dusky Duke charged, he swept aside opposing linesmen as if they were fleas."⁷⁰ Locke plowed over the goal line with seconds remaining in the half to boost Iowa's halftime advantage to 27–0.

It was domination from start to finish. Devine gave the home fans one last enduring memory, adding a four-yard touchdown in the third quarter before being benched for the remainder of the game. At one point in the third quarter, the Hawkeyes drew up a pass to Slater and Duke slipped behind the Hoosier defense, but the passer didn't spot Slater in time to give him a pass reception. Locke scored another Hawkeye touchdown with only minutes left in the game, and Coach Jones pulled Slater, Locke, and several other Hawkeye starters out of the contest at that point to the delight of the crowd. The seniors were lauded as the Hawkeyes kept their perfect record intact with a 41–0 victory.⁷¹

"Slater is undoubtedly the best tackle in the conference at the present time," the *Daily Iowan* concluded. "He has been playing for four years, and he has stopped play after play through his position. He is not as slow as his size would indicate but is down the field on a punt nearly as soon as the ends. When a play is sent on the other side of the line, his favorite trick is to break through the line, cross over, and tackle the man carrying the ball."⁷²

The clamor on Slater's behalf for All-American honors grew by the week. Jim Barnett, sports editor of the *Cedar Rapids Republican*, wrote, "The outstanding fact of the matter is that the playing of Duke Slater, the giant Negro tackle, is the most wonderful line playing ever seen in the country. The big fellow has opened up large gaping holes for the backfield stars to slip through and in every game this season has been a terror both on offense and defense. Slater's playing has not been so noticeable to the spectator in the stands. A lineman's play never is seen to advantage nearly as much as the playing of backfield stars. But without a doubt the big Iowa tackle has shown such wonderful form and such exceptional ability in defense of his position, as well as providing wide paths for advancing runners, to entitle him to a place on the All-American team of 1921. It is to be hoped that the critics of the east as well as the west do not overlook Slater as the greatest tackle ever wearing the moleskins and put him where he belongs on this season's All-American football team."[73]

The Hawkeyes now had a claim on conference and national honors. Iowa and Ohio State were tied atop the Big Ten standings, although the Buckeyes had a non-conference loss. The Hawks had to travel to Evanston and meet Northwestern for their final game in 1921, and the Buckeyes were set to take on Illinois to finish their season. A victory over Northwestern would give Iowa a Big Ten title, their first since 1900, and allow the 1921 Hawkeyes to top that 1900 squad for recognition as the best team in school history. The 1900 Iowa team provided a cautionary tale for the 1921 team, however; the 1900 Hawks had a perfect record until they suffered a 7–7 draw against the Wildcats in their final game.

The 1921 Hawkeyes arrived in Evanston and were greeted by the same kind of muddy field they faced at Purdue. Water was a foot deep on the field in some places. This would be Duke Slater's final game as an Iowa Hawkeye, but the sentimentality of the moment certainly wasn't affecting Coach Jones. "Before the Northwestern game, the last game of the 1921 season, Jones called us together for a pep talk," teammate Craven Shuttleworth recalled. "He pointed to Slater and said, 'Fred, don't think you've made this team yet. I may start you, but you're coming out of there if you do anything wrong.'"[74]

Several Hawkeye fans made the trip to suburban Chicago to watch the game, and they were delighted after the opening kickoff when Slater tossed his helmet to the sideline and played bareheaded one last time. The Hawkeye offense wasted no time getting ahead of the Wildcats. Iowa worked the ball down to the Northwestern 35-yard line, where Aubrey Devine shot a beautiful pass to his brother Glenn for a touchdown. Four minutes into the game, Iowa had an early 7–0 lead.

In the second quarter, the Hawkeyes made their big plays behind Slater, just as they had all season. Iowa faced a third down and one situation three yards from Northwestern's goal line. Aubrey Devine followed Slater to get a first down one yard from the end zone, and then Locke took it over from there for Iowa's second touchdown of the game. The Hawkeye defense was impenetrable, and Iowa took a 14–0 margin into the halftime locker room.

Most of the second half was spent in Northwestern territory with the Hawkeyes threatening, but Devine threw two interceptions near the Wildcat goal line to waste scoring opportunities. Hawkeye ball carriers slipped on several carries in the game as the field deteriorated into a mud pit. Since the circumstances were identical to those Iowa faced against Purdue earlier in the year, they adopted the same strategy when the fourth quarter rolled around; the Hawkeyes relied on their outstanding defense and simply ran the clock to protect their 14-point lead.

As the game drew to a close and it became apparent that an Iowa victory was near, Hawkeye fans received news that Illinois had upset Ohio State, 7–0. The ensuing celebration by the visiting fans shook the stands as word spread around the stadium. Iowa's 14–0 victory over Northwestern would not only clinch the first perfect season in school history but also Iowa's first outright, undisputed Big Ten championship.[75]

Several thousand fans met the Hawkeye team at the train station when they returned to Iowa City. An impromptu parade was thrown, with cars and trucks hauling the players to the town center. An enormous bonfire was lit at the intersection of Clinton and Washington streets downtown, and fans gathered to participate in a "snake dance" and recite school songs and chants.

Meanwhile, the *Courier* praised Slater as one of the game's stars, noting, "Slater particularly was of great help to his eleven, opening big holes in the line and breaking up Northwestern plays at their inception."[76] The *Daily Iowan* concurred. "Most of the gains through the line were made through holes that Slater opened, while there was no chance of making any ground through him as he spilled Northwestern backs for losses every time that a play was sent against him."[77]

Two days after the game, Howard Jones received a formal invitation from the Tournament of Roses committee to play the Pacific Coast champion California Bears on New Year's Day in Pasadena in the 1922 Rose Bowl. The Big Ten generally didn't allow their teams to participate in bowl games, but the conference had waived that rule the previous season for Ohio State. The Buckeyes played in the 1921 Rose Bowl and were shellacked, 28–0, and the Big Ten wasn't about to grant the Hawkeyes a second waiver.[78] Slater admitted years later that he regretted not having an opportunity to play in the Rose Bowl.[79]

Critics across the nation lauded Duke Slater's performance in 1921. He was a unanimous all–Big Ten selection, joining Aubrey Devine and Lester Belding as the first Hawkeyes to ever be named all-conference in three straight seasons. One *New York Times* sportswriter provided a good example of the unanimity that existed concerning Slater's place on the all-conference team. Of the two tackles on his all–Big Ten team, he wrote, "Here in one position there is a chance for argument. The other is simple. It is Slater of the University of Iowa, who was a tower of strength on the defense and who seldom failed to open up holes for his backs to go through. Slater possesses every quality that a good tackle should possess. His work throughout the season stood out in such a way as to make it impossible to overlook him for the place."[80]

Kenneth Clark of the *United Press* agreed, saying that in selecting an all–Big Ten team, "it is best to start building, as the champion Iowans did, from one man — Duke Slater, the giant Negro tackle. All experts concede Slater is the greatest tackle who ever trod a western gridiron."[81] Walter Eckersall officially gave Slater his third all-conference nod in the *Chicago Tribune* while hinting at even wider recognition. "Slater should be a candidate for All-American honors," he wrote. "There is little about line play that he does not know."[82]

Duke was so talented that he often overshadowed his teammates. "Iowa's left tackle [George Thompson] might be regarded as a star were it not for the fact that he is eclipsed by Iowa's right tackle, Slater, a Negro player two sizes larger than Jack Johnson," Walter Trumbull wrote in the *New York Herald*. "Slater is a law student who stands well in his classes, and who stands a giant bulwark in any football line. He is the most powerful tackle we have seen upon a football field this year."[83] Unfortunately for Slater, his teammates occasionally overshadowed him as well. "The Hawkeye Negro has sort of been forced to take the background due to the publicity given Aubrey Devine but, nevertheless, he is about the greatest tackle in the collegiate football world of today," the *Appleton Post-Crescent* noted.[84]

7. A Championship for the Hawkeyes (1921–1922)

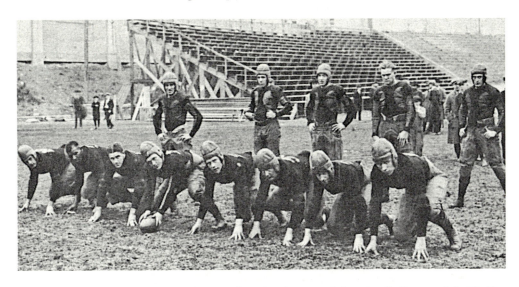

The 1921 Hawkeye football team went undefeated and captured the school's first outright Big Ten championship. Slater, wearing jersey number 15, can be seen in the front row. Crouching front row from left: Lester Belding, Duke Slater, Leo Kriz, John Heldt, Paul Minick, George Thompson, Max Kadesky, Chester Mead. Standing second row from left: Glenn Devine, Gordon Locke, Aubrey Devine, Glenn Miller, Craven Shuttleworth (courtesy Gary Herrity).

As December began, the football team members were honored weekly with banquets and tributes. Duke Slater was invited to dinners held by the Clinton Kiwanis and the Waterloo Rotary Club. "Duke Slater, the dusky giant from Clinton ... ranks with Devine as one of the greatest football players in the country," the Rotary Club announcement read. "In the four years that he has been playing at Iowa, he has made an intensive study of the lineman's job and has developed his huge bulk into one of the greatest offensive and defensive units ever seen on a gridiron. Much of Iowa's ability to charge opposing lines for gains during the past season has been laid at the door of Slater, and opposing teams made it a rule to put three and four men against the Iowa tackle generally to no avail."[85]

The Iowa City Lions Club, on the other hand, used the team's popularity as a fundraising tool. The Lions had a set of 13 "football dolls" made modeled after the 13 main players on the 1921 Hawkeye squad and auctioned the dolls off for charity. Over 100 dollars was raised, with Slater's doll topping the list by selling for 22 dollars. Devine and Locke's dolls were the next most popular, selling for 15 dollars each. "This seems to be the final proof that Duke is the most popular man on the team with the ladies," the *Daily Iowan* observed. "No less than two weeks ago, the *Daily Iowan* [was] harassed with University women clamoring for pictures of the squad. When given a picture, everyone looked first for Duke's likeness."[86]

Meanwhile, the All-American selections started to roll in. Bill Evans of the *Newspaper Enterprise Association* and Roundy Coughlin of Wisconsin's *Capital Times* began the movement by selecting Slater as a first team All-American. Walter Trumbull of the *New York Herald* gave Slater the same honor a week later. Although famed sportswriter Grantland Rice didn't pick an All-America team, he did a position by position analysis of college football players in 1921 and stated that Slater was his choice as the top tackle in the nation.[87]

Coach Jones endorsed the selections, saying, "I have had a number of All-America men in my experience, and I feel very strongly that either Slater or Devine are without a doubt of All-America caliber. Slater is a man weighing 210 pounds, has an exceptional offensive charge, and is a first-class defensive player. In the past two or three years, I have never seen a man who is as strong an offensive player as Slater, and we have played Illinois, Chicago, Minnesota, Nebraska, and Notre Dame."[88] Jones reiterated, "Slater is one of the greatest, if not the greatest, tackle I have ever seen in action. No All-America team would be complete without him."[89]

Knute Rockne echoed those exact sentiments. "No All-American team will be complete unless it includes Duke Slater. No better tackle ever trod a western gridiron," Coach Rockne declared. "This fellow Slater just about beat my team single-handed in the only contest we lost. Realizing the great strength of Slater, and the fact that he knew how to use that strength to intelligent advantage, I had four of my players massed around Slater throughout the game. Occasionally my boys would stop the big tackle, but those times were the exception. Usually he made such holes in my strong line that fullback Locke would go through for long gains, often standing straight up as he advanced the ball."[90]

The *Press-Citizen* added, "The experience of Coach Rockne was only what other western mentors were up against. In every game Iowa played, no opposing tackle was able to make the slightest headway. In fact, other teams usually burned up three or four men in an effort to stop Slater. Bob Zuppke, coach at Illinois and one of the most resourceful in the business, adopted tactics similar to those employed by Rockne but with no more success."[91]

Finally, Walter Eckersall, the most prominent sportswriter outside of the east coast, made his All-American selections. He, too, named Duke Slater a first team All-American. "Slater, the colored Iowa player, is placed at left tackle. The Hawkeye did not meet his match during the season, despite some opponents rearranged their attacks so that two and three players were delegated to keep him out of plays," he wrote.[92]

The biggest All-America team of all, however, was the one selected by Walter Camp. Slater had been just the third Hawkeye ever named by Camp when he was given a third team All-American spot in 1919. In 1921, however, Camp selected Aubrey Devine as a first team All-American and relegated Duke Slater to the second team behind Charles McGuire of Chicago and Russ Stein of Washington & Jefferson College.

The response to Camp's selections was swift. Bill Evans said, "The west will take strong exception to the selection of McGuire instead of Slater. The Chicago tackle is a great player, but Slater is generally considered one of the greatest tackles the west has ever turned out. The selection of Stein of W. & J. as the other tackle will be the subject of much dispute by eastern experts."[93] Hunk Anderson, who played against Stein in the NFL, was adamant that Stein wasn't in the same class as Slater.[94] The *Times-Tribune* confirmed, "Eastern critics expressed surprise when Stein of Washington & Jefferson was selected for tackle over Slater, the big colored boy from Iowa. It is agreed in both the east and west that Slater is among the great tackles of history."[95]

Coughlin expressed not surprise but outrage. "Camp has the right idea on his All-American teams. He waits till everybody else in the world picks his, then he picks somebody else." He continued, "Slater, the big colored tackle of Iowa, being left off Camp's All-American team is causing an awful yell among the football circles in Madison. It is a shame to think that a man that stands head and shoulders above all other tackles in the country today has to lose his great playing ability just because he is a colored man."[96]

In fairness to Camp, it is unlikely that he was racially motivated to omit Slater as a first team All-American; Camp had recently selected Fritz Pollard of Brown and Paul Robeson of Rutgers to his All-American first teams. Instead, Slater's snub almost certainly had to do with Camp's well-known bias towards Eastern players. Aubrey Devine was the first non–Gopher Camp had ever chosen as a first team All-American from west of the Mississippi River, and Camp had never named two teammates west of Michigan as first team All-Americans in the same year. The eleven players he selected for the All-America first team in 1921 came from eleven different schools, so when he chose Devine as his quarterback, he probably felt he had no room for Duke on the team.

Hawkeye fans were unswayed by any explanation. "A traveling man was telling me yesterday that in Iowa City where the University of Iowa is located, to start a fight, all you have to do is mention Walter Camp's name," Coughlin reported. "He says they are bitter that Slater, the big colored tackle, was left off the first team on Camp's selection. They are telling feats he has done in games this year that no other tackle has even come close to doing."[97]

Duke later admitted one of his most bitter disappointments was being relegated to the second team by Camp.[98] But in the end, Camp was outnumbered, as nine critics selected Slater as a first team All-American. The *Davenport Democrat & Leader* reported, "On the Iowa campus there is a feeling that because Slater is a Negro, he did not get the consideration he deserved in some quarters, but Duke's friends, including Coach Rockne of Notre Dame, may take solace in the fact that nine first team selections ... represent at least a fair estimate of the opinion the sports world holds of Slater's abilities."[99]

Duke Slater's selections in 1919 and 1921 made him just the third African American to be twice named an All-American by Walter Camp. William Henry Lewis, a Harvard center, accomplished the feat in 1892 and 1893, while Minnesota's Bobby Marshall earned All-American honors in 1905 and 1906. No African American after Slater would claim two All-American selections by the Walter Camp Foundation until Cal Jones in 1954 and 1955. Being named an All-American was a very rare feat for a black player in that era, but Duke didn't care for such distinctions. Of his All-American selections, he said, "The American phase of it is what appeals the most. It doesn't say anything about race."[100]

Leslie's Weekly, a popular national weekly magazine, gave Duke Slater his highest honor of the 1921 season. They named their top players in each major sport, selecting Babe Ruth in baseball, Jack Dempsey in boxing, Jim Thorpe in pro football, and Duke Slater in college football.[101] "At last, Duke Slater has received full justice. He has been picked by *Leslie's Weekly* as the champion football player of the year. This is perfectly logical for he was the keystone lineman of the Iowa team and the maker of brilliant backfield men. Too much cannot be said for the giant tackle, for he is one of the cleanest players in American football," the *Cedar Rapids Republican* wrote.[102] "Duke Slater, Iowa's big Negro tackle, won the name of being the greatest maker of holes in opposing lines that ever wore a football suit in the country," the *Press-Citizen* declared.[103] "It took a long time for the big black boy to get recognition, but he has certainly come into his own at last."[104]

The 1921 Hawkeye team had a strong claim as the greatest football team in the nation. The Hawkeyes were the undisputed champions of the Big Ten Conference and defeated Notre Dame. Rockne's Irish later handed Missouri Valley Conference champion Nebraska their only loss, which established Iowa as the clear champions of the Midwest. Coach Rockne had the greatest respect for the Hawkeye aggregation; five months before his death, he called Iowa's 1921 team the greatest team he faced in his career.[105]

There was no decisive champion on the east coast. Like Iowa, Lafayette College of Pennsylvania and Cornell University were undefeated and untied, but both accomplished the feat while playing a subpar schedule. Cornell, the champions of the Ivy League, didn't play any of the league's "Big Three" football schools—Harvard, Yale, or Princeton—in the 1921 season, instead running up lopsided scores against inferior competition. Grantland Rice declared that in his opinion, Iowa could defeat any team from the East.[106] Meanwhile, the champions of the south, Centre College of Kentucky, lost in the Dixie Classic to Texas A&M, 22–14.

California was the Pacific Coast Conference champions and the undisputed champions of the west coast. When the Tournament of Roses was prevented by the Big Ten from selecting Iowa, they chose tiny Washington & Jefferson College to oppose California in the 1922 Rose Bowl. Washington & Jefferson was naturally a heavy underdog; one sportswriter sarcastically quipped, "All I know about Washington and Jefferson is that they're both dead."[107] Nevertheless, Washington & Jefferson held California to a scoreless tie in the game, and the consensus opinion was that California was badly outplayed. The Golden Bears were held to just two first downs for the entire game, and Washington & Jefferson had a 40-yard touchdown run negated on a controversial offside penalty.

Grantland Rice remarked in the *New York Tribune*, "Our vote for the four greatest football machines in America goes to California, Iowa, Notre Dame, and Penn State."[108] Of those four teams, only Iowa finished with a perfect record. "One who has seen all the strong teams of the Middle West and some of the big ones of the East feels quite safe in predicting that the eleven from the University of Iowa would beat any football team in the country today," declared James Crusinberry of the *New York Daily News*. "Duke Slater, right tackle, stands out far above all linemen of the West. Out in a drug store window in Iowa City is a photo snapped during a scrimmage of the Iowa-Notre Dame game. It shows Slater on all fours, blocking four Notre Dame men from the hole he has opened in the line, and Locke, with the ball, is plunging unmolested through the hole. That picture showed one instance of what Slater does dozens of times in every game."[109]

The 1921 Hawkeyes not only went undefeated; they never trailed at any point during the season. Iowa defeated two schools—Notre Dame and Illinois—that each claimed national championships two years earlier. The Hawkeyes had a tremendous defense; in Iowa's six major games in 1921, no school scored more than seven points against them. They allowed just three touchdowns in their last six games; one was midway through the fourth quarter in a 35–0 game against Minnesota, and another came on literally the last play of the game in Iowa's victory over Purdue.

Offensively, Iowa's scores on the season were misleading. Iowa won narrow but respectable victories over solid opponents in Illinois and Notre Dame, and Iowa's contests with Northwestern and Purdue were played in terrible field conditions that hindered scoring. In their other three games, the Hawkeye offense scored 134 points. When asked specifically about the possibility of Iowa's offense facing Cal in the Rose Bowl, Indiana coach Jumbo Stiehm said, "California could not shut out Iowa, nor do I think California could beat Iowa. No team in the country could keep the Locke and Devine combination from scoring."[110] This statement was made before Cal's scoreless performance in the Rose Bowl, and afterwards, Coach Stiehm's opinions resonated.

National championship claims in college football are usually inconclusive. The NCAA does not crown an official champion in major college football, and no major organization selected a national champion in 1921. Twelve years later, historian Parke Davis selected the

1921 Hawkeyes as a national championship team, and the NCAA recognizes Iowa in the Official NCAA Records Book as one of five schools with a legitimate national championship claim in 1921. Although several modern national championship selectors have shunned the 1921 Hawkeyes for whatever reason, there is no doubt that Iowa was one of the greatest teams in college football in Duke Slater's senior season.

Since Slater wasn't eligible for the 1922 track season, he occupied himself with boxing matches against former teammates John Heldt and Leroy Kinney. In April, Duke won the university's intramural heavyweight boxing title by defeating John Weisensee in a bout at the school's armory, winning every round.[111] On May 17, 1922, the champion Hawkeyes took the field for the final time together in a scrimmage against the underclassmen. Duke Slater, the Devine brothers, and Lester Belding were honored in a Senior Day celebration. Classes were cancelled in the morning in honor of the event, and a parade was held for the four stars, terminating at Iowa Field where the scrimmage took place.

It was a fitting farewell to Slater, who ended his four-year college career with an overall record of 23–6–1. The Hawkeyes had won their last ten games and their last 13 home games when Duke left school. But another meaningful accomplishment that should not be overlooked occurred when Duke graduated with his B.A. degree in May 1922. Considering his economic background and the rampant racial discrimination of the time, earning a college degree was not an insignificant achievement. Academically and athletically, Duke Slater set an example for others to follow. That would continue as he blazed a trail into the National Football League.

Chapter 8

Coloring the Line (1922–1923)

With a college degree in hand, Duke Slater had to decide what his next step would be. Slater had already begun taking classes at the University of Iowa law school, but he needed a job to continue to fund his tuition. He was approached by several high schools and colleges with coaching vacancies, including Clinton High School, which wanted his help as a line coach.[1] Most notably, however, Coach Howard Jones offered Duke a job as his line coach at Iowa, an opportunity that strongly appealed to Slater.

Duke also received pitches from multiple professional football clubs. The best of these offers came from Walt Flanigan, owner of the NFL's Rock Island Independents. Slater's only reluctance toward playing for Rock Island concerned the coaching opportunity at Iowa. He asked Flanigan if he could do both, attending practices in Iowa City and arriving later in the week for Rock Island's games. "I'm quick at picking up signals," Duke argued. "I'll be in great shape, too."[2]

Flanigan, however, had been burned by similar arrangements in the past, and he rejected any situation which would cause Slater to miss the team's daily practices. Perhaps as a negotiating tactic, Flanigan stated that in addition to playing for the Independents, Slater could serve as line coach for the Rock Island club.[3] The chance to serve as an NFL line coach while continuing to play football was more attractive than Jones' offer, so Slater signed a contract with the Independents. He agreed to a salary of $1,500 for the ten-game 1922 season; that sum made him one of the highest paid players on the Rock Island team.[4]

As his career with Rock Island progressed, Slater's position as line coach was never again mentioned. The coaching position was likely abandoned after Flanigan sold his ownership interest in the team, if it was ever recognized at all. Slater initially pledged to continue his law school classes while playing for the Independents, but he soon shelved that idea to focus on football.[5] He joined the team's training camp and prepared for a preseason exhibition against the Moline Indians.

The Cleveland Panthers, a semi-pro organization, tried at the last minute to lure "Iowa's chocolate colored star" away from Rock Island.[6] "Duke Slater will be in the Rock Island lineup against Moline Sunday," Flanigan declared in an effort to squelch the rumors. "The big colored tackle is at our camp on Rock River and has absolutely no intentions of jumping to the Cleveland Panthers or any other team."[7]

The Rock Island press was thrilled to have him signed and delivered. "Slater is one of the most powerful men in football today," wrote James L. Hughes of the *Rock Island Argus*. "His name was heralded throughout the length and breadth of the land as one of the real line wonders of the game."[8] Against Moline, he lived up to his advanced billing by playing the complete game in the 26–0 exhibition victory.[9] "His foes shiver when he sneezes," the *Davenport Times* wrote of the intimidating Slater.[10]

The first NFL game of Duke Slater's career was at Douglas Park, the home field of the Independents, and the opponent was the Green Bay Packers. The previous season, Rock Island gave Green Bay their first home defeat in five years, and the Packers were looking to return the favor in Rock Island. The Packers were led by their coach and captain, halfback Curly Lambeau. The Independents, conversely, were led by their coach and captain, quarterback Jimmy Conzelman, but the strength of the Rock Island team was in its line. Slater was joined at tackle by Ed Healey, a skilled lineman with a fiery temper, while the talented Jug Earp held down the center position. "Duke Slater is counted on to be a tower of strength in the Rock Island line," the *Davenport Democrat & Leader* declared.[11]

Slater admitted being skeptical of professional football at first but said he didn't realize as much spirit could be developed in the pros as his Rock Island teammates were showing daily. In addition, the talent level impressed Duke. "I never imagined so many first class players could be assembled on a single team," Slater said. "I certainly wish Aubrey Devine could be with us this year. Behind such a line, I believe there would be no limit to his ability to advance the ball."[12] Slater also changed his mind about the importance of headgear. "Hunk taught me to use a helmet," he said. "When I got into pro ball, I wore everything I could get my hands on."[13]

Four African Americans competed in the NFL prior to Duke's arrival with Rock Island: ends Bobby Marshall, Paul Robeson, and Inky Williams, and halfback Fritz Pollard. But on October 1, 1922, Duke Slater became the first black lineman in NFL history when he lined up at tackle against the Green Bay Packers. The game turned into a great battle between Conzelman and Lambeau. Rock Island took an early 6–0 lead on a fourth down touchdown pass by Conzelman, and he added a field goal for a nine-point lead early in the second quarter. Lambeau countered with a long pass that set up a Packer touchdown to cut their deficit to 9–7.

The Independents drove the ball right back at Green Bay and had a first and goal at the Packer four-yard line when Slater took a hard hit and was forced to call timeout. For a man who had not taken timeout in his last three years in college, taking one in the first half of his first pro game made it apparent that the NFL presented a new challenge for the powerful Duke. When play resumed, it took two plays for the Independents to push over another touchdown, restoring their nine-point advantage to 16–7 at halftime.

With only minutes remaining in the contest and Rock Island clinging to a 19–14 lead, Green Bay got the ball back for one final chance at a game-winning score. Slater drilled Curly Lambeau on a pass attempt, but he was penalized 15 yards for roughing the Packer legend, which gave the Packers a first down on the Green Bay 31-yard line. Undeterred, Slater broke through and knocked down Lambeau's pass attempt on the very next play as well, and two more incompletions forced Green Bay to punt the ball. Rock Island was able to run out the clock and secured a dramatic victory over the Packers in Slater's first NFL game.[14] Duke Slater played all sixty minutes in the win.

Things wouldn't get any easier for Slater, as Rock Island's next opponent was the Chicago Bears. In his career, Duke would face the Bears more frequently than any other opponent. Rock Island considered the Chicago Bears their greatest rivals and a decided jinx. In two NFL seasons, the Independents had only been tagged for four defeats; the Bears franchise was responsible for three of them.

The Bears were co-owned by George Halas and Edward "Dutch" Sternaman. Halas was the team's head coach and starting end, while Dutch Sternaman was one of the Bears' starting halfbacks. Dutch's brother, Joe Sternaman, was the team's dynamic quarterback. Halas sent Burt Ingwersen, a former Bears lineman and then the coach of the freshman team at the University of Illinois, to the Rock Island–Green Bay game to scout the Independents.

Slater was touted as a player of "extraordinary ability" after his performance against the Packers, but the linemen of the Bears might give him flashbacks to the brutal Notre Dame game of 1921.[15] Chicago featured Hector Garvey at left guard, and Hunk Anderson, who Slater described as "a rough piece of furniture," started for the Bears at left end.[16]

The two rivals battled to a deadlock for nearly thirty minutes, but just as the first half was coming to a close, Chicago halfback Pete Stinchcomb outran the entire Rock Island team for a 37-yard touchdown. The half ended after the ensuing kickoff, and the Rock Island crowd at Douglas Park sensed the "Bears jinx." But Slater gave momentum back to the Indees in the third quarter. He dropped Joe LaFleur for a loss and then stopped Dutch Sternaman for minimal gain on third down to force a Chicago punt. Rock Island took over and drove down to the Bears' 14-yard line. On second down, "the crowd was thrilled to see Slater take out the entire left side of the Bears' line and [fullback] Buck Gavin crash headlong through the opening, bowl over the secondary defense, and somersault over the line," the *Argus* noted.[17] Conzelman failed to tie the game on the extra point, though, and Rock Island still trailed, 7–6.

On the Bears' next possession, Slater tackled Dutch Sternaman for no gain to force another punt, but a costly fumble by Gavin halted Rock Island's next drive. In the fourth quarter, the Bears advanced to the Rock Island 23-yard line, and although Slater dropped Sternaman to bring up fourth down, Dutch calmly booted a 30-yard field goal to give Chicago a 10–6 lead. Rock Island threatened to take the lead, moving the ball down to the Bears' 12-yard line at one point, but a Conzelman fumble ended the threat. Chicago held on for a 10–6 victory to keep their supremacy over the Indees intact.[18]

Furious over the loss, Rock Island management cut their starting center, Jug Earp. They also signed several new linemen and were eager to unleash a new offense against Evansville after two low-scoring games. "The fans are ripe to see some scoring and they don't care who the victim is," the *Argus* reported. "They want to satisfy themselves that the Independents really are a scoring machine of the class that was developed two or three years ago."[19]

The result was an offensive performance for the record books, and the Evansville Crimson Giants were the victims. Conzelman rushed for a ten-yard touchdown in the first quarter, and he added a second touchdown run early in the second period. Trailing 13–0, Evansville failed to generate any offense on their next possession and was forced to punt the ball away. Duke Slater crashed through the line and blocked the punt, and the Independents recovered at Evansville's 14-yard line. Fourteen yards later, Conzelman rushed for his third touchdown of the day, giving Rock Island a commanding 20–0 lead.

The touchdowns just kept coming, one after another. Before the final gun sounded, the Independents tacked on six more rushing touchdowns. Conzelman added two of those in the fourth quarter, and Rock Island ran away with a dominating win by a final score of 60–0.[20]

"As usual, Duke Slater played the same style of ball that has annexed much football glory to his name," reported the *Davenport Democrat & Leader*. "On the defensive, Slater has been shifted to the end position and his work in this department yesterday was exceptionally strong. On the offensive, Slater opened wagon wide holes for Flanigan's backs."[21]

Those wagon wide holes Slater provided led to a record-setting day by Rock Island's backfield. Conzelman's five rushing touchdowns set an NFL record for rushing touchdowns in a single game; today, the mark still ranks second in NFL history. As a team, Rock Island notched nine rushing touchdowns, setting an NFL record for team rushing touchdowns that still stands ninety years later. Slater played all sixty minutes in the historic victory. He and left end Tillie Voss were the only two Independents who had played all sixty minutes in each of the first three games of the season.

The fans and media may have been impressed with Duke Slater's play, but Doc Alexander was not. Alexander, the coach and captain of Rock Island's next opponent, the Rochester Jeffersons, confidently predicted a Rochester victory. One reporter asked, "How about Slater? Who'll play against him?"

"Who do you birds figure Slater is, anyway?" Alexander snapped. "Do you people figure he's the first lineman that ever played football? Well, I'm here to tell you our regular man will play against him — and no one else."

A few minutes after Captain Alexander spoke, though, word spread that Alexander was assigning two Jeffs with the task of containing Slater. "Since the easterners arrived in Davenport Tuesday afternoon, they have schemed, plotted, and planned ways and means of stopping the giant Negro from wrecking their defense," the *Davenport Democrat & Leader* remarked. "Slater, however, had two opponents in every game last season when he was a member of the Iowa University team and that fact will not disturb the big tackle."[22]

Douglas Park in Rock Island was covered with mud for the Rock Island-Rochester game. The slippery conditions kept Rock Island off the scoreboard for most of the first half, but Conzelman raced 10 yards for a touchdown late in the second quarter to give the home team a 6–0 halftime lead. In the second half, Rock Island's offense snapped to life. Conzelman crashed over the goal line for a one-yard touchdown, and Gavin added two touchdowns in the fourth quarter to secure a 26–0 triumph for Rock Island.[23] Alexander apparently had no comment after the game.

The Independents had a 3–1 record on the season at home, but now they took to the road for the first time. The team was scheduled to make a two-week road swing through Wisconsin, first playing the Green Bay Packers and then traveling to Milwaukee to take on the Badgers. The Packers were winless on the season and would be playing without their leader, Curly Lambeau. Odds heavily favored Rock Island to come away with their second victory of the season over the Packers.

For this reason, the resulting scoreless tie was a major disappointment for the Rock Island fans.[24] Conzelman was likely overconfident of the victory or especially fearful of the Badgers, since he started the Packer game with a group of reserves in the backfield. One early scoring chance was ruined when Walt Brindley, Rock Island's reserve quarterback, threw the ball well over the heads of two receivers who could have strolled in for a touchdown. By the time Conzelman and the rest of the starting backfield came off the bench and into the game, Green Bay had found a weakness in Rock Island's formations and stifled their offense.

Jug Earp was quickly picked up by Green Bay after he was released by Rock Island earlier in the season. Not surprisingly, Earp played an inspired game against his former club. The Independents were forced to change all of their offensive signals on account of Earp's presence with the Packers, but their new signals caused massive confusion for the Independents' offense. Conzelman missed two field goals for Rock Island, and Duke was singled out for blame in the disheartening tie. "Slater, the giant Negro tackle, failed to prove a tartar," the *Argus* sighed.[25] James Hughes of the *Argus* found blame elsewhere, sug-

Ringwood Park in Clinton, Iowa Field in Iowa City, and Normal Park in Chicago have all been torn down, but Douglas Park in Rock Island, Illinois, still stands. Duke Slater played home games at Douglas Park as a member of the Rock Island Independents from 1922 to 1925. Today it is a public park.

gesting that some team members were staying out late and imbibing too much "soda pop."[26]

If the disappointing performance against Green Bay was due to Conzelman's reluctance to reveal his plays to the Milwaukee Badger organization, it was a miscalculation. The Badgers had a very strong team indeed, bolstered by African American stars Fritz Pollard and Paul Robeson. The press, in fact, hyped the matchup as a duel between "two giant men of color," Slater and Robeson.[27] But a severe rainstorm in Milwaukee coupled with only a handful of fans braving the weather in the stands forced the cancellation of the Rock Island-Milwaukee game. Slater hadn't seen the last of the Milwaukee Badgers on the 1922 season, however.

The Independents returned home to face the Dayton Triangles in the last game of the year at Douglas Park. This was a grudge match for Rock Island, as the Triangles were the only team other than the Bears to hand them an NFL defeat. Dayton triumphed over Rock Island in 1920 by a 21–0 score, and several of those Triangles were still on their roster. The 1922 Triangles claimed to be an even stronger squad than the 1920 edition. Their greatest success in 1922 was a tie with the Canton Bulldogs in a game where many felt they outplayed Canton; the Bulldogs were undefeated and well on their way to the 1922 NFL title.

The Triangles were led by quarterback Herb Sies, who played high school football in Davenport before becoming an All-American at the University of Pittsburgh. As a former Davenport player, he relished a chance to beat the Independents. "Two years away from the rivalry of the tri-cities has been almost too much for me," Sies wrote. "You all know I never did waste much love on Rock Island. Just place your bets on Dayton and you won't go wrong."[28] Meanwhile, the *Argus* stated, "The duel between Duke Slater at right tackle for Rock Island and Russell Hathaway at left tackle for Dayton promises to be highly interesting for the fans."[29]

Half of Douglas Park was covered with mud and water ankle deep as the game with Dayton was set to begin, and the other half of the field was only slightly better. That may not have been a coincidence, since Dayton used the forward pass extensively in their 1920 defeat of Rock Island. The home team used the conditions to their advantage, overpowering the Dayton line on their way to two rushing touchdowns and a 17–0 halftime lead.

Duke Slater assumed the kickoff duties for the Independents in this game, taking over the role from Ed Healey. Slater kicked off to start the third quarter, and a drizzling rain began to fall. A few minutes later, Mike Casteel put the game away for Rock Island with the only touchdown of his NFL career, a dazzling 35-yard run. Two costly fumbles by Dayton in the fourth quarter led directly to Rock Island scores, and Rock Island proved that there were no hard feelings toward Dayton by punching across one final touchdown as time expired in a 43–0 victory.[30] When the smoke cleared, Rock Island handed Dayton their worst loss in franchise history, and the Independents had their revenge for that 1920 defeat.

Speaking of revenge, the 4–1–1 Independents had only one loss in 1922, and their final scheduled game of the season was a rematch with the team that gave it to them. Rock Island traveled to Cubs Park to take on the Bears in Chicago. The winner of the Independents-Bears contest would take over second place in the league standings behind the winner of the game between the Chicago Cardinals and Canton Bulldogs. If Rock Island were to defeat the Bears, they planned to ask the winner of the Cardinals and Bulldogs for a game to decide the 1922 NFL championship.

Duke Slater's performance against the great Bears' linemen was considered a key factor in Rock Island's chances for victory. "The Bears figure they can win again Sunday if their line can hold the terrific pounding of the Rock Island all-star trio of backs," the *Argus* reported. "But the work of the two superb tackles, Ed Healey of Dartmouth and Duke Slater of Iowa, must be considered. These men are capable of opening wide holes for their backs to go through."[31]

Both teams had trouble scoring in the rematch. Three missed field goals kept the Independents scoreless in the first half, while the Bears' best scoring chance of the half came with seconds to play. The Bears had the ball, second and goal, at the Rock Island eight-yard line. They lined up for a possible field goal, but the Bears ran a fake field goal instead. Dutch Sternaman swung a pass out to Pete Stinchcomb, and Stinchcomb was tackled for a two yard loss. Before the Bears could attempt a real field goal on third down, the half ended and the scoreboard continued to show no points.

Rock Island feared all week the possibility of Dutch Sternaman getting a chance to kick a winning field goal, and those fears turned out to be well-founded. A potential game-winning field goal by Sternaman with six minutes remaining sailed wide of the goalposts, but the Bears soon got the ball back and gave Dutch another chance. With just one minute left in the game, Dutch booted a 20-yard field goal to give Chicago a 3–0 victory.[32]

Slater's first NFL game in the town where he had grown up attracted a large number of his fans. The *Davenport Democrat & Leader* reported, "Duke Slater, former star tackle at the University of Iowa, had many admirers in the crowd, and he played his usual brilliant game."[33] Though Duke played well, his team didn't. It was a sorry offensive display for Rock Island, the team that led the NFL in offense in 1922. The Independents only had one first down the entire game, and none in the game's final three quarters.

Several Independents blamed Conzelman's poor play at quarterback for the loss to the Bears. In response, team owner Walter Flanigan sent a telegram to Conzelman, firing him.[34] But the problems in the Rock Island organization ran much deeper than Conzelman. The Independents had planned to play a game against the Minneapolis Marines, but the game was canceled when several Rock Island players indicated they couldn't play for Flanigan.[35] This dissatisfaction was caused by the fact that many members of the squad had only been paid sixty percent of their salary for the year. The Rock Island team disbanded for the year, and many of the Independents dispersed to other league teams.

The future of the Independent franchise was in doubt. A financial audit revealed that the Rock Island club was several thousand dollars in debt. In an effort to raise some money, Flanigan did something unprecedented. Tackle Ed Healey joined the Chicago Bears after Rock Island disbanded, so Flanigan sold his contract to the Bears organization for 100 dollars. It was called the first sale of a professional football player ever on record.[36]

Jim Conzelman, relieved of his duties with Rock Island, signed a contract to play with and coach the NFL's Milwaukee Badgers for the rest of the 1922 season. Though many of Rock Island's players would no longer play for and with Conzelman, Duke Slater wasn't one of them. He signed a deal to play the last two games of the season with Conzelman and the Badgers.

The Badgers were led by Fritz Pollard, and Slater was one of Pollard's greatest admirers. When he arrived in Milwaukee, Slater approached Fritz and said, "So you're the great Pollard! Well, I'm going to play with you, and I feel that is a great honor." Pollard feigned ignorance and asked, "What's your name?" After Duke identified himself, Fritz replied, "Where did you go to school?" Of course, Pollard knew exactly who Slater was, but Fritz couldn't resist kidding the big lineman. The two African American football stars would forge a close friendship in the years to come.[37]

Slater and Pollard played with the Badgers on Thanksgiving against the Racine Legion. Milwaukee was "heavily reinforced" by the additions of Slater and Conzelman, but the Badgers failed to muster any offensive firepower and dropped a 3–0 decision to Racine.[38] Milwaukee's final game of the year was against the undefeated Canton Bulldogs. Slater endured sixty minutes opposing Link Lyman, but the rest of the Badgers were hopelessly outclassed. Pollard and Robeson, who were having issues with Milwaukee's ownership, failed to appear for the game, and the Badgers received a decisive 40–6 beating from the powerful 1922 NFL champions.[39]

Despite the losing experience as a member of the Badgers, Slater suited up for one final game of the season. Pollard arranged for a group of African American stars to go up against a white all-star team headed by his Badger teammate, Dick King. The game held at Schorling Park in Chicago was likely the first of its kind, in which an all-white team played against a team consisting entirely of African American stars. Fritz Pollard's All-Star team featured Fritz and his brother, Frank Pollard; Napoleon and Virgil Blueitt; NFL players Robeson, Slater, Ink Williams, and John Shelburne; and future NFL players Dick Hudson and Sol Butler.[40] The *Iowa City Press-Citizen* declared, "Never in the history of football has so strong a Negro aggregation gathered on a gridiron as this bunch of all-stars."[41]

The weather was frigid on the day of the game, which suppressed the fan turnout. Schorling Park's turf was frozen, hard, and unforgiving, so participants on both teams played cautiously to avoid injury. The game remained scoreless in the third quarter, when

King's All-Stars made a serious challenge, driving down to Pollard's four-yard line. On fourth down, Slater broke through and tackled the ball carrier for no gain, ending the threat. Pollard's All-Stars then took the ball down the field and scored the game's only touchdown on a 20-yard pass from Pollard to Robeson. Pollard's All-Stars secured a 6–0 victory, and post-game accounts credited Slater and Robeson's play in opening up holes as being key to the win.[42]

"Duke Slater Goes to Jail for Fraud," the headline screamed, while the subheading read, "Famous Colored Iowa Football Star Passes Worthless Check in Sum of $10." Slater was taken to jail briefly on March 31, 1923, because a $10 check he gave to a furniture company bounced. He was arrested at his home at 320 West Tenth Street in Davenport.[43] The matter was quickly resolved when he paid the debt, but it served as a clear reminder of the scrutiny Slater now lived under as a high-profile African American celebrity.[44]

Duke remained in the Tri-Cities over the offseason of 1923 and tried his hand at other sports. He had been an impressive amateur boxer at Iowa, so he decided to make his professional boxing debut on July 26. "I am anxious to see what I can do as a professional boxer," Duke announced. "I would like to make it one of my sidelines. I can keep in condition by boxing and when football season rolls around, I'll be in the best of shape. During the winter months, I'll box regularly if I get a chance."[45]

His first professional fight was against a local white heavyweight, Battling Walker. The *Davenport Democrat & Leader* reported, "Although far from being a finished boxer, Slater is a terrific puncher. He has a left uppercut which, when it connects, is capable of flattening the toughest of 'em."[46] The fight, which was held at Palmer School Arena in Davenport, was scheduled to go six rounds. It lasted two. Slater was knocked out in the second round by Walker and promptly retired from professional boxing.

Slater found baseball a much less punishing sideline. He spent several months in 1923 playing with a black baseball squad called the Illinois Colored All-Stars. Slater played the catcher position.[47] But football was always Duke's first love, and when the Independents broke for camp in 1923, he was at the front of the line. "Slater was one of the main cogs in the Independents' forward wall last year and this being his second year in the professional game he should do wonders in bolstering up the defensive power of the Independents line," the *Democrat & Leader* noted. "Slater has made his home in Davenport all summer and through playing baseball during that time he will be in the pink of condition when the season opens."[48]

The Independents were ecstatic to have Slater back. The club's financial audit exposed massive debts, and those debts compelled Flanigan to sell his interest in the Rock Island franchise before the 1923 season. Arch H. Bowlby took over the daily management operations of the team. Most of Rock Island's players scattered to other league clubs after the 1922 season, and these players could not or would not rejoin the Independents in 1923. Incredibly, only two players from Rock Island's 1922 roster returned for the following season — long-time center Louis Kolls and Duke Slater.

Bowlby quickly put his stamp on the team. He signed Herb Sies, the man who purportedly hated Rock Island, as his team captain and signed Johnny Armstrong to take over Conzelman's place at quarterback. He also traded Tillie Voss, the only man other than Slater to play every minute of every game for Rock Island in 1922, to the Toledo Maroons for former Notre Dame fullback Robert Phelan.

Thanks to a manufacturing mix-up at the jersey factory, the Independents were unable to obtain their usual green and white jerseys and had to wear temporary red and white uniforms for their first two games. Perhaps those new uniforms were to blame for Rock Island's lackluster performance in the opening exhibition with the local Moline Indians. The Independents trailed at halftime before scoring a safety and a touchdown in the third quarter to squeak out a 9–6 victory.[49] "He was a big man, powerful hands and arms," one of the members of the Moline Indians, "Bugs" Anthony, later said of Duke. "I'll also say this, Duke was the cleanest pro I ever opposed."[50]

Rock Island's NFL opener in 1923 was a home tilt against their old nemesis, the Chicago Bears. Slater prepared for a tough afternoon going directly up against Healey, his former teammate at tackle, as well as the rugged Hunk Anderson. Considering their subpar scrimmage performance and the "jinx" the Bears had on Rock Island, hopes were not high on Rock Island's side. But Bowlby changed that in a hurry.

Ten minutes before Rock Island's team took the field against the Bears, Bowlby signed Sol Butler to a contract. Butler was a well-known African American halfback who had attended Rock Island High School. His primary interest was track and field, and Butler competed in the 1920 Olympics. He had been a favorite to win gold in the running long jump, but he pulled a leg tendon in the preliminaries and withdrew from the competition. Butler had often mentioned that he didn't particularly care for pro football. However, his level of comfort with several players in the Rock Island lineup, including Slater and Butler's former college teammate, quarterback Johnny Armstrong, persuaded him to give the NFL a try.[51]

Sol's appearance in the Independents' lineup was a complete surprise to the media and fans at the game, and he took the field to a roar of approval from the home team's fans. He proved to be the star of the game for the Independents. Late in the first half, Butler entered the game for the first time and promptly intercepted a pass by Sternaman at the Bears' 39-yard line. After two plays lost seven yards for Rock Island, Armstrong lofted a pass to Butler that gained 20 yards and gave the Independents a first down. The Bears, knowing Butler was the key to Rock Island's drive, "endeavored to knock him out," according to the *Argus*.[52] That plan backfired, as the Bears were penalized 15 yards for unnecessary roughness on Butler. The penalty put Rock Island in field goal range, and Sies booted a 20-yard field goal with seconds to spare in the first half.

Three points was all Rock Island needed, because their defense was outstanding all game long. The Bears never seriously threatened in the second half, and the Independents had their first victory over Halas' club, 3–0.[53] The "Bears jinx" had been shattered. "They said it couldn't be done, but it was," the *Argus* declared with glee.[54]

Naturally, hopes were high for Rock Island's second game of the season versus the Cleveland Tigers. Butler literally never practiced with the team prior to the Bears game, so with a week to prepare and practice together, it was hoped that the Independents could put together a dominant performance against the Tigers. However, Cleveland had a strong squad. In an unusual twist, through some kind of arrangement between the Tigers and the Chicago Bears, Hunk Anderson was loaned to the Tigers for this game, so Duke Slater clashed with the scrappy lineman for the second straight week. It would be the only NFL game Anderson played outside of a Bears uniform.

Rock Island, back in their familiar green and white uniforms, found themselves in another defensive struggle against Cleveland. The Independents started Butler off the bench in the third quarter, but even he couldn't spark Rock Island's offense. The scoreless game nearly ended in disaster for the Indees. On the final play of the game, the Tigers had the ball at midfield. Doug Roby, a former Michigan star who years later would become the president of the U.S. Olympic Committee, dropped back to pass and spotted a Cleveland receiver running wide open behind the defense for a potential touchdown. But Roby barely overthrew his teammate at the Rock Island ten-yard line as time expired, and the game ended in a scoreless draw.[55] The *Democrat & Leader* declared, "Slater performed brilliantly on the line."[56]

Although everyone acknowledged that Cleveland outplayed Rock Island, the Independents were still undefeated. Their next opponent was the Rochester Jeffersons, who had been blown out the previous week by the Chicago Cardinals, 60–0. Rochester management assured the media in Rock Island that they were signing several new players and would be much more competitive against the Independents.

They weren't. The game was a rout from the start as Rock Island jumped out to a 14–0 lead after one quarter. Slater, who returned the opening kickoff six yards, handled the kickoff duties as Rock Island's backup kicker. On the first play of the second quarter, Duke Slater made the first known pass reception of his football career. He snagged a pass from Armstrong for a gain of 16 yards to the Rochester 20-yard line, which set up another Rock Island touchdown and a 21–0 lead.

A few minutes later, Waddy Kuehl plunged into the end zone from one yard out to give Rock Island another touchdown. Since Sies, the regular extra point kicker, was out of the game taking a rest, the Independents turned to Slater for the extra point try. Duke's kick sailed wide, but Rochester was flagged for being offside. Under the rules of the time, Slater's extra point was ruled successful on account of the Rochester penalty. Duke had just scored his first NFL point, to the delight of the Rock Island crowd.

The Green and White tacked on four touchdowns in the final period, handing Rochester their second consecutive blowout defeat by a 56–0 score.[57] Slater's kicking proved to be one of the most entertaining aspects of the game. "The fans like to see Duke Slater kick. Duke enjoys it just as much as they do, too," the *Argus* reported.[58]

With three weeks off until their next scheduled league game, the Independents kept busy with two exhibition matches. The first was a home game against the Miners of Hibbing, Minnesota. The Miners featured Rube Ursella and Bobby Marshall, two former Independent stars. Ursella was the star quarterback and head coach of Rock Island in 1919 prior to the formation of the NFL. That season, he scored 99 points for the Independents on a team that claimed the national pro football championship. Ursella and Marshall were also members of the Rock Island squad the following year. Along with Fritz Pollard, Bobby Marshall was one of the first two African American players in the NFL when the league formed in 1920. Marshall suited up at his usual end position opposite Slater.

Attendance for the Hibbing game was boosted by several hundred Hawkeye alumni. A large contingent of Iowa fans living in Illinois traveled to Iowa City for Iowa's homecoming game on Saturday. They saw the Hawkeyes' school record of twenty consecutive wins, which started when Slater was in school, snapped on a game-winning field goal by Red Grange of Illinois. On their way home, the Hawkeye rooters visited Rock Island to see alums Max Kadesky, George Thompson, and Duke Slater in action for the Independents. But it was a non–Hawkeye, Johnny Armstrong, who was the star of the afternoon for the Green and White. Armstrong threw two touchdown passes to halfback Bill Giaver and ran for a third to lead the Independents to a 27–7 victory.[59]

Their second exhibition game in two weeks took Rock Island on the road for the first time all season. The Independents went to Omaha to play the Olympics, and local fans excitedly welcomed the visiting Rock Island squad. Fans organized a large parade with the mayor leading the crowd to the football field for the game. Omaha officials wrote the Rock Island club a letter which stated, "It has been a long time since the fans here have had the opportunity of seeing a big professional team in action, and everyone is on edge for the visit of the Independents. The colored people here are all excited over the coming of Duke Slater and Sol Butler with your team and are working hard to get out a real delegation. There is no question but that we will have a capacity crowd."[60]

In fact, a good crowd of 4,500 fans showed up to watch the Omaha Olympics battle "the team that beat the Chicago Bears." Rock Island lived up to their advanced billing early; two Armstrong touchdown passes and a safety gave the Independents a 15–0 halftime advantage. Omaha gave the home crowd a thrill in the third quarter when a 68-yard pass resulted in the first offensive touchdown yielded by the Independents all year. However, Kadesky would catch a 19-yard touchdown pass late in the game to finish off a 22–6 victory for Rock Island.[61]

Slater fared well against the Olympics' Ed Shaw, a second team all-pro with Rock Island in 1920 and a member of the undefeated 1922 NFL champion Canton Bulldogs. Shaw scored two touchdowns in that embarrassing 40–6 defeat of Slater's Milwaukee Badgers the previous season. As a member of the Olympics, Shaw was very impressed with Rock Island's 1923 aggregation. He praised his former club profusely after the game, stating that Rock Island was the best pro team he had ever seen. He also expressed the opinion that the Independents could defeat his other former team, the Canton Bulldogs, a claim that delighted Rock Island supporters.[62]

Nevertheless, storm clouds were on the horizon. Giaver tore a ligament in his shoulder in the Omaha game, and his future playing status was questionable. In addition, Sol Butler was released from the team. According to the *Argus*, Butler asked for his release so he could return to Chicago and attend to a clothing store he co-owned after his business partner there fell ill.[63] The losses of Giaver and Butler robbed Rock Island of their two best backfield players.

Meanwhile, Rock Island returned to NFL action with a match versus the Milwaukee Badgers. The game with Milwaukee pitted Duke Slater against several players he was teammates with at the conclusion of the 1922 season. One of them, Jim Conzelman, was salivating for revenge after his firing by the Rock Island club the previous year. "It is a settled fact that Conzelman will force his men to the utmost to gain a victory over the Rock Island machine," the *Argus* reported. "It would no doubt mean a whole lot to him to humble the team of his former connections and put it on the wrong side of the ledger in the year's record."[64]

Sies successfully booted a 35-yard field goal to get Rock Island on the scoreboard first. Milwaukee failed to counter, missing four field goals in the first half. Conzelman accounted for two of the Badgers' missed kicks, while fullback Ben Winkleman missed the other two. But in the third quarter, Winkleman redeemed himself by scoring on a three-yard touchdown run, and Rock Island trailed for the first time all season, 7–3. While the Badgers were having success running the ball, the Independents struggled to put together a running game without Butler and Giaver. To make matters worse, Phelan, Rock Island's leading rusher in the game, was sidelined early in the fourth quarter with an ankle injury.

Phelan was also the regular punter for the Independents, and with around six minutes remaining in the contest, Rock Island had to punt. The best punter still in the game for the Green and White was Frank DeClerk, who played center. Armstrong shifted to the center position while DeClerk dropped back to punt. However, Armstrong's snap was far off target, and DeClerk could only fall on the ball at the Rock Island six-yard line, where Milwaukee took over. Six yards later, the Badgers had another rushing touchdown and an 11-point lead. The touchdown sealed the game for the Badgers, and Conzelman punished his old squad with a 14–3 victory.[65]

Rock Island's struggles continued in their next game against the Minneapolis Marines. Marine quarterback Ave Kaplan booted two long field goals, each from over forty yards away, to give his team a 6–0 lead at halftime. Ironically, it was a Marine field goal attempt that saved the day for Rock Island. Midway through the third quarter, Kaplan tried to add to Minneapolis' lead with a field goal try, but the attempt was blocked. Rock Island's Max Kadesky scooped up the ball and sprinted sixty yards the other way. With the ball at the 26-yard line, Phelan made several strong runs before Armstrong plunged in for the game-tying touchdown. Sies missed the extra point, however, and the score was knotted at 6–6.

That wasn't the last of Sies' kicking woes. After Rock Island tied the score, Sies had five opportunities to give the Independents the lead, but he missed all five of his second half field goal attempts, and the game ended in a 6–6 draw.[66] Rock Island settled for a tie despite racking up 13 first downs compared to just four for Minneapolis.

The Independents slogged through two straight lackluster performances, and they weren't filled with confidence as they went to Cubs Park to face their arch-rivals, the Bears. Chicago was looking to avenge their season-opening loss, and the Indees couldn't use Sol Butler as a weapon in the backfield this time. Slater had his hands full with the usual suspects — tackle Ed Healey, guard Hunk Anderson, and the Bears' center, George Trafton.

Rock Island drew first blood in the third quarter when Sies drilled a 25-yard field goal for a 3–0 lead, but a few minutes later, Chicago fullback Oscar Knop made the play of the game. He intercepted an Armstrong pass and returned it thirty yards to the Rock Island 20-yard line. Dutch Sternaman did the rest, running for an eight-yard touchdown one minute into the final quarter and giving the Bears a 7–3 advantage. Rock Island's final scoring threat ended when they turned the ball over on downs at the Chicago 25-yard line with under three minutes left in the game, and the Independents suffered a 7–3 defeat.[67]

Ed Healey and Duke Slater waged a tremendous battle and were the stars of the game on the line. Healey played aggressively against his former team — a little too aggressively, it turned out, as he was ejected in the fourth quarter for unnecessary roughness. On the other side, the *Argus* declared, "Duke Slater played one of his best games of the season against the Halas men. He stopped the Bears a number of times at his station and figured prominently in Rock Island holding the Chicagoans at various occasions."[68]

The final game at Douglas Park for the 1923 season was a rematch of the Independents' tie game with the Minneapolis Marines. The visitors featured African American halfback Dick Hudson, who was given a tryout by Rock Island before the season. The Independents released him before he played a game due to their depth at the position at the time. Hudson played admirably against his former club and led the Marines in rushing. But Slater and the Indees played well too, and in a bizarre coincidence, the final score of the Rock Island-Minneapolis game was identical to the outcome two weeks earlier — a 6–6 draw.[69]

Sporting a 2–2–3 league record, it appeared Rock Island's season was over. But Manager Bowlby scheduled an exhibition in Michigan against the Lansing Durant Stars, a team that claimed to have been undefeated over the last two years. The contest wasn't an official league game, and in fact, the salaries for the Independent players were not guaranteed. Durant agreed to pay for the visiting club's expenses; however, the players' actual salaries would be paid from the gate receipts—and only if Rock Island won the game.

Not surprisingly, a fierce battle ensued. Giaver, who had healed from his shoulder injury, proved to be the player of the game for Rock Island. He scored on a four-yard touchdown run in the second period to give the Green and White a seven-point advantage. The score was still 7–0 with two minutes left in the game when Durant scored the necessary touchdown, but Giaver crashed through the line and rushed the Durant kicker into a missed extra point attempt. That preserved an eventual 7–6 victory for Rock Island and secured everyone's paychecks.[70] Giaver didn't monopolize all the accolades; the *Argus* credited Slater as "a tower of strength on the defense for the Independents."[71]

There was one more temptation Bowlby could not resist. George Halas invited Rock Island for a game at Cubs Park as a tiebreaker to settle the season split between the two teams. Rock Island felt it was at full strength for their third and decisive game with the Bears, and they accepted the challenge.

The matchup was a disaster from start to finish. The Bears jumped out to a 13–0 lead in the second quarter before the Independents put together their only successful drive of the day. Kuehl took advantage of broken Bears' coverage and ran untouched for a 30-yard touchdown reception, but the 13–7 deficit was as close as Rock Island could get. Joe Sternaman added a field goal and a rushing touchdown to push Chicago's lead to 23–7. To add insult to injury, the Green and White were driving for one final score on the season, but Knop intercepted Armstrong's pass and ran 75 yards the other way for a touchdown as time expired on the season. His return was a microcosm of Rock Island's difficulties in a painful 29–7 defeat.[72]

It was a very disappointing end to an otherwise solid season for the Independents. At the end of the year, Duke Slater was rewarded with his first all-pro selections. He was a first team all-pro selection by E.G. Brands of *Collyer's Eye Magazine*, while the *Green Bay Press-Gazette* and the *Canton Daily News* each made him a second team all-pro choice.

Slater and Max Kadesky were the only two Independents to play every minute of every NFL game in the 1923 season, although Kadesky missed the exhibition game against Lansing. Duke Slater had played every minute of every Rock Island game for the past two years. The Independents enjoyed solid success in Duke's first two seasons with the club, but Rock Island's best year in the NFL was right around the corner.

Chapter 9

The Greatest Independent (1924–1925)

Duke spent another off-season in Davenport and again kept in shape by playing baseball. He served as the captain of the all-black Iowa Tigers in 1924, and he played for the Tigers in the summer of 1925 as well.[1] But football was always Slater's claim to fame, and when the fall of 1924 arrived, Slater signed his third one-year contract with the Rock Island Independents.

Team manager A.H. Bowlby wanted to make another big splash, just as he did by signing Sol Butler in 1923. Bowlby caused a minor stir with local fans by bringing former Rock Island star Rube Ursella back to the Independents and naming him team captain.[2] Rube coached the Indees in their exhibition opener against the Moline Indians. Rock Island knocked off Moline, 7–0, on a touchdown run by fullback Buck Gavin.[3] The *Argus* reported Slater "tore a wagon-sized hole" in the Moline line on the Independents' game-winning drive.[4]

The exhibition win was overshadowed, however, by the stunning news that Bowlby signed Jim Thorpe to a contract. Thorpe was renowned as one of the greatest athletes that ever lived. He had been a college football All-American at Carlisle Indian School in 1911 and 1912 and was quite possibly the most famous football player in the world in 1924. By the time he signed with Rock Island, he had already played eight seasons of professional football, and at a presumed age of 36, he was past the prime of his career. But Thorpe was still famous and supremely talented, and his signing was met with great excitement in Rock Island.[5]

With Ursella and Thorpe at halfback and Johnny Armstrong back at quarterback, the Independents had a potent backfield. The 1924 club started the season at home facing their arch-rivals, the Chicago Bears. Thorpe's presence on the squad attracted a huge crowd of over 5,000 spectators to the game. Even the mayors of each of the Tri-Cities— Moline, Davenport, and Rock Island—were on hand to witness the contest.

The game was a defensive struggle, with Healey and Hunk Anderson battling Duke Slater for sixty grueling minutes. Thorpe took center stage for the Green and White, blocking a Dutch Sternaman field goal attempt and leading a long drive down the field just before halftime. Thorpe was not perfect, though. He threw an interception at the Bears' 35-yard line as the first half expired and missed a 30-yard field goal in the second half. After an exhausting battle, Rock Island and Chicago settled for a scoreless tie to begin the season.[6]

It was a decent outcome for the Indees, considering that Jim Thorpe only arrived in Rock Island the day before the Bears game. The Racine Legion were the next team to come to Douglas Park, and the Legion featured former Rock Island halfback Bill Giaver. The home fans hoped for a much better offensive showing with a week to integrate Thorpe into the game plan, but it took three more quarters for the offense to arrive. In the fourth quarter, one of Giaver's replacements in the Rock Island backfield, Buck Gavin, finally rushed for a one-yard touchdown and the Independents' first score of the year. Thorpe added a field goal later in the period to lead the Green and White to a 9–0 win.[7]

Duke Slater played another strong sixty-minute game in the victory. He was one of only three African Americans in the NFL in 1924; the other two, Sol Butler and Ink Williams, both played for Rock Island's next opponent, the Hammond Pros. The media hyped Williams' skills at end and Butler's return to the Tri-Cities. However, Williams unexpectedly failed to appear for the game, and Butler wasn't much of a threat to his former team. Sol fumbled Rock Island's first punt of the game at the Hammond seven-yard line, which led to the first Independent touchdown of the game.

The addition of Jim Thorpe made the 1924 Rock Island Independents championship contenders. Pictured is Duke Slater, crouching for the team picture (courtesy Simon Herrera).

The other Pros were no match for Rock Island's defensive firepower, and the Green and White seized a 20–0 lead on the first play of the fourth quarter. With the game firmly in hand, Jim Thorpe was pulled from the blowout. Duke Slater then took over the kickoff work from Thorpe, and he booted the ball over the Hammond goal from midfield each time.[8] Gavin added a third touchdown with a few minutes left in the game to give Rock Island a 26–0 decision over the Pros.[9]

Armed with an offense to match their powerful defense, the 1924 Independents were legitimate contenders for the NFL title. There were only five undefeated teams in the league, and as luck would have it, two of those five — the Rock Island Independents and the Dayton Triangles — were scheduled to square off at Douglas Park. For the third straight week, a prominent former Independent opposed the Green and White. Duke Slater matched up against Dayton's Herb Sies, who was returning to the Tri-Cities after serving as Rock Island's captain in 1923.

Rock Island played like a championship team in their fourth game of the season. Johnny Armstrong launched a pass to Rube Ursella that set up the Independents' first touchdown. Buck Gavin gave Rock Island a 13–0 lead with his sixth scoring run of the season, and in the fourth quarter, Jim Thorpe dazzled the crowd with a long touchdown pass to cap off a 20–0 victory over Dayton.[10] Meanwhile, Duke Slater set the Independents' club record with his 19th career NFL start in the Green and White.

Only three teams in the NFL were still undefeated on October 20: the Cleveland Bulldogs, the Duluth Kelleys, and the Rock Island Independents. Local fans were calling the 1924 squad the greatest Independent team in history.[11] "Foes of the Rock Island Independents in the last few weeks have been giving them but little trouble," the *Argus* noted confidently. "The Green and White now is a well-organized team, and fans are entertaining thoughts of national professional football honors this year."[12]

Rock Island headed to Kansas City to face the Blues in their first road tilt of the year. The Blues were a new franchise and winless in their history. They had only scored three total points in their previous three losses, while Rock Island had not surrendered a point in four NFL games. Fans in Kansas City were excited to see the exploits of Jim Thorpe and Joe Little Twig, two Native Americans on Rock Island's roster. Slater, on the other hand, wasn't welcome, as there was a "gentleman's agreement" that black players didn't play NFL games in Missouri, a very hostile state towards African Americans.[13]

Duke Slater was listed as a "probable starter" by the *Rock Island Argus* the day before the game and accompanied the team to Kansas City.[14] However, he was denied the right to go upon the field by officials of the Kansas City club, and for the first time in his NFL career, Duke found himself scratched from the lineup.[15] Slater had started 19 consecutive NFL games for Rock Island, a club record. Not only that, he played all sixty minutes in each of those 19 games. The team would feel his absence, since he was the only player who had played every minute in all four of their games that season.

In any event, Duke Slater was benched for a football game for the first time since his sophomore year of high school in 1913. Joe Kraker took Duke's place in the starting lineup, but the other ten starters in Rock Island's lineup were the same ones that started the Dayton game. Chuck Corgan, Kansas City's quarterback, dropkicked a field goal early in the contest for the first points scored on the Green and White all season. Still, it looked as though Rock Island would get through the game unscathed when a two-yard touchdown pass from Armstrong to Ursella gave them a 7–3 lead after three quarters.

However, the Independents' line collapsed in the fourth quarter without the services of their sixty-minute tackle. Corgan followed perfect blocking from his teammates and raced forty yards into the end zone to give the Blues the 10–7 lead. After an Armstrong interception, "Kansas City made an opening in the Rock Island line large enough to drive a horse and wagon through and [Charley] Hill dashed away for another touchdown," the *Argus* reported.[16]

Now trailing 16–7, Rock Island drove into Kansas City territory before losing the ball on downs. The Blues took over possession, and on their first play, Hill sprinted 30 yards through the Independent line. The Blues pounded Rock Island with six more running plays, overpowering the defense to gain their third touchdown of the quarter with seconds to play. Kansas City left the field with their first win and handed Rock Island a blowout loss, 23–7.[17]

The convincing loss was considered one of the biggest upsets of the 1924 NFL season.[18] Rock Island blamed their defeat at Kansas City in large part to Slater's absence.[19] "[The Blues] plunged through the Islander line, weakened by the absence of Duke Slater, for healthy gains and in the last quarter opened up and swept the Independents off their feet," the *Argus* noted.[20] "The Independents Sunday looked like a different team than the one which swept through the first games in easy style."[21]

Duke returned to the lineup just in time for another great confrontation with the Chicago Bears. In addition to reactivating Slater, the Independents bolstered their lineup with a new acquisition in the wake of the Kansas City loss. Joe Guyon, who was largely responsible for dealing Slater's Clinton High team a loss a decade earlier, arrived in Chicago the day before the Bears game and signed a contract to become Duke's teammate with the Independents.

The Green and White failed to score in their first matchup against the Bears, so in the rematch, Rock Island reached into their bag of tricks to get on the scoreboard. Rock Island had the ball, third down and ten, at the Chicago 30-yard line. Duke Slater, who shifted into the backfield just before the ball was snapped, took the handoff. That caught the Bears' defense completely by surprise, since none of the defenders expected the massive Slater to be running with the ball. Duke juggled the handoff but regained possession and charged 21 yards down to the nine-yard line on the first carry of his NFL career. His run set up a short 15-yard field goal by Thorpe, and Rock Island carried a 3–0 lead into halftime.

The second half was highlighted by several skirmishes where fists were thrown. Both teams missed multiple field goals, but Dutch Sternaman connected on a 40-yard attempt midway through the final period to tie the game. The Bears and Independents ultimately settled for their second draw of the season, this one ending with a 3–3 score.[22]

Afterwards, the *Argus* applauded Duke Slater's contribution to his team's only score, and it noted that he "opened large holes" for Rock Island on offense.[23] "Slater is playing even greater football than when starring in the [Big Ten] conference," the *Chicago Tribune* proclaimed.[24] As the Independents prepared for their next game, a rematch with the Legion in Racine, Wisconsin, they spent the week practicing the Slater play that set up their only score against Chicago.

Rock Island trailed Racine, 3–0, in the third quarter when the game turned on a big play. Johnny Mohardt, the ex–Notre Dame star playing halfback for Racine, took the handoff at his own 21-yard line, and his blockers split away from him. Rock Island end Mike Wilson, who also dabbled in pro baseball with the Pittsburgh Pirates, knocked the ball loose from Mohardt's grasp. Duke Slater scooped up the football and carried it three yards to the Racine 15-yard line before being brought down. Slater's fumble recovery gave Rock Island their best scoring chance of the game, and Armstrong took advantage by breaking two tackles on a broken play and scrambling across the field for a nine-yard touchdown. Racine couldn't crack Rock Island's stifling defense in the fourth quarter, and the Independents captured a 6–3 victory.[25] The *Argus* saluted Slater as "one of the boys who did some tearing work on the defense."[26]

The Independents returned to Douglas Park for their most anticipated game of the year. The team that handed them their only defeat, the Kansas City Blues, came to town, and since the game was in Rock Island, they would need to face Slater in the line. The Blues brought the same lineup they used to upset Rock Island in Missouri. This matchup was highly publicized as a game of redemption for the Indees collectively and Duke personally. Local fans predicted the game would stand as "Duke Slater's greatest day" and that "the giant Negro tackle will play the most outstanding game of his career."[27]

Although Rock Island held a 3–0 halftime lead thanks to a Rube Ursella field goal, the home fans were apprehensive because of how the Blues dominated the fourth quarter of the teams' previous meeting. In this game, however, the Independents came out even stronger in the second half. Joe Little Twig, the big Rock Island lineman, flopped on a Kansas City fumble in the end zone for the first Independent touchdown. Rock Island's defense smothered the Blues the whole game, and with minutes remaining, Gavin punched ahead for a one-yard touchdown run and a 17–0 final score.[28] Slater went all sixty minutes in a physical, hard-fought game, Rock Island's fifth shutout of the season. The victory was understandably rewarding for Duke Slater, who set the franchise record with 22 NFL games played in the Green and White.

Rock Island still had only one loss on the season. Just three other teams—the Cleveland Bulldogs, the Chicago Bears, and the Duluth Kelleys—could say the same. The Bulldogs promised to send a contract to Rock Island to set up a Thanksgiving Day game at Douglas Park if the Independents won their next game versus the Duluth Kelleys. Duluth presented a big challenge for Rock Island, however. The Kelleys were unique for having three brothers, Bill, Joe, and Cobb Rooney, on the same squad.

Duluth halfback Wally Gilbert found one of those Rooney brothers, Bill, on a 30-yard touchdown pass in the second quarter. It was the first touchdown scored against Rock Island in the eight NFL games Slater was allowed to play. Gilbert added a 40-yard field goal a few minutes before the quarter ended to increase Duluth's lead to 9–0. In the second half, Rock Island outplayed the Kelleys and countered their speed advantage, but mistakes cost the Indees. An incomplete pass by Armstrong in the end zone ended one fourth-quarter drive after the Independents had advanced to the Duluth eight-yard line. Later, Thorpe fumbled the ball away to end a Rock Island drive at Duluth's five-yard line. Rock Island suffered a disappointing 9–0 loss to end the NFL regular season and knock them from title contention.[29]

If not for their lopsided loss to Kansas City, Rock Island would have still been in the running for the NFL title. A one-loss Independents team could have challenged the Bulldogs or the Bears for the league championship even with a loss to Duluth. Rock Island's defense yielded just one touchdown and 15 points in eight NFL games with Slater in the lineup, an average of less than two points per game. Without Duke, the Independents lost, 23–7, surrendering three touchdowns. Rock Island finished the season ranked third in the NFL in total defense, but when Slater played, the Independents easily had the league's best defense.

Excluding the Kansas City game, Duke Slater again played every minute of every game for Rock Island in the 1924 regular season. Slater was the only Independent player to play eight complete games in 1924, and he surely could have made it nine if he had been permitted to take the field in Kansas City. Duke was named a second team all-pro by the *Green Bay Press-Gazette* for the second time after the 1924 season, becoming the first player in Rock Island franchise history to earn multiple all-pro selections.

Rock Island had one of their best squads in team history, so Bowlby tried to generate some extra cash by setting up a post-season exhibition on Thanksgiving Day at Douglas Park against the Kenosha All-Stars. The All-Stars were a collection of players from the Kenosha and Hammond NFL squads, including Herb Sies and Ink Williams. Thorpe missed the game with a shoulder injury, so Slater handled the kickoff work for the Green and White. One of his kickoffs drilled a Kenosha defender, and Slater, speeding down the field to cover the kick, dove and wrapped his arms around the ball. That gave the Independents possession at midfield in one of the game's more entertaining plays. Rock Island went on to defeat Kenosha, 10–6, on a Johnny Armstrong touchdown pass and a 20-yard Ursella field goal.[30]

Still, cracks in the Rock Island fan base began to appear. Bowlby's attempt to raise revenue with the exhibition backfired when one of the smallest crowds in team history—only 1,500 fans—showed up for the Thanksgiving Day affair. The bitterly cold weather was blamed for canceling the final home game of the season with the Minneapolis Marines, but the poor attendance at the Kenosha game likely influenced that decision as well. Since it appeared Rock Island's season was over, Slater reunited with Aubrey Devine to play for an All-West team in the "Grid Grad" game on December 6. The game was held at Dunn Field in Cleveland, Ohio, and the proceeds of the game went to charity.[31]

Just as the Independents were about to disband for the year, Jim Thorpe stepped in. Indee management was finished with the team for the season, but Thorpe, who had experience running independent teams, began working out a post-season schedule for what remained of the squad under the Rock Island banner. Thorpe arranged for the Independents to make a number of post-season appearances in the south in late December and early January. He also reached an agreement with the Bears organization to stage a December game in Chicago that would decisively settle the season series between the two clubs, which consisted of two tie games.

To prepare for the Chicago game, Thorpe negotiated a road exhibition against the Clinton Legion. The contest was a fun homecoming game for Duke Slater. He went back to his old high school hometown for his first organized football game there since 1915. Thorpe didn't play in the game, but he bolstered the squad by signing several new players, including Evar Swanson, who played the 1924 NFL season with the Milwaukee Badgers. Rock Island had enough strength on the roster to defeat the Legion, 13–0.[32] As usual, Slater played all sixty minutes in a warm return to Clinton, Iowa.

The Clinton game was merely a tune up for Rock Island's third match of the year with the Chicago Bears. The Cleveland Bulldogs won the NFL title, per league rules, by having the best record in the league on November 30. However, the Bears defeated the Bulldogs in a December exhibition and were now claiming to be the rightful NFL champions. For their part, Rock Island was simply trying to break the deadlock in their season series with Chicago.

7,000 fans watched the Bears battle Rock Island, and many were surely surprised at the result. Rock Island had the ball in Chicago territory most of the afternoon. Swanson, their newest acquisition, was the star of the game for the Independents. In the game's biggest play, he intercepted a Bear pass and sprinted 35 yards to a Rock Island touchdown. Ursella missed five field goals that would have padded the lead even more, but the strong wind blew many of his attempts off-line. Still, the Bears didn't seriously threaten Rock Island's 7–0 lead until less than two minutes remained in the game. Joe Sternaman carried the ball into the end zone from 12 yards away to give the Bears a touchdown, but he fared no better than Ursella against the wind. His extra point attempt pushed wide, and the Independents held on for a 7–6 triumph.[33]

"An all-star team of professional football players, including the famous Duke Slater, Sunday defeated the Chicago Bears, 7–6," the *Lincoln State Journal* reported.[34] The Bears, of course, claimed the loss had no bearing on their NFL championship claims. On the other hand, the Rock Island organization was more than willing to make a title claim of its own. After the Chicago victory, the Independents immediately left for a barnstorming trip in the south, playing several games in Texas. The team referred to itself as "Jim Thorpe's Rock Island national champions" during their trip, an obvious reference to their victory over the Bears.[35] Despite all that, the NFL officially named the Cleveland Bulldogs the 1924 league champions.

Football fans that saw "Jim Thorpe's Rock Island national champions" in Texas were deprived of seeing the whole team in action, however. Duke Slater stayed behind in Chicago and didn't accompany the team on their holiday tour, owing to racial conditions in the South. It seems somehow fitting that abhorrent racial conditions prevented southern fans from seeing the full roster of the so-called "national champions" in action, since those same prejudices in Kansas City likely cost Rock Island a shot at a proper NFL championship in the first place.

9. The Greatest Independent (1924–1925)

When Duke Slater signed his fourth one-year contract with the Independents in 1925, he was already one of the most decorated players in franchise history. He held club NFL records for games played, games started, complete games, and all-pro selections. Duke was also a financial draw for the Indees. Club manager Arch Bowlby bolstered Rock Island's roster by signing former college All-Americans Eddie Novak and Chet Widerquist, and the team began promoting their two new acquisitions, along with Slater, as their "famous All-American trio."[36]

In the fall of 1925, Slater decided to resume his law school courses at the University of Iowa after a three-year absence.[37] A rumor spread that Duke might miss games due to academic conflicts, but those concerns were quickly addressed. "Duke Slater's studies at the law school at the University of Iowa will not prevent him from appearing with the Islanders," the *Argus* confirmed. "He has arranged morning classes and will come to Rock Island three days a week for the afternoon practice sessions handed out to the Green and White crew. He will be at his old position in the line."[38]

For the third consecutive year, Rock Island opened the season at Douglas Park versus their rivals, the Chicago Bears. The Bears were out for blood after having their spurious 1924 national championship claims thrown into question by the Independents. Slater had his hands full as always with Healey and Trafton. Hunk Anderson wasn't in uniform, but the Bears just filled his spot with Jim McMillen, the former Illini star.

Duke Slater kicked off to George Halas to begin Rock Island's sixth NFL season. As usual, the two teams battled to a defensive stalemate. The Independents got their big break midway through the third period, recovering a fumble at the Chicago 36-yard line. After a series of nice runs, Armstrong passed to Dutch Hendrian, who raced toward the corner of the end zone. Rock Island fans cheered loudly as they thought Hendrian had scored a touchdown, but the officials ruled that he stepped out of bounds at the one-yard line. The Indees had first and goal from there and still believed a touchdown was imminent, but Gavin fumbled on the ensuing play, and Chicago dodged a major scoring threat.

Both teams missed several field goals, including a 50-yard attempt by Dutch Sternaman that sailed wide of the uprights as time expired. The game ended in a scoreless draw, the third tie in the teams' last four meetings.[39] Duke Slater recovered a fumble in the game and played ferociously on defense. Slater and his linemates were praised for stopping "most everything that came their way."[40]

The second game of the year was against the Dayton Triangles. In one of the most boring games ever played in Rock Island, the Independents battled to their second scoreless tie of the season.[41] Douglas Park was completely covered in mud, and neither team seriously threatened to score or even attempted a field goal during the entire contest. "Duke Slater furnished a little of the colorful part of the game in the second quarter when he picked up a Dayton back and threw him over the line for a loss," wrote the *Davenport Democrat & Leader*.[42] Duke earned praise for his defensive work on special teams as well. "Slater was down on punts before the ends," the *Argus* marveled.[43] But while the Independent defense played well, Rock Island mustered virtually no offense against a Dayton team that would lose all seven remaining games on its schedule.

Rock Island fans had given the 1925 squad lackluster support and attendance in their first two games, and Bowlby responded by hiring a new full-time manager for the team. George H. Johnson, brother of New York Yankee shortstop Ernie Johnson, took over full-time management of the Rock Island club. In ceding the management position to Johnson, Bowlby struck an ominous tone about the future of professional football in Rock Island.

He mentioned that the game with the Bears in Rock Island drew only 2,000 fans, while Chicago's game in Green Bay the following weekend attracted 7,000. "Whether the Tri-Cities continue to enjoy the benefits in publicity and brand of professional football exhibited by their team is altogether up to the fans," Bowlby warned.[44]

Rock Island couldn't match up to Green Bay in the stands, but they hoped to have better luck on the field. The Packers came to Douglas Park looking to hand the Independents their first loss of the year. Green Bay was still led by iconic player-coach Curly Lambeau, but their backfield was even stronger with the emergence of a spectacular halfback named Verne Lewellen. Furthermore, the Packers were unique because six of their eleven starters were playing at least their fourth straight year with the franchise. That familiarity and chemistry was rare in that era and made them a dangerous squad.

A strong wind blew through Rock Island on the day of the game. The team with the wind at their backs on offense possessed a distinct advantage, and Rube Ursella used that wind to assist a 25-yard field goal kick with two minutes remaining in the first half. The kick proved crucial, because Rock Island's defensive line held like a stone wall. Just like the Independents' previous two foes, Green Bay failed to mount a serious scoring threat all day. Rock Island pitched a shutout for the third straight game, but they finally got a victory in the bargain as well with a 3–0 defeat of the previously unbeaten Packers.[45]

The 1925 Independents left the confines of Douglas Park for the first time to take on the Duluth Kelleys. Few teams ventured to frigid Duluth in northern Minnesota, but Rock Island was looking for payback against the team that severely damaged their 1924 NFL championship aspirations. Duluth's seldom-used field was small and cramped, and a fence behind the goal line created a bizarre problem in the second quarter. Rock Island advanced the ball to Duluth's two-yard line, where they faced fourth and goal. Because of the proximity of the back fence to the field of play, the teams agreed to move the ball back to the 12-yard line and consider the ten-yard line the goal line to give the players more operating room. Halfback Roddy Lamb dropped back and found Armstrong wide open for Rock Island's first touchdown on the season.

Notably, Duke Slater faced African American star end Bobby Marshall in this game. Every single player on Duluth's roster was in his twenties except the reliable Marshall, who was an astonishing 45 years old. Following the Rock Island touchdown, Slater kicked off to Marshall, who returned the ball 12 yards. On the next play, Rock Island recovered a Duluth fumble, which soon led to a second touchdown pass from Lamb to Armstrong.

Rock Island took a 12–0 lead, and that was sufficient for a defense that hadn't allowed a point all year. The Kelleys' best scoring chance came with less than four minutes to play in the game. Duluth advanced the ball to the Rock Island 13-yard line, but Slater broke through and drilled Wally Gilbert for a five-yard loss. The Independents soon took over possession and ran out the clock on their first road victory of the season.[46]

Rock Island was still unscored upon after four games, joining the Akron Pros and Detroit Panthers as the only undefeated teams in the NFL. It took the Independents two whole days to return by train to Rock Island from Duluth, which meant a short week of practice. Rock Island needed all the practice they could get, because next on the schedule was a trip to Green Bay and a rematch with the Packers.

Cold rain and bitter wind greeted the Green and White when they took the field in Green Bay in front of 7,000 Packer fans. The first half was a punting exhibition, with neither team able to overcome the weather conditions to make a serious scoring attempt. Around halftime, the rain began to taper off, and by the start of play in the third quarter, both teams were greeted with clear skies. Five minutes into the third quarter, Rock Island punted to quarterback Charlie Mathys, who was dropped in his tracks by Slater at his own 44-yard line.

From that point forward, the Packers morphed into an offensive juggernaut. They directed runs toward the guards and interior of the Rock Island line and began to rack up long gains. Lambeau ended the drive by tossing a ten-yard touchdown pass to fellow halfback Marty Norton, the first points scored against the Independents all year. In the final period, the Independents were doomed by errant passes. Lamb threw two interceptions, both of which were returned inside of Rock Island's 25-yard line. Both miscues soon led to touchdown runs by Green Bay's fullback, Myrt Basing. Rock Island was pummeled into accepting a 20–0 defeat from the Packers, the Indees' worst loss since the final game of the 1923 season.[47]

George Johnson reacted to the humiliating defeat by signing Evar Swanson, star of the 1924 upset of the Bears, for the rest of the season. Rock Island rapidly began preparations for their next opponent, the Kansas City Cowboys. The Cowboys were the new name of the Kansas City Blues, but thankfully, the game was scheduled to be played in Rock Island, so Duke was cleared to play. He had a difficult task, too; lined up opposite Slater in this game was Kansas City's star tackle, Steve Owen.

The game with Kansas City turned into another defensive struggle for the Independents. For the sixth time this season, Rock Island kept their opponents off the scoreboard by halftime. However, for the fourth time in 1925, the Green and White didn't score by halftime, either. The game was still tied, 0–0, with eight minutes remaining when Ursella finally got Rock Island on the scoreboard with a 26-yard field goal. But Kansas City returned Slater's kickoff to their own 48-yard line, and eight plays later, guard Roy Andrews booted a 35-yard field goal to tie the game, 3–3. Rube Ursella tried to win the game with a 23-yard field goal in the final minute of the game, but his drop kick fell short of the crossbar by inches. Rock Island and Kansas City finished in a 3–3 tie.[48]

Slater was praised after the game for his efforts in breaking through the Kansas City line, batting down passes and nailing Cowboy runners for losses. But it wasn't Rock Island's performance on the field that agitated club management. George Johnson and A.H. Bowlby publically expressed displeasure at the game's meager 1,500 attendance. "We are losing money every day we play at home," Bowlby declared. "Last season with a team that was not as strong as our 1925 aggregation, we had almost double the attendance."[49] The dissatisfaction of team management over apparent fan apathy was reaching the crisis point in Rock Island.

Before a trip to Chicago to take on the Bears, Bowlby kept his team in the news by reacquiring the services of Jim Thorpe. Rock Island worked out a trade with the New York Giants prior to the season where Thorpe would play three games for New York at a salary of $200 a game. After those three games, the Giants had the option of extending the contract or letting Thorpe's rights revert back to the Independents. Thorpe's play in New York was hampered by a knee injury, so the Giants released him back to Rock Island.[50] "We don't care what New York thinks of Thorpe," Bowlby bragged. "He may be 39 years old, but he certainly has a lot of football left in him."[51]

The Independents hoped Jim Thorpe would be a difference maker against the Bears, but the game started poorly for Rock Island. Thorpe, under duress from a rushing Bears lineman, got off a poor punt that only traveled 20 yards. This gave the Bears great field position and set up a 20-yard field goal by Joe Sternaman late in the first quarter. Walquist made a beautiful 30-yard run in the third period that led to another Sternaman field goal, and Rock Island trailed, 6–0.

The Independents' offense struggled all game against the powerful Bears, but the Independents received one big chance midway through the fourth quarter. Armstrong dropped back and lobbed a thirty-yard pass to a wide open Joe Little Twig, who had nothing between him and the Bears' end zone. But the ball slipped through his hands and fell incomplete. That play epitomized the Green and White's offensive woes on the day, and they suffered their second defeat of the season, 6–0.[52]

The Rock Island organization had much greater concerns than just a single loss to the Bears. Their upcoming home game with the Hammond Pros was viewed as a litmus test of the viability of professional football in Rock Island. Management declared it a "homecoming" game and sought to bring back several Independents from years past. A.H. Bowlby flatly stated that if attendance at the Hammond game was poor, "the team will not play another game this year and will not operate in Rock Island next year."[53] "Football fans of the tri-cities are to be given their last chance to keep the National Professional Football League franchise in this community Sunday," the *Argus* warned. "If only a small crowd turns out, the Islanders will complete their road schedule and then give up the National franchise."[54]

A heavy snowfall hit late in the week, however, and Hammond's club officials decided the field wasn't in good enough condition to stage a game, so it was cancelled. Rock Island was supposed to head for Kansas City to take on the Cowboys for the second time on the season, but the Cowboys agreed to give up their return game and stage the contest in Rock Island. All of Rock Island's "homecoming" plans were just delayed one week and postponed until the Cowboys game. Even the mayor of Rock Island, Walter Rosenfield, appealed to the public to turn out for the Rock Island–Kansas City match. The club was so desperate to drum up interest that they ditched their signature green and white jerseys and changed their colors to maroon and white for the rest of the season.[55]

Relocating the game from Kansas City was great for Slater, as there would now be no controversy when he suited up to play. On the field, he once again squared off against Steve Owen. Ursella kicked a 41-yard field goal midway through the first quarter to give the Maroon and White a 3–0 lead. From that point, however, the half belonged to the Cowboys. In the second period, halfback Chuck Corgan caught a short pass, shrugged off three tacklers, and bolted 62 yards for a touchdown and a 6–3 Kansas City lead. Later in the quarter, a 45-yard pass reception, again by Corgan, set up Charley Hill's four-yard touchdown run. Rock Island went into the locker room trailing, 12–3, and for all practical purposes, it looked as though professional football in Rock Island might be finished.

The Indees' outlook brightened somewhat when reserve halfback Vince McCarthy turned a short pass from Armstrong into a 23-yard score, but they still trailed at the beginning of the fourth quarter, 12–10. However, Rock Island played their finest fifteen minutes of the season to end this game. Novak plunged forward for a three-yard touchdown, giving the Independents a 16–12 lead. On their next possession, Rock Island was forced to punt, but Slater dropped the Kansas City return man, Al Bloodgood, in his tracks at his own 12-yard line. Two plays later, Armstrong intercepted a pass and ran 18 yards for another Rock Island touchdown.

The Independents weren't finished. Armstrong and Lamb each tacked on touchdown passes, and Rock Island waltzed away with a decisive 35–12 triumph.[56] Four fourth-quarter touchdowns paved the way for the big Indee victory. Facing the possible end of their franchise, Duke and his Rock Island teammates played an inspired second half of football. "Slater looked like an All-American," the *Argus* reported. "He was down on numerous punts, and the receivers were smacked sure before they could step."[57]

Unfortunately, the game only drew 1,500 fans, and A.H. Bowlby was irate. "We bowl over one of the strongest teams in the league by an overwhelming count," he fumed, referring to the 1–4–1 Cowboys. "We lost $1,500 on the victory because of empty stands. Are there any real sports lovers in the Tri-Cities?"[58]

Bowlby set up a town hall meeting to discuss the franchise's issues with local fans, and the event quickly turned acrimonious. He was forced to address widespread complaints held by fans of the team, as well as several nasty rumors regarding players' training habits and desire. One such rumor suggested that Slater's law school classes, which caused him to travel back and forth from Iowa City three days a week, were hampering his physical training. Bowlby angrily shot down the charge, saying, "Rock Island's players do train, and I would invite you any day to Douglas Park between 1:30 and 3 o'clock for proof. The three men who are not with the team all the time keep themselves in shape, and their work in each week's game is ample proof."[59]

Despite the low turnout for the Kansas City contest, management agreed to stage one more home game, this time against the Milwaukee Badgers. The Milwaukee game, too, was considered a litmus test of Rock Island's status in the NFL. "Everything is down to bedrock on the pro football proposition," the *Argus* reported. "After more than a month of warnings and threats, the management of the Independents is awaiting the final showing tomorrow."[60]

Overshadowed by the chaos off the field was the fact that Jim Thorpe had been released by the Indees after just two games on the 1925 roster. That meant Thorpe wasn't in the lineup for the last NFL game played in Rock Island, but reliable Duke Slater anchored the team at the right tackle position as usual. He trotted onto Douglas Park and faced his former team, the Milwaukee Badgers, but only 1,200 Rock Island fans joined him to watch the Independents play the hapless Badgers in freezing temperatures.

With club records for NFL games played, NFL games started, complete games, and all-pro selections, Duke Slater had the most decorated tenure of any Rock Island Independent. He is pictured in his number 16 jersey, which he wore in the 1924 and 1925 seasons.

The Indees jumped out to an early 12–0 lead and dominated in the second half. The Badgers were stopped on their first second-half possession and forced to punt to Lamb, who fielded the ball and weaved his way for a 90-yard touchdown. Lamb's long return gave Rock Island a comfortable 19–7 lead, and the Independents would roll from there. They added three more touchdowns in the final period of play to down Milwaukee, 40–7.[61] The Independents scored 75 points in two weeks, their best two-week offensive stretch since they rolled up 86 points on Evansville and Rochester in consecutive weeks in 1922.

With the franchise's future in doubt, Rock Island went on the road to play in a familiar setting for modern fans of the NFL. The Detroit Panthers hosted the Independents on Thanksgiving Day, November 26, 1925. It was the first NFL game ever played on Thanksgiving in the city of Detroit, a tradition which was later adopted by the Lions franchise and has continued for over eight decades. In 1925, Detroit had only one loss on the season and was contending for the NFL title behind the play and leadership of Coach Jim Conzelman. The Panthers displayed a powerful offense, but the Rock Island defense had been the team's strength all season, so the game presented a contrast of styles.

The Panthers struck first on a 24-yard field goal by Gus Sonnenberg, and Detroit maintained a 3–0 advantage after three quarters. But the Independents had threatened to score all game, and midway through the fourth quarter, Rock Island received a break. Sonnenberg got off a poor punt that gave the Independents possession at Detroit's 34-yard line. Slater and Widerquist opened huge holes for Roddy Lamb, who took it over the goal line from six yards out to give Rock Island the lead, 6–3. An Armstrong interception on the ensuing possession sealed an upset victory for the Independents that knocked Detroit out of the running for the NFL championship.[62]

Duke again played all sixty minutes in the Rock Island victory, and observers marveled at his durability. The NFL's grid notes, which were published across the country, featured a snippet about Slater. "Four years of pro football hasn't slowed up Duke Slater at all," National Pro Grid Notes reported. "The ex–Iowan, who was an All-American in his day, still continues to more than hold his own with any player who faces him. Slater is one of the bulwarks of the Rock Island line."[63]

Despite their shaky financial status, the Independents were surprisingly in the hunt for the 1925 NFL title with only two losses. "Another victory ... will put [the Independents] back on near-even footing with the Bears in fourth place," the *Argus* noted. "Then in event of a few post-season victories, who knows but that Rock Island might again finish at the top, as she did last year?"[64] Seizing the opportunity, Rock Island arranged a game with another two-loss team, the Chicago Cardinals, in an attempt to climb the NFL standings.

Slater, a veteran of ten games against the Chicago Bears, had never faced the Cardinals. The game at Comiskey Park gave Duke his first opportunity as an NFL player to visit Chicago's South Side, the neighborhood where he was raised as a child. A constant, heavy snow fell during the entire Independents-Cardinals contest. The play of the game came in the first quarter. Lamb, backed up inside his own five-yard line, fumbled the ball. Eddie Anderson, the ex–Notre Dame star, recovered it for the Cards; it was one of Anderson's three fumble recoveries on the day. It was a short distance for halfback Hal Erickson to travel to punch in the game's first touchdown run.

Both teams traded punts back and forth for most of the game in the snowy conditions, and Erickson's touchdown loomed large. With less than a minute remaining in the game, Lamb almost redeemed himself. Cardinal quarterback Ike Mahoney punted to Lamb on the Rock Island 10-yard line, and Lamb burst up the field, nearly breaking free for a game-tying touchdown. But Chicago's magnificent halfback, Paddy Driscoll, saved the day by dragging him to the ground after a 55-yard return, and Armstrong's pass was intercepted on the last play of the game to seal a 7–0 defeat for Rock Island in their final game in the NFL.[65]

It was a disappointing end to the season for Rock Island, as they held Chicago to just two first downs the entire game, but Anderson's three fumble recoveries were enough to steal a win. The loss dashed any dim hopes Rock Island may have had toward winning the 1925 NFL championship. In fact, the Cardinals went on to win the disputed league title over the Pottsville Maroons. Pottsville defeated the Cardinals on December 6 to finish with the league's best record and seemingly clinch the NFL title, but they were suspended from the NFL a week later when they played an unauthorized exhibition game in Philadelphia. Chicago proceeded to win two games against hastily constructed teams, which boosted their overall record above Pottsville's. The NFL decided to award the 1925 championship to the Cardinals over the Maroons, a decision that remains controversial.

Duke Slater, as he had in every game during the 1925 season, played all sixty minutes without relief. Only he and George Thompson played every minute of every game for the 1925 Independents. Slater's work against the great Driscoll drew praise. The *Argus* stated, "Driscoll was handed some rough treatment and just about halted entirely. [Slater] dumped him for some losses on several occasions, but as ever before Paddy was back on his feet, ready to go again. They named him right when they started to call him 'Paddy,' for he seems to have all kinds of them on. He is never hurt."[66]

For the third consecutive year, Duke Slater was an all-pro selection. *Collyer's Eye Magazine* selected him as a first team all-pro, while the *Green Bay Press-Gazette* relegated him to their second team for the third consecutive season. Duke became the only Independent to make three all-pro teams. "The greatest lineman who ever played under the Independents' banner was Duke Slater, great Negro star of Iowa," the *La Crosse Tribune and Leader-Press* reported. "The Duke was respected and liked by opponents and was a veritable idol among his teammates."[67] The greatest Independent of all time had another stellar season, but the future of his franchise was in serious jeopardy.

Chapter 10

Sweet Home Chicago (1926–1927)

Red Grange, widely considered the greatest college football player of his generation, signed a contract with the Chicago Bears the day after his last college game in 1925. He agreed to participate in a 19-game barnstorming tour over the span of ten weeks that paid him around $100,000. Grange and the Bears played in front of huge crowds; during his first eight games as a pro, he played before an estimated 200,000 fans.[1] Naturally, Grange and the Bears bypassed Rock Island and the Independents' small fan base on this tour.

Red and his business manager, Charles C. Pyle, realized how lucrative Grange's talents were, and they sought to monetize his popularity with an audacious request. Pyle and Grange asked for their own NFL franchise in New York City. Rock Island, which had missed out on the opportunity to cash in on Grange–mania, was enthusiastically in favor; they hoped a visit from a New York team led by Grange was just what the franchise needed to boost their flagging attendance. The New York Giants, however, were appalled that Grange sought to encroach on their territory, and the rest of the NFL sided with them. When the NFL refused Pyle's proposal in February 1926, he concocted an even bolder scheme. He immediately announced the formation of the American Football League, a new professional gridiron association that would compete directly with the NFL.

After the Independents failed to draw 2,000 fans for either of their final two home games in 1925 despite multiple appeals and threats, it became apparent that Rock Island had a bleak future in the NFL. This strengthened the appeal of Grange's AFL, and Arch H. Bowlby and Rock Island management decided to gamble that the AFL would evolve into a league superior to the existing NFL. The American Football League, conversely, relished the opportunity to poach one of the NFL's founding franchises. On July 16, 1926, the Rock Island Independents were introduced as one of the nine members of the new American Football League.

The AFL had seven "resident" franchises and one traveling team, the Wilson Wildcats, which played all their games on the road. The Independents were a mix of the two—they were to host their first three games in the Tri-Cities before finishing the year as a traveling team, playing their final twelve games on the road. Manager Bowlby eased concerns about the long road trip by chartering an $11,000 Northland bus, which was touted as a real advantage over travel by train.

Duke Slater had a memorable off-season. Most notably, he married Etta J. Searcy of Muscatine, Iowa. Etta and Duke had much in common. Etta was a graduate of the University of Iowa; she attended Iowa Wesleyan for the first three years of her college career before transferring to Iowa City and graduating in 1921.[2] Like George Slater, Etta's father, V.A.

Searcy, was a minister, and Reverend Searcy performed the marriage ceremony at a church in Madison, Illinois.³ Duke had met his wife a few years earlier, and Etta would be her husband's constant support in the decades that followed.

In addition to getting married and continuing his law classes in Iowa City, Slater managed and played third base for the Iowa City Blackhawks, the local all-black baseball team. He also reported that a summer's work in brick and concrete made him more solid than ever before. "Duke Slater's labor during the summer included the wheeling of concrete. Someone said that the morning Duke came on the job, all the other concrete-wheelers were laid off, for Duke wheeled away the entire contents of the mixer at one shot," the *Argus* joked.⁴ "He has carried more brick during the past few months than it would take to erect another structure as big as the Safety Building."⁵

The Rock Island club was ecstatic to have Duke on board as they embarked on their first season in the AFL. "Fred 'Duke' Slater, the greatest lineman ever turned out by Iowa University, has been signed to play right tackle with the Rock Island Independents," reported the *Democrat & Leader*. "He has been started in every game of the schedule, excepting one Kansas City game, and has never lost a minute's time in any contest. He is a mountain of strength on the right side of the line. Opponents prefer to try for gains somewhere besides through Slater. He is well-known to Tri-City fans and the announcement of his return to the Independents lineup will gratify those studying the strength of the Rock Island Independents this year."⁶

Although the franchise retained the Rock Island name, the AFL Independents played their home games at Browning Field in nearby Moline. The team did restore the classic green and white jerseys, however. The Independents felt they had a big advantage over the other AFL teams, because while some other franchises were starting from scratch, Rock Island was an established organization that had been continuously operating for years. The Independents were also able to retain several players from their NFL days. "You can take it from Duke Slater that the Independents will be stronger this year than before. Duke said the other day, 'Ah believe we never did have so good a team as we got this year.' There's word from an All-American. You can weigh it yourself," the *Argus* reported.⁷

Their opening game was against the AFL's traveling team, the Wilson Wildcats. The Wildcats were listed as being from Los Angeles, although since they played all road games, they could have been listed as being from anywhere. The Wildcats' roster was filled with players from western schools, including their headlining player, George "Wildcat" Wilson.

In a bold move, Manager Bowlby shelled out $500 to sign college football legend Elmer Layden, one of Grantland Rice's "Four Horsemen of Notre Dame," to a one-game contract. The acquisition didn't exactly pay huge dividends for Rock Island. In the opening quarter versus the Wildcats, Layden had a punt blocked deep in Rock Island territory. The Indee defense managed to hold the visitors out of the end zone, but end Jim Lawson kicked an easy 16-yard field goal to give the Wildcats an early 3–0 lead.

The following period, Johnny Armstrong took control of the game for the Green and White. He completed a long pass near midfield to halfback Wes Bradshaw, who slipped and fell at the five-yard line. A few plays later, Armstrong ran in the game's only touchdown to give Rock Island the lead. The second half saw no scoring, although Rock Island was fortunate when one of the Wildcats dropped a sure touchdown pass at the Independents' goal line. Nevertheless, Rock Island held on to a 7–3 victory in their AFL debut.⁸

Armstrong, fresh off his strong performance against the Wildcats, was named Rock Island's coach for the rest of the year. Slater's work in the line was critical to the win. "The

Duke held up his end of the game," the *Argus* noted. "Slater was through the line more than once, and there were two men on him most of the time as usual, too."[9] Moving the games to Moline didn't help the Independents' attendance, however; only a modest crowd of 2,500 fans saw the contest.

Fortunately for Bowlby, a much better crowd of 5,000 fans turned out to see the league's marquee team, Red Grange's New York Yankees, the following week. After an early interception of Grange, Rock Island had great field position. But the game's momentum changed in an instant when Wesley Fry, a tough fullback from Iowa, picked off Armstrong's pass and ran 82 yards the other way for a Yankee touchdown. On the first play of the second quarter, Grange caught a 12-yard pass for another New York touchdown and a 14–0 lead. The Yankees put on an impressive first half performance, considering the conditions. Rain made Browning Field soggy and slick, and by halftime, every player on the field was covered in mud from head to toe.

In the second half, things just got worse for the home team. A fumbled punt gave the Yankees excellent field position, and Grange shook off five tacklers and raced to the end zone to increase New York's advantage to 20–0 midway through the third period. Fans flocked for home with the Yankees comfortably ahead, Grange on the bench for the entire fourth quarter, and a pouring rain dampening everyone's interest. The Yankees added another touchdown as time expired to win, 26–0.[10] Overall, the margin of victory and the weather created an underwhelming spectacle in Rock Island.

Duke Slater matched up with Yankee lineman Paul Minick. Minick had been Slater's teammate at Iowa, and the two Hawkeyes were good friends. He was a rookie for the Yankees, and he was literally playing for his place in pro football against Rock Island and Slater. "My future, the money I needed, was dependent on my showing in this first game. Duke knew this," Minick recalled. Since the game was out of hand in the second half, Slater took care not to embarrass his friend. "He took pains to make me look good," added Minick. "When the game was over, people told me how I had played Slater even. But I knew it was just another example of Duke's kindness of heart."[11]

The Independents' final home AFL game of the year was against the Chicago Bulls, who featured a familiar foe. Joe Sternaman, the man who tortured the Indees on so many occasions as a member of the Bears, was the owner, coach, and captain of the Bulls. Sternaman was flanked by fellow Chicago standouts Johnny Mohardt and Eddie Anderson.

Duke Slater actually sat out of one scrimmage during the week of the Bulls game, a highly unusual occurrence. He had been suffering from an "infected side, due to irritation."[12] The injury didn't prevent him from being in the lineup versus the Bulls, however. Squandered scoring opportunities were the story of the Chicago game for Rock Island. The Independents drove to the Bulls' one-yard line, and on fourth and goal, the Indees shoved the ball into the end zone. However, the referee ruled that the play was dead before the ball crossed the goal line, and the Bulls avoided an early deficit.

At the beginning of the second quarter, one of the Bulls' backs smashed head-first into Duke, and Slater had the wind knocked out of him for a few seconds. Duke called for time-out for the first time since his first NFL game in 1922. Rock Island fans were convinced there had to be a conspiracy. One woman in the stands called for the referee to examine the headgear of the player that hit Slater. "There must have been iron or something in the fellow's headguard!" she exclaimed.[13]

Sternaman kicked an 18-yard field goal in the second period, and Chicago led, 3–0, going into the fourth quarter. Rock Island blew two scoring chances with interceptions deep in Chicago territory, and it looked as though Sternaman's famous kicking might sink the Independents yet again. But with ten minutes left in the game, Slater and the other Rock Island linemen began to rip gaping holes in the Bulls' line. Eddie Novak rushed for repeated gains, capped by a six-yard touchdown run. The final touchdown in front of the home crowd allowed the Green and White to leave Rock Island as winners, defeating Chicago, 7–3.[14]

The *Democrat & Leader* declared Slater "did practically all the work on the line and opened holes in the Bull wall big enough for a string of box cars."[15] It reported that while Novak made most of the gains, any member of the Rock Island backfield could have powered through the massive holes Slater created. "In fact, the whole Indee backfield could have gone through most of the openings," the *Democrat & Leader* reported.[16] Despite calling for timeout in the first half, Slater stayed in the game and again played all sixty minutes in the last professional football game held in the Tri-Cities.

Hours after the Chicago game, the Green and White loaded up the fancy Rock Island Football Club bus and departed on their long road trip. They were scheduled to play twelve road contests and hoped their profits offset the money the team lost on their two non–Grange home games. The team set out for Cleveland, Ohio, but in an ominous sign, the much-publicized charter bus blew a flat tire nine miles west of Toledo. Lots were drawn among the players to decide who would fix the rear tire, and Slater drew the short straw. Duke fixed the tire all right, but upon examination, he put the lugs back on so tight that he bent the wrench.[17] Like so many rival linemen, the wrench was a victim of Slater's brute strength.

The Independents eventually made it to Cleveland and took on the Panthers in their first road game of the year. Cleveland had long been an independent team, and in 1922, they tried to pry Slater's services away from Rock Island before he pledged his loyalty to the Independents. Now a member of the AFL, the Panthers were a squad to fear. They began the game by executing a dominating drive down the field, capping it off with halfback Dave Noble smashing ahead for a touchdown.

The Panthers held that 7–0 advantage right before halftime when Coach Armstrong made a tactical error. With only seconds remaining in the half, he chose to call up a trick play on fourth down and four from Rock Island's 37-yard line. Tackle Dick Stahlman was sacked on the pass attempt, resulting in a five-yard loss and a turnover on downs. The Panthers immediately drilled a 41-yard field goal just before the end of the half to extend their lead to 10–0.

Cleveland added two touchdowns in the third quarter to seize a 23–0 lead. Reserve quarterback Ave Kaplan passed to Bradshaw for a 16-yard touchdown in garbage time with the game out of reach; those were the last points scored by the Independents in major professional football. Ultimately, the Cleveland Panthers cruised to an easy 23–7 victory.[18]

The Indees hopped on the bus and headed for Philly to take on the Quakers, and the players greatly enjoyed riding the Rock Island charter. It provided plenty of room for big Duke Slater, whose hunger matched his size. "Windows in the big bus were kept wide open during the trip to Philadelphia from Cleveland," the *Argus* declared. "The fresh air gave the boys extra large appetites. No one knows how big Dale Johnson's and Duke Slater's checks were for lunch yesterday noon."[19]

While in Philly, Slater spent the week with Canton's Sol Butler, who was in town for a game against the Frankford Yellow Jackets. That same week, the *Philadelphia Inquirer* printed an interview they conducted with Red Grange. In it, Grange, the most famous football player in the world, called Duke Slater the greatest tackle he had ever seen. "They can bring all the tackles in the country," Grange said, "but this fellow Slater is the best of them all. Slater is a marvel and is so strong and powerful that he seems to sweep one-half of the line aside when he charges. I've played against Slater, and I know what I'm talking about. Eddie Tryon also declares Slater is one of the sweetest looking tackles he ever faced."[20]

The Philadelphia Quakers were one of the AFL's strongest teams and near the top of the league standings. A major blunder cost the Independents dearly against the Quakers. Already trailing, 3–0, Armstrong attempted to pass near his own goal line in the second quarter. Philadelphia's Adrian Ford intercepted the pass and returned it 18 yards for the game's only touchdown. Rock Island's defense stood tall, but the offense was nowhere to be found in their 9–0 defeat.[21] Still, Slater and his line mates impressed onlookers. The president of the AFL, "Big Bill" Edwards, watched the game from the sidelines and decreed that Rock Island's line was the most powerful he had ever seen.[22]

The fledgling AFL handed Rock Island a schedule designed to maximize weekend games by giving them a Saturday-Sunday doubleheader. The city of Philadelphia prohibited football on Sundays, so the Independents played the Philadelphia Quakers Saturday afternoon. The team then drove to Newark, New Jersey, by late Saturday night to play the Newark Bears on Sunday. The winless Bears had the poorest fan support in the league. When Slater and his teammates took the field for the game, they were greeted by a cold rain and a muddy field. The poor weather helped ensure a meager attendance of about 400 fans.

The few fans in the stands who braved the lousy conditions were rewarded with a horribly-played game. The Bears had little talent, while the Independents were tired from travel and their game against the Quakers. By midway through the first quarter, players on both sides were covered in mud. Bradshaw got close enough to attempt a field goal at the start of the fourth quarter, but his 26-yard attempt sailed inches below the crossbar. The teams battled to a scoreless draw in the pouring rain.[23] Slater "starred for Rock Island" against Newark, and Duke trudged off of the field, having played two complete football games in two days.[24]

Rock Island had a week off before they were scheduled to play a Sunday-Tuesday doubleheader against the Brooklyn Horsemen and Grange's New York Yankees, respectively. Most of the Independents used the time off to enjoy the sights of New York City, but Slater instead accompanied Red Grange and Quakers' coach Bob Folwell to Philadelphia Friday to watch the Tuskegee-Lincoln college football game.[25] Grange and Slater joined a crowd of 35,000 to see two of the top black college football teams in the nation play a terrific game. Tuskegee and their star halfback, Ben Stevenson, secured a 20–16 win en route to an undefeated season and the black college national championship.

A torrential downpour caused the Rock Island-Brooklyn game to be cancelled anyway, and that rainstorm ensured a wet field when the Independents tangled with the Yankees on November 2.[26] The rematch was even less competitive than the teams' first meeting in Rock Island. Trailing 14–0, Slater continued to fight valiantly, tackling Grange for a five-yard loss which helped end a New York scoring threat in the second quarter and then catching a ten-yard pass from Armstrong for a first down. But on the very next play, Armstrong's pass was intercepted by Tryon, who ran it back 25 yards for another New York touchdown. The Yankees added two more fourth quarter touchdowns— one of them on a dazzling, classic Grange run— and New York pummeled Rock Island, 35–0.[27]

Duke Slater, the only African American in the American Football League, wasn't immune to racial prejudice in this league, either. Slater diffused many of these situations with humor and a calm temperament, but being one of the most physically imposing athletes on the field was an advantage as well. Leo Kriz, a member of the 1926 New York Yankees, recalled an incident from the Rock Island–New York game. "One of our boys, a Southerner, started to get rough with Duke, trying to kick him when he was down," Kriz said. "Duke just looked up at the fellow and said in a quiet voice, 'Look, man, don't do that, because I don't want to hurt you.' The guy stopped the dirty play right there."[28]

Meanwhile, the AFL was in dire straits. Newark and Cleveland both left the AFL to play an independent schedule, so the league was down to only seven teams. Cleveland's departure left the Philadelphia Quakers without an opponent on November 6. The Independents, who were originally supposed to play the Quakers November 13, raced back down to Philly to take Cleveland's place on the schedule.

The Quakers had a powerful squad, and they improved their roster even further with the addition of halfback Glenn Killinger. Rock Island, on the other hand, was weary from the long road trip and playing on short notice. The Independents played Philadelphia even in a scoreless first half, but everything fell apart for the Green and White after halftime. Rock Island threw six interceptions, with Killinger snagging four of them. Philly's defense never wavered as they blanked the exhausted Independents, 24–0.[29] It was the fourth straight shutout suffered by Rock Island, an ignoble record for a once proud franchise.

The Independents' schedule was in ruins as Brooklyn and Boston were the next two teams to bail on the AFL. There were only five stable franchises left in the league—Rock Island, Philadelphia, New York, Chicago, and Wilson's traveling team. Rock Island had just played New York and Philadelphia, the only two remaining franchises on the East Coast, so the Indees had no choice but to head for home on their charter bus. Through it all, the players enjoyed their trip west, joking and singing as they traveled. At one point, the bus stopped while the players got out and chased a herd of cows from the road.[30]

Several team members sensed the end of the Rock Island franchise and left the squad when they returned to Illinois. The remaining Independents, including Slater, stopped in Chicago and awaited instructions from team management. Rock Island's next game was scheduled for November 21 at the Chicago Bulls, and the Independents were negotiating with the Wilson Wildcats for a game in the Tri-Cities on November 28. While Rock Island's players were idling in Chicago, representatives of the NFL's Chicago Cardinals contacted Independent players Duke Slater and Chet Widerquist about possibly joining their squad. Widerquist immediately accepted the offer and left Rock Island's club, and few could have blamed Duke for doing the same. However, Slater told the Cardinals that while he was interested in the opportunity, he felt a responsibility to stay with the Independents until the end of their season, despite the shaky status of the franchise and the AFL as a whole.[31]

Although much of the roster was gone, what remained of the Rock Island Independents met at Comiskey Park in Chicago on November 21, 1926, to take on their old nemesis, Joe Sternaman, and the Chicago Bulls. In the final game for Rock Island in major professional football, Sternaman's renowned kicking toe fittingly sunk the Green and White one last time. His first quarter field goal eventually gave Chicago a 3–0 victory on a snowy, cold day.[32] But just as fittingly, Duke Slater was on the field for the full sixty minutes, defending the Independent goal line to the very end. "Duke Slater smeared plays, one right after the other," the *Argus* declared, "and when the Bulls approached the Rock Island goal, he was in there like a big stone barrier."[33]

In 1926, the NFL had two Chicago teams. The Bears and Cardinals shared the Windy City in much the same way baseball's Cubs and White Sox still do today. The Bears were the city's more popular team, representing the white collar North Side. The Bears' name was even a take off of the moniker of the Cubs, and the Bears played their home games at Cubs Park, which was later renamed Wrigley Field. The Chicago Cardinals, on the other hand, represented the city's gritty, blue collar South Side and used Comiskey Park for many of their home games in the 1920s. The Cardinals and Bears had a spirited rivalry, which culminated every year in an annual inner-city game on Thanksgiving for Chicago bragging rights.[34]

The Chicago Cardinals were awarded a controversial NFL title in 1925 over the Pottsville Maroons. However, the Cards were struggling in 1926. The AFL's Bulls introduced a third team into the Chicago market, and they took up residence in the Cardinals' South Side turf. The Bulls actually stole the Cards' turf, literally; they offered Comiskey Park a far better lease agreement before the season and won exclusive rights to use the Cards' field. As a result, the Cardinals were banished back to Normal Park, a much smaller venue they used prior to 1922. They had outgrown Normal Park years earlier, and being forced to host games there again severely hurt their attendance and revenue.

The Cards started the 1926 season by winning five of their first six games, but injuries led to a four-game losing streak and a 5–5 record on the year. With their annual showdown with the Bears looming, Cardinals owner Chris O'Brien wanted to strengthen his roster. The demise of the Independents gave O'Brien exactly what he needed—a chance to sign an all-pro on the cheap. Duke Slater made $175 a game for the Independents, but when he signed with the Cardinals, he took a pay cut to $125 a game.[35]

African American players generally couldn't be overly choosy when it came to pro football opportunities, but the Chicago Cardinals were the perfect team for Duke Slater. He was raised on the South Side of Chicago; in fact, Normal Park was built on top of a vacant lot where Slater played street football as a youth. It was located in the same neighborhood where his grandparents and parents had lived in the first decade of the 1900s. Duke felt very comfortable on the South Side, and his signing meant a return to his home town.

Rock Island failed to arrange a game with the Wildcats, so the Independents' AFL season was over. Duke Slater remained in Chicago after Rock Island's contest with the Bulls, and O'Brien signed him for the final two games of the Cards' season. After playing on November 21 with the Indees, Duke was set to play on November 25 in the Cardinals' annual Thanksgiving matchup with the Bears. Since Rock Island considered the Bears their greatest rivals, Slater had no problem adjusting to the Cardinals-Bears rivalry.

The only issue was that the Cardinals were already strong at the tackle positions. Left tackle Bub Weller was a second team all-pro in 1926, while right tackle Fred Gillies had been a long-time Cardinals mainstay who held the respect of everyone in the organization. As a result, Chicago actually considered shifting Slater to the end position.[36] The Cardinals ultimately decided to keep the starting lineup the same in the interest of continuity and just play Slater off of the bench for the rest of the season.

On November 25, 1926, Slater came off of the bench for the first time in his NFL career as he made his debut with the Chicago Cardinals. He substituted at right tackle and teamed with Gillies to form a powerful tackle combination for the Cards. With the help of Slater and an assist from Mother Nature, the Cardinals battled the Bears to a scoreless tie. Rain soaked Cubs Park, which made moving the ball difficult. Former Independent halfback Roddy Lamb followed behind Slater for multiple first downs including one at the Bears'

21-yard line, but the Cardinals never got close enough to score. Defensively, however, Slater and Gillies kept former Cardinal star Paddy Driscoll on his heels and prevented him from taking over the game.[37] Recording a tie against the undefeated Bears was a solid showing for the 5–5 Cardinals.

In the final contest of the 1926 season, the Cardinals hosted the Kansas City Cowboys. Slater was not in the starting lineup for the second consecutive game, and that very quickly proved to be a mistake. On Kansas City's second offensive play of the game, Rufe DeWitz ran to the side of the field occupied by Weller, the Cards' left tackle, and scampered 75 yards for a touchdown. Slater soon entered the contest in place of Weller, but the damage was done. Duke and the Cardinal defense shut down Kansas City from that point forward, but the mud that covered the field kept Chicago from generating enough offense to even the score. Only a late Cardinals' safety prevented the shutout as Kansas City held on for a 7–2 victory.[38]

Several all-pro teams were announced after the season, but many of these teams included only NFL players. Slater was selected to two of the all-pro teams that actually considered AFL players; he was a first team all-pro choice by the *Chicago Tribune* and a second team selection by *Collyer's Eye Magazine*. Wilfrid Smith announced Duke's all-pro selection for the *Tribune*, writing, "Slater, who started the season with Rock Island and finished with the Chicago Cardinals, is one of the best tackles who ever donned a suit. His phenomenal strength and quickness of charge make it almost impossible for his opponents to put him out of any play directed at his side of the line."[39]

Duke Slater and the Rock Island Independents parted on the best of terms. Slater stayed with the Independents to the very end, even as other players bailed out. Following his two games with the Cards, he returned to play in post-season exhibitions with the Independents, including a December scrimmage in Des Moines against the Valley Junction Independents.[40] Manager Dale Johnson announced that Rock Island would play the 1927 season in the AFL, but the entire American Football League folded after just one season, and Rock Island was finished with professional football at a national level.[41] After five years in the Tri-Cities, Duke Slater moved his wife and home permanently to Chicago's South Side. Slater had a bright future with the Cardinals, but other African Americans were seeing their opportunities slip away.

A seismic shift took place in professional football that off-season. Red Grange's American Football League collapsed after one year of challenging the NFL. His New York Yankees franchise was added to the NFL, but the rest of the AFL disbanded. Despite their victory, the National Football League was financially damaged by the challenge to their supremacy in professional football, and the league elected to make drastic changes.

In the 1926 season, there were 22 NFL teams, and many of them were located in relatively small towns. The league tightened its roster to just 12 franchises for the 1927 season, eliminating financially weaker teams and focusing more on large cities on the East Coast over smaller towns in the Midwest. The resulting purge of franchises concentrated the existing talent onto fewer teams, making the surviving franchises stronger on the field and at the ticket office.

The mass elimination of franchises in smaller Midwest towns had racial consequences, however. In 1926, there were five African Americans playing professional football. In addition to Slater with Rock Island, Ink Williams and Dick Hudson played for Hammond, Fritz Pollard suited up for Akron, and Sol Butler was on Canton's roster. Hammond, Akron, Canton, and Rock Island were all relatively small towns, and their football franchises didn't survive the NFL's restructuring in 1926. Williams, Hudson, Butler, and Pollard all saw their NFL careers come to an abrupt end.

The NFL was growing from its disorganized origins into a well-run sports league, but the top professional sport in the eyes of the average American fan was still baseball. Baseball had maintained a ban on African American players for decades, and by the late–1920s, many owners in the National Football League were receptive to the idea of following their lead. The elimination of several franchises gave owners an opportunity to rid the league of its remaining black players.

By 1927, every African American was cast out of the NFL — except Duke Slater. There are several reasons Slater remained. He was frequently described as one of the "cleanest" players in the game, someone who didn't take cheap shots or get involved in fights, regardless of how he was treated. Slater was a law student, exceedingly intelligent and well-spoken, like his father before him. As a result, he was beloved by his teammates and respected by opponents. Duke also didn't attract attention to himself through either his words or actions. Unlike Williams, Hudson, Butler, and Pollard, Duke was a lineman, so he wouldn't steal headlines or take attention away from his white counterparts. Finally, he was a fan favorite, a star gate attraction and a magnet to crowds wherever he played.[42]

Duke Slater returned to the South Side of Chicago with the Cardinals in 1926, and by 1927, he was the only African American in the National Football League.

But the main reason why Duke Slater was able to break across the forming color line was sheer talent. Duke was easily the most decorated African American football player of all time. He made the all-pro team in 1926 for the fourth consecutive season; no other African American had ever been named all-pro more than twice. Furthermore, he had been the only African American to make the all-pro team in 1924, 1925, or 1926, so he was still in the prime of his career.

Race aside, Duke was one of the greatest linemen in the NFL in the 1920s. As writer Manque Winters explained, "[Slater] was so good that if he were rejected, not only could owners' integrity and morality be questioned, but also their sanity."[43] The Chicago Cardinals saw him as a hometown player who performed at a high level for a reasonable price. Because of this, the Cardinals knew if they passed on him, some other franchise would pick him up. Duke Slater's level of excellence singlehandedly prevented a color ban from forming in the NFL and kept the door ever so slightly ajar for other black athletes.

Slater earned the starting spot at right tackle for the Chicago Cardinals as the 1927 season began. Fred Gillies retired before the season, which allowed Duke to work his way into the starting rotation. Cardinals owner Chris O'Brien was so pleased with Slater that he claimed his tackles were the best in the NFL.[44] The Cards also brought in legendary coach Guy Chamberlin to be a player-coach of the squad. Chamberlin had been the head coach of four of the previous five NFL champions, so his arrival sparked high hopes for the 1927 Cardinals.

Those hopes were dashed very early in the year when the Cards dropped an exhibition game to Hammond, 6–0. Slater was back to his old tricks, however, playing all sixty minutes in the exhibition despite a constant shifting of players elsewhere in the lineup. The season opener for the Cardinals was a match against their old rivals, the Bears. Duke had his hands full with the usual Bears' players in their line — including Lyman, Trafton, McMillan, and Healey.

For more than three quarters, neither team came close to scoring, but the Bears seized control in the final period. They got close enough to attempt a 45-yard field goal, and the Cards' old hero, Paddy Driscoll, drilled it to give the Bears a 3–0 lead. According to the *Tribune*, that field goal "broke the stiff defense the Cardinal line had presented to that time."[45] The Bears later drove eighty yards for a game-clinching score, with Driscoll carrying three yards for the only touchdown in a 9–0 victory.[46]

Although the opening loss to their rivals stung, the Cards needed to refocus quickly because their next game was a grudge match with the Pottsville Maroons. The Cardinals were awarded the 1925 NFL championship over Pottsville, a decision the Maroons loudly and angrily protested. The two teams didn't meet in 1926, so this contest was their first encounter since the disputed ruling was handed down. The Maroons had a 20–4–2 record in their previous two NFL seasons, so they were a formidable challenge. They took out their frustrations on the Cardinals early. The Maroons blocked a punt attempt by halfback Hal Erickson and fell on it in the end zone for a touchdown when the game was only three minutes old. However, the Cardinal defense, which played well for three quarters the previous week, shone on this day. They recovered a Maroon fumble in the second period, which allowed the offense to finally get on the scoreboard. Halfback Rollin Roach, playing in the only game of his NFL career, rushed for one career touchdown to cut the deficit to 7–6 at halftime.

In the third quarter, the passing game paid dividends for the Cardinals. Chicago used steady passes to move down the field, eventually scoring on quarterback Ben Jones' touchdown run for a 13–7 advantage. The Cardinals' defense was airtight and refused to allow Pottsville any offensive points on the day. Increasingly desperate, Pottsville filled the air with passes, and with minutes remaining, Chicago reserve center Bill Springsteen returned an interception to Pottsville's one-yard line. Paul Hogan punched over a short touchdown run in the last game of his pro football career for the Cards' final touchdown. Even though Slater missed the extra point attempt, Chicago scratched out a 19–7 victory.[47] In his fourth game, Duke finally had his first win in a Cardinal uniform.

Slater's endurance in the rugged battle was significant. He was the only Cardinals player to play the entire game, yet at the end of the match, Duke was the one still going strong. "Duke Slater was instrumental in halting the Maroon attack late in the game when he kept charging through, hurrying the passer," the *Chicago Herald-Examiner* remarked.[48]

The Cardinals sought to make it two victories in a row against the perennial cellar-dwelling Dayton Triangles. Most of the day was frustrating for the Cards, as they repeatedly squandered scoring chances. The first half ended with the Cardinals in possession of the ball one yard from the Dayton goal line. In the fourth quarter, a Bub Weller 35-yard field goal try banged off of the upright and fell away. It looked as though the Cards, whose defense limited the Triangles to only two first downs, would settle for a scoreless draw with Dayton.

On their final drive, however, the Cardinals' offense got on the same page and drove down the field. Faced with a fourth down, halfback Red Strader plunged over the goal line with less than thirty seconds remaining in the game to give the Cardinals a 7–0 victory.[49] The *Chicago Tribune* sounded more relieved than impressed. "There was no doubt about the Cardinals' superiority over the invading eleven but there was considerable doubt in the minds of the 3,000 fans whether the Cards ever would be able to overcome their self-imposed handicap of fumbling and poor generalship to score," recapped the *Tribune*.[50]

Chicago left Normal Park for the first time in 1927 and traveled to Green Bay for one of the most important matchups of the NFL season to date. The Packers and the Cards each only had one loss administered by the league-leading Bears, so the winner would be right back in the NFL title hunt. Unfortunately for the Cardinals, the showdown turned into a one-sided affair. The Packers scored a touchdown early in the second period on a trick play to take a 6–0 lead into halftime, and the Cardinal offense couldn't gain traction all day. Verne Lewellen, the Packers' sensational halfback, tacked on a touchdown in the fourth quarter to lead Green Bay to a convincing 13–0 victory.[51] Duke Slater played all sixty minutes for the fourth straight game.

The Cards got back in the win column with a blowout exhibition victory over Spring Valley before staging their most anticipated game of the year. Chris O'Brien believed a visit from Red Grange and his New York Yankees would draw a huge crowd and put the Chicago Cardinals in the spotlight. He hyped the game and even moved the site of the contest from Normal Park to Soldier Field with the expectation of a huge gate. His best laid plans were derailed, however, when Grange was severely injured two weeks earlier while playing against the Bears. O'Brien tried to sustain interest by concocting a "Presentation Day" at the last minute that featured Red being presented a crate of apples at halftime, but the fans were understandably dissatisfied. Despite frequent chants for Grange from the crowd, the star failed to make an appearance in the actual game.

The fans saw an uninteresting if competitive football game in Grange's absence. Slater shifted to the left tackle position and spent sixty minutes battling New York's terrific rookie lineman, Mike Michalske. The Cardinals' passing attack led to two touchdowns in the third quarter; unfortunately, one of those was an interception Wesley Fry returned sixty yards for a New York score. Eddie Tryon kicked the extra point for the Yankees. Several Chicago passes later led to a one-yard touchdown run by halfback Hap Moran, but the Cards missed their extra point try, which proved to be the difference in the game. "The Chicago Cardinals pro football team celebrated Presentation Day yesterday at Soldiers' Field," the *Tribune* noted. "Shortly after, the Cardinals, without any ceremony, presented the Yankees with the ball game, the final score being 7–6."[52]

Ironically, the Cardinals got the excitement they so desperately missed the week before when they returned to Normal Park to host the Packers on November 6. Green Bay easily handled the Cardinals earlier in the year, but the Normal Park crowd was vociferous and ready for an upset. The odds of seeing such a result grew in the second quarter, when Lewellen, one of the league's best punters, shanked a kick in Green Bay territory. With the benefit of good field position, Chicago quarterback Mickey MacDonnell fired a risky pass downfield, and Red Dunn of the Packers was in position for an interception. But the ball grazed off of his hands and into the arms of Weller, who raced in for a Chicago touchdown just before halftime.

The Cards maintained their 6–0 lead midway through the fourth quarter, when the powerful Packers ramped up their offense and drove down the field. Lewellen redeemed himself for his errant punt by slamming ahead with a five-yard touchdown run, and Red Dunn was also given a shot at redemption. Dunn, who played for the Cards the previous season before being released, had an opportunity to send his former team down to defeat. But his extra point attempt was blocked, and Green Bay had to settle for a draw with the scrappy Cardinals.[53]

Reducing the number of NFL franchises in 1927 produced more rematches during the season between existing clubs. Duke Slater got another sixty minute dose of Mike Michalske when Chicago went to New York for their second game with the Yankees. Their previous meeting was fairly dull, but this game turned into one of the roughest of the season. Red Grange tried to play for the Yanks, but the hitting was too fierce and he had to leave. Eddie Tryon, the former Colgate All-American, had one of his best days in pro football in Grange's absence, scoring two touchdowns on a short run and a reception from "Wild Bill" Kelly. But the physical game took its toll. Tryon was carried from the field after his second score, and Yankee halfback Bullet Baker was sent to the hospital with two fractured ribs. Regardless, the Cards' offense was helpless against the Yankee defense, and New York added a third touchdown in the second half. The Cards got a late score, but they were thoroughly defeated, 20–6.[54]

The physical battle with the Yankees was nothing compared to the Cardinals' next test. The Frankford Yellow Jackets fell under Philadelphia's "no football on Sundays" law, so Chicago accommodated them by traveling to the east coast for a Saturday-Sunday doubleheader. In the first game, Slater was matched against Frankford's veteran lineman, Rudy Comstock. The scoreboard showed some bizarre scores in this contest. The Cardinals fell behind, 5–0, when the Jackets got a field goal and Chicago's Roddy Lamb fell on his own fumble in his end zone for a safety.

Chicago responded with a ten-yard touchdown run by Ben Jones for a 6–5 halftime lead, and they padded the advantage with a safety of their own in the next quarter. With time running down in the game, the Cards were clinging to a strange 8–5 lead, and it looked like they might snap their four-game winless streak. But Chicago's big dreams were dashed by a tiny player. Frankford reserve quarterback Henry Homan had the nickname "Two-Bits," because he was one of the smallest players in NFL history at 145 pounds. Two-Bits Homan made two brilliant catches on long passes on the same drive; his second catch was an 18-yard reception for a Yellow Jacket touchdown with mere minutes left on the clock. It was the decisive score as the Cards fell short again, 12–8.[55]

The loss was a major disappointment, and the Cardinals had to leave immediately for the Polo Grounds to play the league-leading New York Giants the following day. Duke Slater and New York's Steve Owen were paired against each other again, but the Cardinals were exhausted from the effort they gave against Frankford. The Giants also had one of the best teams in the NFL in 1927, and it showed on the field. New York scored three touchdowns in the first quarter en route to a lopsided 28–7 victory.[56]

Chicago's two NFL teams were headed in opposite directions. The Cardinals returned from the long road trip winless in their last six games, while the cross-town rival Bears were atop the league standings. As the two teams met for their annual Thanksgiving Day game, fans didn't expect the Cardinals to be able to keep the Bears close. The Southsiders surprised spectators with a fast start. Early in the game, Mickey MacDonnell grabbed a punt and returned it 55 yards to the Bears' 20-yard line. "On the next play, he shot through the left side of the Bear line behind Duke Slater and was stopped seven yards from the goal line," the *Tribune* noted.[57] The Bears halted the Cardinal drive there, but the gains resulted in a field goal by end Evar Swanson and an early 3–0 lead.

Just as they did for Rock Island in 1924, Swanson's points sunk the Bears. For all the Cardinals' offensive woes on the season, their defense played admirably in several games in 1927. That defense loomed large against the Bears, protecting the three-point lead for sixty minutes and shocking the city with a 3–0 upset victory.[58] The defeat dropped the Bears from the top of the league standings behind the Giants, and the *Herald-Examiner* called the result "the greatest upset of the current National Pro Football League season."[59]

The Cards had the city's attention after their startling win, so O'Brien moved their final game of the season versus the Cleveland Bulldogs to Soldier Field. The Bulldogs featured the league's most prolific passer in star quarterback Benny Friedman, and O'Brien hoped Friedman would attract a large crowd to the stadium for a memorable game. However, the contest quickly turned into one to forget for the home team. Friedman lived up to his advanced billing and more, passing for four touchdowns and absolutely torching the Cardinals in a 32–7 victory.[60]

Most of Chicago's players had given up by this point in a losing season. "The Cardinals surpassed their own record for indifferent football," the *Tribune*'s Wilfrid Smith hissed after they were annihilated by the Bulldogs. However, Duke continued to give maximum effort. "During the first half, Slater seemed the only Cardinal linesman who had ambition to hurry Benny's passes, and the Duke generally was bumped out of the play," noted Smith.[61] As the only African American in the NFL, Duke Slater wasn't just playing for personal pride; he made sure his play and work ethic left little room for criticism.

The Chicago Cardinals ended the season with a 3–7–1 record and few bright spots. Undoubtedly, Slater was one of those. The veteran tackle played every minute of every game for the Cards, piling up eleven complete games; no other Cardinal completed more than eight. Duke also made the all-pro team for the fifth consecutive season. He was a first team all-pro selection by the *Cleveland Press*, but he was again bumped down to the second team by the *Green Bay Press-Gazette* for the fourth time in his career.

Duke Slater's first full year with the Chicago Cardinals was a success from an individual standpoint, but his play was in direct contrast to the struggles of the Cardinal team as a whole. However, major changes to the Chicago franchise were on the horizon. Those changes would culminate in Duke Slater's greatest moment in the NFL.

Chapter 11

Last Man Standing (1928–1929)

On June 4, 1928, Duke Slater graduated from the University of Iowa College of Law. He started taking classes toward his law degree while he was starring for the Hawkeye football team. After a brief hiatus as he began his career in the NFL, he resumed classes in 1925 and spent his off-seasons in Iowa City studying and taking odd jobs to pay his college tuition. For example, newly-elected president Herbert Hoover returned to his birthplace of West Branch, Iowa, in 1928 to make a speech about agriculture. Since there were no major restaurants in West Branch, Slater attended to the crowd's needs by running a chicken sandwich concession near the event.[1] Earning his law degree was the culmination of years of manual labor, menial jobs, and rigorous coursework, but he finally achieved a dream his father helped set in motion fifteen years earlier.

Duke was the only African American in the National Football League in 1927, a distinction of which he was not proud. He made sure he wouldn't have to stand alone during the 1928 season by lobbying for Harold Bradley to get a shot with the Cards. Bradley briefly attended the University of Iowa as a lineman, where he was understandably hyped as "another Duke Slater," but he left school after one year without ever playing for the Iowa varsity.[2] "I believe Duke had something to do with him signing with the Cardinals," his son Harold Bradley Jr. recalled. "There certainly was some kind of connection."[3]

Through that connection, the first black lineman in NFL history helped convince the Cardinals to make Harold Bradley the second. "If the Chicago Cardinals have nothing else to boast about, they are at least unique in one respect and that is that they are the only team in the Professional League which carries on its roster two colored players," the *Wisconsin Rapids Daily Tribune* reported.[4] "It is said by opponents that when the two get working together side by side that it takes a good combination to stop them," added the *Appleton Post-Crescent*.[5] Unfortunately, racial diversity was all the 1928 Cardinals could brag about, because the team simply had little talent. "Outside of Slater, the Cardinals boast of no other All-Americans and in that respect they are unique among teams in the National League, for practically every spoke in the wheel has three or four All-American selections in their lineups," the *Daily Tribune* noted.[6]

The Cardinals hired respected former tackle Fred Gillies to coach the squad. They opened the season against the Bears with Harold Bradley starting at right guard next to Slater at right tackle. The season began disastrously. Cards halfback Hal Erickson took the opening kickoff and tried to lateral to a teammate, but the Bears recovered and took over at the Cardinals' 26-yard line. The Cardinals stopped the Bears on downs at the one-yard line, but they were then forced to punt deep in their own territory, and the punt was blocked out of bounds for a safety.

Driscoll returned the ensuing kickoff beyond midfield, and after a few first downs, Joe

Sternaman faked an inside run, circled outside, and sprinted for a touchdown. The score was 9–0 just a few minutes into the season, and the Cardinals couldn't generate a serious scoring chance all afternoon. The Bears blocked another punt late in the fourth quarter, and Laurie Walquist converted a short touchdown run to make the final score 15–0.[7]

The linemen bore the brunt of the blame for the loss. "The Cards may or may not have a fast, high-scoring backfield, but that cannot be decided until they are seen in action behind a line," reported the *Southtown Economist*. "With the exception of Ralph Claypool and Duke Slater, two Cardinal All-Americans, the Southtown line was sadly wanting in Sunday's game."[8] To add further insult, the Cards followed their loss to the Bears with an embarrassing exhibition loss to the Chicago Mills, 7–6, on a missed extra point.

A visit from the hapless Dayton Triangles was just what the Cardinals needed. After a scoreless first half, Slater kicked off to Dayton's 35-yard line, and two plays later, Erickson made the play of the game for Chicago. He intercepted a short pass and galloped 35 yards down the sideline for a touchdown. The Cards squandered several other scoring chances, but fortunately for them, Dayton's offense was even more inept. One defensive touchdown was enough to beat the Triangles, 7–0.[9] Remarkably, that turned out to be the Cardinals' last home game of the season.

Chicago's next contest was in Green Bay, where Slater had had little success. Those frustrations continued, as this game was a disaster for the Cardinals. Packer halfback Eddie Kotal had one of his greatest games in an NFL uniform, getting Green Bay on the board first with a 40-yard touchdown run and then catching a pass down to the Cardinals' one-yard line. He then handed the starring role back to Verne Lewellen, who was quite accustomed to it. Lewellen plunged for a one-yard score and added a second touchdown from two yards away in the final quarter. Chicago was only inside Green Bay's 30-yard line once all day, and Slater was held in check by a Packer line that included guard Paul Minick. The Packers blew out the Cards, 20–0.[10]

The Cardinals had a 1–2 record three games into the season. For reasons that may never be fully understood, the Chicago Cardinals organization inexplicably took the next month and a half off from the NFL. It's possible O'Brien simply couldn't schedule any opponents because teams that traveled to Chicago preferred to play the Bears rather than travel to Normal Park. The league's 1927 reorganization also eliminated several local franchises from the Midwest that would typically serve as the Cardinals' opponents. In addition, O'Brien was facing financial difficulties running the club, which became apparent after the season.

Slater remained active in football despite the Cards' woes. Harold Bradley played against Dayton as a reserve lineman, but after two games, he was released by the Cardinals. Those were the only two games of his NFL career. Following Bradley's release, Slater was again the only African American in the National Football League. Since NFL owners were maintaining a color line only Slater was able to penetrate, Fritz Pollard organized a club of aspiring young African American players flanked by NFL veterans like Ink Williams, Sol Butler, and Pollard himself. Fritz Pollard's Chicago Blackhawks scrimmaged against semi-pro teams in interracial games, and Duke suited up for the Blackhawks while the Chicago Cardinals were on their six-week hiatus.[11]

When they finally returned to NFL play, the Cardinals were a broken team. They reunited on November 24 for another Saturday-Sunday doubleheader on the East Coast. The Frankford Yellow Jackets were near the top of the league standings, and Chicago did well to trail only 6–0 at halftime. A spectacular play broke the Cardinals' tough resistance as the second half began. Duke Slater kicked off to the Jackets, and the kick was caught by Frankford's Indian star, Fait "Chief" Elkins, at the two-yard line. Elkins had track star speed, and he displayed it by returning the second half kickoff 98 yards for a touchdown, which broke every known league record at the time.[12] Chief's sparkling run paced Frankford to a 19–0 victory over the Cardinals.[13]

Chicago immediately headed for Yankee Stadium, where the second half of their doubleheader was against the New York Yankees. Duke renewed acquaintances with Mike Michalske, New York's star lineman. The Cardinals-Yankees game was a fight to avoid joining the Pottsville Maroons and Dayton Triangles in the NFL cellar. The 1–3 Cardinals kicked off to the 1–7–1 Yankees, and New York immediately sliced through the weary Cardinal defense with a long touchdown drive. Chicago had no chance to win, because the backfield simply couldn't generate any offense. Their best scoring chance came in the third quarter, when a New York fumble gave the Cards the ball at the 18-yard line. The offense actually went backwards before turning the ball back over to the Yankees.[14]

The Cardinals finally wore down from their second game in two days. New York halfback Red Smith zipped for a touchdown in the fourth quarter to pad the Yanks' lead to 13 points. One last desperate attempt to score in the final seconds backfired on the Cardinals when "Wild Bill" Kelly intercepted a Chicago pass and returned it 46 yards another New York touchdown. The Cards were shut out and defeated by the same score on consecutive nights, 19–0.[15]

All that remained of the Cardinals' miserable season was their Thanksgiving rivalry game with the Chicago Bears. In one final attempt to light a spark under his struggling team, O'Brien signed 41-year-old Jim Thorpe to a one-game contract. But not even Thorpe could resurrect the Cardinals' moribund offense. After a scoreless first period, the Bears hammered the Cardinals in the second quarter. On consecutive possessions, the Bears blocked punt attempts by the Cards that led to easy touchdowns. The first block led to an eight-yard scoring run by Joe Sternaman, and Bears lineman Bill Fleckenstein blocked the second and returned it 15 yards himself for the touchdown.

The Bears weren't finished; they added two more touchdowns before halftime. The Bears had piled up 28 points in a single quarter, and their reserves tacked on another touchdown right before the final whistle to deliver a blowout 34–0 victory.[16] It was the most lopsided victory in the nine years of the Cardinals-Bears series, and it was also the final game of the legendary Jim Thorpe's career. Now a shadow of his former athletic self at 41 years old, Thorpe played only half the game and left the NFL behind for good after a marvelous career.

1928 was a complete nightmare for the Cards. They finished 1–5 in only half of an NFL season. They had one of the worst offenses in NFL history; the 1928 Cardinals failed to score an offensive touchdown the entire season. The only touchdown for Chicago in six games was a defensive score against winless Dayton that resulted in the Cards' only victory.

Duke Slater was the only Cardinal to play complete games in all six contests in 1928. He continued to shine, but his play was overshadowed by the struggles of his squad. "The team lacked speed in the backfield and strength in the line," author Joe Ziemba observed. "There were no marquee names in the lineup, except perhaps for the reliable tackle Fred Slater."[17] For the first time since his rookie year, Duke Slater failed to make any all-pro teams after the 1928 season. This wasn't a reflection of Slater's play; his omission was due to the fact that his team played only a half of an NFL season and fared so poorly when they did play. The Cardinals' disastrous year forced major changes within the organization.

The Cardinals were losing money hand over fist. Although he loved his team dearly, team founder Chris O'Brien had no choice but to sell the franchise to wealthy Chicago physician David Jones. Dr. Jones promptly pledged to bring a winning team to the South Side. His first step toward that goal was overhauling the Cardinals' roster, and this presented a perfect opportunity to purge the league of its only African American player. However, first and foremost, Dr. Jones had promised to win games, and he wasn't about to release a man considered by many to be "the greatest colored football player that ever lived."[18] Jones only retained three players from the failed 1928 Cards, but one of the three men he kept on the roster was their "peerless tackle," Duke Slater.[19]

Dr. Jones' decision was made easier because the other players in the NFL admired Slater. The *Milwaukee Sentinel*, in a misguided attempt at a compliment, said, "Slater is regarded by other players as as white inside as he is black outside." The *Sentinel* went on to praise Slater's "fairness and cleanness," and he was dubbed the backbone of the Cardinals' franchise.[20] Duke was also intelligent and an upstanding member of the community; he passed the Illinois bar exam in 1929 and had just opened a law practice on the South Side. Those factors, combined with the fact that Slater was still one of the best linemen in the league, were enough to convince Jones to keep him in a Cardinal uniform.

David Jones cleaned out the entire Cardinals organization and started fresh. His next order of business was hiring former Duluth Eskimos owner Ole Haugsrud as his team manager and former Eskimos coach Dewey Scanlon as his team's head coach. These moves allowed Jones to sign Ernie Nevers, a superstar who sat out the 1928 NFL season with injuries. Nevers was a standout for Stanford in college and one of the most popular college football players from the West Coast. He then became a first team all-pro fullback with the Eskimos in 1926 and 1927. Like Slater, Nevers possessed legendary durability; he played 14 NFL games and 15 exhibition games with Duluth in 1926 and was on the field for 1,711 of a possible 1,740 minutes that season.[21]

Jones had plenty of other ideas on how to improve the club and attract interest. He moved the Cardinals' home games from Normal Park back to Comiskey Park, the larger venue the Cards used before 1926. He also had the team attend a preseason camp in Coldwater, Michigan, to prepare for the season. It was the first out-of-town preseason training camp in NFL history, designed by Jones to get his entirely new roster of players on the same page before the games began.

Slater was extremely popular with the folks in Coldwater. "Much has been said relative to Duke Slater. Duke, Negro, is the comedian of the squad because of his ready answer to anything that his teammates shoot at him," wrote the *Daily Reporter*. "Slater knows his football on the field only. One never hears of his conquests from his own lips. On the gridiron, he is just plain poison to his opponents."[22]

Duke's shoes also continued to attract interest. One newspaper article reported that Slater had yet to be knocked off his feet. When he heard this claim, legendary sportswriter Grantland Rice looked Duke over and replied, "Why should Slater ever be knocked off his feet? Look at them!"[23] Meanwhile, it was reported that Slater's shoes were so large they inspired the University of Iowa to set up a display at the school's Field House. A glass case enclosed the shoes he wore in his final varsity game, and over the case read an inscription, "Who Will Fill Them?"[24]

Nevers was busy playing professional baseball and unable to join the Cardinals in Clearwater or for the beginning of the 1929 season. The team was consequently upset in a preseason exhibition by the Canton Bulldogs, 6–0. In response, Slater shifted to the left tackle position before the first regular season game. The Cardinals opened 1929 on the road in Buffalo against the Bisons, and Duke made sure Chicago put the scoring woes of the previous season behind them. In the first quarter, the Bisons were forced to punt. Slater broke through the line and blocked the kick, which the Cards recovered deep in Bison territory. Even though the offense wasn't able to advance the ball, Slater's block set up a successful 40-yard field goal by Chief Elkins, who the Cards had acquired from Frankford. Elkins' kick gave the Cards their first offensive points since 1927.

Buffalo tied the game in the third quarter with a field goal, but the Cardinal defense was playing well. A few minutes later, Chicago forced another Buffalo punt, and this time, MacDonnell fielded the kick and sprinted 65 yards for a much-needed Cardinal touchdown. The Bisons repeatedly threatened in the fourth quarter, even driving down to the Cardinal two-yard line at one point. But the defense had an answer for every Buffalo charge, and Chicago kept the Bisons out of the end zone for a 9–3 victory.[25]

Next on the schedule were the powerful Green Bay Packers. Slater hadn't emerged victorious over a Green Bay team since his first NFL game in 1922, but the Packers still feared Duke's abilities. "This year, the Cards are bringing such stars as Duke Slater, the giant Negro tackle," the *Post-Crescent* reported.[26] "[Slater] is back on the job again and is in fine shape.... He is regarded as one of the greatest tackles in the country."[27]

For most of the contest, the scoreboard read like a baseball game. The Cardinal defense took charge early, backing Green Bay up to their own goal line. The Packers mixed up their signals, and the center snapped the ball into the end zone; Green Bay recovered, giving Chicago a two-point safety. The Cards held their advantage until Red Dunn booted a 40-yard field goal in the third quarter to give the Packers a 3–2 lead.

Chicago's offense continued to fail them, however. The team hadn't scored an offensive touchdown since 1927, and that streak continued in this game. The defense fought valiantly, thwarting several Packer scoring attempts. But Green Bay halfback Verne Lewellen was again a thorn in the Cardinals' side. Like Slater, he was an attorney by trade, and he had been elected district attorney of Brown County the previous off-season. District Attorney Lewellen pressed a four-yard charge against the Cardinals into the end zone to seal the victory late in the fourth quarter. The Packers missed the extra point, resulting in a 9–2 victory for Green Bay.[28] Interestingly, in over ninety years of NFL play, it is the only game that has ended with a final score of 9–2.

In the wake of the loss, Duke Slater's continuing football career became the subject of several newspaper articles. "Duke Slater Goes On in Pro Racket in Spite of Years," one headline read. "The gigantic bulk of Duke Slater, famous tackle on four University of Iowa football teams, still looms darkly above rivals on middlewestern gridirons," the *Waterloo Courier* reported.[29] These articles then marveled at Slater continuing a football career that began 16 years earlier. Duke was one of the veteran players in the NFL, and his longevity at a time when the sport was known for very brief careers astonished observers.

Chicago's offense was in desperate need of help, and it got some when the team arrived in Minneapolis. Their game with the Red Jackets would be the first to feature Ernie Nevers in a Cardinals uniform. Nevers showed a bit of rustiness, however. Following a scoreless first half, he had a punt blocked, and Minneapolis recovered in the end zone for a touchdown. But he soon got on track, tying the game with an electrifying 75-yard touchdown pass to Don Hill. It was a spectacular way to register Chicago's first offensive touchdown in two years.

The game was tied, 7–7, midway through the fourth quarter. Minneapolis' player-coach Herb Joesting, an excellent fullback affectionately nicknamed the "Owatonna Thunderbolt," countered Nevers with a 40-yard pass to end Ken Haycraft, who was tackled within a yard of the Cardinal end zone. The Red Jackets then quickly retook the lead on a one-yard touchdown run. But Nevers wasn't finished. He drove Chicago down to Minneapolis' one-yard line, but on fourth and goal, the Cardinals tried to run for the game-tying touchdown. The referee marked the ball one foot short of Minneapolis' goal line, and that became the decisive call in Chicago's 14–7 loss to the Red Jackets.[30]

Chicago's offense was clearly revitalized by the addition of Ernie Nevers. In the line, Duke performed admirably against Minneapolis' enormous 235-pound tackle, Herbert "Chief" Franta. The *Chicago Defender* wrote, "The Slater-Franta duel provoked great interest from the football writers and fans. Experts claimed that more inside football was shown on their side of the line than had ever been displayed before."[31]

The Cardinals and Nevers sought to use their contest at Wrigley Field versus the Bears as a litmus test of their newfound strength. As usual, the rivalry game was a ferocious defensive battle, and Duke Slater played sixty grueling minutes of outstanding football. The Cardinals won the statistical battle in the first half; their best attempt at a score was a 30-yard field goal Nevers pushed wide of the goal posts. The Bears reversed their fortunes in the second half, outgaining the Cardinals and intercepting a pass deep in Cardinals' territory with minutes to play. But Paddy Driscoll's 35-yard field goal attempt came up short, and the game ended in a scoreless tie.[32]

The final score was a draw, but it was received like a win for the Cards. The city's football fans were impressed by Dr. Jones' reorganization of the franchise, and the presence of Nevers on the South Side club elevated the Cards' second-class status within the city. "Practically unchallenged in the pro football field in Chicago since its inception, the Chicago Bears found out yesterday that they have more than a casual competitor in the Cardinals this season," the *Herald-Examiner* reported.[33]

The Cardinals' improved play provided an electric atmosphere at Comiskey Park when they faced the undefeated Green Bay Packers. Energized by the crowd, the home team fought valiantly on defense. In the first quarter, Lewellen seemed to be headed for an easy touchdown, but the opening closed quickly and he was met head on at the one-yard line. Lewellen fumbled the ball and the Cards recovered possession. The defense was playing so well that the Packers had to resort to trickery to get on the scoreboard in the second quarter. Green Bay had a fourth down at Chicago's 15-yard line, so Lewellen dropped back into field goal formation. But he ran the ball away from Slater on a fake field goal play and scampered 15 yards for a touchdown.

Duke and his teammates played terrific defense for most of the game. "A smashing Cardinal line turned back [Green Bay's] attack yesterday with the exception of the second period score," the *Tribune* noted.[34] However, Lewellen kept Chicago on their heels with long punts, and the Cards didn't put together a sustained drive until the last half of the final quarter. With four minutes left in the game, Nevers fired up the offense. Chicago faced fourth and 11 from the Packers' 29-yard line, and Nevers fired a long pass toward end Chuck Kassell. Two Green Bay defenders collided, and Kassell sprinted in for a dramatic touchdown. But Nevers' extra point attempt sailed wide, and the undefeated Packers escaped their closest scare of the season with a 7–6 victory.[35]

It was an impressive showing against the eventual NFL champion Packers, and the Cards were full of confidence. However, a road game with the Frankford Yellow Jackets was next on the schedule, which meant another Saturday-Sunday doubleheader. For the second time on the year, Slater was moved to the left tackle position. This meant he wasn't going directly against Frankford's head coach and tackle, Bull Behman, but he wouldn't have an easy time wrestling with veteran lineman Rudy Comstock.

In Frankford, Chicago was victimized by weather and poor timing. The Yellow Jackets got on the scoreboard early in the first quarter with a one-yard touchdown run on fourth down by fullback Wally Diehl. That score was important, because the skies soon opened and dumped a heavy rain on the players for the remainder of the game. The field was rapidly covered in mud, and respectable play became impossible. Frankford added two points in the third quarter when Nevers bobbled a wet football and dove on it in the end zone. The Cards suffered another loss, 8–0.[36]

The Cardinals were a much-improved team, but this fact wasn't showing up in the standings. They had a record of 5–17–3 in the 25 games Slater had played with them,

A Chicago Cardinals jersey allegedly worn by Duke Slater is on display at the Pro Football Hall of Fame. Interestingly, Slater wore five jersey numbers in games during his seasons with the Cardinals, and none of them were #10. Duke wore #14 (1926, 1927, and 1930), #16 and #91 (1928), #7 (1929), and #47 (1931).

an abysmal 26 percent winning percentage. From the time Duke suited up at Clinton High School in 1913 through his fourth season in the NFL with Rock Island, he always played for winners, or at least respectable teams. All this losing wasn't something to which Slater was accustomed, but everything was about to change.

The turnaround in their fortunes began, interestingly, with the first night game in NFL history. The Cardinals lost to Frankford on Saturday, November 2, and they were scheduled to play the Providence Steam Roller the following day. But the heavy rainstorm that caused such a problem for both teams against Frankford also rendered Providence's home field unplayable. Nevers was a major star, however, and the Steam Roller didn't want to see Nevers and company leave town without cashing in at the ticket office. Since floodlights had recently been installed at a nearby soccer stadium, Kinsley Park Stadium, the two teams agreed to move their postponed game there and play the following Wednesday night.

The gimmick of night football attracted a huge crowd. The ball itself was painted white to help the players locate passes, which gave the round football the appearance of a large egg. Aside from that, the game progressed fairly normally. Nevers proved his star power by igniting Chicago's offense, and the Cards finally snapped out of their slump. He passed to Kassell for a long touchdown and added a 33-yard field goal in the second quarter. He also scored Chicago's second touchdown by driving through the line in the final period. Nevers ultimately had a hand in all of the points in Chicago's 16–0 victory.[37] The *Chicago Tribune* declared, "It was one of the greatest individual exhibitions of football ever turned in by an individual player."[38] Duke Slater played all sixty minutes in the NFL's first night game on November 6, 1929. But those performances by Nevers and Slater were only the beginning.

The Cards returned to Comiskey Park for a rematch with the weak Minneapolis Red Jackets. Minneapolis only had one win on the season, but it was their 14–7 victory over the Cardinals in the teams' first encounter. Slater was paired against Chet Widerquist, his old Independent and Cardinal teammate, in the upcoming game; Duke was labeled as an "old standby ... playing better than ever."[39] Dr. Jones bolstered his team by acquiring center Bill Stein, and that move paid immediate dividends when he blocked a Minneapolis punt in the first half of his first game with the Cardinals. The Red Jackets' punter recovered the ball in the end zone for a Chicago safety, and the Cards had a 2–0 lead.

They maintained that slim two-point margin going into the final period. After a long battle, the Chicago linemen finally wore down their opponents in the fourth quarter. The Cardinals ran the ball on several plays to within eight yards of the goal line when quarterback Cobb Rooney took a lateral from Nevers. Rooney stiff-armed a Jacket defender and sprinted the remaining distance for a clinching Chicago touchdown. The Cards won again, 8–0, for their first two-game winning streak since early in the 1927 season.[40]

The consecutive victories combined with a visit from the undefeated Green Bay Packers attracted the largest Cardinals home crowd since their championship season of 1925. Fifteen thousand fans filed into Comiskey Park to see if Nevers could lead Chicago to an upset of the Packers. The Cardinals battled hard for four quarters, and Green Bay held a slim six-point lead until midway through the fourth quarter. Chicago apparently hadn't learned from their previous loss to the Packers, and Green Bay again successfully ran a fake field goal play for a touchdown. This time it was the Packers' terrific end, LaVern "Lavvie" Dilweg, whose score finally broke the stiff resistance of the Cardinal defense. The undefeated Packers had to fight, but they scraped out a 12–0 victory, their third of the year over the Cards.[41]

Duke Slater went a third round with Green Bay's outstanding left guard, Mike Michalske, and the Cardinal linemen gave a good accounting of themselves. "The Packers had trouble with their line smashing plays yesterday, a determined Cardinal line, from tackle to tackle, holding [fullback Bo] Molenda in check. But Green Bay gained consistently on wide runs and its passing was brilliant," the *Tribune* noted.[42]

Chicago had a much easier test in their home finale. The winless Dayton Triangles came to town, and only three hundred fans even bothered to show up in the chilly, windy conditions. Slater paired off against Hobby Kinderdine, Dayton's durable lineman best known for kicking the first extra point in NFL history in 1920. Ernie Nevers once again shined, running for a touchdown in each of the first three periods to help Chicago to a 19–0 victory.[43] The game lacked excitement, but a few Cards' fans kept things interesting by organizing a cheering section in the stands to root for their inept opponents. The Dayton Triangles had been the dregs of the league for years, and this defeat was their final one in the NFL. Seventeen of Dayton's 18 players, including Kinderdine, retired after the game; end Harold Fenner appeared in one game for the Portsmouth Spartans in 1930 before leaving the NFL.

But the Cardinals moved on. They had won three of their last four games, which put them right next to the Chicago Bears in the league standings. A win of their annual Thanksgiving showdown would guarantee the Cards a better record than their cross-town rivals; in their ten years in the NFL, the Cardinals had only finished above the Bears in the standings once, their championship year in 1925. The game was billed as a duel between Ernie Nevers and Red Grange, who had returned to the Bears organization he played for in 1925. Nevers was still disappointed with his lack of offense in the teams' first meeting, which ended in a scoreless draw. "I told my players, the next time we meet the Bears, we'll beat the hell out of 'em," he recalled. "I knew we could. I just knew it."[44]

Duke suited up for the battle with the Bears at left tackle rather than his usual position at right tackle. Eight thousand fans arrived at Comiskey Park to watch the game, and what they witnessed was historic. The Cardinals had the ball at the Bears' 20-yard line six minutes in when Nevers made the game's first score. "Big Duke Slater blasted open a hole off the tackle slot for Nevers to go the rest of the way," author Paul Michael wrote.[45] Nevers added a second touchdown before the end of the first quarter as "the Cards scored quickly again behind the blocking of Slater."[46]

The Cardinals led, 13–0, and they used several tricky plays in the second quarter, including a triple pass and a reverse, to get back down to the Bears' six-yard line. "But in the end it was brute power that bulled it in, with Slater charging ahead of Nevers off tackle from the six," Michael observed.[47] Nevers' third touchdown gave the Cards a 20–0 advantage at halftime.

At the beginning of the second half, Red Grange's brother Garland broke a tackle and outraced the Cardinal defenders to the end zone, cutting the deficit to 20–6. But late in the third quarter, Nevers quickly swung momentum back over to the Cardinal sideline by making a fourth touchdown run. The Cards were now well in control of the game, but Ernie Nevers wasn't finished. He ran for two more touchdowns in the final quarter, giving him six rushing scores and forty total points. When he left the game to a rousing ovation, he had established several NFL records en route to an incredible 40–6 victory for the Cardinals.[48]

Nevers' forty points in a single game set an NFL record that still stands today, over eighty years later. His six rushing touchdowns are also a league record; it broke the existing mark Slater helped Jim Conzelman set against Evansville in 1922. Slater was a major reason for Nevers' record-setting performance as well. "People said that as the game went on, Nevers actually would point directly at the spot in the line where he would be running, and even then, he couldn't be stopped," Cardinals owner William Bidwell later recalled.[49]

The *Chicago Tribune* effusively praised Nevers but also noted, "The Cardinal line was the foundation on which these ball carriers built their successes. There was no question of its superiority, and it played no favorites."[50] Of all the men on the Cardinal line that day, only one of them was with Ernie Nevers from start to finish — Duke Slater. Duke played his eleventh straight complete game of the season in the historic victory. "Slater Rips Gaps in North Sider's Line as Ernie Shatters Pro Precedent," the subheading read in the *Chicago Herald-Examiner*. "Duke Slater, the veteran colored tackle, seemed the dominant figure in that forward wall which had the Bear front wobbly. It was Slater who opened the holes for Nevers when a touchdown was in the making."[51]

Over eighty years later, the Cardinals-Bears Thanksgiving contest in 1929 is remembered as one of the greatest games of all time. A survey of over 2,340 newspaper and magazine sports writers selected it as one of the ten greatest NFL games to take place before the 1970 merger.[52] Duke later called that game the greatest thrill of his professional football career.⁵³ For his part, Ernie Nevers never forgot Slater's role in his performance that day. When asked about his record-setting display, he often replied, "What about the horses up front? They made it all possible."⁵⁴

Nevers, Slater, and the rest of those horses finished the season admirably. Spectators flocked to the Polo Grounds to see what Nevers would do for an encore as the Cardinals met Benny Friedman's New York Giants. The Giants were 9–1–1 on the season, and Duke was up against their combination of tackle Steve Owen and end Ray Flaherty. The Cards and Giants put on an electric contest. The home team jumped out to a 14–0 lead on two Friedman touchdown passes, but Chicago countered with a Nevers touchdown pass and a safety just before halftime to go to the locker room down, 14–9.

Early in the second half, the Cardinals' offense sustained their positive momentum. Chicago took the lead on a touchdown run by Gene Rose, and Nevers looked to break the game open early in the final period. He intercepted a Friedman pass and returned it to the one-yard line, and then Nevers bowled into the end zone to give the Cardinals a 21–14 advantage. Twenty-one straight points had given the Cardinals control of the game, but the Giants struck back. The marvelous Friedman engineered an 80-yard drive for a game-tying score, capped by a touchdown run from halfback Tony Plansky. Plansky then secured his place as the hero of the game, booting a game-winning 42-yard field goal as time expired to give the Giants a thrilling 24–21 victory.⁵⁵

The loss dropped the Cardinals' record to 5–6–1 with one game to play. They needed a victory to finish the season at .500, and standing in their way were the Tornadoes of Orange, New Jersey. For the final game of the year, Slater assumed the left tackle position for the fourth time in 1929. This put him against the Orange Tornadoes' second-year tackle, Bob Beattie.

The Cardinals took over the game in the first half, jumping out to a 14–0 lead on two touchdown passes by Nevers. With minutes remaining in the second quarter, the Tornadoes frantically tried to pass to get on the scoreboard before halftime. Duke dropped back, intercepted a Tornado pass at the line of scrimmage, and dashed forty yards to the end zone. Two weeks after his remarkable game against the Bears, Duke Slater scored the only touchdown of his NFL career. Slater's touchdown gave the Cardinals a 20–0 advantage, and Nevers added a rushing touchdown in the second half to pace Chicago to a 26–0 victory.⁵⁶ It was their largest margin of victory on the season, and it secured a .500 record for the Cards. Chicago finished the season with five victories and two respectable losses to the league-leading Packers and Giants in their final seven games.

Duke Slater played the complete game in all 13 of the Cardinals' contests in 1929; he was the only Chicago player to do so. For his efforts, Duke was named an all-pro for the sixth time in seven seasons. The *New York Post* named him a second team all-pro, while the *Green Bay Press-Gazette* relegated him to their second team for an astonishing fifth time. The *Chicago Tribune* chose Slater as a first team all-pro, however. "Slater Seems to Get Better," the *Tribune* declared in making the selection. "Slater, the oldest in service of the [all-pro] eleven, seems able to continue indefinitely. It was the former Hawkeye star who inspired the Cardinal line and led the defense throughout the season."⁵⁷

Of course, not even Duke Slater could continue to play football indefinitely. But as his NFL career wound down, there could be no doubt that the only African American in the National Football League was now a legitimate star.

Chapter 12

A Brilliant Finish (1930–1931)

Duke Slater was the only African American in the NFL for most of the late–1920s, but his presence prevented the establishment of a full color ban. In 1930, the Staten Island Stapletons followed the Cardinals' lead and signed guard David Myers to strengthen their line, giving the league a second black player. Slater, meanwhile, continued to anchor the Chicago Cardinal line. "Duke Slater, colored tackle, will be the mainstay of the Cardinal forward wall again," the *Southtown Economist* reported when Duke arrived for his ninth NFL season.[1]

Ernie Nevers was a national sensation after his great game on Thanksgiving in 1929, and Dr. David Jones rewarded him by naming him player-coach of the 1930 squad. They opened the year with a blowout exhibition win over the Sturgis Wildcats, 30–0.[2] The Cards proudly used 35 players, a sign of things to come. Dr. Jones also sought to cash in on Nevers' heightened fame with an aggressive schedule. The Cards had an unenviable start to the 1930 NFL season with six straight games on the road.

Chicago's season opener illustrated the difficulty of their schedule. The Cards started the season in Green Bay against the defending NFL champion Packers. Before the game, the Packers raised the 1929 NFL championship pennant. The strength of Green Bay's team was on the left side of their line, where tackle Mike Michalske paired with guard Cal Hubbard to form a powerful combination. However, Slater shifted to left tackle for this game, which put him on the other side of the line away from the two Hall of Famers.

The Cardinals' worst nightmare came true early in the Packers game when Nevers came down with an ankle injury. With Nevers limited, Green Bay's defense was impenetrable, and they kept the ball in Chicago territory all day. Two plays into the second quarter, Lewellen ran 10 yards for a Packer touchdown and a 7–0 lead. Things got no better for the visitors in the second half, as Dilweg caught a forty-yard touchdown pass to push the Green Bay advantage to 14 points. "Slater turned in a good day's work for the Cards," the *Chicago Tribune* noted.[3] Nevertheless, when it became apparent the Cardinals were headed toward defeat, Lou Gordon came into the game, replacing Slater. It was the first time in Duke's long pro football career that he failed to finish a game he started. After thirty consecutive complete games, Slater took a rest, and Chicago took the loss from Green Bay, 14–0.[4]

The Cardinals had several players in addition to Nevers injured in the Green Bay game, which hampered the squad as they traveled west to Minneapolis for a meeting with the Red Jackets. Minneapolis halfback Oran Pape was simultaneously the hero and the goat in this matchup. He made a spectacular run in the third quarter for an eighty-yard touchdown, and the home crowd was ready to celebrate an upset victory. But in the fourth quarter, Pape fumbled near midfield and the Cards recovered. Behind the blocking of Slater, Bill Boyd scored on a five-yard touchdown run to tie the score, 7–7. After sixty minutes, Chicago settled for a draw with Minneapolis.[5]

Two road games to start the season was only the beginning. Dr. Jones then arranged for the Cards to play four games in ten days during a grueling swing through the East Coast. The first stop was in Portsmouth, Ohio, and the locals were aware of Duke. "Another great lineman on the Cardinal lineup is Duke Slater," the *Portsmouth Times* reported. "He was one of Iowa's greatest tackles and will no doubt keep [Spartan tackle Dud] Harris amused in Sunday's contest."[6]

The game against the Spartans was a defensive slugfest. The Cardinal defense stopped Portsmouth on several occasions, including a first quarter stop after the Spartans advanced to Chicago's three-yard line. The Cards couldn't sustain any offense, either. Nevers, who was already playing through pain coming into the game, reinjured his ankle and was forced to the sidelines. He rushed back in and tried to play in the fourth quarter when it looked like the Cardinals might have a scoring drive under way, but Chicago's offense stumbled and the game ended in a 0–0 draw.[7] The highlight of an otherwise boring game was Dr. Jones getting roundly booed by the Portsmouth fans for protesting several calls.

Three days later, the Cardinals took the field against the weak Newark Tornadoes. Newark was only 1–5–1 on the season, but the Cards had to play with the usually-durable Ernie Nevers watching in street clothes. Chicago was able to grab the advantage early, because Duke Slater overpowered the left side of Newark's defense. "The Cardinals found the left side of the Newark line weak and tore through that side to pave the way for the first touchdown," the *Tribune* observed.[8] Gene Rose, starting in place of Nevers at fullback, ran behind Slater for a 25-yard touchdown in the second quarter. Later in the period, Rose added another touchdown, this time from two yards away, to give the Cards a 13–0 halftime advantage. The Cardinals' defense, meanwhile, continued their outstanding play. They stopped Newark on downs at the Chicago 20-yard line to end the Bears' best scoring chance and notched a 13–0 shutout for their first win of the year.[9]

Duke never lost his sense of humor and relayed what was called "the best football story of the season."[10] Early in the year, Slater squared off against a former college All-American end making his first start in the NFL. The young man plunged into Duke on the first snap and sent him sprawling. On every play thereafter, he came at Slater with everything he had. He was playing cleanly, giving maximum effort just as he did in college. But even when the ball was going in another direction and neither man had a chance to make a play, the young end kept charging at Duke.

Still, the rookie was helpless against the veteran Slater. Duke, who had played numerous complete games in his career, knew this young man would quickly wear himself out expending so much energy on every snap. Finally, one play sent both men sprawling. As they sat stretched out on the field, Duke wearily raised himself on his elbow, looked at his young opponent, and cracked, "What's the matter, boy? Ain't you made your letter yet?" That good-natured comment drew a laugh from the other veteran players on the field, and Duke took the lad aside and gave him a few pointers about how to have a long career in pro football.[11]

One man who didn't need a lesson on how to have a long career in pro football was Jim Conzelman, the head coach of the Cardinals' next opponent, the Providence Steam Roller. Conzelman, Slater's head coach during his rookie season in 1922, was in his first season as solely a head coach after retiring from play in 1929. His 1930 Providence team was just as scrappy as Conzelman had been as a player. Their game with the Cardinals was bitterly fought in the line, and both teams incurred numerous penalties.

Providence quarterback Frosty Peters got the home team on the board first with a very impressive 51-yard field goal. In the second half, the Cardinals made a critical mistake. Fullback Mack Flenniken of Chicago threw an interception to right guard Frank Racis, who raced 40 yards for a Providence touchdown. The Steam Roller's 9–0 lead proved insurmountable, as the Cardinals' offense was again lost without Nevers. Two long forward passes set up a four-yard touchdown run by Flenniken in the fourth quarter, but the Cardinals still went down to defeat, 9–7.[12] The weary Cards were exhausted from the trip and forced to use several substitutes; Slater was one of only two Cardinals to play the entire game.

The Chicago Cardinals played in the first night game in NFL history in Providence the previous season, and the gimmick was spreading by 1930. Slater and the Cards traveled to New York and opposed the Giants in the first night game ever held at the Polo Grounds. A huge crowd of 15,000 New Yorkers, including former governor Alfred E. Smith, witnessed the spectacle. Duke again faced the Giants' star tackle, Steve Owen. But the Giants also had their star player-coach, Benny Friedman, while the Cardinals' player-coach, Ernie Nevers, was sidelined for the third straight game.

The Cardinals fought hard in Nevers' absence. Flenniken ran for the first touchdown of the game in the second quarter, and even though the Giants scored two rushing touchdowns of their own to make the score 13–6, the Cards refused to quit. Chicago cut their deficit to just one point early in the fourth quarter when Flenniken barreled ahead for his second score of the evening. But Benny Friedman took over down the stretch, rushing for two touchdowns in the final period and leading the strong Giants to a 25–12 victory.[13]

His team lost the game, but Slater won the eternal respect of the Giants organization with his sportsmanship. On one occasion, a Giant player burst through the line, and Slater took pains to avoid "heeling" the player with his spikes. This move saved the ball carrier from a serious injury. When Duke was commended for his action, he simply smiled and said, "The little fellow was stopped. Why should I hurt him?"[14] These sportsmanlike gestures helped endear Slater to even prejudiced crowds.

Saddled with a 1–3–2 record, the Cardinals finally limped home to Comiskey Park for their home opener. Unfortunately, the opponent waiting for them was the Chicago Bears, who remembered Nevers' spectacular performance against them last season. The Bears were loaded with stars in the backfield, including Red Grange and rookie fullback Bronko Nagurski. They also had Link Lyman on the line to counter Duke.

Seven thousand Chicago football fans quickly realized the injury-weakened and weary Cardinals were no match for the Bears. The first score occurred minutes after the opening kickoff when Red Grange took the ball around left end, reversed his field, and outran two defenders for a 38-yard touchdown. Grange rushed for another touchdown later in the first quarter to stake the Bears to a 12–0 lead. Nevers, still bothered by his knee injury, didn't enter the game until the Cards already trailed by 12 points. By that time, it was too late. Nevers rushed for the lone Cardinal touchdown later in the game, but the Northsiders cruised to an easy 32–6 victory.[15]

Slater played his usual rugged sixty-minute game. This contest also marked his first encounter with Nagurski. Duke later recalled one running play where he faced the full brunt of the rookie's power. "He gave the play away," Slater said. "I was in the slot waiting for him. He made my ears ring, [and it] took three or four of us to stop him after a four-yard gain."[16]

The Cardinals had a lousy record, but Nevers' gradual recovery from injury gave them some hope. They had a few days off before another grueling Saturday-Sunday doubleheader, but this was an unusual road-home pair of games. The Cards planned to play the Yellow Jackets in Frankford on Saturday before returning to Chicago for a game against the Portsmouth Spartans on Sunday. Nevers was finally fully healthy, and he promised to be ready for the physical challenge ahead. Even so, he admitted he still got anxious before every game. "The nervous strain is much greater than the physical," Nevers stated. "I'd be all on edge even if we were going out Saturday to play a sandlot team. Everybody's that way, even Duke Slater who's been at it almost as long as anybody."[17]

A powerful wind had a major impact on their first leg of the doubleheader in Frankford. The Cards got the benefit of the wind first, and Nevers took advantage with two rushing touchdowns in the first quarter. With the wind at their backs in the second and third periods, the Yellow Jackets held Chicago at bay and scored a touchdown on a three-yard pass to trim the deficit to 13–7. But when the field reversed again in the fourth quarter, the Cards finally pulled away. Charles "Bunny" Belden, a halfback who was Nevers' teammate with Duluth, entered the contest in Nevers' place. Belden ran through the entire Frankford team for a 78-yard touchdown, and Gene Rose added a 57-yard touchdown run a few minutes later. Rose capped the scoring with a seven-yard touchdown to hand the Yellow Jackets a convincing 34–7 defeat.[18]

Slater played all sixty minutes at right tackle. "Duke Slater, the famous old Iowa tackle, is playing with the Chicago Cardinals pro team this season, and he has plenty of football left in his system, too," the *Daily Observer* declared as it looked forward to Chicago's next game.[19] However, the team traveled back to Comiskey Park, and the next day against Portsmouth, Duke Slater missed a start for the first time since 1926. There was no official explanation for his absence from the lineup, which snapped a streak of 38 consecutive starts.

Without their star tackle in the lineup, the Cards started slowly. Portsmouth's Mayes McLain powered over two tacklers and into the end zone in the first quarter for a Spartan touchdown. The Spartans padded their lead to 13 points a few minutes into the second quarter when halfback Tiny Lewis scored on an eight-yard run. Jess Tinsley, who started at right tackle in Slater's place, was pushed aside on the play, and Lewis ran through the hole Tinsley vacated for the touchdown.

Portsmouth had a 13–0 lead, and Slater sprang off the bench to relieve Tinsley at tackle. With Duke back in the game, the Cardinals instantly responded like a new team. Ernie Nevers punched over a touchdown from three yards out to get the Cards on the scoreboard. Then Nevers took to the air, throwing a 29-yard touchdown pass to Cobb Rooney with seconds left in the half to tie the game, 13–13, at intermission.

The outcome was still undecided midway through the fourth quarter, even after Nevers booted a 30-yard field goal to give Chicago a 16–13 lead. But with five minutes to play, Rooney intercepted a pass in Portsmouth territory, and the Cards drove for the game-clinching touchdown. "Duke Slater opened a hole through which Nevers gained ten yards, and the former Stanford star scored two plays later," the *Tribune* reported.[20] Slater left the bench just in time to guide Chicago to an impressive 23–13 comeback victory.[21]

A 33–6 exhibition road win over the Milwaukee Night Hawks gave the Cardinals three comfortable wins in a row. It also gave them their first break after playing eight games in 24 days. Slater and his teammates had a week off and a chance to catch their breath before welcoming Frankford to Comiskey Park. The Yellow Jackets came to town with a poor 2–9 record, and they were defeated decisively by the Cardinals just one week earlier, but the rematch was a much closer affair.

The key sequence of the game took place in the third quarter. Nevers kicked a long punt down to the Yellow Jackets' five-yard line, but the play was negated when the Cardinals' Kessel and Frankford's Kelly Rodriguez were both flagged for offsetting roughing penalties. Nevers took the Yellow Jackets by surprise when, rather than punt again, he dropped back to pass instead. "Nevers stepped back and arched a 50-yard toss to Belden, who nabbed it, eluded the safety man, and stepped over the goal line," the *Tribune* observed.[22] Frankford never threatened to score in the second half, and the Cards narrowly won their third consecutive league game with a 6–0 victory.[23] The *Tribune* was unimpressed, calling the victory "drab," but it was the first time one of Slater's teams enjoyed a three-game NFL winning streak since the 1924 Independents saw a three-game run snapped with his benching in Kansas City.

The streaking Cards would need to overcome a huge challenge to keep that winning streak going. The New York Giants and their fantastic quarterback, Benny Friedman, had a 9–1 record and victories in seven straight games. They also had the NFL's leading offense, but the Cards kept them off the scoreboard in the first half. Meanwhile, Nevers was in rare form, booming a 65-yard punt in the second quarter that rolled out of bounds at the Giants' one-yard line. On Chicago's ensuing possession, he arched a pass to Bill Boyd for a 20-yard touchdown, and the Cards led, 7–0, at halftime.

Friedman's legendary passing was stifled in the first half, and he left the game with an injury that kept him from starting the third quarter. Some members of the home crowd feared a possible upset, but Friedman's injury only opened the door for Hap Moran. Moran, the former Cardinal, piloted the team brilliantly and lit up the Cardinal defense with his passes. He shot a short pass to reserve quarterback Jack Hagerty, who reversed field several times, changed speeds, and dodged the Cards' safety for a sparkling 65-yard touchdown run. The Cards held onto the lead, however, when Duke Slater broke through the line and blocked Moran's extra point attempt.

The reprieve was short-lived. Less than two minutes later, Moran threw a 35-yard pass and followed it up with a two-yard touchdown run. That gave the Giants a 13–7 lead, and their defense didn't allow the Cards any opportunity to approach a game-winning score as New York escaped with a victory.[24] Slater spent sixty minutes in the trenches battling the Giants' Steve Owen in the loss.

The disappointment of losing to the Giants still lingered when 17,000 fans packed into Comiskey Park to watch the Cardinals' final NFL home game of the year. The Cardinals' test was even tougher than the week before, if that was possible. Green Bay had easily won the 1929 NFL championship with a 12–0–1 record, and the league-leading Packers brought a perfect 8–0 mark into their game against the Cards. They convincingly defeated the Cardinals in the season opener, when Duke shifted to left tackle. For this game, he remained at his usual spot, which put him squarely against Cal Hubbard and Mike Michalske, the Packers' terrific left tackle and guard. Few noticed that left end Lavvie Dilweg would miss the game, because his replacement, Ken Haycraft, was touted highly as a talented player.

The game started as poorly as most Cardinals fans feared, with Gene Rose fumbling the opening kickoff and Green Bay recovering at the Cards' 38-yard line. But the Cards stopped the Packers on downs, and the first quarter ended scoreless. Early in the second quarter, the Cardinals took over at midfield and began a drive toward Green Bay's goal. Using clever passing and running by Nevers, Chicago faced a third down at the Packers' seven-yard line. Nevers swung a short pass over to Bunny Belden, who followed behind Slater and dove into the end zone.

The Cardinals held a surprising 6–0 lead at halftime, but the Packers promptly answered. Green Bay recovered a fumble at the Cardinals' 35-yard line and quickly moved down the field. The Packers earned a first down at the Cardinals' three-yard line. "Three times Duke Slater and Herb Blumer held the Packers' smashes," the *Tribune* reported.[25] But on fourth down, the Packers ran away from Slater to the other side of the Chicago line, and halfback Herdis McCrary crashed into the end zone to tie the game at 6.

The score was still deadlocked at 6–6 in the fourth quarter when Boyd returned a Green Bay punt to the Packer 44-yard line. A series of clever misdirection plays helped the Cards get the ball down within 16 yards of the Green Bay goal, but then the Cardinals reverted to a power running game. "Slater and Blumer continued to anchor a smart, resourceful line," author Joe Ziemba noted. "If all else failed, Nevers would simply plow straight ahead down the field behind the unwavering blocking of Slater."[26] At this crucial juncture, Nevers behind Slater was the key play. Nevers carried the ball on five of the next six plays and finally plunged over the goal line for a 13–6 lead with four minutes remaining in the game.

The Packers took the kickoff, lost the ball on downs, and never regained it. The Cardinals ran out the clock and had possession of the ball on Green Bay's two-yard line when the game ended. Chicago shocked the Packers, 13–6, and handed them their first loss in two years before 17,000 amazed fans at Comiskey.[27] "The thousands who yesterday hoped for victory were stunned when it was achieved," the *Tribune* declared.[28]

Slater claimed his first win over Green Bay since his rookie debut in 1922, and a major reason for the Cardinals' upset over the eventual 1930 NFL champions was Slater's terrific defense. The *Milwaukee Journal* observed, "Haycraft, lauded to the skies as a wonder by Minneapolis and St. Paul writers, failed dismally because he was woefully weak in the most important factor in end play — blocking a tackle. In the Cardinal game, he failed to stop Duke Slater once and a good scoring chance was messed up when the great Iowa Negro star broke into the Packer backfield so often the fans thought he was playing there."[29]

Duke's magnificent performance was greatly praised by critics, but he still suffered from the prejudice of the times. The Cardinals had an exhibition match versus the Memphis Tigers the following week. Slater was still basking in the glow of the tremendous upset over Green Bay when he was benched for the entire game against the Tigers, due to the "southern objections" of the visitors.[30] The Cards won handily without him, but it served as a stark reminder that his successes weren't appreciated everywhere.

The Cardinals' final game of the 1930 regular season was their annual Thanksgiving clash with the cross-town Bears. The Bears still had the talented Red Grange in the backfield, but Bronko Nagurski, their rugged fullback, was injured and unable to play. To take his place, the Bears controversially signed Notre Dame standout Joe Savoldi prior to the game. Savoldi's signing violated league rules, since his college class had not yet graduated; the Bears were later fined $1,000 by the NFL for using an ineligible player.

Nevertheless, Savoldi and Grange led the Bears into the rivalry game with the Cards. The game was a defensive chess match from the start. In the second quarter, the Bears had their first scoring opportunity, facing fourth and one from the Cardinal six-yard line. Red Grange took the ball but was dropped for no gain and a turnover. "Red's mistake," the *Chicago Tribune* noted, "was in running smack into Duke Slater."[31]

Later in the quarter, the Bears were on the move again, and Grange had learned from his previous encounter. The Bears had the ball near the Cards' 20-yard line. "Red slid around the Cards' left tackle — Slater plays on the opposite side of the line — and wound up his excursion five yards from the goal line," the *Tribune* reported. "[Carl] Brumbaugh gained a yard, then Red carried within inches of the line, again at the left tackle."[32] Steering clear of Slater paid off for Grange and the Bears, as Savoldi plowed into the end zone on the next play to stake the Bears to a 6–0 advantage.

Slater was a veteran player now, but he could still impose his will on a game. He lined up opposite Bears lineman Dan McMullen, and Duke was working him over on the line. At the end of the first half, McMullen's good friend, Jack Donoho, went to the exit tunnel to greet McMullen as he left the field. McMullen shuffled toward the locker room holding his shoulder with a look of pain on his face. When he spotted Donoho, he groaned, "Jack, the big n — — r is killing me."[33] Even in his ninth year in the league, Duke was an intimidating physical presence.

Unfortunately for the Cardinals, the Savoldi touchdown proved insurmountable. The second half dissolved into a series of frozen punts and poor offense, with the only highlights being a series of fights and brawls between the two bitter rivals. Extracurricular activities aside, the Cards went down to a 6–0 defeat.[34]

Later in the week, the Cards traveled to Memphis for a return exhibition game against the Tigers. As before, Slater was scratched from the lineup while the Cardinals tacked on another victory.[35] The 1930 season was officially over, but there was one more historic game on the schedule. The Bears and Cardinals agreed to compete for the third time in 1930 in a post-season exhibition, with the proceeds going to charity. Since it was December in frigid Chicago, the two clubs arranged to play the game indoors at Chicago Stadium. The layout inside the stadium presented some challenges, however. The field was only 80 yards long, so the officials frequently walked off twenty yards based on who had the ball to simulate a regulation field. Also, due to the proximity of the crowd to the field, field goals were outlawed in this game.

The Chicago Bears and Chicago Cardinals met on December 15, 1930, for the first indoor game in NFL history. The Bears scored early in the first period when a long pass set up halfback Joe Lintzenich's one-yard touchdown run. It was a 7–0 game at halftime, and in the third quarter, a 71-yard punt by the Bears pinned the Cardinals near their own goal line. A bad snap led to Nevers being tackled in his own end zone for a safety, and the Bears expanded their lead to 9–0.

Because the Cardinals were forbidden from kicking field goals, those extra two points loomed large. Nevers rushed for a four-yard touchdown halfway through the fourth quarter, but the Cards' rally fell short as the Bears won, 9–7.[36] Slater played his usual sixty-minute game, and the event was a smashing financial success. The teams raised $2,000 for unemployment relief from an estimated attendance of 10,000 fans. The indoor game was so popular that the Bears repeated the gimmick two years later, when they faced the Portsmouth Spartans in the first NFL playoff game.

Duke Slater was again an all-pro for the seventh time in eight seasons. The *Chicago Daily Times* and *Chicago Herald-Examiner* each chose Duke as a first team all-pro, and *Collyer's Eye Magazine* put him on their second team. The *Green Bay Press-Gazette* again recognized him at a lower level, placing him on their all-pro third team. Regardless, Slater became the first lineman in NFL history — of any race — to earn seven all-pro selections. He was just the second player overall to gain seven all-pro nods, joining fellow Chicago legend Paddy Driscoll. "The years apparently have dealt kindly with Fred W. 'Duke' Slater," the *Globe-Gazette* reported when making the announcement.[37] Slater, finishing his 16th season of organized football, was a perennial all-pro, but his NFL career was slowly winding down.

Duke Slater returned to the Chicago Cardinals for his fifth full season with the team and his tenth in the NFL in 1931. Slater was now a legend in the game of football. This became strikingly clear when Pop Warner named Duke to his all-time All-America football team in *Collier's Magazine* that season.[38] Slater was also a professional football institution; his tenth season in the league ranked him third in NFL history.

Dr. Jones hired Roy Andrews to coach the 1931 Cardinals team. Nevers led the Cardinals the previous season, but Andrews had compiled a 24–5–1 coaching record for the New York Giants over the previous two seasons. He was fired when the Giants twice finished second in the league behind the Green Bay Packers, but Jones wanted to see what Andrews could do in Chicago. The Cards were initially impressive under Andrews' tutelage. They ran up lopsided victories over Chicago Harley-Mills and the Pullman Panthers in two exhibition games. But again, Slater was being conserved. He came off the bench at right tackle against the Panthers in the Cards' 31–0 victory.[39]

The NFL opener for Chicago was at Universal Stadium in Portsmouth, Ohio, against the local Spartans. The Cards controlled the first half, keeping the ball in Spartan territory and scoring first on a 27-yard field goal by Nevers late in the half. But the 3–0 lead evaporated in the third quarter, when fullback Tony Holm and quarterback Glenn Presnell each scored a touchdown for the Spartans. Portsmouth dominated the second half in yardage and first downs en route to a 13–3 victory.[40]

Dr. Jones was irate over the loss and Andrews promptly resigned, restoring Nevers to the head coaching position. Nevers had plenty of time to work with the squad, as the Cardinals took several weeks off. By the time the 0–1 Cards went to Green Bay, the Packers were already 4–0. The two-time defending NFL champs were a formidable foe, but the Cards immediately summoned memories of their epic upset the previous season. Several Cardinals broke through the line to block a Lewellen punt in the second quarter, which led to a Nevers touchdown pass. Though Nevers pushed a 35-yard field goal attempt wide of the goalposts late in the half, Chicago took a 7–0 lead to the halftime locker room over a stunned Green Bay squad.

In the second half, however, the Packers responded like champions. They started the second half with a vengeance, quickly scoring the tying touchdown on a pass reception by star halfback Johnny "Blood" McNally. The ensuing punt by Nevers was blocked, and Lewellen ran for a touchdown to give Green Bay the lead. The Packers piled on in the fourth quarter, with McNally notching two more touchdowns. It was a replay of Chicago's trip to Green Bay the previous year, and again, Duke Slater left the game in the fourth quarter of a blowout loss. He was replaced by Tom Cobb, who finished out Chicago's 26–7 defeat.[41] "The giant black no longer strikes terror in the hearts of the opposition," the *Wisconsin State Journal* said of Slater, "but Duke still has the biggest feet in football."[42]

The large-shoed Slater and his teammates returned to the Windy City to oppose Link Lyman and his Chicago Bears at Wrigley Field. The game was nearly an exact replay of the Cards' game versus Green Bay. The Cardinals shot out to a 7–0 halftime lead on the strength of a Nevers touchdown pass, but they collapsed in the second half. Grange and Nagurski took turns carving up the Cardinal defense. Grange notched two third quarter touchdowns and added a third in the fourth quarter, while Nagurski shook off several tacklers on a 62-yard touchdown run. The Cards trailed 26–7, which was actually the final score in their loss to the Packers. Nevers added a meaningless touchdown run with under a minute left to make the final score look better at 26–13.[43]

Chicago possessed an 0–3 record and needed some positive momentum. Since they didn't have a league opponent lined up for the coming week, the Cardinals traveled to Rock Island, Illinois, for an exhibition against the Rock Island Green Bush. "Duke Slater, first string tackle, will be playing in the city that gave him his start in professional football," the *Tribune* observed.[44] The Green Bush were a semi-pro outfit that had succeeded the Independents in organized football, and the game gave Duke a chance to revisit some great moments of his early pro career.

In a warm homecoming for Slater, Duke played in front of the home crowd in Rock Island one final time. The Cardinals defeated the Rock Island Green Bush, 45–13, on the strength of seven Chicago touchdowns.[45] One of the Cards' touchdowns was tallied by Duke Slater; although it was only an exhibition game, the touchdown stood as the final points Slater scored in professional football.

The Cardinals were still winless in NFL play, however, and they traveled to Ebbets Field in Brooklyn to try to reverse their fortunes against the 2–6 Dodgers. The game featured a matchup of the NFL's only two African Americans. Slater got the start at right tackle and lined up across from Brooklyn's David Myers at left guard. Duke's Cardinals struck first. A 40-yard punt return in the second quarter by Bunny Belden started their drive. Then Ernie Nevers took over, running on four straight plays before launching a 23-yard touchdown pass to Chuck Kassell. Brooklyn tied the score when fullback Jack McBride passed to Stumpy Thomason, who weaved his way down the field through the Chicago defense and into the end zone.

Nevers broke the 7–7 tie in the second half. He finished off a 65-yard drive with a touchdown run to give the Cards a 14–7 advantage going into the fourth period. The Dodgers tried to rally on offense in the final quarter for a tying score, but their drives into Chicago territory were repelled by the Cardinal line. "Big Duke Slater ... rose to the occasion to quell the Dodgers' [fourth quarter] attack," the *Herald-Examiner* reported, and Chicago held on for their first NFL victory of 1931 by a 14–7 count.[46]

The Cards continued their road swing by stopping in Cleveland to play the Indians. Slater was moved to left tackle in this contest to counter Cleveland's massive 235-pound tackle, George "Babe" Lyon. Nevers controlled the game from beginning to end. He opened the second quarter with a long pass to halfback Milan Creighton at the Cleveland three-yard line and later smashed over the goal line for Chicago's first score and a 7–0 lead. Later in the period, he duplicated the feat. Nevers completed a long toss from midfield to Bill Boyd down at Cleveland's two-yard line before driving over the goal line himself for another Card touchdown. The Indians had no answer for Nevers' short touchdown runs, and the Cards coasted to a 14–6 victory.[47] "That dusky destroyer, Duke Slater ... was as easy to slap down as a gorilla," sportswriter Bill Ritt observed. Ritt interviewed a star end who had the misfortune of crossing Slater, and the player's torso was covered with black and blue bruises. "Believe it or not," the end groaned after the game, "that big colored boy wasn't trying to rough me. He wouldn't get mad. He'd just get those paws on me and — ow!"[48]

Another exhibition victory over the Grand Rapids Maroons gave the Cardinals their fourth win in a row. Confident, they returned to Chicago for their "home" NFL opener against the Green Bay Packers. Dr. Jones was constantly searching for ways to drum up interest in his Cardinals, and one of his zany ideas in 1931 involved moving the team's home games from Comiskey Park to Wrigley Field. Relocating to Wrigley turned out to be a terrible idea. First, sharing Wrigley with the Bears created scheduling conflicts that delayed the Cardinals' home opener until November 15. Second, it infuriated the local fan base, who felt their franchise was abandoning the South Side by moving north to Wrigley.

The 1931 Chicago Cardinals were Duke Slater's final NFL team, concluding a brilliant decade in pro football. Slater is in the third row, far right, wearing #91. In the middle of the photo, fourth from left in the second row wearing #44, is Ernie Nevers (courtesy Matt Fall).

The Cards welcomed the Packers to Chicago in front of a relatively sparse crowd, but the Cardinal players had bigger concerns than fan outrage. The Packers were 9–0 and once again atop the NFL standings. They still remembered their loss the last time they visited the Cards, and they were out for a road win, wherever the location. Slater had a challenge with star end Lavvie Dilweg lined up against him; Dilweg didn't play in the Cards' upset the previous season.

The Cardinals started strong against Green Bay. The home squad began a 52-yard drive to the Packer end zone, culminating with a 24-yard touchdown pass by Nevers on fourth down. Nevers wasn't perfect, however. Green Bay broke through and blocked one of his punt attempts, and Packer end Tom Nash recovered in the end zone to cut Chicago's lead to 7–6. That was the score at halftime, but the Cards had led at halftime in Green Bay, too, and went on to lose the game.

Midway through the third period, the Cards proved they were serious about their upset bid. They put together a long drive to the Green Bay goal line, and Rose added to Chicago's lead by following Slater the final five yards into the end zone for a touchdown. The Cardinals now led, 14–6, and as time ticked away, the Packers grew increasingly desperate. Green Bay began to fill the air with passes in an attempt to bridge their eight-point deficit, but their quarterback, Paul Fitzgibbon, was intercepted by Chicago end George Rogge, who returned the ball to the Packers' 10-yard line.

A lateral and two incomplete passes lost four yards, and the Cards had fourth and goal from the 14-yard line. Nevers decided to go for it, and he passed to a wide-open Kassell for a Chicago touchdown and a 21–6 lead. For the second time in 1931, Duke Slater was benched at the end of a blowout game against the Packers, but this departure was much sweeter. Green Bay scored a touchdown on the Chicago reserves, but the Cardinals clinched a decisive 21–13 upset of the previously undefeated Packers.[49] For the second consecutive year, Slater and his Cardinals had done the unthinkable, knocking off an undefeated Packers team that was headed for their third straight NFL championship.

Green Bay's loss to the Cards dropped their record to 9–1, but they still led the NFL standings over the 10–2 Portsmouth Spartans. The Cardinals were anxious to avenge their season-opening defeat at Portsmouth, and the Spartans arrived in town a week after the Packers. The game was advertised as a duel between Ernie Nevers and Portsmouth's fantastic rookie quarterback, Dutch Clark. Although Nevers garnered most of the attention, the Spartans still feared Slater's offensive power. "Duke Slater is at left tackle, and it will be a pretty hard matter to get around him," the *Portsmouth Times* observed.[50]

A heavy rain soaked Wrigley Field leading up to the contest, and an inch or two of mud covered the field at game time. Footing was particularly good near the north end zone at Wrigley, which was left field during baseball season, but the south end zone was a muddy mess. The Spartans began the first quarter facing the good end of the field, and they were soon rewarded. A blocked punt gave Portsmouth good field position, and on fourth and goal from the four-yard line, Dutch Clark made his first mark on the game by circling around end for a touchdown.

The Cardinals, however, got the better end of the field in the second period, and they too took advantage. Belden made a wide run for an 11-yard touchdown, and Nevers tied the game with the extra point, 7–7. Later in the quarter, the Cards marched 80 yards down the field on the Spartan defense. On third and goal from the two, Nevers stretched for the goal line and barely got the ball across before being thrown back. That gave the Cards the lead, 13–7, at halftime.

In the third quarter, Portsmouth moved toward the solid end of the field again, and they turned a disastrous play into a great one. Clark dropped back to punt from the Spartans' 41-yard line, but the snap was off target. Dutch recovered the errant snap, eluded a tackler ten yards behind the line of scrimmage, and took off up field. On the broken play, he reversed field twice and improbably raced the final thirty yards untouched for an electrifying 59-yard touchdown. He missed the extra point, but Portsmouth tied the game going into the fourth quarter, 13–13.

The Cards were out of the mud for the final quarter, however, and they quickly ramped up their own offense. On fourth and two from the Spartans' six-yard line, Nevers powered ahead for five yards, giving the Cards a first down. On the next play, he carried it one more yard for the touchdown and a 20–13 lead. Nevers' touchdown was seemingly devastating, since all the points had been scored at the good end of the field. The Spartans now had to get a touchdown at the muddy end of the field in order to tie the game.

Portsmouth halfback Glenn Presnell, who had several excellent seasons with the Spartans and Detroit Lions, had been breaking off long punt returns all day. With three minutes remaining, he fielded a punt from Nevers and nearly scored with it, racing up the sidelines to the Chicago 20-yard line. Three plays bogged down in the mud, but on fourth down, Clark tossed to left end Bill McKalip in the right corner of the end zone for the touchdown. The Spartans were a drop kick extra point away from a tie.

Clark left the game in favor of Gene Alford, who would attempt the tying score. Standing ankle deep in mud, Alford dropped the ball for the drop kick. The ball plopped in the mud and didn't bounce at all, and the kick went nowhere. Chicago held on to win, 20–19.[51] In consecutive weeks, the Cardinals defeated two teams that would finish first and second in the final 1931 NFL standings; the Portsmouth defeat handed the 1931 NFL title right back to the Packers. Slater played all sixty minutes in the win. It was the first four-game league winning streak of Duke Slater's pro football career.

In possession of a winning record in November for the first time in five years, the

Cards geared up for their annual Thanksgiving game against the Bears. The winner would take over third place in the NFL standings behind Green Bay and Portsmouth, the Cardinals' two latest victims. The Cardinals had three losses on the year, and they had exacted revenge for the first two in the past two weeks. A victory over the Bears would make the cycle complete.

Bronko Nagurski was hurt for the Bears, so they featured Herb Joesting at fullback, and of course, Red Grange still wore the Bears' colors. The Bears took advantage of a major penalty in the first half. The Bears faced fourth and inches at the Cardinals' eight-yard line when quarterback Carl Brumbaugh fumbled and lost four yards. This would have resulted in a turnover, but the Cardinals were flagged for being offside on the play, which gave the Bears a first down. Two plays later, the "Owatonna Thunderbolt" struck the Cardinals for a touchdown.

Near the middle of the second quarter, the Cardinals drove to try to tie the score, but after advancing to the Bears' 13-yard line, Nevers threw an interception. The Bears brought the ball back out to midfield and had possession at the Cards' 45-yard line with seven seconds left in the half. It appeared that the Cardinals would head to the halftime locker room trailing by six points, as there was only time for one last play. Grange shot through a hole in the line, shook off three tacklers, and sped 45 yards for a demoralizing touchdown.

The Bears led, 12–0, at halftime, and that score deflated the Cardinals. The Bears added a third touchdown in the third quarter to extend the lead to 18 points. The Cardinals were routed, 18–7.[52] Duke Slater played all sixty minutes in his 22nd and final career matchup with the Chicago Bears as a player.

Two days later, the Cardinals welcomed the Cleveland Indians to Wrigley for their final game of the 1931 NFL season. The Cards played Cleveland on Saturday to accommodate the Bears, who needed to use the field the following day. No one knew it at the time, but this would be the last game in the NFL for two Cardinal legends—Ernie Nevers and Duke Slater.

Nevers made a dramatic impact in his final NFL game. The Cards kept the ball in Cleveland territory for most of the first half, and in the second quarter, Nevers gave them control of the game. After two long passes to Milan Creighton, Nevers plunged over the goal line himself for a Chicago touchdown. Later in the period, the Cardinals executed a methodical sixty-yard drive against the Cleveland defense and capped it with Nevers' second touchdown run from one yard out.

The Cards maintained their 14–0 lead until the fourth quarter. Chicago gained great field position near midfield after a Cleveland interception, and Nevers promptly tossed a pass to reserve halfback Les Malloy for 44 yards and the final Cardinal touchdown of the season. The home team prevailed, 21–0, over the Indians.[53]

The win gave Chicago a 5–4 record, their first winning season in six years. The Cardinals also finished fourth in the NFL standings behind the Packers, Spartans, and Bears; it was the highest finish of Slater's decade-long career. Without fanfare or acclaim, Nevers and Slater fittingly walked off an NFL field for the final time together as champions.

Duke Slater concluded a brilliant decade in the NFL in 1931. He ranked second in league history with seven all-pro selections behind only the famed Paddy Driscoll. Duke was third in NFL history with ten seasons in the league, and his 96 starts in pro football ranked fourth all-time. His durability was legendary—Slater played ninety-nine games in professional football and never missed a single contest due to injury. The only missed game of his career came in 1924 when he was benched due to racism, not the quality of his play.

Furthermore, in over ninety of those ninety-nine league games, Duke Slater was on the field for every single minute of play. And he accomplished all of this despite being a constant target for opposing teams as one of the few — and for most of the late–1920s, the only — African Americans in the National Football League.

Less than a week after the Cleveland game, the *Olean Times* reported, "Dr. David Jones may land a lineman to take the place of Duke Slater."[54] Duke faced the reality of retirement from pro ball. "I hung up my suit in 1931 when I realized that football is a young man's game," Duke said.[55] Lew Byrer of the *New York Telegram* waved farewell to Duke by writing, "As long as I've played and watched football, the greatest tackle I ever saw was Duke Slater of Iowa. He was colored and received little credit."[56]

Chapter 13

Fighting Against Exclusion (1931–1940)

Duke Slater's NFL career was over, but he was far from finished with football. Duke played with Fritz Pollard's Chicago Blackhawks in 1928 when he wasn't suiting up for the Cardinals. Every year since then, Pollard had taken his Blackhawks on the road during the fall and winter months, and in 1931, the squad was headed to California.[1] With African Americans a rarity in the NFL, such all-star squads were more important than ever. Immediately after the conclusion of the 1931 Cardinals season, Duke signed on with the Blackhawks and accompanied the team to Los Angeles. The *Los Angeles Times* noted that it was the first appearance in Los Angeles for Slater, the Blackhawk "standout."[2]

The Blackhawks were heralded as the first team comprised entirely of African Americans to ever visit the West Coast.[3] The team featured Duke Slater, Fritz Pollard, Sol Butler, Ink Williams, Dick Hudson, Joe Lillard, and several others as star attractions. Slater, Pollard, and Williams functioned as the three managers of the team.[4]

The organization encountered difficulties immediately. When the players arrived in California on December 18, they discovered that promoters had already canceled their first scheduled game. But Marshall Duffield, an All-American quarterback for Howard Jones at USC, rounded up a team of Coast Stars to oppose the Blackhawks on December 27. The match was moved to L.A.'s White Sox Park, but the last minute change of venue limited attendance to only 800 spectators.

The Blackhawks were given a loud ovation when they trotted onto the field in their red jerseys, and then they proceeded to jump all over Duffield's Coast Stars. Lillard intercepted a Stars' pass and dodged and weaved 45 yards for the game's first touchdown. Butler added a twenty-yard touchdown reception a few minutes later, and Hallie Harding scored a third touchdown for the Blackhawks. Although the Coast Stars notched a touchdown of their own in the second quarter, they got no closer in the second half, and the Blackhawks claimed a 20–6 victory.[5] The crowd reportedly "yelled at every move made by Lillard and Slater, who were big favorites."[6]

The Blackhawks played two more games the following week, winning one game against an unspecified opponent before traveling to San Pedro to battle the San Pedro Longshoremen. Trona Field was reduced to a sea of mud, and neither team was able to make any headway due to the uncertain footing. The game ended in a scoreless tie due to the lousy conditions and drew even fewer spectators than the Blackhawks' previous two games.[7]

With such meager attendance, Blackhawk players began worrying about their salaries. The bus to the coast cost the players over three hundred dollars each, and only $47 had been raised for each player before the trip.[8] The players expected to earn over one thousand dollars each in revenue from these West Coast contests, but the poor attendance left them with far less.[9] Players began to bail, grabbing any ride back east they could find. Pollard's Chicago Blackhawks played a few more games on the coast before disbanding, but many of the players were left penniless and stranded on the West Coast for some time.[10]

Duke found work despite the dissolution of the Blackhawks. By January, Ernie Nevers and several other Chicago Cardinals stars were playing post-season exhibitions in California as well. Nevers' National Collegiate team was scheduled to take on Nate Barragar's Southern California All-Stars at Wrigley Field in Los Angeles, so Nevers acquired Slater's services for the January 17 game. Nevers' team won on two second-half touchdowns, 14–0. Contributing to the National Collegians' shutout victory was Slater, whom the *L.A. Times* called "immovable on defense."[11]

Duke then traveled with Nevers to San Francisco for a charity game at Kezar Stadium the following week.[12] Nevers' All-Star team faced an All-Star team led by Frank Carideo, a famed Notre Dame quarterback. Many sources didn't have Slater in the starting lineup for Nevers' team, and Slater was omitted from the game program. In one of these charity games, several players on the opposing team threatened to boycott the event if Slater suited up with Nevers' club. Nevers, upon hearing this, told those in charge of the game, "If Slater doesn't play, I won't play. It's both of us or neither." Since Ernie Nevers was the main financial attraction in these games, that threat carried significant weight and would cancel the entire event if carried out. The opposing players backed down, the game went on as scheduled, and Duke played.[13]

Ernie Nevers suffered a wrist injury in the 26–14 victory over the Carideo All-Stars and then stunned observers by announcing his retirement from professional football. "It just went to show that a football player's playing days are numbered," the *Oakland Tribune* observed. "Duke Slater, of course, goes on year after year, but the Duke is unusual. Most of them live to regret having played football too long."[14] Few newspapers were yet aware that Duke's NFL career was over as well.

Ernie Nevers and Duke Slater only played three seasons together with the Cardinals, but the two forged a lifelong friendship that transcended race. "Whenever Duke went to California, he had to stay with Ernie Nevers," Sherman Howard recalled. Howard also believed Duke's friendship with Nevers legitimized Slater in the eyes of otherwise prejudiced football fans. "When a guy like Ernie Nevers is one of your greatest boosters, everybody has to pay attention to that," Howard said. "For many years, Ernie was one of his best friends. They were very, very close, and that's quite something."[15]

Duke returned to Chicago and settled into life on the South Side. Because of their education and success in integrated athletic competition, Slater, Pollard, Ink Williams, Paul Robeson, and others formed an elite circle in Chicago's African American community. These men spent many evenings together at nightclubs and traveled to the East Coast as their schedules allowed.[16]

Despite his retirement, Duke Slater's connections to football still ran deep. He and Fritz Pollard spent the 1932 season assisting Foster Branch in his coaching of the Ambassador A.A. club in Chicago, composed of former high school and college stars.[17] The team fared well, losing only two games all season. Slater also took a few jobs as a college football official. He worked as a referee for the annual Wilberforce-Lincoln college football game at Cole's American Giants baseball park in Chicago.[18] 6,000 fans turned out in a downpour of rain to witness the 7–7 tie.[19] Officiating was a difficult job, according to Slater; after one game, he said he never worked so hard in all his life.[20]

On the field, opportunities for African Americans were dwindling. Slater and David Myers retired from the NFL after the 1931 season, but Slater's career with the Chicago Cardinals was such an unqualified success that they signed Joe Lillard in 1932. Lillard was the only African American in the NFL that season and was joined in the league by Ray Kemp of the Pittsburgh Pirates in 1933.

However, Lillard didn't have Slater's remarkable ability to rise above prejudice. He retaliated physically and angrily when he received a cheap shot or a late hit on the field. While such a reaction is understandable and justified, rival players knew they could bait him into an altercation. Even Lillard's teammates shunned the fiery halfback. The *Pittsburgh Courier* wrote, "Rumor has it that Joe did not fit in with the [Cardinals] as did Slater or other colored stars before him."[21] Lillard was expelled from the league in 1933 after a brawl in which he responded to a punch thrown by an opposing player with a retaliatory uppercut.

Joe Lillard became a perfect example for segregationists who argued that blacks and whites shouldn't mix on the football field.[22] Since 1927, many NFL owners had sought an opportunity to eliminate African American players from the league, and by 1933, no player with Slater's unique blend of talent and temperament was around to stop them. Two short years after he retired, the door Slater held open for years finally slammed shut, and the NFL became whites-only.

This narrative that blacks and whites shouldn't mix in football naturally ignored Slater's career, because Duke Slater was widely acknowledged as a gentle, well-mannered player. The *Associated Press* wrote in 1934, "The immense Duke Slater [was] one of the greatest tackles football ever developed. Duke was the idol not only of those who knew and respected ability, but who had a weakness as well for sportsmanship, good nature, and manliness, regardless of race or color. He never lost his temper, never lost the grin that continually split his huge face, and never was more than an arm's length, either, from the man with the ball."[23]

In an attempt to expose the foolishness of the segregationists' claim that blacks and whites could not play football peaceably, Slater assembled and coached a team called the Chicago Negro All-Stars in 1933. Duke's Chicago Negro All-Stars played several local semi-pro teams and used Slater's fame to help draw crowds. "The greatest Negro gridder in history leads his famous Chicago colored stars to Roosevelt Field Sunday afternoon," the *Hammond Times* reported before a 20–0 loss to the East Chicago Gophers. "The Duke ... has had no superior in professional football."[24]

The team lasted just one season before football took a back seat to economic realities. Faced with worsening conditions caused by the Depression, Duke Slater was forced to do the unthinkable. He closed his small law practice in 1934 and left his beloved city of Chicago. Slater considered several offers to coach college football but instead decided to take a job as football coach and athletic director at Douglass High School in Oklahoma City, Oklahoma.[25] The main allure of this job for Slater was an opportunity to break into a prominent Oklahoma law firm.[26]

Although African Americans were being shut out of the NFL, college football was soon captivated by an electrifying black halfback at Slater's alma mater. Ozzie Simmons made his Big Ten debut for the Hawkeyes on October 6, 1934. He helped Iowa dominate the favored Northwestern Wildcats, 20–7, by rushing for 166 yards and adding 138 yards on punt and kick returns. Simmons quickly became the talk of the African American sports community and the entire sporting world.

Numerous myths and stories began to emerge about how Ozzie and his brother Don arrived in Iowa City. One was that "the ebony hand of one Fred Slater" was involved; it claimed that Slater, as a "leading colored attorney in the southwest," saw Ozzie playing football every week in Fort Worth and convinced him to go to Iowa.[27] Another stated that Simmons contacted Iowa coach Ossie Solem and asked if African American players would be given a chance to compete, and "Solem replied, pointing out how Duke Slater ... had won fame at Iowa."[28] In truth, a former Iowa alumnus, who was neither a college athlete nor an African American, saw Ozzie playing high school football and convinced the Simmons brothers to go to Iowa.[29]

However he got there, Ozzie Simmons energized the Hawkeye football program and the entire Big Ten. He was tabbed as a second team All-American as a sophomore, even though Iowa had a subpar season in 1934. He became the second black football player to earn All-American honors at Iowa, following Duke Slater. Slater met Simmons for the first time at an Iowa game the following year, and the pair became fast friends.[30] Ozzie began to look up to Duke as a mentor, and their close friendship continued for the rest of their lives.

Duke supported Ozzie's career at Iowa by becoming one of his biggest fans. In 1935, Slater returned to Iowa City to watch Simmons in the Hawkeyes' homecoming game against Minnesota. Duke was part of a huge African American congregation at the football game. Iowa City's black population at that time included just nine families, but the homecoming game of 1935 lured nearly 350 African Americans to the Hawkeye campus to watch Ozzie. The school held a homecoming dance at the city park, and Slater joined the Simmons brothers, Homer Harris, Ed Gordon, and other African American Hawkeye sports stars as the guests of honor.[31] Beginning in 1935, Slater made his attendance at Iowa homecoming an annual tradition for nearly three decades.

Slater could see how much of an impact African American sports stars had on the Hawkeye campus, but it was difficult to effect change while living in Oklahoma. Fortunately for Duke, he was offered a job in November 1935 that returned him to the South Side after only a one-year absence. He was appointed assistant corporation counsel for the city of Chicago and credited with making "just as big a success in law as he did on the gridiron."[32] The move back to the Midwest and his proximity to Iowa City allowed Slater to more easily assist his alma mater in recruiting African American athletes.

His new job had other benefits as well, including standard vacation hours. In the fall of 1936, Duke Slater spent his two weeks vacation in Iowa City to serve as Ossie Solem's line coach before the football season. "This squad looks pretty good, but maybe I can pass out a few pointers to the linemen," Slater said.[33] He was just the third African American in major college football history to serve as an assistant coach, after California's Walter Gordon and Fritz Pollard, who was a volunteer backfield coach for Northwestern for two seasons.[34]

The Iowa coaching job was the fulfillment of a dream for Slater and one of his most cherished honors.[35] At long last, he was able to take the position Howard Jones offered him back in 1922. Duke said he was "having the time of his life" helping his alma mater.[36] "A dusky giant ... stood a step behind Ossie Solem, watching the University of Iowa football squad go through its paces," the *Mason City Globe-Gazette* reported.

"Duke Slater was back."[37]

Unfortunately for Iowa and Ozzie Simmons, 1936 was a disappointing year for the Hawkeye football squad. Simmons even briefly quit the team after a blowout loss to Minnesota. He got into a dispute with Coach Solem and felt he was shouldering too much of the blame for the team's poor season. Hawkeye fans sided with Simmons and pleaded for "one of the best-liked and adored men the school has had since Duke Slater" to rejoin the team.[38] Ozzie quickly relented and finished out the season with the Hawkeye football squad.

Once the season was over, Simmons immediately declared himself eligible for pro ball and signed with the semi-pro American Giants. He made his professional debut November 26 against the Calumet Stars. Simmons was the star of the game, scoring a touchdown and helping the Giants earn a 6–6 tie. Slater officiated the contest as a field judge. Simmons then returned to school in Iowa, while openly harboring dreams of playing in the NFL for the Chicago Cardinals or the Detroit Lions.

The College All-Star game was an annual exhibition that pitted a team of top college stars against the previous season's NFL champions. By 1937, no African American had yet made the College All-Star team, and Ozzie seemed to be a natural candidate. Many in the media falsely believed that Simmons' game with the American Giants made him ineligible for the team, but when it was confirmed that Ozzie was eligible for the College All-Star game, Slater helped organize a campaign to vote him in. "If every race fan votes for him, he certainly will be the first of his race to gain the honor," the *Chicago Defender* reported. "The game was inaugurated after Duke Slater was through at Iowa; otherwise the famous tackle would certainly have made it."[39]

The voting drive came up well short of gaining Ozzie a spot on the team, which left many African Americans discouraged. Their frustration only grew when Simmons received absolutely no interest from an NFL team, as all league franchises were locked into the color ban. Simmons, considered by many "one of the top open-field runners in the first seventy years of college football," was completely shunned by the National Football League, and his exclusion was a clear signal to all black athletes that the color line wasn't going away. As author John Carroll asked, "If Simmons could not get a contract or even a tryout with an NFL team, then what black player could?"[40]

Duke Slater needed to do something to ensure that men like Ozzie had a future in professional football, so he went back to coaching. Duke agreed in 1937 to serve as the head coach of the Chicago Brown Bombers, an all-star team of African Americans shunned by the NFL. The Brown Bombers were named after the famous "Brown Bomber," boxer Joe Louis. John Whitaker of the *Hammond Times* made the connection between Louis and Slater, and he felt Louis made the more lucrative career choice. "Not all the tough guys have been smart enough to play in the league that really pays off on toughness. The most Slater ever got was $200 per afternoon while playing for the Chicago Cardinals. With those gorilla arms and panther legs, the Duke should have been chasing Dempseys and Tunneys right out of the ring," he wrote. "Yessir, Felix, the Duke was the mightiest of all the colored men, whether they be Brown Panthers, Brown Bombers or Black Giants."[41]

Shortly after agreeing to coach the Brown Bombers, it became obvious Slater wouldn't be confined to the sidelines. "Coach Duke Slater may be in the starting lineup against the Austin Bears," the *Defender* declared. As a coach, Slater took the same hands-on approach as his college mentor, Howard Jones. "The former star linesman of the Chicago Cardinals and All-American player from Iowa has been showing a desire to get back into the game by the way he has been jumping into the tackle position while coaching members of the forward wall," noted the *Defender*.[42] Duke lined up for a competitive football game just shy of his 39th birthday, which was an extreme rarity in that era.

Ozzie Simmons was offered a spot on the Bombers, but he chose instead to join the

Paterson Panthers of the American Association. Besides Slater, the biggest name on the Brown Bombers' roster was Sol Butler, who held down one of their backfield spots. The team practiced at American Giants Field and hosted their first game there on October 10. The opponent was the Calumet All-Stars, and they were coached by Fred Gillies, Slater's teammate and coach on the Chicago Cardinals.

The All-Stars blocked a punt on the Bombers' 25-yard line shortly after the second half started, which led to a touchdown pass and a 7–0 lead. Slater came into the game in the third quarter as a substitute for the Bombers, and they immediately responded, completing three passes for fifty yards to put the ball in scoring position. Anderson, the Bombers' fullback, crashed into the end zone for a one-yard touchdown, but Butler's extra point attempt was blocked. That miss cost the Bombers, as they suffered a 7–6 defeat.[43] Though Slater may have played sparingly in other semi-pro games, his participation in the loss to the Calumet All-Stars is the last known appearance of Duke in a football uniform.

The Brown Bombers later managed a 7–7 tie against the Brandt Florals, although the date of the game was unknown.[44] On November 7, the Bombers traveled to Wisconsin to play the La Crosse Lagers, the reigning champions of the Northwest Professional Football League, in a non-conference game. The *La Crosse Tribune and Leader-Press* reported, "Duke Slater, who gained All-American mention at Iowa, is the outstanding star [of] one of the most colorful football attractions in the Midwest."[45] Although billed as a "player-coach," Duke stayed on the sidelines for this game and focused on coaching. Dick Hudson appeared in the lineup of the Brown Bombers in this contest, which was played in front of the Lagers' largest home crowd of the season.[46] La Crosse pulled out a 7–3 victory.[47]

The Brown Bombers were also members of the Windy City Football League, a small league of six Chicago clubs.[48] They played one game against the Alderman Kells on November 18.[49] The result of that game and of any other league games the Brown Bombers may have played is unknown. Three days later, Duke coached the Bombers in another game against the Lagers.[50] Though the Bombers were bolstered by the addition of Don Simmons, they fell to La Crosse in the rematch, 7–0.[51]

On November 30, they dropped a 7–0 decision to the Des Moines Comets, the eventual champions of the Northwest Professional Football League.[52] The Brown Bombers ended their season December 3 with their only known victory of 1937, traveling south to Nashville and defeating the Silver Streaks by a 13–7 score in front of a crowd of over 4,000 fans. Two touchdown passes by fullback Anderson gave the Bombers a 13–0 lead, and while a touchdown with only five minutes remaining cut the lead to six points, Chicago was able to hold on for the win.[53] It was a significant victory for an all-black squad to come away with a win in Nashville, a distinctly southern town.

The Chicago Brown Bombers ended the year with a known record of 1–4–1, although records of several other scores and opponents will likely never be found. Despite the overall record, the Bombers were competitive in every game and gave a fine account of themselves. Duke Slater was the biggest name and the most notable draw for this new All-Star squad, and his popularity had been critical in getting the organization off the ground. He later turned over the coaching of the squad to former Bomber players like Shag Jones, but it was Duke's coaching and leadership that established the Chicago Brown Bombers as they began a noteworthy four seasons of existence.

Duke Slater, the founder of the Chicago Brown Bombers, sat ringside at Yankee Stadium in New York to watch the real Brown Bomber, Joe Louis, defeat Max Schmeling for the heavyweight championship on June 22, 1938.⁵⁴ The attorney also spent a little time in court as a defense witness for Benny Friedman, who was being sued by "Wild" Bill Fleckenstein. The legendary Friedman suggested in a newspaper article that Fleckenstein, a Bear lineman, was the dirtiest player in pro football. Fleckenstein sued for damages over the allegation, and several former NFL players, including Duke, testified Fleckenstein was, in fact, a dirty player. Slater was seen as a reliable witness to Wild Bill's actions, since "Duke was known as one of the most peaceful men in the game when playing professional football unless his deadly tackling is to be considered an offense."⁵⁵ Despite Slater's testimony, Friedman was found guilty of damaging Fleckenstein's reputation and ordered to pay the monetary equivalent of Fleckenstein's good name — six cents.

The problem of the NFL's color ban persisted, and in August 1938, the sports department at the *Chicago Defender* hatched a plan — organizing a team of black All-Stars to challenge either the Washington Redskins or the Chicago Bears. Halas and the Bears accepted the offer, and a game was scheduled for September 23 at Soldier Field to benefit three Chicago charities. Duke Slater was the first man named to the All-Stars' coaching staff.⁵⁶ He served as an assistant to Ray Kemp, who was chosen to lead the Negro All-Stars.⁵⁷ The All-Stars quickly enlisted some of the best African American football talent available. Ozzie and Don Simmons, Joe Lillard, and several players from southern historically black colleges made up the All-Stars' roster.

The All-Stars suffered from poor organization. Training camp was supposed to begin several weeks before the game, but many players came later. The athletes were forced to provide their own equipment and practice clothes. Every player was supposed to receive $100 for the game plus expenses, but rumors that they wouldn't get paid cut into players' morale. It also led to resentment; some players felt men like Homer Harris, who arrived the day before the game, shouldn't receive the same pay as players who had practiced all month.

The *Defender* reported, "The players looked to such men as Duke Slater, Iowa's famous tackle, to help them. Duke did the best he could, but he was an assistant — not head coach."⁵⁸ Coach Kemp tried to assure the players in the dressing room minutes before the game that they would all receive their money, but many players ultimately were not paid the full amount they had been promised.

On the field, it was a complete blowout. Halas screamed at his players to watch out for Lillard and Simmons in the backfield, but the extreme weakness of the All-Stars' line completely neutralized the playmakers. The All-Stars' line was so poor that Kemp himself had to play most of the game, leaving the sideline coaching to Duke. "Without a doubt, Kemp, with the assistance of Duke Slater, Iowa tackle and All-American tackle of all times, did a good job of coaching with what they had," the *Defender* said.⁵⁹

Unfortunately, what they had was a disorganized squad, lacking in physical bulk and team unity. The Bears scored at will, recording touchdowns in every quarter. Chicago was able to block two All-Star punts when their line simply couldn't hold off the charging Bears. The All-Stars' best scoring chance came in the fourth quarter, when a long pass to a wide-open Simmons hit him in the hands and was dropped. The Bears kept their foot on the gas the whole game and registered a commanding 51–0 victory.⁶⁰

It was a fairly clean game despite the decisive loss. Fate Johnson of the All-Stars was warned twice by the referee in the first quarter about his rough play. The Bears' players told him they wanted to play a clean game, but said, "If you want the other kind, we can play that kind, too."⁶¹ Johnson was quickly benched by Kemp and Slater for the rest of the game to avoid any further incidents. One of the All-Stars was kicked in a pileup as well, but Halas sought him out after the game and took him to the Bears' locker room, where the player who kicked him apologized and the men shook hands. All in all, the exhibition illustrated that players of both races could play together amicably, even if the final score was lopsided.

Duke Slater spent the rest of 1938 focusing on his legal career. He was a principal speaker at a Democratic mass meeting in Chicago Heights, and he also continued to serve as an official for high school football games.[62] In addition, Duke was a leader in the community. The Morgan Park district chose an honorary mayor every year, and Slater was elected in 1938.[63]

The College All-Star game continued to exclude African American players into the late–1930s. In 1939, Duke offered his support to a campaign to get a player such as Brud Holland of Cornell, Bernie Jefferson of Northwestern, or Horace Bell of Minnesota into the game.[64] All three were eventually selected as reserves, breaking the color line at the College All-Star game. David Ward Howe of the *Chicago Defender* reported that the enthusiastic campaign of Windy City supporters was instrumental in voting the three men in.

The appearance of Holland, Jefferson, and Bell on the All-Stars roster was a groundbreaking event that set the stage for breaking down the NFL's color ban as well. "It might be somewhat embarrassing to have a race lad stand out in this game subsequently to attract attention to the fact that professional football draws the 'color line,'" Howe wrote. "If then a race lad stands out in the game, what will be the attitude of the owners of the professional teams? Will they then offer the race star a chance to enter professional football or will they continue to draw the line? The All-Star Game might well serve to arouse public sentiment behind a campaign to place race men in the pro league and if so, it will have served another fine purpose. Then, too, the game itself would probably benefit for there are many fans of all creeds and colors who have been awaiting a chance to see another brilliant performer like Duke Slater of the old Chicago team."[65]

For all of Duke Slater's positive attributes, he wasn't the most skillful driver. He had been involved in a traffic accident two years earlier when he struck a girl who Duke said ran out in front of his car; thankfully, the girl's injuries were not serious.[66] On August 30, 1939, Duke attended the College All-Star game at Soldier Field and watched the color ban come down at the event. He was driving home from the game when his car caromed off a fire hydrant before striking a tree. It was reported that he "narrowly escaped death" in the incident. Slater was rushed to the hospital by ambulance for lacerations to the face, and he was kept away from all visitors with the exception of his wife for several days.[67]

When he recovered, Slater immediately went back into coaching. The Chicago Comets were an all-star black football team sponsored by Kenneth Campbell, a vehicle tax inspector. Slater coached the Comets in 1939 along with player-coach Don Simmons. The Comets had a much better record than Slater's 1937 Brown Bombers. The Comets won their first three games in shutouts, defeating the Joliet Devils, 38–0, Winkler A.C. of Chicago, 24–0, and the Macomb Eagles, 10–0.[68] The victory over Macomb was particularly impressive, as they were the semi-pro football champions of the Midwest at the time.[69] Their unblemished record took its first hit on October 29, however, when they faced the powerful Des Moines Comets. Billed as the "Chicago Negro All-Stars," probably to avoid confusion between two teams with the same nickname, the Chicago organization proved to be the inferior Comets, absorbing a 33–0 loss from the Des Moines club.[70]

The Chicago Comets played at least two more confirmed games. They played in Spring

Valley, Illinois, on November 5, but the opponent and outcome of the game is unknown.[71] The Comets also notched one more victory when they defeated a squad from Kenosha, Wisconsin, 28–12, on November 26. On an unfortunate note, end Don Simmons suffered a broken jaw in that game which put him in the hospital for a week.[72]

Duke was trying to create opportunities for African Americans not only at the professional level, but collegiately as well. In the 1920s, Iowa's football program recruited Arlington Daniels, Ledrue Galloway, Harold Bradley, and Wendell Benjamin. All four of these athletes were African American linemen, and all of them were, at one time or another, compared to Slater or considered "the next Duke Slater." Slater's fame as the greatest black football player of all time helped Iowa in its recruiting of several standout black athletes in the 1920s and '30s, including as the Simmons brothers and Homer Harris. By the late-1930s, however, Slater began to transition into an active recruiter on Iowa's behalf. He started seeking out talented African American athletes and selling them on the advantages of playing in Iowa City.

Duke and the Simmons brothers started by visiting Lee Farmer, an 18-year-old Proviso High School track and football star who shattered the Illinois state record with a long jump over 23 feet and won the 100-yard dash. Although Farmer was only a high school junior, the three former Iowa stars already began the recruitment process to get Farmer to Iowa City.[73] Their sales pitch worked. Lee Farmer attended the University of Iowa and the "protégé of Duke Slater" eventually stole the spotlight at the 1942 Big Ten track and field championships. He won the 60-yard dash and broke the conference broad jump record twice—once in the preliminaries and then again in the finals to take the conference championship.[74] Farmer was also named captain of Iowa's 1943 track team, but he only participated in one meet that year before being inducted into the army.

On the football field, Slater convinced James J. Walker, an all-state high school tackle from South Bend, Indiana, to head for Iowa. Walker was a talented three-sport athlete, but he wasn't recruited by his home town school, Notre Dame, because of his race. Walker considered Duke his favorite athlete of all time, which surely helped Slater's sales pitch.[75] "They say around here that big Jim Walker, 21-year-old Negro tackle on the University of Iowa football team, will be a second Duke Slater before his collegiate competition is finished," the *Carroll Daily Herald* announced. "Big Jim worships Slater. It is Duke who makes it possible for Walker to attend the university. During the summer, he works at jobs that Slater gets for him in Chicago."[76]

Jim Walker went on to become a member of Iowa's 1939 Ironmen team. Although Walker was injured early in the season, the 1939 Iowa squad went on to have one of the greatest seasons in school history. Their season, coincidentally, was highlighted by an upset victory over Notre Dame. Slater, the hero of Iowa's victory over the Irish eighteen years earlier, watched with tears streaming down his cheeks as halfback Nile Kinnick scored Iowa's lone touchdown in a 7–6 upset.[77] Kinnick and his Ironmen would rapidly supplant Duke's 1921 squad as the most beloved team in school history, but Slater was nevertheless thrilled for his alma mater's success. Through his recruiting of prominent black athletes, he would remain a very important contributor to that success.

In January 1940, Governor Henry Horner of Illinois appointed Duke Slater as an assistant Illinois commerce commissioner.[78] Slater was only in this new job for a little over a year before returning to his previous position with the corporation counsel's office.[79] Nevertheless, Fay Young of the *Chicago Defender* wrote, "No news of recent date has elated your columnist as much as the announcement that Fred Slater, known to all his cronies and the followers of Big Ten football as Duke, had been appointed by Governor Henry Horner of Illinois as assistant commerce commissioner. Slater goes down in history as the greatest of tackles and never is there an All-American eleven of all times mentioned without his name on it.... In the pro circles, he was stamped 'the greatest tackle of his day.' The plaudits in the crowds in pro football were as great as those in college circles, for wherever he played and against whom he played, Slater had the reputation of playing a clean, sportsmanlike game."

Young then recounted a story of meeting Slater at Young's Chicago home. Duke placed his boots outside the door, and Young told him to bring them inside, worrying they might get stolen in such a rough neighborhood. "No chance," Slater retorted. "Nobody could wear them but me — they are too big!" Young had failed to consider one of the side benefits to having abnormally large feet. "But they weren't any bigger than Duke's heart," Young wrote. "It is good to look back over the years and to know this one and that one who have played the game and are now making good. It does away with the old saying that an athlete's brain is in his feet or legs."[80] David Condon of the *Chicago Tribune* agreed. "Duke Slater wore size 16 shoes, extra width. That was the size foundation necessary to support a man of the Duke's heft and heart," Condon wrote.[81]

Slater continued to be active in the local Democratic Party in 1940. He served on the steering committee to host the National Colored Democratic Convention in Chicago on July 12 to 14.[82] He also helped oversee the creation of the American Negro Exposition that summer at Chicago Coliseum. Henry A. Wallace, the Secretary of Agriculture and candidate for Vice President, visited Chicago for the event and was greeted by a committee of prominent Chicagoans, including Slater. At the exposition were murals and portraits of notable African Americans, and a Hall of Sports where trophies won by Joe Louis and others were displayed.[83]

Duke and Etta took a trip to California in August to visit his aunt, Jennie Graham, in Los Angeles and attend an A.M.E. dinner in Oakland.[84] When Duke returned to Chicago, he was offered another coaching opportunity. A Chicago bondsman, W.A. Donaldson, organized an all-star team of African American players called the Chicago Panthers. Slater took the head coaching job for the Panthers and began assembling some of the best talent around. He signed Ozzie and Don Simmons to the team and added Bobby Vandever, a black halfback who had been a star with the Des Moines Comets, and Fred Smith, a reserve end for Iowa's 1939 Ironmen squad.

When the Panthers took the field at Mills Stadium against the Waukegan Collegians on September 11, they had another famous name in the lineup. Kenny Washington, a star halfback who dazzled spectators in the 1940 College All-Star game, was waiting in Chicago for a possible contract offer from George Halas and the Chicago Bears. Washington suited up for Slater's squad while he awaited a response, and with his help, the Panthers rolled over the Collegians, 42–0.[85] However, it became apparent soon after the game that Halas would be unable to break the color ban and sign Washington, so he left the team and returned to the west coast.

The Panthers, meanwhile, kept rolling. They played the Sioux City Olympics on September 29 and the Merrill Foxes on October 9, and while the scores of these games are unknown, the Panthers were undefeated until they were beaten by the Detroit Pioneers on October 12. The Pioneers tackled Vandever for a safety on a punt attempt and emerged victorious, 2–0.[86]

Two days later, the Panthers played the Toledo Grills; the outcome of this game, too, is unknown.[87] Vandever then led Slater's team against his former squad, the Des Moines Comets, on October 20. But Vandever wasn't enough for the team billed as the "Chicago Black Panthers" to avoid their second known loss by a 20–7 score in front of 4,000 fans in Des Moines.

The Panthers followed that loss with two victories. They defeated the Jefferson Park Bulldogs on October 23, 19–6, and then followed that game with an 18–13 victory over Edison Park four days later.[88] The final confirmed game for the Panthers was in Fort Madison, Iowa, against a team of prisoners at the state penitentiary on November 3.[89] One player later declared that their record in 1940 was 9–2.[90]

The exposure Slater was generating for African American football players was beneficial, but it had to be frustrating that no black players were able to break through at the NFL level. Kenny Washington's performances at the College All-Star game and with the Chicago Panthers didn't lead to a tryout with the Bears. Furthermore, Ozzie Simmons' short stint with the Panthers was his final foray in professional football. Banned from the league due to his race, Simmons would never grace an NFL roster, despite being one of the most talented players of his era. His skills were undeniable; the scene with Halas screaming at his Bears to carefully watch Ozzie was evidence of that. But unlike Washington and Lillard, whose NFL careers were cut short due to the color ban, Simmons' entire career was taken away by a league that wanted nothing to do with African Americans.

Duke Slater spent his coaching tenure with the Panthers weighed down by personal tragedy. On October 4, 1940, George Washington Slater, Jr., died in Chicago at age 67 from

Duke Slater mentored several African American athletes in his lifetime. Perhaps the most prominent was Ozzie Simmons, an All-American halfback at the University of Iowa in the mid–1930s. Simmons' prime landed squarely in the midst of the color ban in professional football, so he never played a single game in the NFL (© University of Iowa-CMP Photograph Service).

complications of an operation. Duke's parents lived in Edmonton, Canada, for much of the 1920s before returning to Des Moines in 1930.[91] Reverend Slater soon relocated to Council Bluffs, Iowa, and headed an A.M.E. church there. He was a prominent community leader and activist in that town for several years. George achieved a major victory in 1932 by leading a lobbying effort that pressured several local restaurants to remove signs stating, "No Colored Trade Solicited."[92] Duke's parents lived with him and his wife in Chicago shortly before George's death. After the funeral, Duke's stepmother Missouri returned to Clinton and passed away a few years later.

It would be up to Duke to advance his father's vision of racial equality and increased opportunities for the black community. In an era where African Americans in the sports arena were still subject to arbitrary bans on their participation in professional football and baseball, were forbidden from eating and living with white teammates, and were subject to numerous forms of discrimination, Duke Slater had found a way to rise above. Now he was actively working to improve the conditions for those that followed.

Reverend Slater had a profound impact on Duke's life. George was an advocate of education to the end. While in Council Bluffs in 1937, he achieved a goal he sought for more than forty years, graduating from the University of Nebraska at Omaha with a Bachelor of Arts degree. Even in his mid-sixties, he expressed an interest in continuing his education and obtaining a master's degree in theology. George Slater's emphasis on intellectual improvement and his unshakeable commitment to accomplishing his goals obviously had an impression on his son Fred, and so much of Duke Slater's success can be attributed to George's guidance.

As George Slater finally received his college degree, reporters at the commencement ceremony asked him what he was feeling. His response exuded a sentiment his son could take to heart as he fought against racial exclusion in professional sports. "It took a long time," George said, "but I never gave up hope."[93]

Chapter 14

From the Field to the Bench (1941–1951)

Less than twelve months after Duke's father passed away, Slater suffered the loss of another mentor. On July 27, 1941, his college coach, Howard Jones, suddenly collapsed and died of a heart attack. Jones had always been tough on Duke. He was a stern disciplinarian, and his players considered it praise to escape his criticism. "Jones always had you in hot water. At times you didn't know whether you were on the club or not," Slater recalled, saying he felt that way up to and including his final game against Northwestern in 1921.[1] "Jones was hard to please," Duke continued. "I never felt I satisfied him."[2] Coach Jones maintained psychological leverage over his pupil by never calling him by his nickname and always referring to Slater as Fred.[3]

Years later, Southern California took on Notre Dame in Chicago, and Coach Jones stayed at the Del Prado Hotel. Some of the 1921 Hawkeye team members bumped into each other in the lobby of that hotel and were chatting when they spotted Jones talking to his friends. The Hawkeye players went to greet their old coach. Slater recalled, "It came my turn to shake hands with him and in answer to the remark that I also played for Jones, I said, 'Yes, I guess I played a little football with you, Coach.' Jones' reply was, 'Yes, you did, Fred, but you could have played a whole lot more.'"[4] Although he never seemed to admit it to Duke himself, Jones proclaimed Slater's greatness to others. "He could knock down two men with one arm and then grab the ball carrier with the other and throw him for a loss," Jones remarked.[5] He said he never coached a lineman who made so few errors on either offense or defense. "In Slater's case," Jones clarified, "you might translate 'so few' as 'none.' He was simply never out of position, never fooled by a fake, never mistaken on where the opposing ball carrier was going, never late on his offensive charge."[6]

Howard Jones constantly referred to Tom Shevlin, an All-American lineman at Yale, when he wanted to teach Slater a particular technique. Duke reminisced, "Jones was always talking about Shevlin. It got so I wished I could have seen him play."[7] But after Duke's career, Jones no longer dwelled on Shevlin. "One of the secrets of [Jones'] success was the establishment, in his own mind, of performance standards based upon the best men in each position that he had ever coached. He was continually attempting to bring his present players up to the standard of the best player in the past," Aubrey Devine explained. "This was particularly true in connection with his linemen of which Slater of Iowa was his standard. Although he developed many outstanding linemen, several of which were of All-American caliber, he never, in his own mind, developed one that equaled or exceeded the performance of Duke Slater and always, up to the date of his death, used Slater as his ideal example of what a great lineman should be."[8]

In January 1942, a speaking engagement made Slater realize the impact he could have on the lives of Chicago youth. He was invited to speak to 670 members of the Illinois State Training School for Boys at St. Charles. All of the boys were "inmates" or juvenile delinquents, and almost all of them were raised in poverty or broken homes. Duke openly talked to the boys about how he tried to quit school, about the death of his mother when he was 11 years old, and about growing up in poverty. Of course, the boys then learned how Slater made it all the way through law school and "became one of the greatest football stars of all time."[9] Duke was notably impressed by the occasion and promised to try to bring Joe Louis, world's heavyweight champion, to address the boys as well. Slater would become a frequent speaker to youth groups in the ensuing decades, imparting his life story to young people.

The experience also altered his coaching priorities. Duke spent most of the 1930s coaching semi-pro African American teams, including the 1938 Negro All-Stars against the Chicago Bears. Three years later, he sat on the bench in a similar game and gave encouragement to the Colored All-Stars, an all-star squad organized to oppose the New York Yankees at the Polo Grounds.[10] This group of All-Stars, coached by Benny Friedman and assisted by Joe Lillard, made a much better showing than Slater's team did; the 1941 Negro All-Stars led the Yankees after three quarters, 20–17, before falling, 24–20.[11]

But by 1942, Slater turned from semi-pro coaching and focused on youth football. Inspired by the kids of St. Charles, Duke volunteered to coach their football team that year.[12] During World War II, Slater became involved in the Chicago Sports Association. A six-school league was formed to teach youngsters ranging from ten to 15 years old the fundamentals of football. The schools trained for eight weeks before embarking on a regular schedule that included exhibitions between the halves of pro games.[13] Duke coached the Washington Park school in 1944 and 1945 and helped coach the Columbus Park team in 1946.[14] His Columbus Park squad played at halftime of one of the Bears-Cardinals games in 1946.[15]

Duke retired from his sporadic coaching positions after World War II. For him, coaching was always something he did out of necessity in the interest of expanding opportunities for African American athletes, but it wasn't something he wanted to pursue as a career. Slater called coaching a hazardous job which took a special technique he never felt he had. "The whole future of a coach and his family can depend on what a 17-year-old athlete does in one game," he marveled.[16]

Racial unrest moved to the forefront in Chicago during World War II. One of the most notorious incidents in Chicago surrounded the 1943 shooting of a 16-year-old African American boy by a white policeman. The officer claimed he shot the boy in self-defense, because the boy had thrown rocks at the officers. The local NAACP called for action, and Slater contributed money to a citizens' fund to pursue legal action against the officer.[17] Attorney Slater also headed a citizens' committee of nearly 200 Morgan Park residents who protested the police department's decision not to press charges.[18]

The war also saw racial barriers in sports begin to crumble. In 1944, Bill Willis became the first African American to earn a starting spot in the College All-Star game. It was noted that Willis was "more than able to take care of himself," at one point slapping "one of those 'Duke Slater tackles'" on a Chicago Bear ball carrier.[19] He would go on to have a notable pro football career, first in the All-American Football Conference and later in the NFL. When Willis was named an all-pro with the Cleveland Browns in 1950, he became the first black lineman to earn all-pro honors in the NFL since Slater in 1930.

The NFL's color ban was finally shattered in 1946 as Kenny Washington and Woody

Strode were signed by the Los Angeles Rams. That re-integrated the league after a 12-year ban on African Americans, and the pioneers that re-integrated the league after the war started to overshadow pre-war players like Slater. Kenny Washington is often credited as being the first "modern" black player in the NFL. While the qualifier makes the statement technically correct, calling Washington the first "modern" black player naturally led to confusion. Spike Claassen, an *Associated Press* writer in New York, joked, "What was Duke Slater back there with the Chicago Cardinals in the mid-1920s? A cheerleader?"[20]

A trickle of African Americans started to appear in the NFL, but at the college level, Duke's involvement was creating a flood of opportunities. He passionately recruited for his alma mater, guiding Obern Simons, a fast Chicago halfback, to Iowa's football squad in 1945.[21] But he also assisted African Americans that didn't wind up choosing the Hawkeyes. Claude "Buddy" Young was one of the greatest young black athletes of the Midwest, and Slater was the featured speaker at a victory banquet where Young was awarded a football scholarship to the University of Illinois.[22] Duke more or less adopted Young and served his chief advisor.[23] Slater attended several of Young's games at Illinois, including a game against Great Lakes in 1944 where Young helped the Illini secure a 26–26 tie by scoring on a 93-yard touchdown run.[24]

Yet the effects of Duke's mentorship were felt most acutely in Iowa City. The University of Iowa developed a national reputation as a place where African American athletes could excel, and Slater was largely responsible for that. Duke had guided several athletes to Iowa, and his protégés soon started finding recruits of their own. While in the Coast Guard, Jim Walker met a multi-talented African American football player named Emlen Tunnell. Walker raved about his days in Iowa City and told Tunnell the gridiron tales of Duke Slater and Ozzie Simmons. "So I knew blacks got a fair shake there," Tunnell later said of his decision to attend Iowa.[25]

Tunnell described what the University of Iowa had become. "I had never seen so many Negro guys in one place in my life. This was on the University of Iowa practice field in the autumn of 1946. There were 325 candidates for the football team, many of them war veterans, and 58 were Negroes," Tunnell recalled. "Most of those Negro boys had come to Iowa for the same reason I had. They knew they would be given a chance to play. Great Negro players were part of a tradition at Iowa, going way back to the days around World War I. Fred 'Duke' Slater, who is a judge now in Chicago, was an All-American tackle at Iowa right after the first war."[26]

Duke Slater's athletic prowess was known far and wide, and in 1946, he earned one of the greatest honors of his college football career. On September 1, he was named an all-time All-American by a nationwide poll of 600 sportswriters, coaches, and other critics. The eleven players selected as the greatest football players of all time congregated at Wrigley Field to accept the award at a charity exhibition game between the New York Giants and the Chicago Bears. In a halftime ceremony, Slater, the only African American chosen, received his award along with Jim Thorpe, Red Grange, Don Hutson, Willie Heston, Bronko Nagurski, and others. It was a tremendous honor for Slater, who, according to Sec Taylor of the *Des Moines Register*, "played as much tackle at Iowa under the Howard Jones regime as anybody has ever played anywhere, anytime."[27]

1946 also marked the 25th anniversary of Iowa's great 1921 team, and the squad met for their 25-year reunion at the Iowa-Notre Dame game. Just as he had been on the field, Slater was one of the leaders of the team at the reunion. "After joining the Hawkeyes at the training table, Slater, who is remembered as the leading songster of the group, couldn't resist the temptation to gather the men for one more round of songs," the *Press-Citizen* reported.[28]

Although Duke was long removed from his football days by 1947, he still occasionally flashed his old athletic ability, playing for the Iowa City Blackhawks, a local all-black baseball team, that summer.[29] But most of his athletic accomplishments were limited to the past tense. "Duke Slater's prodigious feats at tackle are Hawkeye legends now," the *Daily Iowan* wrote. "Slater had everything a great tackle should have and more. How opposing backfield men hated to try his side of the line!"[30]

Duke was more than just a great former athlete; he served as an ambassador for his race in the face of persistent bigotry. As an African American who competed in sports against mostly white opponents, Duke Slater was able to reach out to white audiences and break down racist stereotypes in a way few other African Americans could. When Duke joined Jackie Robinson to speak at a fundraising dinner, it was clear both men's accomplishments greatly transcended sports.[31]

"One Negro star on the gridiron or baseball diamonds with white fellow teammates preaches a better interracial sermon than a hundred orators," Lucius C. Harper wrote of Slater and Robinson. "The field of sports has truly contributed its worth in battling race prejudice. It reaches the multitude. The orator's voice, pleading for justice and fair play, is limited in scope. A Jackie Robinson playing in a World Series will be viewed with more interest and renown in white American homes than President Truman's signing of an antilynch bill. Sports have always preached a sermon of goodwill wherever a black man has been given the opportunity to take part in them. It is one way to crush prejudice in the heart of the average white who will listen to no other argument on the subject."[32]

Wendell E. Green was the first African American elected to the Cook County Municipal Court in 1942. Still, a storm of protest swept over Chicago in the mid–1940s for failing to give consideration to the nomination of more black judges. A group of three independent black attorneys ran for the Chicago judicial bench under the banner of the Progressive Party and pledged to "Wipe out Jim Crow from the Courts."[33]

While that movement failed to gain traction, the Democratic Party in Chicago took notice. As a concession, they agreed to nominate a second African American to the city's municipal court in a January 1948 meeting at the Morrison Hotel. Duke Slater was given the choice of seeking the bench or taking another political office; Slater decided to place his name on the judicial ballot.[34]

Duke was an ideal candidate. He had lived for several years in the 19th Ward's small, affluent black community, and he served as the Democratic machine's supervisor for the ward's 18 black precincts.[35] Slater was admired by white voters for his athletic prowess and the "gentlemanly" way in which he played. Black voters, conversely, salivated at the opportunity to get another African American on the city bench. The black community admired Slater for the fact that, despite his success, he stayed true to his roots and remained an active part of his South Side neighborhood. His nomination to the bench meant Slater would be even more involved on the political scene. Duke was chosen to speak at an NAACP-sponsored Emancipation celebration in Waterloo, Iowa, on August 3, 1948. In a powerful speech which channeled the fiery sermons of his father, Duke Slater began with a brief review of events and progress in the movement toward "real achievement of the Emancipation declared in 1863" and noted that "the issue of human rights or civil liberties has come upon us with a tremendous crash in the last few years."

He then pressed for the audience to demand advancement in the civil rights movement. "We must use all possible means and all techniques to get this job done. We ought to see that the politicians carry on with the civil rights issue; we must see that they don't make a political football out of it," Slater said. But he then challenged the Waterloo crowd to eliminate racial prejudice by starting at home. "It's up to you to assume the responsibility," he continued. "At a time when all our major political parties have the issue before them, when the leaders are sensing the need for action on the racial inequalities, WE must work.... Make your ideas work in Waterloo. That's where the progress starts—in the thousands of individual communities. Not in Washington, DC, but in Waterloo. People are ready and willing to listen to reason and justice and fact. So now is the time to work."[36]

Duke worked to build support for his nomination to the Chicago courts by giving speeches all over the Windy City. He saw the judgeship as a chance to extend his influence well beyond the gridiron. "Slater is a well-built man with an understanding and usually serious face," the *Chicago Tribune* noted. "It was football ... that made Slater famous, but his aim is to be remembered as well, or better, as a public servant and benefactor of his race. This was the goal set for him by his late father, an Iowa minister, Slater says, and he has spent his last 20 years pursuing it."[37]

Despite Slater's enormous popularity, he wasn't assured of an election victory. His candidacy was heavily tied to the electoral fates of other Democrats on the ticket, and Slater attended several fundraisers for the re-election campaign of President Harry Truman with the hope of making history.[38] On November 2, 1948, both Truman and Slater did so. President Truman's late surge in Illinois gave him an upset victory in the 1948 presidential election over Thomas Dewey. The surge of votes in Chicago, especially among minority voters, helped elect Slater as Municipal Court judge as well.[39] Duke Slater racked up over 960,000 votes, a testament to his popularity in the city.[40] He was now just the second African American judge in Chicago history. Three weeks later, he attended a tribute banquet for Paddy Driscoll, and the old players in attendance responded by giving Duke a standing ovation when he entered the room.[41]

Duke Slater was sworn in as a Cook County Municipal Court judge on December 13, 1948, in Room 902 of City Hall. The courtroom was crowded with admirers and dignitaries, including Judge Green, who cut his own re-election ceremonies short in order to be present. The bench had been covered with beautiful floral pieces, which Slater sent to patients at various Chicago hospitals after his inauguration.

Superior Court Judge John Bolton performed the installation ceremonies. With his wife and other relatives looking on, Duke was praised by business, civic, and religious leaders, as well as many of the judges before whom he had practiced as an attorney. Judge Duke Slater was overcome by emotion and said, "Facing this occasion seems harder to me than a football game." But he pledged to do his best to uphold the good records of all the judges that had come before him. Slater then heard his first case that very morning. Not surprisingly, Judge Slater got right to work.[42]

"The spectators, mostly colored, rise as one as the bailiff raps the Municipal court into session on Chicago's great South Side," wrote Art Snider of the *Chicago Daily News*. "A bulky man with tremendous shoulders and a serious but warm face emerges from a side door and lumbers toward the bench. Lawyers and court attendants address him as Judge Slater. Thousands of football fans would know him better as Fred 'Duke' Slater, Iowa's all-time, All-

American tackle on the fabulous 1921 championship team." Snider admitted being "taken back by his stateliness and dignity for a moment" as he was writing the article.[43]

Slater very much enjoyed being a judge and handled about 35 civil and criminal cases a day in 1949.[44] He wasn't all about work, however; his favorite sport at this point in his life was golf, and he kept his putting form sharp in his judge's chambers with his trusted club and a glass on the parlor carpet.[45] His new occupation led to a few colorful plays on words. "Duke Slater, one of Iowa's all-time great football players, is now a referee — but he makes his decisions on a court bench instead of the football field," the *Des Moines Register* reported. "At Iowa, Slater did not spend much time 'on the bench.' Most of every game he was on the football field."[46]

His new job also gave him a newfound power that protected him against some forms of prejudice. He and Wendell Green were attending a party when two red-faced Chicago police detectives arrived at the property, looking for a shakedown. The detectives barged into the house, only to return a few minutes later. One bystander outside asked the detectives if they had the pleasure of meeting the two esteemed judges while they were inside. The officers uttered a profanity-laced response and quickly left the scene.[47]

There were other perks to his job as well. Every year, the Bud Billiken parade and picnic attracted hundreds of thousands of revelers on Chicago's South Side. The 1949 parade drew almost half a million spectators. The parade was led by Illinois governor Adlai Stevenson, Chicago mayor Martin Kennelly, and John Sengstacke, publisher and editor of the *Chicago Defender*. Following close behind were prominent Chicago citizens, including Jesse Owens, Ralph Metcalfe, and Judges Irvin Mollison, Herman Moore, Wendell Green, and Duke Slater.[48]

Judge Slater occasionally gave his fellow judges flashbacks. Roger Kiley, the Notre Dame end from 1921, was a judge in Chicago's appellate court. "I passed a ghost in the Hall of Records the other day," Kiley said. "Duke Slater came by and I instinctively moved over to let him go through."[49] Kiley, who scored Notre Dame's only touchdown in that 10–7 loss, could recall the game decades later. "I can still hear Slater saying, 'Big day today, Aub' and 'Right through here, Aub,'" he admitted.[50]

Yet as Slater became further removed from his playing days, some observers gradually began to overlook his impact on the game. *Ebony Magazine* asked 38 sportswriters and radio broadcasters in August 1949 to name the top ten black athletes of all time. Fritz Pollard was the only football player selected, placing ninth in the voting. "Although the selectors chose only one pro football player, it is surprising that they so completely overlooked the Iowa star of the early '20s, Duke Slater. There are many men who played against Slater who swear he belongs on the all-time All-American team," Pat Harmon of the *Cedar Rapids Gazette* lamented. "Perhaps the fact that Pollard as a halfback attracted more publicity than Slater led to his selection. In looking back 28 to 35 years, it's easier to remember the headlines than the small type."[51]

For those that still remembered him, however, Duke Slater was held up as an example for others to follow. After hearing several stories about the frequent carousing of Buddy Young, a gossip columnist for the *Chicago Defender* advised, "Please, Buddy, don't make the mistake so many of our other big-time athletes have made.... Copy after Judge Duke Slater and forget about apeing the others, won't you, Buddy?"[52] The *Defender* cited Slater and Jesse Owens as two outstanding examples for future athletes to emulate.[53]

"In this day and age of young athletes with their hands out waiting for the best 'deal,' Duke Slater's story is a striking contrast," Tait Cummins of the *Cedar Rapids Tribune* wrote.

"Every day while he was in college, Duke peeled spuds for a living. Just try to get a third-string water-boy to stoop to peeling potatoes for his college education today. Duke did it!" He concluded, "There's a moral there someplace, kids, but with offers flying high, wide, and handsome from colleges below the Mason-Dixon line, it's hard for today's athletes to see the sense in doing it the hard way like Duke did. But it made him a man."[54]

The South Side neighborhood where the Slaters lived was as rough as ever. Judge Slater's car was stolen and later recovered stripped of all four tires.[55] Still, Slater simply focused on improving the area where he lived. He attended a cornerstone laying ceremony for a new Washington Park YMCA. The new building cost over a million dollars and was designed to serve thousands of young people on the South Side.[56] He also served on the board of directors of a group called the South Side Boys Foundation, which was created to help young Chicago athletes find direction. Slater was joined on the board of directors by Jesse Owens, Ralph Metcalfe, Joe Louis, and others.[57]

Judge Slater was also visible in political circles. The Jefferson Jubilee, a large Democratic rally, was held in May 1950, and Slater was seen conversing at the convention with Judge Wendell Green and Senator Paul Douglas. President Harry Truman gave the keynote address, and it was attended by several prominent Democratic politicians including Adlai Stevenson.[58] Months later, a third African American Democrat joined Green and Slater on the Municipal Court bench, Henry C. Ferguson.[59]

While they gained a fine judge in Ferguson, the Chicago courts lost a great jurist in May 1951 when Judge Mike McKinley passed away. Judge McKinley was a hugely influential figure in Slater's life; more than any other individual, McKinley was responsible for bringing Duke to Iowa, and it was Slater's "greatest admiration and respect" for his mentor that led him into the judicial field.[60] That respect was mutual. "Judge McKinley thought Duke was just the tops on everything," Sherman Howard recalled.[61]

Duke also got his passion for the Hawkeyes from McKinley. Judge McKinley founded the Chicago Alumni club of Iowa and helped create four four-year scholarships to the university.[62] One of his favorite sayings when the subject of football recruiting came up was, "Maybe we better confer with Coach Slater first. He's the head coach, and I'm just a third-rate assistant." Mrs. Slater testified that McKinley would call Duke at all hours of the night to pick his brain about football matters.[63] Judge McKinley's involvement with the University of Iowa throughout his life paid enormous dividends in bringing outstanding individuals, including Duke Slater, to the Hawkeyes.

1951 marked the opening of two significant Halls of Fame. First, the *Des Moines Register* launched a State of Iowa Sports Hall of Fame. The Iowa Sports Hall of Fame recognized athletes who were either born in Iowa or who gained prominence while competing for an Iowa school. Nile Kinnick, Aubrey Devine, Jay Berwanger, and Elmer Layden joined Slater as the five football players inducted in the inaugural class.

"No Hawkeye in history has been held in higher esteem," Bert McGrane of the *Register* wrote in his induction article. "Big Duke had tremendous hands. And feet. Every inch of him was man and muscle. Benign in appearance, kindly, courteous, good natured, his mild manner didn't seem to match up to his massive bulk. Any mildness in his makeup left him when he crossed the side stripe of a football field, however. He was plain poison out there and it mattered not whether he was tearing up an enemy line on offense or closing in on a ball carrier on defense." McGrane concluded, "They still rank Duke with the top tackles the game has known."[64]

More notably, the "Football Hall of Fame" opened in 1951. This Hall of Fame was devoted to college football players and would come to be known as the College Football Hall of Fame years later, particularly after the Pro Football Hall of Fame opened in Canton in 1963. The College Football Hall of Fame inducted 54 members in their inaugural class. Duke Slater joined his coach, Howard Jones, fellow Hawkeye Nile Kinnick, and rival coaches Zuppke, Stagg, Rockne, and Doc Williams in the first Hall of Fame class. Duke Slater was the only African American elected to the College Football Hall of Fame in its inaugural year, but astonishingly, that fact went almost completely unnoticed by the national media.

Nevertheless, his induction was merely a confirmation of his status as one of the all-time greats in the history of football, and entering alongside his deceased former coach, Howard Jones, made the moment doubly sweet. "Fred 'Duke' Slater was one of those unusual young men who come along about once in a coach's lifetime," Mervin Hyman wrote.[65] His old Clinton teammate Burt Ingwersen, a longtime coach himself who succeeded Jones as head coach at Iowa, agreed with that sentiment. "Every line coach dreams of walking onto the field some afternoon and finding another Duke Slater out there ready to go to work," declared Ingwersen. "I've played against and coached a lot of good linemen, but that Slater topped them all."[66]

Chapter 15

Truly Superior (1951–1959)

Hall of Famer Duke Slater was an extremely popular guest speaker in the 1950s, giving dozens and dozens of speeches every year. At these speaking engagements, he related his unique experiences in sports and used athletics to make observations about society as a whole. Slater appreciated his responsibility as an athlete to serve as a role model for youth. At a tribute to Drake star Johnny Bright, Slater declared, "Sports exerts its influence in our country. An athlete, whether he's a star or not, is someone's hero and sets a pattern for others."[1]

Duke enjoyed telling high school students he had more fun playing football in high school than anywhere else, because a youth then is giving his all just because of his love for the game. "In high school, an athlete is also closer to his coach and teachers," Duke remarked.[2] He paid high compliments to high school coaches, since they can have a tremendous impact on a young athlete's career.[3]

Following his father's lead, Slater counseled young athletes about the importance of education. "Time has long passed when dummies can get along. Today one must have the know how," Slater stated.[4] He also felt the Hawkeye State was a land of opportunity. "Iowa is a great state. Young men here have a fine opportunity to go on in school to prepare themselves for future life," he said. "If the youngsters are taken care of, we will have no fear of the future."[5]

Duke appreciated that his alma mater prepared him for his future. "I'll always be grateful to the University of Iowa, not only for giving me a chance to play football but also for a fine education in law," Judge Slater said.[6] Reflecting back on the 1921 team, Slater was proud of the fact that they were a well-educated group, with five starters on the squad going on to become lawyers.

He was also happy the 1921 Hawkeye team featured home-grown talent. "I think it's important to note that every man on that starting team came from someplace in Iowa," Slater remarked. "I have always said that Iowa produces the best football players in the country, if we could only keep them at home. Jay Berwanger, Bob Saggau, Sonny Franck, [Elmer and Mike] Layden, [Bob] O'Dell—they are only a few of the dozens that have gotten away."[7]

Of course, Slater had become one of Iowa's best recruiters of out-of-state athletes, directing Chicago kids to Iowa City. He playfully acknowledged his role in educating youngsters about the cultural advantages of Iowa. For example, Mike Riley of Minneapolis was a player he directed to Iowa in 1950. "I just happened to know his mother who lives here in Chicago," Duke grinned.[8]

Duke said he stayed so close to the game because he felt he owed a lot to football.[9] He admitted football was more interesting and harder to master in the 1950s than it had been three decades earlier. "The defense is smarter. It has to be to keep pace with the tricky offenses developed," he said.[10] "The forward pass has done it. In my day, we ran with the ball and threw only in desperation. Nowadays, with the rules allowing a forward pass any place back of the line of scrimmage, the defense is up against it."[11] Even so, he confessed to being "pleased as punch" over an NCAA ruling that banned the two-platoon system. "It means the game will again be played as it was meant to be played," Duke said. "The past few years most of my time at a game has been spent consulting the scorecard and watching mass substitutions."[12]

Duke clearly mourned the passing of the sixty-minute player. He rarely left the football field in his playing days, and he applied that same durability and tenaciousness to his job as a judge. He was recognized for having the best attendance record among all judges in the Chicago Municipal Court in 1952 and again in 1956.[13] Slater attributed these accomplishments to his years in athletics. "Football is a rugged, demanding sport," he said, "and it teaches you to put every effort forth. The finest thing about playing is that you retain a lot of the give and take the rest of your life."[14]

That was the type of enduring lesson Slater believed sports taught athletes. In his quiet, sincere way, he cited the values of football as a training for citizenship.[15] Slater declared that in his experience as a judge, he rarely found anyone running afoul of the law that had been blessed with good sports training.[16] Still, he felt the values instilled by high school and college sports were a byproduct of the athletic team's connection to the larger educational institution, and he warned against commercializing college sports. "We can't justify a wholly commercialized athletic contest," the judge remarked. "These contests should be closely supervised by the college authorities."[17]

Another lesson Slater learned on the field concerned the dispensability of athletes. "After our unbeaten season in 1921, everyone thought Iowa was going to plunge to the bottom [of the standings] in 1922 because several of us regulars—men like Aubrey and Glenn Devine, Lester Belding, and I—had graduated," Duke recalled.[18] "I heard it so much I began to believe it myself.... It made me feel pretty big."[19] Duke even visited an Iowa practice early in the 1922 season. "I really felt sorry for Coach Howard Jones, because he had only a handful of experienced players left," he said.[20]

But the following season, Iowa exceeded expectations. "Playing without the Devines, Belding, and Slater, Iowa went out and won itself a Big Ten title and went undefeated," Slater recalled.[21] "They won all their games and never missed us at all."[22] He used Iowa's 1922 season to teach a lesson to his listeners. "There's always someone to take your place, no matter how good you are.... You're never so good that you can't be done without," he declared.[23] "You will be missed but will always be replaced."[24]

Duke was frequently asked about the greatest players he had ever seen. "Ernie Nevers was the greatest of them all. He could pass, kick, and run," Duke said.[25] "The fellow had everything, including a great desire to play. He was emotional, and he played his heart out in every game."[26] He called Bronko Nagurski the hardest back to stop and wryly said no pro player was overpaid when Bronko was on the opposing side.[27] "Nagurski had more sheer power than any other man I have ever seen," he admitted.[28]

Duke recognized other stars as well. "I played with Jim Thorpe, the Carlisle Indian, after he was 41 years old," he said. "As good as he was then made me really wonder just what he really did in his hey-day."[29] Among college players, Duke found Earl Martineau and Herb Joesting of Minnesota to be exceptionally tough athletes.[30] He named Ken Strong the best pro back he played against and Joe Stuydahar the top lineman he ever saw. "[Don]

Hutson, [Guy] Chamberlin, and [Bill] Hewitt were great ends," Duke added. "George Trafton and Bulldog Turner were great centers. Hunk Anderson was the best guard I ever saw."[31]

Duke very rarely spoke of the rough treatment he received while playing football, but he did mention he had his shins kicked often and finally improvised shin guards by stuffing several magazines under his knee-high socks.[32] While he may not have openly discussed it, his friends saw the evidence of Slater's years of rugged play. "I used to look at his knees and I'd see all those bruises and everything," Sherman Howard recalled. "In those days, they just had open spikes on the shoe. They didn't have the cover on the spikes that they have today. Duke said, 'If you put your hand down, guys would step on your hand with their spikes.' They didn't have the cleats on them like they have now."[33]

Duke's speeches were typically very well-received. His talks were frequently greeted with a standing ovation and followed by a long autograph session.[34] After one speech at Oelwein High School, Judge Slater was called "a tremendous man, both in stature and mind" and one of the finest men ever to give a talk at the small Iowa school.[35] Pat Harmon of the *Cedar Rapids Gazette* called his speech at a banquet for several Cedar Rapids schools "one of the finest talks we have ever heard at an athletic dinner."[36]

John O'Donnell of the *Davenport Democrat & Leader* marveled at Duke's poise and humility during a radio interview. "Duke, whose name is legend at Iowa City, talked modestly of his days with the Hawks," O'Donnell wrote. "Years after being named one of the greatest tackles in the country, his interest in Iowa football is still razor sharp." Noting that Slater wasn't one to boast, O'Donnell called Duke the One-Man-Line of the Howard Jones regime at Iowa. "The man has a golden voice, an impish smile, and the quality of humility," he concluded. "He not only entertained his listeners, he charmed them."[37]

Racial prejudice couldn't always be escaped, however. Just before he passed away, Judge Mike McKinley was invited to be the guest speaker at his alma mater, Postville High School. They were dedicating a new gymnasium, and McKinley asked Slater to accompany him and speak as well. However, McKinley first needed to call ahead and find special accommodations for his friend. McKinley and Slater had to wait to make their plans until the Commercial Hotel agreed to house the black star.[38]

Duke Slater felt sports could be a vessel to break down such barriers of discrimination. He believed athletics increased racial understanding by providing a forum where different races could interact. Duke's father, George Slater, once wrote, "Contact and education soon removes ... the prejudice that is due to the dislike of unlikes," and sports allowed such contact to take place.[39] "Think correctly, and men aren't different," Duke observed. "What makes men different are the ways in which they think."[40]

It wasn't just men who received support from Duke. Slater made a surprise appearance at a meeting of the Cook County Bar Association's "Portias," or women of the legal profession. He lent his support to the organization and greeted the female lawyers in attendance. One of the women Slater talked to was B. Fain Tucker, who won election to the bench in 1953 as the first female Circuit Court judge in Chicago.[41]

Judge Slater's wisdom and professionalism on the bench defied racist stereotypes. His judicial decisions "have caught the favorable attention of all Chicago and have forced many a heretofore prejudiced individual to admit that culture, intelligence, courage, and knowledge of the law does not lie in race alone," the *Chicago Defender* declared.[42] "Judge Slater ... is most popular as a city judge and is admired and loved by everyone," it continued. "He is a good judge of human nature."[43] When Duke Slater's name again appeared on the voting ballot in 1954, he was convincingly re-elected to a second term as a Municipal Court judge.[44]

That same year, Duke found himself back in a familiar setting. As a youth, Slater grew up playing football in a vacant lot on Racine Avenue. Twenty years later, a football field, Normal Park, had been constructed over his childhood playground to serve the Chicago Cardinals. Duke played several NFL games in the same spot where he learned football as a boy twenty years earlier until the Cardinals abandoned Normal Park after the 1928 season. In an improbable twist, the field was torn down decades later and a new police court was erected over the grounds. Remarkably, Judge Slater's chambers were transferred to that very police court in 1954. Duke Slater's personal journey over a half-century—from poverty-stricken youth to NFL player to prestigious jurist—had come full circle in the exact same location.[45]

Meanwhile, Duke continued to have an impact on sports at his alma mater. Slater worked to guide Sherman Howard, Earl Banks, Mike Riley, and Harold Bradley, Jr., among others, to the Hawkeye football squad. Duke's recruiting efforts

Duke Slater gave several speeches to youth groups and other organizations during the 1940s and '50s. This photograph was taken during one of Slater's many visits back to Clinton in the 1950s (courtesy Gary Herrity).

were not limited to football, either. William McKinley "Deacon" Davis was one of the most talented basketball players in Illinois, but everyone assumed he would be attending Tennessee A&I University in Nashville, because his uncle, Walter S. Davis, was the president of the historically black college.

Deacon Davis went to Iowa instead. "All the charms that Uncle W.S. could dangle in front of him didn't match the eloquence and persuasive powers of one Judge Fred 'Duke' Slater," wrote sportswriter Fay Young. "We have no thought that the judge's size scared young Davis into going to Iowa, but our good friend Slater can put things over just like he bowled over opposing linemen."[46] Davis became an impact basketball player for the Hawkeyes and recruited his friend Carl Cain to Iowa City. Cain served as a lynchpin of Iowa's "Fabulous Five" teams that made two appearances in the NCAA Final Four.

Duke Slater was widely considered the greatest lineman in Iowa history, but that status was challenged in the mid–1950s by a young African American from Steubenville, Ohio. Calvin Jones was immediately hailed as "Iowa's new Duke Slater" as a sophomore in 1953, and by his junior season, he was a consensus first team All-American.[47] "Iowa's New Duke

Slater (Calvin Jones) Is as Effective," the *Cedar Rapids Gazette* declared. The paper put up a picture of a Cal Jones block next to the photo of Slater's "famous block" against Notre Dame in 1921. The caption below the photos read, "Ranking right along with Nile Kinnick, there's another legend at the University of Iowa called Duke Slater and another in the making in Calvin Jones. The above pictures show why."[48]

While African American athletes were embraced in Iowa, opportunities for black jurists in the Hawkeye State were much more limited. Judge Slater threw his support behind Des Moines attorney Luther Glanton, a candidate in the city's municipal court election. Glanton was attempting to become the first African American judge in the state of Iowa. On November 4, 1955, Judge Slater gave a speech to a nonpartisan group of 130 people at the Hotel Des Moines. In it, he hoped that on Election Day, "people of Des Moines will find themselves, along with other great communities, big enough to overlook some of the silly prejudices and place men in office because of their ability alone."

"In all places where Negroes have been elected to the judiciary, they have given a good account of themselves," Slater continued. "The Declaration of Independence says all men are created equal. It doesn't say 'all white men' or 'all Catholics' or 'all Jews.' It says 'all men.'"[49] With Slater "blocking" for Glanton, the Des Moines attorney made history, sweeping into office as Iowa's first black judge.

Roi Ottley of the *Chicago Tribune* hailed Judge Slater as a Chicago success story. "Judge Slater's roots are deep in the community and reach back into the last century," he added, pointing out that Duke was a third-generation Chicagoan. "It always seems appropriate when a man from the sidewalks of Chicago develops sufficiently to be elevated to the bench. It thus can be said a native is judging his peers."[50]

Judge Slater was lauded for not having a single legal decision reversed by the Appellate Court.[51] Ottley continued, "He is now sitting in the Wabash Avenue court, in the heart of the South Side, which is considered one of the busiest police districts in the world and one that is woefully undermanned. Before him come the problems of the community and he meets each one with a sympathetic but firm judicial eye. Judge Slater has found his work challenging and especially rewarding in the fact that people place trust in his judgment. Nor is there any grumbling in the community about the decisions he makes. The reason, perhaps, is that he knows his law and also brings sociological insights to his judgments."[52]

Duke used his athletic fame to make a difference in the lives of Chicago youth. In February 1956, he joined Ernie Banks, Rogers Hornsby, Gene Baker, and others at a Youth Foundation Program where Chicago children could meet sports heroes and watch a film of the Yankees-Dodgers 1955 World Series.[53] The following month, Duke helped to organize the Chicago Varsity Club, which was designed to help local kids. Charter members of the group included Slater, Ink Williams, Dick Hudson, Ralph Metcalfe, Fritz Pollard, Ozzie Simmons, and Jesse Owens. Slater was elected as the club's first president.[54] At their first club meeting, Slater and the Varsity Club presented a trophy to Coach Phil Woolpert of the San Francisco Dons and his star player, Bill Russell. Russell accepted the club's award as the top college basketball player in the nation.[55]

Duke was also a popular guest speaker at historically black colleges and universities. He was frequently asked to speak at Wilberforce University, and one year he delivered the keynote address at the Founders' Day banquet at Lincoln University in Jefferson City, Missouri. Therefore, it was not unusual when Slater was invited to Baton Rouge to be the special convocation speaker at Southern University in May 1956. He agreed to deliver a tribute to "Ace" Mumford, the retiring head coach and athletic director at Southern.[56]

Thirty-five years after he had been named a college All-American, Slater spoke just minutes from the campus of Louisiana State University, which was still eighteen years away from having their first African American football player. A large crowd of admirers gathered to hear Slater talk, including Eddie Robinson, the legendary Grambling College coach.[57] "Participation in athletics prepares men and women for life situations," Slater said. "There are four principle things that athletics teaches a youngster. These are:

1. Champions are people who can think
2. One is not indispensable
3. [Athletics] emphasizes cooperation, and
4. Ability knows no color."[58]

His last point was a lesson the Southeastern Conference would need another decade to learn.

The 1956 football season was a special one for Slater's Iowa Hawkeyes. Two years earlier, Duke had been honored at halftime of the opening game in Iowa City and given a plaque commemorating his induction into the Football Hall of Fame. When asked about the 1954 Hawkeye squad, Slater, always a fan, confidently predicted, "We're going to win this game and go on to the Rose Bowl." Though Iowa rallied to defeat Michigan State that day, the Hawkeyes fell short of a conference championship. A Hawkeye fan reminded him of his prediction months later, but Slater just grinned and replied, "I didn't say what year, did I?"[59]

As it turned out, Duke's prediction was two years too soon. He was in attendance in 1956 when the Hawkeyes clinched the school's first Rose Bowl berth with a 6–0 victory over Ohio State. Duke joyfully milled around the Hawkeye locker room, slapping the players on the back for a job well done and joining in the celebration.[60] Slater's pride in the team shone through when he declared that his 1921 team could not defeat the 1956 club. "I don't mind if the 1921 team is pushed back into the limbo of antiquity," he conceded.[61]

Thirty-five years after Duke Slater had been denied a chance to play in the 1922 Rose Bowl, he attended his first Rose Bowl game to watch his beloved Hawkeyes. "I'll be with the spectators this time," he said. "Back on Jan. 1, 1922, I would have been at tackle."[62] There was noticeable hurt in his voice when he talked about how he missed an opportunity to play in the Rose Bowl. But he was quick to point out that life had been good to him and that he had no complaints.

Duke reflected on the progress African Americans had made in his lifetime. "There is a chance for everybody now," he said. "Maybe things aren't perfect, but they're better. You can see it in athletics particularly. You hardly ever saw a Negro player in my days as an athlete. Now it's unusual when you see a team without one or more Negroes."[63]

At the 1957 Rose Bowl, one fan asked Duke how he thought players of his day would stack up against players in 1956. He smiled and said, "Oh, I think we could stay in there a few minutes at least."[64] Reporters, on the other hand, wanted to know what Slater thought about the starting lineup Iowa coach Forest Evashevski had chosen. Duke joked, "Let's let Evy run the club today. We've been coaching it all year." Slater was content interacting with fans and being one himself.

Duke trudged through the crowd up to row 45 before game time carrying two carnival pennants, one an Iowa pennant and one a Rose Bowl pennant. A fan asked, "What goes there, Duke, with all the flags? You look like the United Nations!" Slater replied with a wide grin, "Oh, I'm just having some fun today."[65] Slater was mobbed by autograph seekers but finished signing just before the game, and he thoroughly enjoyed the Hawkeyes' 35–19 victory over Oregon State for their first Rose Bowl victory.

In the wake of the game, sportswriter Bill Evans conducted a long interview with Slater and discussed a wide range of topics. Naturally, Duke brainstormed creative ideas on how to spice up football, proposing a plan to give teams a quarter or half a point for a first down.[66] He also talked about his den, which he dubbed "The Iowa Room," which was filled with pictures, framed awards, and other athletic items relating to his football heyday.

In more serious matters, Duke embraced a somewhat libertarian view of narcotics, expressing his opinion that it was almost impossible to prevent drug addiction but that regulating its distribution would yield much social progress. Slater said, "If legal machinery could be set up to try to eliminate the profit angle from drug traffic and to regulate sale, such a plan might be effective in reducing smuggling and other law violations attendant to narcotics."[67] He mentioned that he went into politics to help his people, and he discussed his charity work. Mrs. Slater told Evans that "the phone is always ringing" with people who "want him to help with a project."[68]

Slater's latest project was serving as chairman of a committee to honor Abe Saperstein, founder of the Harlem Globetrotters, with a testimonial dinner in April 1957. Slater attended and helped arrange dozens of political and athletic banquets over the years for civic leaders, high school teams, and notable athletes. He participated in banquets honoring athletes such as Jackie Robinson and Larry Doby, and he served on a banquet committee that put on a dinner recognizing Jesse Owens on the silver anniversary of his Olympic performance of 1936.[69] But the Saperstein tribute turned out to be one of the largest banquets Slater was responsible for organizing.

The $100-per-plate dinner doubled as a fundraiser for the City of Hope Medical Center in California.[70] The dinner at the Sherman Hotel attracted 750 people, including luminaries such as Jackie Robinson, Larry Doby, Ralph Metcalfe, Jesse Owens, Big Ten commissioner Tug Wilson, former MLB commissioner "Happy" Chandler, Charles Comiskey, and Chicago mayor Richard Daley.[71] Also attending the tribute to Saperstein was nearly every former Globetrotter, including all 31 members of the original 1927 Globetrotter team.[72] Slater was congratulated for making the tribute "one of the most memorable civic events ever held in Chicago."[73]

Judge Slater interacted with some of the biggest names in the African American community. He was a frequent guest at the annual Robert S. Abbott Award ceremonies, where he mingled with notables including poet Langston Hughes and attorney Thurgood Marshall.[74] In May 1958, Slater attended a huge tribute for Branch Rickey at the Grand Ballroom of the Conrad Hilton Hotel. Duke joined Jackie Robinson, Governor William Stratton, Ernie Banks, Frank Robinson, Ralph Metcalfe, William L. Dawson, Joe Louis, Illinois state representative Corneal A. Davis and many others in honoring Rickey.[75]

A few months after honoring Rickey, it was Slater's turn. For years, James A. Peterson, president of the bottled water firm of Hinckley and Schmitt, planned an annual football luncheon in Chicago immediately before the College All-Star Football Game. Peterson selected one player every year to honor at the luncheon and published an accompanying book that told the athlete's life story. Previous players so honored included Harry Kipke, George Gipp, Red Grange, Walter Eckersall, and Jim Thorpe. Duke Slater was Peterson's choice in 1958.

On August 13, 1958, Slater arrived as the guest of honor at his testimonial luncheon, and it attracted a larger crowd than any prior Peterson banquet. Red Grange, who was honored at the first Peterson luncheon, was the master of ceremonies for the Slater tribute. Guests present included Hawkeye teammates Glenn and Aubrey Devine, Gordon Locke, Lester Belding, and Bill Kelly. Burt Ingwersen, Duke's Clinton High School teammate, and Elmer Layden and Joe Guyon, his teammates with the Rock Island Independents, were also on hand. Several opponents took part in the tribute as well, including Jim McMillen of Illinois, Charles McGuire of Chicago, Roger Kiley and Hunk Anderson of Notre Dame, and Laurie Walquist of Illinois. Others in attendance included Clinton Osborne, Stub Barron, and Chicago mayor Richard Daley.[76]

Locke recalled that Slater could knock down two men with one of his long arms and grab the ball carrier with the other. Other speakers mentioned that Slater's tremendous reach, combined with the size of his feet, made it almost impossible to get around him or knock him over.[77] Mayor Daley declared, "Judge Slater, as a judge, sportsman, and gentleman, is doing the kind of job in the courts that he did on the football field."[78] Slater spoke at the end of the evening, closing his remarks by stating, "As we move toward a better world, I believe that the people connected with sports will play a tremendous part in our advance toward better understanding."[79]

The Chicago newspapers gave tribute to Duke as well. "Judge Slater, one of the greatest blocking backfield men in football history, has been acclaimed as both 'a leader of men and boys in Chicago,'" stated the *Defender*. "Judge Slater's life and career are another forceful lesson that leadership is primarily a matter of example. And Duke Slater has been a worthy example to all America."[80] The *Daily News* added, "Judge Duke Slater, we salute you—not only as a great football player but as a leader in your community."[81]

Celebrities often enlisted Judge Slater's assistance in legal matters. For example, he performed the September 4, 1958, wedding ceremony of jazz singer Sarah Vaughan to former college football standout Clyde Atkins.[82] It was the second marriage for Vaughan, one of the greatest jazz singers alive. Sarah didn't have a bridesmaid, however, so trumpeter Dizzy Gillespie volunteered his services. When Dizzy was asked how he felt about the wedding, he replied, "I'm nervous; I've never been a bridesmaid before."[83]

Slater maintained an active interest in all sports and was an avid baseball fan. The Negro Leagues were nearing extinction as Major League Baseball slowly poached the league's best players, but it still existed in 1958. The East-West Classic of the Negro American Baseball League was held at Comiskey Park that year, and Duke Slater and Jackie Robinson were recognized on the field prior to the game. The two sports legends then watched the game from the box seats.[84]

Meanwhile, the 1958 World Series pitted the New York Yankees against the Milwaukee Braves. Slater and several other notable African Americans were rooting for the Braves and their star right fielder, Hank Aaron. Duke even traveled with several friends to Milwaukee to watch games six and seven of the Series.[85] After game six, he attended a party thrown by Milwaukee physician George H. Lane along with Cubs star Ernie Banks.[86] Unfortunately for Slater, his Braves blew a 3–2 series lead and lost to the Yankees in seven games.

The outlook was much better for Duke's Hawkeyes, however. Iowa won the 1959 Rose Bowl for their second victory in Pasadena in three years. The decisive play of the game was a Rose Bowl record, 81-yard run by African American halfback Bob Jeter. But not surprisingly, it was the linemen who captured Duke's attention. He said, "The thing I noticed in the Rose Bowl game was the tremendous line play, and that's a sign of great coaching. In particular, I noticed the blocking of Gary Grouwinkel and John Nocera. We all were excited by Jeter's great run, but we tended to forget those boys 25 yards back up field who threw the blocks to get him loose."[87]

Duke and Ozzie Simmons attended a testimonial dinner two weeks later to honor Iowa coach Forest Evashevski. "When Duke arose in response to Milo Hamilton's introduction," columnist Dan Burley wrote, "the house came down. Secret of why they and everybody else likes him — Dignity, man, dignity! And incidentally, all man, too! You get the same impression when you watch Duke in public that you got watching Jack Johnson, Rube Foster, Willis Ward, Harry Wills, Paul Robeson, Joe Louis, Jackie Robinson, Levi Jackson, Ralph Metcalfe, and Jesse Owens in public view!"[88]

Slater received high recognition for his civic work in 1959 when he was elected to the Executive Board of the Chicago Boy Scout Council at a meeting held at Edgewater Beach Hotel. The president of the Chicago Scout Council, Wayne A. Johnston, announced, "The Chicago Council, Boy Scouts of America, is proud to have fine citizens such as Judge Slater serve on its executive board. There is no greater service a man can give to our community than that of working with its greatest resource, youth. This executive board is a hardworking group and the abilities exhibited by Judge Slater will be an important asset. The job is a big one and the challenge is worthy of his skill."[89]

First and foremost, however, Judge Slater was an advocate for increased civil rights from his seat on the bench. His keen legal mind was on display when he returned to Clinton, Iowa, to address the Clinton County Bar Association's annual meeting in 1959. "The vital, stabilizing role that lawyers have played in the development of this nation was cited by Judge Fred W. 'Duke' Slater of Chicago," the *Herald* reported. "Utilizing his resonant voice, the Chicago municipal judge ... paid special tribute to the part the legal profession has played in the growth of the nation. Judge Slater also briefly touched upon the issues of segregation and integration. He said he felt the U.S. Supreme Court members had exhibited remarkable courage in their position on the racial matters. He stated that Gov. J. Lindsay Almond, Jr. of Virginia deserves special commendation as he had his own deep-seated convictions but was magnanimous to go along when he found the highest courts and the law of the land at variance with him."[90]

Judge Slater approached the end of his second six-year term in the Municipal Court. He was still one of only three African American judges in the Chicago courts, and none of them were members of the Superior Court system, the highest judicial circuit in Chicago. With over a decade of experience on the bench, Slater was a perfect candidate to become Chicago's first African American Superior Court judge. He and Republican George S. Barnes were nominated by the Chicago League of Negro Voters through their respective parties for election.[91] Two weeks later, the Cook County Bar Association, composed of 400 African American lawyers, endorsed six black candidates for the Superior Court. Slater led the Bar Poll with the highest number of votes cast; only two missing votes kept it from being unanimous.[92]

The support of the Chicago NAACP was instrumental in Slater's judicial campaign. In January 1959, he conducted the oath of office for the officers and board members of the branch.[93] Four months later, Slater served on the faculty for a six-week study course run by the NAACP designed to help black patrolmen in the Chicago police department pass the examination for police sergeant.[94] Not surprisingly, Judge Slater's Superior Court candidacy earned the endorsement of the Chicago NAACP. Slater was lauded by the group as being "well-qualified and acceptable to an overwhelming number of the voters." The *Defender* noted, "Judge Slater has been a Chicagoland hero for more than 35 years."[95]

On November 3, 1959, Duke Slater won election to Chicago's Superior Court.[96] He became the first African American to ascend to the Superior Court in Chicago history.[97] Duke Slater was a pioneer on the football field and in the legal field, and his election to the Superior Court served as the crowning judicial achievement of an extraordinary man.

Chapter 16

Death of a Pioneer
(1959–1966)

"Fred 'Duke' Slater ... had many a great day on the football field. But none was greater or more memorable than the one here this week when he was elevated to the bench of the Superior Court of Cook County," Bill Evans reported.[1] Friends, relatives, and dignitaries jammed the courtroom of Judge John F. Bolton to witness the ceremonies. The crowd included Duke's wife, Etta, and his father-in-law, 96-year-old V.A. Searcy. Several members of Duke's family flew in from Los Angeles for the occasion. Football luminaries included Max Kadesky, Clinton Osborne, Judge Roger Kiley, and Erwin Prasse, a Chicago native and captain of Iowa's 1939 football team. Slater, looking physically fit, was given a standing ovation when he entered the courtroom.

The principal speaker at the event was Chicago mayor Richard Daley. "The community is fortunate in having a man like you to ascend the bench," the mayor said. He praised Slater as a "fine and dedicated public official [who] will fulfill all the definitions of a great judge."[2] Other high-profile speakers gave tributes as well. County clerk Edward Barrett predicted Slater would display the wisdom of Solomon as a jurist. State Rep. Corneal Davis called the occasion a history-making event and said, "As he has been superior in the past, he will be superior in the future." Reverend J.A. Portlock of Slater's Bethel A.M.E. Church even expressed hopes that Slater would ascend to the U.S. Supreme Court.[3]

Duke became so overwhelmed with emotion over the outpouring of support that he was only able to speak for a short time before tears swelled in his eyes and he was forced to sit. He paid tribute to his family, his church, local organizations, and his friends. Although Duke was aware that he was making judicial history for African Americans in Chicago, he was satisfied that he earned the position because of his character and wisdom rather than the color of his skin. "The thing that pleased me most about this," Slater commented, "is that nothing was said about my race."[4]

Not everyone was pleased about Slater's appointment. State's Attorney Benjamin S. Adamowski loudly criticized Slater's judgment just days after his election to the Superior Court. Adamowski considered the prosecution of illegal gambling rings one of the great priorities of his term in office. The previous year, two men were brought before Judge Slater on gambling equipment possession charges. The men were initially stopped for running a red light, and police searched their trunks to find the equipment. Judge Slater acquitted the men after ruling that searching their trunk without a warrant violated both the U.S. and Illinois Constitutions, adding that police could only search a vehicle "as they can see it" unless they obtain either a warrant or consent. The practice of local police searching glove compartments and trunks of cars stopped for minor violations had drawn complaints on the South Side for some time. Adamowski openly protested the decision and immediately ordered a probe to determine whether the gamblers could be indicted on similar charges.[5]

From then on, Adamowski's office sought to obtain the necessary warrants for their gambling stings from Judge Slater, but another dispute quickly followed. The State's Attorney's office set up a raid on a suspected gambling site and pushed for Duke to sign the search warrants quickly. "I think at the time it was a question of secrecy. They wanted to make the raid before it became known publicly what was about to happen," Slater recalled.[6]

The judge hastily signed a search warrant for Adamowski's office, a move he later came to regret when he discovered that the basis for their raid was a newspaper story. Officers in the raid seized money from a safe as evidence, but the cash couldn't be directly tied to any gambling activities at the location. Nevertheless, the men were brought in on gambling charges and taken before Slater.

Judge Slater acknowledged he shouldn't have authorized the warrants on a newspaper article alone. He was also unimpressed by the evidence the raid uncovered. "If it had been money taken from a dice game or some other form of obvious gambling, it would have been different, but not money from a safe," the judge declared.[7] Regardless, when he heard the justification for the raid, he reconsidered and quashed the evidence. Slater's reversal drew sharp condemnation from Adamowski at the time, and these disputes led to Adamowski fiercely criticizing Slater's election to the Superior Court. Judge Slater was asked in turn for his opinion of Adamowski, but the judge tersely offered no comment.[8]

Despite Adamowski's objections, Slater was a Superior Court judge. Since he was assigned to hear criminal cases in the Superior Court, Judge Slater tried some of the most heinous cases in the city. He noted that long-standing racist attitudes often cheapened the value of a black person's life, resulting in light sentences for African Americans convicted of murdering one of their own. Those attitudes were slowly changing, and Judge Slater vowed to continue such progress by enforcing stiff sentences against convicted African American murderers.[9] In his first month on the job, Judge Slater sentenced a man to fifty years in prison for rape and found another man guilty of stabbing his roommate to death during a quarrel over 35 cents.[10]

However, Judge Slater also followed the rule of law. When a Dubuque woman was hospitalized in Chicago in critical condition and alleged it was due to a botched abortion, her Peoria doctor was arrested and charged. The doctor testified he only treated the woman for an innocuous infection, and on February 9, Judge Slater acquitted the doctor of the charges.[11] Slater also acquitted three defendants of murder in two separate cases in his first six months on the bench.

In June, Judge Slater heard a case brought by convicted robber Richard Morrison. Morrison accused police lieutenant Sigmund Wroblewski of accepting $2,500 to fix an auto theft charge. When Slater acquitted Wroblewski of bribery on July 5, 1960, Benjamin Adamowski's chief assistant, Frank Ferlic, went on the attack. Ferlic criticized those four acquittals by Slater, assailing Slater's "disgraceful conduct" and calling the acquittals "gross miscarriages of justice."

Ferlic declared, "We are not allowed a change of venue from judges like Fred Slater. Mayor Daley has erred in almost 99 percent of the judges he has put on the slate. The selection of Fred W. Slater was one of the more grievous errors committed by the mayor."[12]

Of the Wroblewski case, Ferlic said the evidence presented by the state went unchallenged, undenied, and corroborated.[13] He continued, "The testimony that a lieutenant of police accepted a bribe was corroborated, and the charge remains undenied. The court did not follow the law or the evidence. This is part and parcel of what is called Cook County justice."[14] Ferlic announced he was sending a letter to the Chicago Bar Association recommending incompetence on the part of Slater.[15]

Judge Slater told a reporter he regretted having to defend his decisions through the newspapers, and he said that he didn't intend to make a habit of doing so. But he then blasted Ferlic's charges as "hot air" and explained his position on the Wroblewski case. Slater acquitted Wroblewski, in part, because the judge said he wouldn't believe Morrison "on a stack of Bibles." He said of Ferlic, "He's downstairs in his big office, and he never hears the evidence or the testimony. I have to make the decision on the basis of what I hear in the courtroom, not from what the grand jury reports."[16]

Slater also responded to Ferlic's statement that 23 men and women agreed to indict Wroblewski. "An indictment is not a trial," the judge said. "If one must be guided by the grand jury, what is the necessity of the trial? The only people who go before the grand jury are the state's witnesses and the prosecuting witness. The public must understand that this is not a trial." He added that this was all he intended to say on the matter, since he didn't want to engage in a running feud with the State's Attorney's office. Nevertheless, Judge Slater challenged Ferlic's threat to send a letter suggesting his incompetence, declaring, "If he has anything against me, let him bring it before the bar."[17]

The State's Attorney's office continued to find fault in Slater's allegedly light sentences. The following month, Slater sentenced six city employees to probation after being convicted of stealing $437 of electric cables. Adamowski recommended a year or two of imprisonment, contending that the thefts were aggravated because the men were in a position of trust as city employees. Judge Slater instead opted for probation since the men had no prior criminal records. When he heard Slater's sentence, Adamowski replied, "This is another example of how the courts are preventing us from sending criminals to jail. It's a shocking indictment of the entire city system."[18] Slater, conversely, maintained his typical good humor. When told Adamowski was "up in the air" over his ruling, Slater cracked, "Where did he land? On his head or on his feet?"[19]

The criticism of Judge Slater's rulings died down considerably when Adamowski was roundly defeated in his re-election campaign in November 1960. Slater had no further troubles with Adamowski's successors at the State's Attorney's office. However, in December 1960, the judge was transferred from the Criminal Court to hear civil suits, and the media interpreted the move as punitive. One daily newspaper charged that Slater was being exiled to the county's judicial Siberia because his rulings embarrassed Democrats.[20]

For his part, Judge Slater was unperturbed by the news. "It is a well-known fact that newly-elected judges are always sent to Criminal Court. I don't know anything about being exiled," he replied. "I enjoyed my work here and I am going to enjoy it where I'm going."[21] Mayor Richard Daley assailed the newspaper reports as inaccurate and malicious, suggesting that the story was an attempt to turn "certain groups" against his administration. He declared that contrary to being exiled, the move should be considered a promotion, since, as Slater suggested, new judges typically began in criminal court before being assigned to civil courts.[22]

On the heels of his battles with the State's Attorney's office and the controversy over his court transfer, the Joint Negro Appeal prepared a major tribute dinner for Judge Slater at the Grand Ballroom of the Sherman Hotel. The JNA, a large volunteer organization composed of fifteen different community welfare agencies, was citing Duke for his contributions to charitable and youth-serving causes. Judge Slater received a plaque honoring him as an "outstanding All-American athlete, civic leader, and distinguished jurist."[23]

Over 500 people appeared at the JNA tribute. Attorney Frank H. Uriell lauded Judge Slater as "a generous, kind, and helping individual [and] truly an All-American gentleman."[24] One of Duke's longtime friends testified that Judge Slater had always been for the individual on the bottom, particularly youngsters facing a lifetime of restricted opportunities, and this quality of compassion and sympathy was what made him such a merciful judge.[25]

But the surprise of the evening was an appearance by Mayor Daley, who used the occasion to publicly support Slater after a tumultuous initial year in the Superior Court. Daley expressed complete confidence in his judgment, affirming that he had the highest regard for the judge and didn't "know another man who has served two courts as well as Judge Slater has."[26] Daley blasted the press for reporting that he felt Slater was an embarrassment to the Democratic administration. "Nothing was more contemptible or untrue," Mayor Daley said. "Judge Slater represents the best in citizenship and the best in the judiciary."[27]

Judge Slater soon had company on the Superior Court bench. James B. Parsons was elected to the Superior Court, joining Slater as the second African American in the circuit. Slater and Parsons had dinner in the judges' dining room, an event newspapers called historic, and Duke joined Mayor Daley to speak at Parsons' installation ceremony.[28] Judge Parsons only served on the Superior Court for one year; in 1961, he became the first African American federal judge after being nominated to the U.S. District Court by President Kennedy. Slater served as chairman of a testimonial dinner supporting Parsons' selection to the District Court.[29]

One of the saddest events of Duke's life took place in 1962. His wife, Etta, had been in ill health since September 27, 1960. That day started as a normal one for Judge Slater. He called his wife in the afternoon, and Etta reminded him to bring home some meat from the grocery store for their evening meal. When Duke arrived home shortly after 5 P.M., he discovered Etta in the bedroom, unresponsive and bleeding from a bullet wound in the abdomen.[30] Duke owned a .38-caliber pistol, a standard protective measure in a rough South Side neighborhood.[31] Etta was cleaning the bedroom closet when the gun somehow discharged, entering her upper abdomen and passing through her back. Mrs. Slater was rushed to the emergency room and listed in critical condition.[32]

Etta Slater, had been in perfect health before that incident, never fully recovered. On March 24, 1962, Duke's wife of 35 years passed away in her sleep of an apparent heart attack. Mrs. Slater, an Iowa graduate, once taught school at Langston University and in Kansas City, Missouri. Early in their marriage, Etta was employed by the U.S. Bureau of Health in Chicago and by the Cook County Department of Welfare. She retired in 1942 to become a full-time housewife.[33] Mrs. Slater shied away from the public spotlight, and as a result, relatively little is known about her. But she was a quiet support for her husband during the final years of his NFL career through his years as a lawyer and judge. Etta remains an unsung foundation behind Duke's many accomplishments, and her untimely death was a sad tragedy.

Now a widower, Duke immersed himself with volunteer work in the community. Duke Slater served on the Jesse Owens Education Foundation board of directors; the Foundation gave scholarships to aspiring students regardless of gender, race, or athletic ability.[34] He was also chairman of the City of Hope's Sportsman's Award Dinner, held on April 27, 1963, at the Chicago Sheraton Hotel. Ernie Banks was selected as the group's first award winner.[35] Slater renewed acquaintances at the event with Fred Gillies, Duke's teammate and coach with the Chicago Cardinals.[36]

Judge Slater received several awards for his civic work. He joined Vice President Richard Nixon, New York Congressman Adam Clayton Powell, Jesse Owens, Ernie Banks, and several others in receiving an award in human relations from the Order of Eastern Star.[37] In addition, nearly 300 lawyers, judges, and friends of the Cook County Bar Association honored Slater with an award for his contribution to the legal profession and to the city of Chicago.[38]

The Chicago Committee of One Hundred, an organization of business people, saluted Judge Slater for his contributions in the field of race relations by giving him one of their annual "Good American" awards in 1963. The president of the committee stated, "We are convinced that these public testimonials are more than token recognition of our honorees' contributions in the area of human relations. We believe that they inspire others to move more determinedly toward erasing from the American conscience the ugly scars of racial and religious bigotry." Those honored in addition to Slater included civil rights author Sarah Patton Boyle, Ford Motor Company chairman Henry Ford II, Attorney General Robert F. Kennedy, entertainer Ed Sullivan, Jackie Robinson, and Dr. Martin Luther King, Jr.[39]

Fred and Etta Slater were married for 35 years until her death in 1962. She was buried in Mount Glenwood Cemetery on Chicago's far South Side.

Duke Slater had been the picture of physical health for most of his life. His appendix ruptured in 1941, which left him in serious condition and resulted in an emergency hospital visit that lasted nearly a month.[40] He also underwent surgery at Provident Hospital in 1958 for an undisclosed reason, but for the most part, Duke never had any serious medical problems.[41] The former athlete was still physically fit in his sixties, although his athletic interests were limited to golf; he attended the Choi-Settes Golf Tourney on June 22 and 23, 1963, where he had a nice photo opportunity with two of his golfing buddies, Jackie Robinson and Joe Louis.[42]

Two months later, Duke collapsed on a golf course. He was rushed to the hospital and diagnosed with a heart attack.[43] Slater had three operations at Provident Hospital and was dangerously ill. His aunt, Pauline Slater, came to Chicago from Los Angeles to care for him. Duke lost thirty pounds and spent over three months in the Chicago hospital.[44]

As he slowly recuperated, Duke accompanied his aunt back to her home in Los Angeles. He kept an active interest in football despite his serious health issues. While in California, he visited Pasadena for the 1964 Rose Bowl game between Washington and Illinois and had a reunion with his former Clinton teammate, Illinois assistant coach Burt Ingwersen. The Los Angeles City Council used the occasion of his visit to present Duke with a scroll that depicted highlights of his football and legal careers. A fragile Slater was emotionally affected by the tribute.[45]

Duke was restored to full health by early 1964. The *Gazette* reported, "He is carrying a full load of cases and is looking and feeling fine. He looks and acts as if he could go a full sixty minutes."[46] When Slater returned to work later that year, a constitutional amendment in Illinois reorganized the court system into nineteen unified circuit courts. As a result, Superior Court Judge Slater became Circuit Court Judge Slater. The new Circuit Court of Cook County featured judges, associate judges, and magistrates. There were five African American Circuit Court judges after the reorganization, with Slater as the senior judge of the five.

Judge Slater was transferred to the divorce division and presided over divorce proceedings.[47] In the wake of losing his wife of many years, he was greatly troubled by the perilous state of modern marriages. "Divorce is a serious problem," Duke declared. "It calls for attention. Anything that could conceivably lessen the number of divorces should be tried."[48]

Despite his earlier scuffles with the State's Attorney's office, Duke was a widely respected jurist. Controversy arose in 1964 over the bar poll conducted by the Chicago Bar Association. The poll surveyed Chicago lawyers about the competence of judges, and a vote under 70 percent tagged a judge with being unfit to serve by the bar. The poll was accused of having a racial bias against black judges, especially considering the Chicago Bar Association didn't even admit African Americans until after World War II. In an investigation, it was revealed that Judge Slater only polled a 74.4 rating in the bar poll in 1956, which would have put him reasonably close to being disbarred. The fact that a well-respected judge like Slater scored so poorly added weight to bias charges against the poll.[49]

That was just one of the racial issues brought up in Chicago in the mid–1960s, as the civil rights movement was in full swing. One of the biggest events in this movement occurred when Dr. Martin Luther King, Jr., visited the Windy City in August 1964. King was the featured speaker at the Illinois Rally for Civil Rights at Soldier Field, where 75,000 people sold out the stadium to celebrate the passing of the civil rights bill in the Senate. Sitting on a platform on stage near the center of the field were two dozen prominent guests, including civil rights leader Al Raby, jazz singer Nancy Wilson, and Judge Slater. The crowd roared as Reverend King called for continued demonstrations and an immediate end to segregation.[50] Slater went on to hear King speak on several other occasions as well.[51]

Duke was regarded as a living legend among African American athletes. Larry Whiteside, a sportswriter with the *Kansas City Kansan*, compiled a list of "legendary Negro athletes" for *Black World Magazine* and mentioned Duke Slater, Jesse Owens, Jackie Robinson, Marion Motley, Wilt Chamberlain, and Oscar Robertson. "These men proved to the world that the Negro athlete could hold his own with anyone," Whiteside wrote. "Often theirs was a lonely and thankless fight, but they made their point."[52]

As a sports pioneer for African Americans, Duke Slater was often selected to honor other such trailblazers. He was chosen to present several former Negro League ballplayers with citations for their contributions to baseball at a game between the Indianapolis Clowns and the New York Stars at Comiskey Park.[53] He also helped the Cubs honor a former Negro Leaguer of their own on July 15, 1964, when he appeared at Wrigley Field for "Ernie Banks Day." Joining Slater at the event were several baseball greats, including Hall of Fame Yankee shortstop Phil Rizzuto. Rizzuto was impressed by Slater's response when a reporter asked Duke what he thought of the festivities. "They honored a top athlete and a fine man," Duke said of Banks. Then he echoed Banks' remarks when he said, "I especially liked Ernie's words, 'I am proud to be born an American.'"[54]

Duke Slater was active his whole life in the A.M.E. denomination of churches where his father had been a minister. For decades, Duke Slater attended Chicago's Bethel A.M.E. Church at 4448 Michigan Avenue, where he served on the board of trustees.

Slater was also proud to be an Iowan. He made a habit of attending Iowa's homecoming game every year, where he sat as an honored guest in the box occupied by the governor of the state and the mayor of the city.[55] Duke's heart attack in 1963 forced him to miss the entire season for the first time since 1935, but he pledged to start a new yearly streak in 1964.[56] As promised, Duke attended the Hawkeyes' 1964 season-opening home game against Washington. Members of Iowa's famous 1939 Ironman team were also on hand for their 25-year reunion. On the day of the game, Duke Slater was walking down the street on his way to the stadium when he passed Max Hawkins' house, where the Ironmen were gathered, and one of the Ironmen spotted Duke. "When the word got around, all of the Ironmen came charging out of the house like ants out of the ant hill to greet the Duke," the *Cedar Rapids Gazette* reported. "Guess even the heroes have heroes, huh?"[57]

Duke Slater, a minister's son, had been a man of strong faith all his life. He was a trustee of Bethel A.M.E. Church at 4448 Michigan Avenue in Chicago.[58] He joined in the celebration of the church's 100-year anniversary, and his fundraising helped the church hold a ceremonial dinner to "burn" the church's mortgage.[59] For Christmas in 1965, Duke's church family repaid him by presenting him with a "This Is Your Life" program and reminiscing on all the great moments of his life and career. The pastor of the church said they were honoring Judge Slater because he contributed so much to the church as well as to the community.[60]

The program was held at an appropriate time. Duke entered Wesley Memorial Hospital on March 25, 1966, for a bowel obstruction. Doctors found the obstruction was caused by a tumor, and he was diagnosed with stomach cancer. Slater was soon told his condition was terminal, and after more than two months in the hospital, he informed the medical staff that he wanted to die at home. He returned to his South Side home at 4800 South Chicago Beach Drive on June 1, where he spent the final months of his life.[61] On August 14, 1966, Fred "Duke" Slater's remarkable life came to a close.

Chapter 17

A Legend in His Lifetime (1966–1972)

"Judge Fred 'Duke' Slater, whose death at 67 is also mourned by thousands who never read the sports pages, was one of the great men who made University of Iowa's Hawkeyes great in football," wrote David Condon in the *Chicago Tribune*. "Duke Slater's prominence illustrated that Negroes could win acclaim in the National Football League almost a quarter century before baseball backtracked on its lamentable color line."[1] Though Slater's death transcended sports, fans of the gridiron might have felt his absence the most. "Today the entire football world misses the Duke," Condon continued. "Whenever fine friends gather to talk football, they talk of the likes of Duke Slater. The pioneers of the National Professional League will remember the Duke's rugged career.... That's because football is a grand old game, and because Duke Slater was one of the hardies who made it so grand."[2]

Duke Slater's life was fondly remembered in Iowa City, where he had such a profound influence on the University of Iowa. "It was an honor and a pleasure to have known such a humble and sincere person as the 'Judge' or 'Your Honor,' as his many friends so affectionately called him," Al Miller of the *Cedar Rapids Gazette* recalled. "His deep voice and well-chosen words commanded attention. During a conversation two years ago, he expressed some concern as to why Iowa wasn't able to obtain a larger number of Negro athletes from a town the size of Chicago. But, whether the athletes were Negro or white, it didn't matter to Duke. Iowa athletics and especially football were No. 1 with the Hall of Famer, and he never stopped working to bring the best type of athlete to the Iowa City school. He will be missed."[3]

Slater's recruiting efforts were not lost on one great former Hawkeye coach. "Duke was a great Hawkeye who surely will be missed," Iowa athletic director Forest Evashevski said. "He helped me a great deal during my coaching days at Iowa. Duke was very instrumental in getting quite a few high school players for Iowa. He was a great morale booster."[4] Russ Smith of the *Waterloo Courier* agreed. "Slater, perhaps the best known of all ex–Hawkeyes unless it was the late Nile Kinnick, [was] a great asset to the Hawkeyes in the Chicago area recruiting," Smith observed. "He'll remain an inspiration to other youngsters who'll wear the Gold and Black in the future."[5]

Iowa City wasn't the only place where Duke Slater was seen as a role model. His high school years in Clinton, Iowa, gave Duke an eternal love for the Mississippi River town. Bob Fleischer of the *Clinton Herald* noted that Judge Slater's modesty and work ethic served as an inspiration for Clinton youth. "Duke's greatest achievements were not on the football field but rather in the field of life. Duke, a Negro, had to struggle beyond the prejudices that have too often stopped others. Yet he was accepted, not because of his race or in spite of it, but because he was a true gentleman.... Duke had every reason to become egocentric. Here was a man who rose through tremendous trials to a marked success. He hauled coal and shined shoes long before he became a judge. Yet he was humble and always remembered old friends," Fleischer wrote. "Duke did rise above the petty prejudices of life. He proved his worth as a man, well enough to teach a lesson to the world. Duke, you see, was a big man. He was very special. He'll be remembered that way."[6]

His Clinton teammate, Burt Ingwersen, was amazed at Duke's amiability. "No man who ever knocked over so many people ever had so many friends," Ingwersen said.[7] One of those friends who would never forget his mentor was Ozzie Simmons. "He was the kind of man you'd like to have as your father, your brother, or your friend," Simmons remarked. "Slater had quite a lot of influence on me. He kept me in school because I had several offers to do other things which, in the end, would not have been beneficial."[8]

Meanwhile, all across the Windy City, notables lined up to mourn the passing of one of the most colorful jurists in Chicago's history.[9] Mayor Richard Daley declared, "The passing of Judge Fred Slater is saddening to me and to thousands of his Chicago fellow citizens. He was a real leader of men and a model for youngsters, and he will be greatly missed."[10]

The void in Chicago's courts left by Judge Slater's death was felt, too. Illinois Chief Circuit Judge Samuel Boyle eulogized, "Judge Slater was a good lawyer and a perfect gentleman. He was highly regarded by his associates, a religious man who set a fine example for youth."[11] Judge Robert L. Hunter said Slater "was respected as an honest, intelligent, and fair man who followed the law."[12]

Edward L. Davis served as Slater's court clerk for three years. "This tenure was not without both gratitude and excitement," Davis recalled. "On many occasions, Judge Slater would go way beyond the call of duty to help the poor as well as the rich to solve their problems. It was an extreme pleasure to work with a man so highly respected by people of all races, nationalities, and professions. Judge Slater, or 'Duke' as he was so often referred to, was an asset to this great country of ours."[13] Even the man tasked with sorting out Slater's estate had the utmost respect for his client. "On many occasions, the judge rendered big-brother counseling. It was through people like him that I became a lawyer," said attorney Wilson Frost. He asserted that Slater "was well thought of by the lawyers who practiced in his court and his colleagues on the bench."[14]

The *Chicago Defender* noted, "Slater was one of this city's few jurists who possessed 'street smarts' commensurate with his book learning. It was this quality, coupled with quick wit, which made him one of the people who made Chicago the fabulous city that it is."[15] *Defender* columnist Leonard Foster called Slater "one of the irreplaceables." "Fred 'Duke' Slater was another of those titans who seem to be on the way to extinction," Foster wrote. "We will survive his loss, but the world is a worse place without him."[16]

Phil Rizzuto, who met Slater years earlier at Wrigley Field, eulogized the judge on his national radio show, *Sports Time*. Calling Slater "strong as the proverbial ox [and] a working model of everyday sportsmanship both on and off the field," Rizzuto dwelled on Duke's post-football achievements. "What he earned with his body went towards the nourishment of his brain, in his case, law school," Rizzuto noted. "If you ask, perhaps, what all this has to do with *Sports Time*, my answer is, 'Plenty.' Because any former athlete of national stature automatically is on the spot for as long as he lives. If he becomes a bum in his private life, those who get their kicks from throwing rocks at former headliners have a field day. Apparently they never cast even a pebble at the likes of Superior Court Judge Duke Slater."[17]

Rizzuto continued by marveling at the example Slater set for African American youth. "With all the tensions, racial and otherwise, making the rounds today, Duke Slater must have been a lighthouse in the dark skies of South Chicago! The son of a Negro clergyman, Slater must have been raised to stand on his own two feet! Proud in his knowledge that in America, as in no other country, a man, regardless of creed or color, can advance by the sweat of his brow and the muscle of his mind."[18]

Herb Lyon of the *Chicago Tribune* called Slater "a shining example for all. He proved that racial adversity can be overcome by any dedicated individual, and his whole career was exemplary proof."[19] *Jet Magazine* summarized Duke's life, writing, "During his lifetime, Duke Slater had inspired a legend of greatness that included not only heroic feats on the football field, but a superhuman determination to overcome epic hurdles, and a human warmth and influence which, divine-like, heavily shaped the lives of those he knew."[20]

Duke Slater's body laid in state on August 19 at Bethel A.M.E. Church until his funeral there the following day.[21] His pallbearers included judges, doctors, attorneys, aldermen, and two football players to whom he served as a mentor—Sherman Howard and Ozzie Simmons. Mayor Daley attended the funeral, and tributes were sent by George Halas, Ernie Nevers, and many others.[22] Margaret Culbertson Jetter, a Clinton relative, attended the funeral. "The streets were full of cars and limousines. I have never seen such a crowd at a funeral. The church was packed and there were all kinds of dignitaries," she said. Another of Duke's Clinton relatives, Elizabeth Stewart Jones, said, "There was never a kinder, friendlier man than the Duke. We all loved him."[23]

Slater was buried in Mount Glenwood Cemetery on Chicago's far South Side.[24] He was laid to rest next to his wife, Etta, and just a few feet from cyclist Marshall "Major" Taylor, the first African American to achieve the level of world champion. The epitaph on Duke Slater's tombstone summed up his unparalleled career, labeling him simply as "A Legend in His Lifetime."

For someone who grew up in poverty, Judge Slater died a financially secure man. He emerged from a family that couldn't afford a six-dollar football helmet in his high school playing days to become one of the wealthiest men in his Chicago neighborhood. Duke's job as a judge garnered him $12,000 a year when he took the bench in 1948, and that figure rose in the decades that followed.[25] When he died, he left behind an estate of around $35,000 and a legacy as a true American rags-to-riches story.[26]

Posthumous tributes to Slater began to take shape. The Chicago Varsity Club created a Fred "Duke" Slater award to honor their first president. The Slater Award was handed out for at least five years.[27] Earl Banks, the head coach at Morgan State and a man Slater recruited to the University of Iowa, won the inaugural award; Emlen Tunnell made the presentation.[28]

Duke was still recognized as one of the greatest college football players of all time. To commemorate the 100th anniversary of college football in 1969, the Football Writers Association of America selected 44 players for an all-century squad.[29] Duke Slater was the only Hawkeye chosen and one of seven Big Ten players on the squad.[30] The following year, Duke was picked for an all-time all–Big Ten team by the Big Ten Conference in conjunction with the league's 75th anniversary.[31] That same year, Hawkeye fans chose Slater as the third greatest football player in school history behind Nile Kinnick and Calvin Jones.

The University of Iowa dramatically felt Slater's absence in the spring of 1969. Many black football players were eager to secure more benefits for African American athletes at Iowa, and they threatened to boycott spring practice. With Duke no longer around to serve as a buffer between these athletes and the Iowa coaching staff, the situation reached a boiling point. Sixteen black athletes boycotted Hawkeye football practice and were promptly kicked off the team, dooming the squad to an underachieving season. "Historically, this university has been good to the Negro athlete and the Negro athlete has been good to the university," Al Grady wrote sadly in the *Press-Citizen*. He noted that Slater was one of the earliest and most prominent African American athletes in Big Ten history and that he remained a loyal follower of the Hawkeyes throughout his lifetime. But in a foreshadowing of the eventual marginalization of Slater's legacy, Grady noted, "One should realize and respect that today's black man does not want to be patronized with yesterday's history."[32]

Mount Glenwood Cemetery is the final resting place of Judge Fred W. "Duke" Slater, a legendary athlete and judge.

Duke Slater may have been yesterday's history, but he was still listed among the greatest African American athletes of all time. "The American Negro athlete today is the greatest competitor in the history of organized sports," wrote author Bill Doherty. "He has been the champion since the middle forepart of the century when Jesse Owens, Joe Louis, Satchel Paige, Goose Tatum, and Duke Slater were leading the way."[33] Jimmy Blair, sportswriter for the *Galveston Daily News*, posed the question in 1972 of which black athlete contributed the most as a builder in the world of sports. He named six men—Jackie Robinson, Mel Whitfield, Willie Mays, Jesse Owens, Joe Louis, and Duke Slater.[34]

On September 17, 1971, the Urban League of Chicago organized a charity game at Soldier Field between two historically black universities. In a tribute befitting one of the great African American football players ever, Alcorn State and Grambling squared off for the Fred Duke Slater trophy, which was captured by Grambling after their 21–6 victory. The trophy was accepted at a post-game awards ceremony by Coach Eddie Robinson. "Robinson's pride in accepting the winning team trophy was apparent and well-deserved for a coach whose track record includes 195 victories and only 79 defeats in 29 seasons," the *Chicago Defender* reported.[35]

The University of Iowa grappled with the issue of how to best honor such a loyal and influential alumnus. The university followed the Chicago Varsity Club's lead and created the Duke Slater Award, granted annually to a Chicago athlete. Rick Brooks, a defensive back from Hales Franciscan High in Chicago, was the first recipient in 1970.[36] Initially, the award was just a plaque "presented in the memory of one of Iowa's greatest football players."[37] However, scholarships were soon attached to the award, with Ray Smith and Lorin Lynch receiving the first Duke Slater Scholarships in 1972.[38]

These were meaningful tributes, but the city of Chicago topped them all when it named an apartment complex in Slater's honor. "Judge Slater Apartments" was a senior citizens' complex located at 4218 S. Cottage Grove Avenue in Chicago. The apartments were designed

This apartment complex, located less than a mile from where Slater attended services at Bethel A.M.E. Church, serves as Chicago's living memorial to Judge Duke Slater.

for residents 62 years of age or older, and the complex still exists today. It stands as a lasting memorial to a Chicago icon, and the University of Iowa soon deliberated a similar honor for Slater. That debate would consume the Hawkeye campus in the summer of 1972.

Since 1929, the Hawkeye football team had played their home games at blandly-named Iowa Stadium. Iowa hadn't had a winning season in over a decade, and the football program was in serious need of some enthusiasm. Gus Schrader, the longtime sports editor of the *Cedar Rapids Gazette*, spearheaded a movement to rename Iowa Stadium after 1939 Heisman Trophy winner Nile Kinnick. When an Iowa fan questioned why Kinnick was being singled out for the honor over players like Duke Slater, Schrader's argument had four parts:

1. Kinnick represented, in Schrader's view, "the ideal combination of scholar-athlete, being a Phi Beta Kappa graduate and law student,"
2. Kinnick was the only Hawkeye to win the Heisman, Maxwell, and Walter Camp trophies,
3. Kinnick led a great team at Iowa that brought football success to the state after years of mediocrity, and
4. Kinnick was tragically killed in World War II.[39]

Of course, Slater, too, was an admirable scholar-athlete as a former All-American turned Iowa law school graduate, and the three awards Schrader listed hadn't even been created when Slater played at Iowa. The 1921 Hawkeyes stood alongside Kinnick's 1939 squad as one of the greatest teams in Hawkeye history, and Duke was clearly one of the leaders of that squad. And although Slater didn't have his life cut short by war, he was a racial pioneer who, through his recruiting efforts and image, changed the face of Hawkeye athletics.

Nevertheless, the clamor to name the stadium after Nile Kinnick grew loud enough to demand an answer from the school's administration. On June 5, 1972, University of Iowa president Willard L. Boyd formally announced his recommendation that Iowa Stadium be renamed in favor of both Nile Kinnick and Duke Slater. "Both of these individuals contributed greatly to the University, not simply as football players, but as human beings who exemplified throughout their lives what a University should be," Boyd wrote. He noted that a recent revival of interest in honoring Kinnick required a review of the history of Iowa football. "Such a review instantly brings to mind two great names: Nile Kinnick and Duke Slater," President Boyd said.

Boyd cited Slater as "a tower of Iowa football strength [who] enjoyed the widest acclaim and respect." Like Kinnick, President Boyd called Duke a modest person and a team player. He concluded, "I believe that each of them would consider this action more meaningful in every way than honoring the memory of one of them alone." Boyd's suggestion that Iowa Stadium be officially renamed "Kinnick-Slater Stadium" was placed before the University of Iowa campus planning committee for review.[41]

Gus Schrader responded angrily to what he called "an almost unbelievable suggestion," attributing the idea to political correctness run amok. "If Nile Kinnick had been born black instead of white, we're sure just as many Iowans would have been campaigning to name the stadium after him," Schrader sulked. "And if Duke Slater had been born white instead of black, we feel equally sure the same campaigners still would have preferred Kinnick Stadium to ... Kinnick-Slater Stadium."[42]

Schrader wasn't finished. "We would like to give President Boyd the benefit of the doubt and say he proposed Kinnick-Slater Stadium because he feels the two men were equally qualified to be so honored in Hawkeye football history," he wrote. "However, the evidence suggests he compromised to include a black man for fear of offending a segment of Iowa fans, administrators, and athletes."[43] To Schrader, the proposal of Kinnick-Slater Stadium amounted to little more than racial appeasement.

Naturally, Gus Schrader insisted he had "great affection, respect, and admiration" for Slater, despite having never seen him play. But he then proceeded to list out the reasons he felt Slater was unworthy of having his name on the stadium alongside Kinnick. "We have to point out that Duke never won a football trophy like the Heisman or the Maxwell, as Kinnick did," Schrader wrote.[44] Of course, neither the Heisman Trophy or the Maxwell Award had been created in 1921 when Duke played, but Schrader felt it was appropriate to hold Slater's inability to win nonexistent awards against him anyway.

"It should be noted Duke was one of the THREE All-American players on Iowa's 1921 team," Schrader continued, implying that Devine and Locke's honors meant Slater's role on the team was less than Kinnick's role for the Ironmen.[45] At no point did Schrader consider the fact that Devine and Locke's honors were made possible in part through Slater's tremendous line play. As former Big Ten commissioner Tug Wilson noted, "There was unanimous agreement that, despite the all-around brilliance of the undefeated Hawkeyes of 1921, there would have been a blemish or two on their record were it not for Duke Slater."[46]

Gus Schrader also took care to note that Slater was not a consensus first team All-American, because Slater had been snubbed by Walter Camp. He neglected to mention how controversial that decision was at the time and how it appears to be even more egregious an omission in hindsight. Slater's academic background failed to impress Schrader, either. "While Duke was a good student and later had a fine career in law, he did not make Phi Beta Kappa, as Kinnick did," Schrader argued.[47]

President Boyd wrote a letter to Schrader, defending his suggestion. "I am grateful to you for reading carefully my letter to the committee on the naming of university structures as it states clearly my reasons for suggesting inclusion of Judge Slater's name," Boyd wrote. "I greatly admired both Nile Kinnick and Fred Slater during their lives. Although it was not my privilege to know Nile Kinnick personally, I did see him play. It was, however, my great privilege to have been with Judge Slater on several occasions, the most thrilling of which was at the dedication of the University of Chicago law school several years ago where I had the privilege of representing the University of Iowa. Judge Slater was also serving as a delegate representing the bench of the city of Chicago, and I was greatly impressed by the esteem in which he was held by the members of the bench and bar in Chicago and within the university."[48]

Boyd and Schrader were clearly at a stalemate. Ivor W. Stanley, a Republican in the Iowa legislature, suggested a compromise. "Iowa's new recreation building northwest of the stadium doesn't have much of a name," Ivor reasoned. "Why not name it after Duke Slater — maybe Slater Hall or something like that — and the stadium after Kinnick?"[49]

In fact, attention turned to Iowa's newest residence hall, a 12-story building directly east of the Field House and the nearest residence hall to Iowa Stadium. Built in 1968, the new structure was directly across the street from Rienow Hall and had been temporarily named "Rienow Hall II." Both buildings were named after Robert Rienow, the dean of students when Slater was attending Iowa. Few were opposed to renaming Rienow II, so the university — and in particular, President Boyd — seized on the compromise. On June 15, 1972, Boyd officially endorsed to the Board of Regents that the university rename Iowa Stadium "Kinnick Stadium" and Rienow Hall II "Slater Hall."[50] The Board of Regents approved the proposal, and the University of Iowa planned both dedication ceremonies for the following fall.

"The first University of Iowa building to be named for a black person will be officially renamed and dedicated in a special ceremony," the *Iowa City Press-Citizen* reported in October.[51] When Duke Slater played football at the University of Iowa, he wasn't allowed to live in the dorms due to the color of his skin. Fifty years after he earned his bachelor's degree from Iowa, the university was naming an entire residence hall in his honor.

Rienow II was officially renamed Slater Hall on October 27, 1972. Despite President Boyd's initial concern over locating Slater's next of kin, three of Duke's sisters — Helen Coffey, Annabelle Phillips, and Aurora Hoskins — were in attendance for the ceremony. Two of Duke's nieces, Eliza Wilkins and Letha Coffey, also made it to Iowa City for the event. Boyd presided over the dedication and gave the opening remarks. Letha Coffey then spoke on behalf of the Slater family. She thanked the university for the tribute, concluding her remarks by saying, "My uncle loved this institution."[52] Finally, Slater's grand-nephew, 10-year-old Frederick Slater Davis, cut the ribbon and formally opened the residence hall.

Sports Information Director Eric Wilson used the occasion to reminisce about Duke. "Soft-spoken, polite, almost gentle in his usual weekday actions, Duke was a Saturday terror on the football field," Wilson recounted. "Seldom could he be taken out of a play.

Almost never fooled by foes' maneuvers and among the first down the field under punts, Slater typified the ideal interior lineman. This was true in 1921, his final collegiate season, and would also hold good in 1972, because Slater's mastery of fundamentals and his skill at execution would make him superb even in present day football."

Wilson then recalled an event he attended in Columbus, Ohio. "Amidst the elite in attendance, Duke stood out as the same kindly, modest, gentlemanly giant of his college days," he wrote. "Nothing ever changed him: professional law achievements or election to the National Football Hall of Fame and the Helms College Hall of Fame. Duke Slater had in abundance whatever ingredients go into the makeup of the complete man."[53]

The Slater family was treated royally during the weekend, riding in a car in the homecoming parade. Duke's three sisters were given roses at halftime of the Michigan State football game and received a standing ovation from the Hawkeye fans. The family later acknowledged they were very impressed by the university and the dedication ceremony.[54] Slater Hall would become Duke's permanent tribute from the university he loved.

Chapter 18

Fading from Memory (1973–2012)

Time passes, and legends fade. Clinton High School has tried to keep Slater's legend alive, naming him Clinton's Lineman of the Century in 1969. Bill Misiewicz, a teacher at Clinton High School, has taken a lead role in overseeing the construction of a permanent Duke Slater exhibit. The Slater display should help remind Clinton residents of the incredible accomplishments of one of their native sons, but those accomplishments are now nearly a century old. Many observers might now see Duke Slater as Grady did, yesterday's history. "He should be better remembered," local historian Gary Herrity admitted. "Duke's kind of forgotten. All the people that knew him are gone."[1]

The University of Iowa quickly forgot about Slater as well. In 1972, Iowa Stadium was officially renamed Kinnick Stadium, an event Gus Schrader called "the most satisfying project I ever undertook."[2] Over the last forty years, the University of Iowa has made significant efforts to keep the memory of Nile Kinnick alive. Pictures of him appear on signs all around Kinnick Stadium. In 2006, the university added several tributes to Kinnick during a substantial renovation of the stadium. A relief of Kinnick's touchdown run against Notre Dame in 1939 was carved into the side of the building, and a 12-foot bronze statue of Nile was unveiled at the entrance to the stadium.

On the other hand, no mention of Duke Slater can be found near Iowa's home field. Four decades after the Kinnick-Slater Stadium proposal was scuttled, Duke is completely absent from the grounds at Kinnick Stadium. One wall of the structure is adorned with plaques of every consensus All-American in school history, but thanks to Camp's snub back in 1921, Duke Slater cannot be found there. In fact, no permanent plaque, display, or tribute to Slater can be seen anywhere at the football stadium of the program to which he gave so much.

Since 1972, it has become apparent that naming the stadium after Kinnick and a residence hall after Slater were anything but equivalent tributes. While Kinnick's legacy in Iowa City is alive and well, Slater's accomplishments promptly receded into the background. The University of Iowa maintained a trophy case in the 1970s that displayed the massive shoes he wore to fame at Iowa.[3] The school also had a display at Slater Hall featuring dozens and dozens of pictures of Duke. Both of those displays have long since been torn down, and few even remember their existence.

Slater Hall looks much different today. Tributes to Duke Slater in the residence hall are disturbingly absent. No permanent plaque is affixed to the building, and no photograph of Slater can be found on the walls. No biography of Slater is displayed anywhere in the lobby, letting the residents know why the building is named after him, who he was, or why it is important that he be remembered. The residence hall bears his last name, but aside from that, there is absolutely no mention of him anywhere inside or outside the building.

His former fraternity, Kappa Alpha Psi, created a plaque commemorating Duke in 1983. This marker was designed to be displayed in Slater Hall, but it has since fallen into disrepair. The photograph on the plaque has turned pink with fading and is blurred by smudges of fingerprints. The plaque itself is nowhere on display in Slater Hall; instead, it sits idly in the office of a residence hall administrator who rescued it from otherwise certain neglect. The plaque, which has been obscured from public view, serves as a microcosm of Slater's legacy at Iowa.

Given the complete absence of a visible tribute at Slater Hall, most of the building's residents know little about its namesake. Nearly a dozen students living in Slater Hall were interviewed and posed a question about Duke Slater, and not a single one had any idea who he was. "Who?" one typical student asked quizzically when Slater's name was mentioned. "Never heard of him."[4]

Dedicated in 1972, Rienow Hall II was renamed Slater Hall in order to serve as the campus symbol of Duke Slater's contributions to the University of Iowa.

The Chicago Varsity Club's vaunted Duke Slater Award passed into history along with the club itself, but that's probably a better fate than what awaited the University of Iowa's Duke Slater Award. Iowa's athletic department has nearly 180 fully or partially endowed scholarships that support Hawkeye sports. Examples include the "Nile Kinnick Memorial Scholarship," the "Ironmen Memorial Scholarship," and the "Mr. and Mrs. John V. Synhorst Athletic Scholarship." The Duke Slater Scholarships were designed in 1972 to assist aspiring Hawkeye athletes in much the same way.

Financial considerations changed that. Roy J. Carver, an Iowa industrialist and philanthropist, donated millions of dollars to the University of Iowa. His name is everywhere on the Iowa City campus. The University of Iowa's College of Medicine is named in his honor, as is the basketball facility Carver-Hawkeye Arena. At some point, the Duke Slater Award adopted his name as well, becoming the "Carver Scholarship/Slater Award." It is the only one of the 180 endowed athletic scholarships at the University of Iowa named in this manner, with two seemingly unrelated entities sharing a scholarship name. It's quite likely the Carver family contributed financing at some point to keep the award alive. But it serves as an indignity for Duke Slater, one of the greatest athletes in Iowa's history, to be the only man relegated to second billing on an Iowa athletic scholarship behind a financial booster.

The NFL has done no better in keeping Duke Slater's pivotal role in its history front and center. Joe Ziemba, an author and expert on the old Chicago Cardinals, declared, "Slater is perhaps the most underrated tackle in the history of the game."[5] The Cardinals' franchise has traveled a long road from Chicago to St. Louis to their current home in Arizona. Still, the continued existence of the Cardinals franchise provides a link from Slater's playing days to the current NFL. Duke Slater was the first African American to play for a current NFL franchise when he signed with the Chicago (now Arizona) Cardinals in 1926.

Unfortunately, the Cardinals have occasionally overlooked Slater's important place in their franchise's history as well. The Arizona Cardinals moved into University of Phoenix Stadium in 2006, and their new stadium contains a "Ring of Honor" that recognizes Cardinal greats from all eras of the franchise. Included in the Cardinals Ring of Honor are Slater's contemporaries like Ernie Nevers, Jim Conzelman, and Paddy Driscoll. However, Duke Slater, a trailblazer and one of the greatest linemen of his era, has not yet been similarly recognized.

Duke Slater should have been inducted into the Professional Football Hall of Fame in Canton, Ohio, decades ago. Before the Pro Football Hall of Fame opened in 1963, *United Press International* mentioned Slater as one of nine candidates that had been nominated for election to the new Hall.[6] The other eight have all been elected to Canton. The following year, the *Associated Press* listed Duke and five other "strong candidates" for election to the Hall of Fame.[7] Again, the other five were quickly enshrined, but Slater remains the exception.

For several years, the Pro Football Hall of Fame announced their inductees all at once. Beginning in 1970, however, they began releasing a list of finalists from which the official Hall of Fame class would be chosen. Duke Slater was on the first list of finalists in 1970 and was again listed as a finalist in 1971. Seven players were listed as finalists for the Hall of Fame in both of those first two years. Of those seven, six were eventually welcomed into the Hall of Fame; again, only Slater has been denied.

In 1971, the *Associated Press* yet again listed seven players who were under consideration for the Hall. The players named were Benny Friedman, Ace Parker, Tuffy Leemans, Ward Cuff, Bruiser Kinard, Duke Slater, and Bill Hewitt.[8] Five of the seven were elected to Canton, with only Slater and Cuff omitted. Exasperated, columnist A.S. "Doc" Young asked in 1965, "What'll it take — a racial campaign — to get Judge Fred 'Duke' Slater voted into pro football's Hall of Fame?"[9] One can only imagine how outraged Young would be now, nearly a half century later.

Perhaps a racial campaign would have been in order, because Duke Slater was the greatest African American NFL player prior to World War II. He became the first African American to earn three all-pro selections in 1925; Hall of Famer Fritz Pollard had two, and no other black player had more than one. Slater ended his career with seven such selections, the only African American to do so until Emlen Tunnell earned his seventh all-pro nod in 1955. Tunnell, incidentally, became the first African American welcomed to the Hall of Fame in 1967, but the man who inspired him and so many others to head to Iowa City in 1946 has been forced to wait.

While Duke was the most decorated African American football player of his day, that doesn't tell the whole story. Duke Slater established himself as one of the greatest linemen in the NFL during the 1920s — of any race. He was the first lineman to earn seven all-pro selections when he earned his seventh in 1930. It was a feat only duplicated by six other linemen before 1945. Those other six are in the Hall of Fame.

Slater had astonishing durability. He was famous for playing complete games, going wire to wire in nearly every contest. Duke often discussed how substitutions were much rarer when he played. "You were expected to play the whole game unless you got hurt," he pointed out.[10] While it's true that athletes often played complete games in his era, very few played one complete game after another for an entire season and then repeated those performances season after season as Duke Slater did. He also never missed a game due to injury in his long career, despite being a frequent target as one of the few black players and occasionally the only black player in the NFL.

His durability can be put into perspective when you consider that he only missed three starts of the 99 games he played in his pro football career. His percentage of missed starts to career games played (3.03 percent) is the smallest of any player who completed his career before 1950 (with a minimum of eighty games played). This group includes 100 players and 31 current Hall of Famers. With a minimum of 50 games played, Slater's percentage of missed starts ranks second among 444 qualifying players behind only Dayton Triangles center George Kinderdine.

Slater's omission from the Hall of Fame would startle his contemporaries. Red Grange, arguably the most celebrated football player in history at the time, was asked to choose his personal all-time all-pro team in 1959. Rather than selecting the standard eleven players, Grange named thirteen men he felt were the greatest football players in the first forty years of the NFL. His choices included twelve current Pro Football Hall of Famers—and Duke Slater.[11] Similarly, Ernie Nevers said Slater was one of the five greatest players he ever lined up with or against. The other four — Red Grange, Bronko Nagurski, Walt Kiesling, and Mike Michalske — are all in Canton.[12]

Other legends of football also sang Duke's praises. Fritz Pollard was outspoken that he felt Duke Slater deserved enshrinement in the Pro Football Hall of Fame.[13] Hunk Anderson called Slater "the toughest man I ever faced in football" and the greatest tackle the game had produced.[14] Jim Conzelman singled Slater out as one of the "great players in our league," while former NFL commissioner Elmer Layden called Duke "the greatest tackle I ever saw."[15]

One of Duke Slater's biggest admirers throughout his life was the iconic George Halas. "I can't say too much about Duke Slater as a football player and as a gentleman," Halas once recalled. "In the old Cardinal-Bears games, I learned it was absolutely useless to run against Slater's side of the Cardinal line. They talked about Fordham's famous Seven Blocks of Granite in the mid–1930s and what a line that was. Well, Slater was a One Man Line a decade before that. Seven Blocks of Granite? He was the Rock of Gibraltar."[16]

Modern football historians also agree Slater has been wrongly overlooked. Author Sean Lahman wrote, "Slater entered the NFL twenty-five years before Jackie Robinson broke baseball's color barrier, and you have to imagine that he suffered all of the same indignities, insults, and outright hostility. Of course, the opportunities for abuse had to have been greater while playing a contact sport." On the topic of the Hall of Fame, Lahman added, "Fritz Pollard ... was finally inducted in 2006. The honor came twenty years after Pollard died and nearly eighty years after his career ended. It took too long to correct that oversight, and Slater's exclusion is just as egregious."[17]

ESPN's K.C. Joyner called Slater a "viable Hall of Fame candidate," noting his long career and all-pro selections. "This is even more impressive when you consider the circumstances under which Slater earned those honors. He played during an era where blacks had an incredibly tough time getting a fair shake," Joyner remarked. "If Slater did that well against a stacked voting deck, I can only imagine how well he would have fared with a colorblind accounting of his skills."[18]

Dan Daly of the *Washington Times* named Duke one of the two best tackles of the 1920s and one of the decade's least appreciated players.[19] "How great was Slater?" Daly asked. "Put it this way — He was an interior lineman, and he was well-known."[20] Daly openly advocated Slater for the Pro Football Hall of Fame in 2006, concluding, "The evidence is overwhelming, but for the judge, there has been no justice."[21]

There are many reasons why Duke Slater has been denied justice. The first has to do with the "official" all-pro team. Several sources named all-pro teams during the 1920s, but the all-pro choices by the *Green Bay Press-Gazette* are, in retrospect, considered by many to be the official selections from 1923–1931. Unfortunately, Slater was never chosen as a first team all-pro by that organization, leaving some to claim he had zero all-pro selections. A player who was never a first team all-pro has a difficult case to make to the Hall of Fame.

Whether due to racial bias or simple oversight, Slater's repeated exclusions from the *Press-Gazette* all-pro first team are suspicious. He was denied a place on the *Press-Gazette* first team by Boni Petcoff in 1924, Ed Weir in 1927, and Bob Beattie in 1929. These were Petcoff, Weir, and Beattie's only all-pro selections of their careers. All three men were in their first or second season in the NFL when they were named all-pro, and each was out of pro football within two years. Their selections cannot be attributed to their team's successes either, as none of their teams had winning seasons the year they were named all-pro. As a result, the repeated snubs of the more veteran Slater can only be classified as curious.

Furthermore, Duke Slater was a second team all-pro by the *Press-Gazette* on five different occasions. It seems unusual that he was so consistently one of the four best tackles in the league but never one of the best two. No other player before World War II was a second team choice on the "official" all-pro team more than three times except Slater, who was relegated there an amazing five times. Many players who earned three second team all-pro selections in their careers had several first team mentions as well. For example, Bruiser Kinard had five first team selections and three second team mentions in his career, while Bronko Nagurski made the first and second all-pro teams three times each. But Slater's combination of five second team all-pro selections but zero first team nominations from the *Press-Gazette* is unique among all NFL players before 1945.

Duke Slater was a consistent all-pro performer from 1923 to 1930. The only times in this eight-year stretch where he failed to gain honors was in 1928, when his Chicago Cardinals only played half of an NFL schedule, and in 1926, when he was omitted by some all-pro selectors on account of playing most of the season in the AFL. The *Press-Gazette* never chose Duke as a first team all-pro, but many other organizations did. ESPN and the Pro Football Researchers Association have chosen consensus all-pros retroactively, based on an aggregation of every all-pro team announced in a given year. ESPN named Duke Slater a consensus first team all-pro for the 1925 and 1929 seasons, while the PFRA did the same for 1926 and 1930.[22]

At least the *Green Bay Press-Gazette* admitted Slater was one of the four best tackles in the game in five seasons in the 1920s. By 1969, the Pro Football Hall of Fame wouldn't even concede that much. Members of the Hall of Fame's selection committee choose an all-decade team every ten years, and membership on the All-Decade team is often used as a key component to a Hall of Fame candidate's case for induction. The All-1920s NFL team was chosen retroactively in 1969, and it included four players at the tackle position. Duke Slater was passed over for Ed Healey, Pete Henry, Cal Hubbard, and Steve Owen, who were all already enshrined in Canton at the time.

Duke Slater was awarded seven all-pro selections in his career, six of them in the decade from 1920 to 1929. His six all-pro mentions in the 1920s were the most of any lineman, but he was snubbed from the All-1920s team. The choices of Steve Owen and Cal Hubbard at tackle were particularly perplexing. Owen had been a solid player for the New York Giants and a three time all-pro, but he was much better known for guiding the Giants to a 151–100–17 record and two NFL championships as a coach from 1931–1953. While that certainly merits Owen a place in Canton, it doesn't explain why he was chosen for the All-1920s team over a more decorated player.

Cal Hubbard's selection was even more egregious. Hubbard was a terrific football player for the Packers and Giants, and he was a seven-time all-pro selection. However, he played from 1927–1936, so he only played three seasons in the decade of the 1920s. Furthermore, when he was an all-pro player in 1927 and 1928, Hubbard played end, so he was only a tackle for one season in the decade of the 1920s. Yet he was selected for the league's all-decade team at the tackle position over Slater, a six-time tackle all-pro in the 1920s.

Duke also died without any children who could trumpet his legacy the way Fritz Pollard's family, specifically grandson Fritz Pollard III, have done. Pollard's case was aided by the fact that he played for the 1920 Akron Pros, who won the NFL championship. Unfortunately, this was an unusual occurrence for African Americans before World War II. The most successful franchises in the league at the time didn't want or need black players. The closest Slater came to an NFL championship shot came in 1924, when Rock Island's loss in Kansas City without him cost the team any chance at a title. That Kansas City benching also kept him from reaching 100 games in professional football, as he ended his career with 99 games played in the NFL and AFL.

But the main reason why Slater has not yet been inducted to Canton is simply due to oversight. The voters who elect members to the Pro Football Hall of Fame have a very difficult job. Unlike baseball, pro football's Hall of Fame voters are given a strict cap of two Seniors Candidates every year. As a result, Duke Slater has simply been overshadowed in a long queue of possible deserving players whose careers are more recent than his. All the players that saw him play have passed on, and the Hall of Fame voters have simply chosen to give most of their nominations to more recent retirees who played in the 1950s and 1960s and are still alive to accept the honor. Those are all practical reasons for why Duke Slater hasn't been chosen, but they're also ultimately unsatisfying. At some point, it's time to give a man whose career ended eighty years ago his due.

It would be easy to condemn those associated with the Pro Football Hall of Fame for Slater's prolonged absence from Canton, but they are far from alone in neglecting him. Sports fans in the United States have banished Duke to the history books, while the accomplishments of so many of his contemporaries vividly live on. The same factors that allowed racists to overlook Slater's presence in football during his playing days — his humility, his quiet strength, and his ability to deflect the spotlight — allowed the entire American sporting public, not just Hall of Fame voters, to overlook his unique and remarkable place in history as well.

Slater made it easy for everyone to forget him, and he was so modest that he didn't even mind being pushed into the "limbo of antiquity." But that doesn't mean he should be. This is a man who deserves to be celebrated, rather than have his legacy steadily fade away. Duke Slater was a legend in his lifetime, but he is certainly worthy of remaining one far beyond.

Appendices

A: Records and Point Totals

Duke Slater played 18 seasons of organized football: three at the high school level, four at the collegiate level, ten at the professional level, and one at the semi-pro level. Records and point totals of all known games (including exhibitions) are included in the table below.

Playing Career:		G	Record	Points
1913	Clinton High School	8	7–1	508–50
1914	Clinton High School	9	7–1–1	353–54
1915	Clinton High School	8	7–1	155–26
1918	University of Iowa	9	6–2–1	123–36
1919	University of Iowa	7	5–2	90–44
1920	University of Iowa	7	5–2	142–54
1921	University of Iowa	7	7–0	185–36
1922	Rock Island Independents (NFL)	8	5–2–1	180–27
1922	Milwaukee Badgers (NFL)	2	0–2	6–43
1922	Pollard All-Stars	1	1–0	6–0
1923	Rock Island Independents (NFL)	12	6–3–3	149–87
1924	Rock Island Independents (NFL)	12	9–1–2	118–27
1925	Rock Island Independents (NFL)	11	5–3–3	99–58
1926	Rock Island Independents (AFL)	9	2–6–1	21–126
1926	Chicago Cardinals (NFL)	2	0–1–1	2–7
1927	Chicago Cardinals (NFL)	13	4–8–1	102–140
1928	Chicago Cardinals (NFL)	8	2–6	25–114
1928	Chicago Blackhawks	–	N/A	N/A
1929	Chicago Cardinals (NFL)	14	6–7–1	154–89
1930	Chicago Cardinals (NFL)	16	7–7–2	198–147
1931	Chicago Cardinals (NFL)	13	9–4	257–141
1931–32	Chicago Blackhawks	2	1–0–1	20–6
1932	National Collegians/Nevers' All-Stars	2	2–0	40–14
1937	Chicago Brown Bombers (player-coach)	1	0–1	6–7
Totals				
1913–15	Clinton High School	25	21–3–1	1,016–130
1918–21	University of Iowa	30	23–6–1	540–170
1922–26	Rock Island Independents	52	27–15–10	567–325
1926–31	Chicago Cardinals	66	28–33–5	738–638
1922–31	NFL/AFL League Games	99	38–46–15	925–922
1922–32	All Pro Football Games	126	59–51–16	1,383–1,033

B: The Games

The dates and outcomes of every known game of Duke Slater's playing career are listed below. Not included are any games he played with the 1928 Chicago Blackhawks, which are not available. Games in which Slater didn't participate (such as Englewood in 1913 and Kansas City in 1924) have been omitted. An asterisk indicates an NFL exhibition game.

Playing Record
1913 Clinton High School (Record: 7–1)
Coach Clinton Osborne
9/20 — Rochelle, IL	94–0
10/4 — DeKalb, IL	108–0
10/11 — Rock Island, IL	42–0
10/18 — @Oak Park, IL	14–32
10/25 — Bowen High (Maquoketa, IL)	67–0
11/1 — @Cedar Rapids, IA	26–0
11/8 — Cornell College Freshmen	41–18
11/27 — Keewatin Academy	116–0

1914 Clinton High School (Record: 7–1–1)
Coach Petersen
9/26 — Englewood, IL	27–0
10/3 — @Keewatin Academy	7–27
10/10 — @West Aurora, IL	14–0
10/17 — @Iowa City High, IA	20–0
10/24 — Mount Morris (IL) College	109–0
10/31 — @Davenport, IA	17–7
11/7 — Lane Tech (Chicago, IL)	73–7
11/21 — Dubuque, IA	73–0
11/26 — West Des Moines, IA	13–13

1915 Clinton High School (Record: 7–1)
Coach Craig
9/25 — Englewood, IL	19–6
10/2 — @Rock Island, IL	20–0
10/9 — Dubuque College Junior Varsity	7–0
10/16 — Iowa City High, IA	17–14
10/23 — Sterling, IL	52–0
10/30 — Davenport, IA	0–6
11/6 — Keewatin Academy	5–0
11/25 — Crane High (Chicago, IL)	35–0

1918 Iowa Hawkeyes (Record: 6–2–1)
Coach Howard Jones
9/28 — Great Lakes Naval Station	0–10
10/5 — @Nebraska	12–0
10/12 — Coe College	27–0
10/19 — Cornell College	34–0
11/2 — Illinois	0–19
11/9 — Minnesota	6–0
11/16 — Ames College	21–0
11/23 — Northwestern	23–7
11/30 — @Camp Dodge	0–0

1919 Iowa Hawkeyes (Record: 5–2)
Coach Howard Jones
10/4 — Nebraska	18–0
10/18 — @Illinois	7–9
10/25 — @Minnesota	9–6
11/1 — South Dakota	26–13
11/8 — @Northwestern	14–7
11/15 — @Chicago	6–9
11/22 — Ames College	10–0

1920 Iowa Hawkeyes (Record: 5–2)
Coach Howard Jones
10/2 — @Indiana	14–7
10/9 — Cornell College	63–0
10/16 — @Illinois	3–20
10/23 — @Chicago	0–10
11/6 — Northwestern	20–0
11/13 — Minnesota	28–7
11/20 — @Ames College	14–10

1921 Iowa Hawkeyes (Record: 7–0)
Coach Howard Jones
10/1 — Knox College	52–14
10/8 — Notre Dame	10–7
10/15 — Illinois	14–2
10/29 — @Purdue	13–6
11/5 — @Minnesota	41–7
11/12 — Indiana	41–0
11/19 — @Northwestern	14–0

1922 Rock Island Independents (Overall Record: 5–2–1; NFL Record: 4–2–1)
Coach Jim Conzelman
9/24 — Moline Indians*	26–0
10/1 — Green Bay Packers	19–14
10/8 — Chicago Bears	6–10
10/15 — Evansville Crimson Giants	60–0
10/22 — Rochester Jeffersons	26–0
10/29 — @Green Bay Packers	0–0
11/12 — Dayton Triangles	43–0
11/19 — @Chicago Bears	0–3

1922 Milwaukee Badgers (Record: 0–2)
Coach Jim Conzelman
11/30 — @Racine Legion	0–3
12/3 — @Canton Bulldogs	6–40

1922 Fritz Pollard All-Stars (Record: 1–0)
Coach Fritz Pollard
12/16 — King's All-Stars	6–0

1923 Rock Island Independents (Overall Record: 6–3–3; NFL Record: 2–3–3)
Coach Herb Sies
9/23 — Moline Indians*	9–6
9/30 — Chicago Bears	3–0
10/7 — Cleveland Indians	0–0

Date	Opponent	Score
10/14	Rochester Jeffersons	56–0
10/21	Hibbing Miners*	27–7
10/28	@Omaha Olympics*	22–6
11/4	Milwaukee Badgers	3–14
11/11	@Minneapolis Marines	6–6
11/18	@Chicago Bears	3–7
11/25	Minneapolis Marines	6–6
12/2	@Durant Stars*	7–6
12/9	@Chicago Bears	7–29

1924 Rock Island Independents (Overall Record: 9–1–2; NFL Record: 5–1–2)
Coach Rube Ursella

Date	Opponent	Score
9/21	Moline Indians*	7–0
9/28	Chicago Bears	0–0
10/5	Racine Legion	9–0
10/12	Hammond Pros	26–0
10/19	Dayton Triangles	20–0
11/2	@Chicago Bears	3–3
11/9	@Racine Legion	6–3
11/16	Kansas City Blues	17–0
11/23	Duluth Kelleys	0–9
11/27	Kenosha-Hammond All-Stars*	10–6
12/7	@Clinton Legion*	13–0
12/14	@Chicago Bears*	7–6

1925 Rock Island Independents (Record: 5–3–3)
Coach Rube Ursella

Date	Opponent	Score
9/20	Chicago Bears	0–0
9/27	Dayton Triangles	0–0
10/4	Green Bay Packers	3–0
10/11	@Duluth Kelleys	12–0
10/18	@Green Bay Packers	0–20
10/25	Kansas City Cowboys	3–3
11/1	@Chicago Bears	0–6
11/15	Kansas City Cowboys	35–12
11/22	Milwaukee Badgers	40–7
11/26	@Detroit Panthers	6–3
11/29	@Chicago Cardinals	0–7

1926 Rock Island Independents (Record: 2–6–1)
Coach Johnny Armstrong

Date	Opponent	Score
9/26	Los Angeles Wildcats	7–3
10/3	New York Yankees	0–26
10/10	Chicago Bulls	7–3
10/17	@Cleveland Panthers	7–23
10/23	@Philadelphia Quakers	0–9
10/24	@Newark Bears	0–0
11/2	@New York Yankees	0–35
11/6	@Philadelphia Quakers	0–24
11/21	@Chicago Bulls	0–3

1926 Chicago Cardinals (Record: 0–1–1)
Coach Norm Barry

Date	Opponent	Score
11/25	@Chicago Bears	0–0
11/28	Kansas City Cowboys	2–7

1927 Chicago Cardinals (Overall Record: 4–8–1; NFL Record: 3–7–1)
Coach Guy Chamberlin

Date	Opponent	Score
9/18	Hammond*	0–6
9/25	Chicago Bears	0–9
10/2	Pottsville Maroons	19–7
10/9	Dayton Triangles	7–0
10/16	@Green Bay Packers	0–13
10/23	@Spring Valley Wildcats*	33–0
10/30	New York Yankees	6–7
11/6	Green Bay Packers	6–6
11/13	@New York Yankees	6–20
11/19	@Frankford Yellow Jackets	8–12
11/20	@New York Giants	7–28
11/24	@Chicago Bears	3–0
11/27	Cleveland Bulldogs	7–32

1928 Chicago Cardinals (Overall Record: 2–6; NFL Record: 1–5)
Coach Fred Gillies

Date	Opponent	Score
9/16	@Hammond*	12–0
9/23	Chicago Bears	0–15
9/30	Chicago Mills*	6–7
10/7	Dayton Triangles	7–0
10/14	@Green Bay Packers	0–20
11/24	@Frankford Yellow Jackets	0–19
11/25	@New York Yankees	0–19
11/29	@Chicago Bears	0–34

1929 Chicago Cardinals (Overall Record: 6–7–1; NFL Record: 6–6–1)
Coach Dewey Scanlon

Date	Opponent	Score
9/22	@Canton Bulldogs*	0–6
9/29	@Buffalo Bisons	9–3
10/6	@Green Bay Packers	2–9
10/13	@Minneapolis Red Jackets	7–14
10/20	@Chicago Bears	0–0
10/27	Green Bay Packers	6–7
11/2	@Frankford Yellow Jackets	0–8
11/6	@Providence Steam Roller	16–0
11/10	Minneapolis Red Jackets	8–0
11/17	Green Bay Packers	0–12
11/24	Dayton Triangles	19–0
11/28	@Chicago Bears	40–6
12/1	@New York Giants	21–24
12/8	@Orange Tornadoes	26–0

1930 Chicago Cardinals (Overall Record: 7–7–2; NFL Record: 5–6–2)
Coach Ernie Nevers

Date	Opponent	Score
9/14	@Sturgis Wildcats*	30–0
9/21	@Green Bay Packers	0–14
9/28	@Minneapolis Red Jackets	7–7
10/5	@Portsmouth Spartans	0–0
10/8	@Newark Tornadoes	13–0
10/12	@Providence Steam Roller	7–9
10/16	@New York Giants	12–25
10/19	Chicago Bears	6–32
10/25	@Frankford Yellow Jackets	34–7
10/26	Portsmouth Spartans	23–13
10/29	@Milwaukee Night Hawks*	33–6
11/2	Frankford Yellow Jackets	6–0
11/9	New York Giants	7–13

11/16 — Green Bay Packers 13–6
11/27 — @Chicago Bears 0–6
12/15 — @Chicago Bears* 7–9

1931 Chicago Cardinals (Overall Record: 9–4; NFL Record: 5–4)
Coach Roy Andrews; Coach Ernie Nevers
9/16 — @Chicago Harley-Mills* 25–0
9/20 — Pullman Panthers* 31–0
9/23 — @Portsmouth Spartans 3–13
10/11 — @Green Bay Packers 7–26
10/18 — @Chicago Bears 13–26
10/25 — @Rock Island Green Bush* 45–13
11/1 — @Brooklyn Dodgers 14–7
11/8 — @Cleveland Indians 14–6
11/11 — @Grand Rapids Maroons* 36–0
11/15 — Green Bay Packers 21–13
11/22 — Portsmouth Spartans 20–19

11/26 — @Chicago Bears 7–18
11/28 — Cleveland Indians 21–0

1931–32 Chicago Blackhawks (Known Record: 1–0–1)
Coach Fritz Pollard
12/27 — @Duffield Coast Stars 20–6
1/3 — @San Pedro Longshoremen 0–0

1932 National Collegians/Nevers' All-Stars (Known Record: 2–0)
Coach Ernie Nevers
1/17 — Southern California All-Stars 14–0
1/24 — Carideo All-Stars 26–14

1937 Chicago Brown Bombers (Known Record: 0–1)
Coach Duke Slater
10/10 — Calumet All-Stars 6–7

C: Coaching Career

Duke Slater also had a 13-year coaching career, beginning when he accepted a line coach position from Walter Flanigan with the Rock Island Independents in 1922. He spent five years as an assistant coach at various levels and eight years as a head coach, including four years leading four different semi-pro organizations. Slater's coaching resume is listed below.

Coaching Career

1922	Rock Island Independents (line coach)
1932	Ambassador A.A. (assistant coach)
1933	Chicago Negro All-Stars
1934–35	Douglass High School
1936	University of Iowa (line coach)
1937	Chicago Brown Bombers (player-coach)
1938	Negro All-Stars (assistant coach)
1939	Chicago Comets
1940	Chicago Panthers
1942	St. Charles School
1944	Washington Park youth club
1945	Washington Park youth club
1946	Columbus Park youth club (assistant coach)

The outcomes of every known game of Duke Slater's semi-pro coaching career are listed below.

PROFESSIONAL HEAD COACHING RECORD

1933 Chicago Negro All-Stars (Known Record: 0–2)
10/1 — @Harvey Yellow Jackest 0–17
10/22 — @East Chicago Gophers 0–20

1937 Chicago Brown Bombers (Known Record: 1–6–1)
10/10 — Calumet All-Stars 6–7
10/26 — Cicero Silver Arrows N/A
10/31 — @Des Moines Comets 0–7
11/3 — Brandt Florals 7–7
11/7 — @La Crosse Lagers 3–7
11/18 — Alderman Kells N/A
11/21 — @La Crosse Lagers 0–7

11/23 — Chicago Spokes A.C.	0–19
11/30 —@Des Moines Comets	0–7
12/3 —@Nashville Silver Streaks	13–7

1939 Chicago Comets (Known Record: 4–1)

N/A — Joliet Devils	38–0
N/A — Winkler A.C.	24–0
N/A — Macomb Eagles	10–0
10/29 —@Des Moines Comets	0–33
11/5 —@Spring Valley	N/A
11/26 —@Kenosha	28–12

1940 Chicago Panthers (Known Record: 5–2*)

9/11 — Waukegan Collegians	42–0
9/29 —@Sioux City Olympics	Win
10/9 —@Merrill Foxes	Win
10/12 — Detroit Pioneers	0–2
10/14 — Toledo Grills	N/A
10/20 —@Des Moines Comets	7–20
10/23 — Jefferson Park Bulldogs	19–6
10/27 — Edison Park	18–13
11/3 —@Fort Madison Prison	N/A

*One former Panthers player claimed the team's record was 9–2.

D: All-Pro Selections

Duke Slater was named to numerous all-pro teams in his ten-year NFL career. His all-pro selections are listed below. Note that he made an all-pro team in every season from 1923 to 1930 with the exception of 1928, when the Chicago Cardinals only played half of an NFL schedule. The all-pro teams of the *Green Bay Press-Gazette* are considered by many the "official" all-pro teams from 1923–1930. The *Press-Gazette* only evaluated NFL performances in making its selections in 1926, when Duke Slater played the majority of the season in the AFL.

***All-Pro Selections*[1]**

1923 *Collyer's Eye Magazine*— First Team
1923 *Green Bay Press-Gazette*— Second Team*
1923 *Canton Daily News*— Second Team

1924 *Green Bay Press-Gazette*— Second Team*

1925 ESPN — Consensus First Team
1925 *Collyer's Eye Magazine*— First Team
1925 *Green Bay Press-Gazette*— Second Team*

1926 PFRA — Consensus First Team
1926 *Chicago Tribune*— First Team
1926 *Collyer's Eye Magazine*— Second Team
1927 *Cleveland Press*— First Team
1927 *Green Bay Press-Gazette*— Second Team*

1929 ESPN — Consensus First Team
1929 *Chicago Tribune*— First Team
1929 *Green Bay Press-Gazette*— Second Team*
1929 *New York Post*— Second Team

1930 PFRA — Consensus First Team
1930 *Chicago Daily Times*— First Team
1930 *Chicago Herald-Examiner*— First Team
1930 *Collyer's Eye Magazine*— Second Team
1930 *Green Bay Press-Gazette*— Third Team*

*—"Official" all-pro team

E: African Americans in the NFL

Thirteen African Americans competed in the National Football League before World War II, and Duke Slater was the most durable and decorated of these thirteen. No African American matched his seven all-pro selections until Hall of Famer Emlen Tunnell earned his seventh in 1955.

African American Players in Pro Football, 1920–1945[1]

Name	Seasons	Games	Games Started	All-Pro Selections	"Official" All-Pro Selections
Duke Slater	10	99	96	7	6
Fritz Pollard*	6	49	36	2	1
Ink Williams	6	37	34	1	1
Sol Butler	3	23	13	0	0
Joe Lillard	2	18	12	1	0
Paul Robeson	2	15	13	1	0
David Myers	2	13	11	1	0
Bobby Marshall	2	12	9	1	1
Dick Hudson	3	8	7	0	0
John Shelburne	1	6	6	0	0
Ray Kemp	1	5	0	0	0
James Turner	1	3	2	0	0
Harold Bradley	1	2	1	0	0

*Pro Football Hall of Fame Member

F: Pre-World War II All-Pro Selections

Below is the list of the sixteen players who earned seven all-pro selections prior to World War II.

Most All-Pro selections — 1920–1945[1]

Mel Hein*	13
Don Hutson*	11
Clarke Hinkle*	10
Link Lyman*	9
Lavvie Dilweg	8
Paddy Driscoll*	8
Turk Edwards*	8
Ray Flaherty*	8
Dan Fortmann*	8
Cal Hubbard*	8
Mike Michalske*	8
Duke Slater	7
Bronko Nagurski*	7
Bruiser Kinard*	7
Ken Strong*	7
Tuffy Leemans*	7

*Pro Football Hall of Fame Member

Only seven linemen earned seven all-pro selections prior to World War II. Duke Slater was one of them; the other six are in the Pro Football Hall of Fame.

Most All-Pro selections among linemen — 1920–1945[2]

Mel Hein*	13
Link Lyman*	9

Most All-Pro selections among linemen—1920–1945[2]

Turk Edwards*	8
Mike Michalske*	8
Dan Fortmann*	8
Duke Slater	7
Bruiser Kinard*	7
Ed Healey*	6
George Trafton*	6
Joe Stydahar*	6
Ox Emerson	6
George Christensen	6
George Musso*	6

Pro Football Hall of Fame Member

Slater wasn't selected for the 1920s All-Decade team, despite being one of the greatest linemen of the decade. He made six first or second all-pro teams, the most of any lineman in the 1920s.

Most first or second team All-Pro selections among linemen—1920–1929[3]

Duke Slater	6
Ed Healey*	6
George Trafton*	6
Pete Henry*	5
Link Lyman*	5
Jim McMillen	5
Gus Sonnenberg	5
5 with	4

Pro Football Hall of Fame Member

Chapter Notes

Introduction

1. *Chicago Defender*, 10/17/36.
2. *The Iowan*, Volume 3, No. 1, Oct./Nov. 1954, 26.
3. *Davenport Democrat & Leader*, 4/12/27.
4. James Peterson, *Slater of Iowa*, 36.
5. Kenneth L. "Tug" Wilson and Jerry Brondfield, *The Big Ten*, 115.
6. *Chicago Defender*, 10/17/36.
7. *Iowa City Press-Citizen*, 12/3/21.
8. Kenneth L. "Tug" Wilson and Jerry Brondfield, *The Big Ten*, 115.
9. United Press International, 8/16/66.
10. John McCallum, *Big Ten Football Since 1895*, 201; Mervin Hyman and Gordon White, *Big Ten Football*, 263.
11. Mervin Hyman and Gordon White, *Big Ten Football*, 263.
12. Howard Roberts, *The Big Nine*, 117.
13. John McCallum, *Big Ten Football Since 1895*, 201.
14. *Iowa Alumni Review*, September 1989, 26.
15. David McMahon, "Remembering the Black and Gold: African Americans, Sport Memory, and the University of Iowa," *Sport and Memory in North America*, 77.
16. *Washington Times*, 2/4/2006.

Chapter 1

1. George W. Slater, "Emancipation," *Chicago Daily Socialist*, 12/10/1908.
2. *Chicago Tribune*, 1/9/55.
3. *Chicago Tribune*, 8/16/66.
4. *Waterloo Courier*, 8/16/66.
5. Winston James, "Being Red and Black in Jim Crow America," Fall 1999.
6. *Chicago Tribune*, 1/9/55.
7. George W. Slater, "How and Why I Became A Socialist," *Chicago Daily Socialist*, 9/8/1908.
8. George W. Slater, "How and Why I Became A Socialist," *Chicago Daily Socialist*, 9/8/1908.
9. For more information about Rev. George Slater and his writings on black Christian Socialism, see *Black Socialist Preacher*, by Philip S. Foner.
10. Winston James, "Being Red and Black in Jim Crow America," Fall 1999.
11. George W. Slater, "Negroes Becoming Socialists," *Chicago Daily Socialist*, 9/15/1908.
12. George W. Slater, "The Cat's Out," *Chicago Daily Socialist*, 9/29/1908.
13. George W. Slater, "The Cat's Out," *Chicago Daily Socialist*, 9/29/1908; George W. Slater, "Roosevelt and the Race Problem," *Chicago Daily Socialist*, 12/1/1908.
14. Philip S. Foner, *Black Socialist Preacher*, 294.
15. George W. Slater, "The Colored Man Welcome," *Chicago Daily Socialist*, 1/4/1909.
16. James Peterson, *Slater of Iowa*, 8.
17. Silag, Koch-Bridgford, and Chase, *Outside In: African American History in Iowa, 1838–2000*, 396.

Chapter 2

1. John S. Watterson, *The Football Crisis of 1905–1909: Was It Really a Crisis?*, North American Society for Sports History Proceedings, 2000.
2. *Iowa Alumni Review*, December 1972, 12.
3. Mervin Hyman and Gordon White, *Big Ten Football*, 263.
4. *Mount Pleasant News*, 3/28/53.
5. James Peterson, *Slater of Iowa*, 8.
6. *Mason City Globe-Gazette*, 3/30/57.
7. Clinton County Historical Society, *Clinton (IA): Images of America*, 95.
8. *Cedar Rapids Gazette*, 11/21/49.
9. *Cedar Rapids Gazette*, 11/21/49; *Des Moines Register*, 8/16/66.
10. *Mount Pleasant News*, 3/28/53.
11. *Des Moines Register*, 8/16/66.
12. James Peterson, *Slater of Iowa*, 12.
13. *Clinton Herald*, 9/22/13.
14. *Clinton Herald*, 9/22/13.
15. *Clinton Herald*, 9/29/13.
16. *Clinton Herald*, 10/6/13.
17. *Clinton Herald*, 10/13/13.
18. *Burlington Hawkeye*, 3/28/53.
19. *Cedar Rapids Gazette*, 11/8/49.
20. *Mount Pleasant News*, 3/28/53.
21. *Burlington Hawkeye*, 3/28/53.
22. *Clinton Herald*, 10/13/13.
23. *Clinton Herald*, 10/13/13.
24. *Clinton Herald*, 10/20/13.
25. *Clinton Herald*, 10/27/13; *Clinton Daily Advertiser*, 10/27/13.
26. James Peterson, *Slater of Iowa*, 11.
27. James Peterson, *Slater of Iowa*, 11.
28. *Clinton Herald*, 10/25/13.
29. *Clinton Herald*, 11/3/13.
30. *Cedar Rapids Gazette*, 11/3/13.
31. James Peterson, *Slater of Iowa*, 11.
32. *Clinton Herald*, 11/10/13; *Clinton Daily Advertiser*, 11/10/13.
33. *Clinton Herald*, 11/15/13.
34. *Clinton Herald*, 11/17/13.
35. *Clinton Herald*, 11/17/13.
36. *Clinton Daily Advertiser*, 11/28/13.
37. *Des Moines Capital*, 11/21/13.
38. *Clinton Herald*, 11/27/13.

39. *Waterloo Courier*, 9/11/13.
40. *Clinton Daily Advertiser*, 12/1/13.
41. *Clinton Herald*, 11/24/13.
42. *Clinton Herald*, 11/24/13.
43. James Peterson, *Slater of Iowa*, 11.

CHAPTER 3

1. *Mount Pleasant News*, 3/25/53.
2. *Clinton Herald*, 11/6/13.
3. *Clinton Herald*, 9/28/14.
4. *Clinton Herald*, 10/5/14.
5. *Clinton Herald*, 10/5/14; *Clinton Daily Advertiser*, 10/5/14.
6. *Clinton Herald*, 10/5/14.
7. *Clinton Daily Advertiser*, 10/5/14.
8. *Clinton Herald*, 10/5/14.
9. *Clinton Daily Advertiser*, 10/12/14.
10. *Chicago Tribune*, 8/17/66.
11. *Clinton Herald*, 10/19/14; *Clinton Daily Advertiser*, 10/19/14.
12. *Clinton Daily Advertiser*, 10/19/14.
13. *Clinton Daily Advertiser*, 10/19/14.
14. *Clinton Herald*, 10/19/14.
15. *Clinton Daily Advertiser*, 10/12/14.
16. *Clinton Herald*, 10/26/14; *Clinton Daily Advertiser*, 10/26/14.
17. *Clinton Daily Advertiser*, 10/26/14.
18. *Davenport Democrat & Leader*, 11/2/14.
19. *Clinton Herald*, 11/2/14; *Clinton Daily Advertiser*, 11/2/14.
20. *Davenport Democrat & Leader*, 11/2/14.
21. *Davenport Democrat & Leader*, 11/2/14.
22. *Chicago Defender*, 9/25/58.
23. *Clinton Herald*, 11/9/14; *Clinton Daily Advertiser*, 11/9/14.
24. *Clinton Daily Advertiser*, 11/9/14.
25. *Clinton Herald*, 11/9/14.
26. *Clinton Herald*, 11/23/14.
27. *Clinton Herald*, 11/23/14.
28. *Clinton Herald*, 11/23/14.
29. *Des Moines Capital*, 12/14/19.
30. *Clinton Herald*, 8/17/66.
31. James Peterson, *Slater of Iowa*, 12.
32. *Clinton Herald*, 11/28/14; *Clinton Daily Advertiser*, 11/27/14.
33. *Clinton Herald*, 11/28/14.
34. *Clinton Herald*, 12/3/14.
35. *Mason City Globe-Gazette*, 3/30/57.
36. *Clinton Herald*, 9/24/15.
37. *Clinton Herald*, 9/26/15.
38. *Clinton Herald*, 10/4/15.
39. *Clinton Herald*, 10/4/15.
40. *Clinton Herald*, 10/11/15.
41. *Clinton Herald*, 10/18/15.
42. *Clinton Herald*, 10/22/15.
43. *Clinton Herald*, 10/25/15.
44. *Clinton Herald*, 10/29/15.
45. *Clinton Herald*, 11/1/15.
46. *Clinton Herald*, 11/1/15.
47. *Clinton Herald*, 11/1/15.
48. *Clinton Herald*, 11/8/15.
49. *Clinton Herald*, 11/8/15.
50. *Clinton Herald*, 11/26/15.
51. *Clinton Herald*, 11/26/15.
52. Personal interview with Gary Herrity, 11/8/2011.

CHAPTER 4

1. *Mason City Globe-Gazette*, 3/30/57.
2. *Des Moines Register*, 9/4/66; *Mason City Globe-Gazette*, 3/30/57.
3. James Peterson, *Slater of Iowa*, 12.
4. *The Bystander* (Des Moines), State Historical Society of Iowa, 10/13/16.
5. Dick Lamb and Bert McGrane, *75 Years with the Fighting Hawkeyes*, 58.
6. Mark Dukes and Gus Schrader, *Greatest Moments in Iowa Hawkeyes Football History*, 25.
7. *Des Moines Register*, 9/4/66.
8. James Peterson, *Slater of Iowa*, 38; *Des Moines Register*, 9/4/66.
9. *Waterloo Courier*, 8/16/66.
10. *Mason City Globe-Gazette*, 4/1/57.
11. *Iowa City Citizen*, 11/27/17.
12. *Capital (WI) Times*, 9/25/18.
13. *Waterloo Courier*, 9/18/18; *Waterloo Courier*, 9/20/18.
14. *Des Moines Register*, 5/7/64.
15. *Chicago Defender*, 11/20/48.
16. *Iowa City Press*, 9/30/18; *Waterloo Courier*, 9/30/18.
17. *Iowa City Press*, 9/30/18.
18. *Waterloo Courier*, 9/30/18.
19. *Iowa City Citizen*, 10/5/18, quoting the *Chicago Tribune*.
20. *Iowa City Press*, 10/7/18; *Iowa City Citizen*, 10/7/18.
21. *Iowa City Press*, 10/7/18.
22. For more information about the Spanish flu outbreak of 1918, see the terrifying *The Great Influenza: The Epic Story of the Deadliest Plague in History*, by John M. Barry, or *America's Forgotten Pandemic: The Influenza of 1918*, by Alfred W. Crosby.
23. John C. Gerber, *A Pictorial History of the University of Iowa*, 106–107.
24. *Cedar Rapids Gazette*, 11/17/99.
25. *Iowa City Press*, 10/14/18; *Cedar Rapids Gazette*, 10/14/18.
26. *Iowa City Press*, 10/14/18.
27. *Iowa City Citizen*, 10/21/18.
28. *Iowa City Press*, 10/30/18.
29. *Chicago Tribune*, 8/17/66.
30. *Cedar Rapids Gazette*, 11/4/18; *Iowa City Press*, 11/4/18.
31. *Chicago Tribune*, 8/17/66.
32. *Iowa City Press*, 11/4/18; *Cedar Rapids Gazette*, 11/4/18.
33. *Iowa City Citizen*, 11/9/18; *Des Moines Daily News*, 11/10/18.
34. *Des Moines Daily News*, 11/17/18; *Cedar Rapids Gazette*, 11/18/18.
35. *Des Moines Daily News*, 11/17/18.
36. *Cedar Rapids Gazette*, 11/18/18.
37. *Cedar Rapids Gazette* 11/25/18; *Iowa City Press*, 11/25/18.
38. *Iowa City Press*, 11/25/18.
39. *Iowa City Press*, 12/2/18; *Iowa City Citizen*, 12/2/18.
40. *Des Moines Daily News*, 12/4/18.
41. *Waterloo Courier*, 12/9/18.
42. *Iowa City Citizen*, 12/9/18.
43. *Des Moines Daily News*, 12/8/18.
44. *Iowa City Citizen*, 12/18/18.

CHAPTER 5

1. *Mason City Globe-Gazette*, 4/1/57.
2. *Mason City Globe-Gazette*, 9/14/36.

3. *Mason City Globe-Gazette*, 4/1/57.
4. *Iowa City Citizen*, 3/20/19.
5. *Waterloo Courier*, 5/12/19.
6. *Des Moines Daily News*, 8/18/19.
7. *Cedar Rapids Gazette*, 9/24/19.
8. *Nebraska State Journal*, 12/23/38.
9. *Daily Iowan*, 10/5/19.
10. *Nebraska State Journal*, 12/23/38.
11. *Iowa City Citizen*, 10/6/19; *Cedar Rapids Gazette*, 10/6/19.
12. *Iowa City Citizen*, 10/6/19.
13. *Iowa City Citizen*, 10/6/19.
14. *Iowa City Citizen*, 10/20/19.
15. *Iowa City Citizen*, 10/20/19.
16. *Des Moines Capital*, 12/14/19.
17. *Iowa City Citizen*, 10/18/19.
18. *Iowa City Citizen*, 10/20/19.
19. James Peterson, *Slater of Iowa*, 20.
20. James Peterson, *Slater of Iowa*, 20.
21. *Mansfield (OH) News*, 12/14/49.
22. *Burlington Hawkeye*, 10/26/19; *Waterloo Courier*, 10/27/19.
23. *Waterloo Times-Tribune*, 10/26/19.
24. *Iowa City Citizen*, 10/29/19.
25. *Cedar Rapids Gazette*, 11/3/19.
26. *Waterloo Courier*, 11/03/19.
27. *Waterloo Times-Tribune*, 11/8/19.
28. *Waterloo Courier*, 11/10/19; *Cedar Rapids Gazette*, 11/10/19.
29. *Waterloo Times-Tribune*, 11/12/19.
30. *Iowa City Citizen*, 11/12/19.
31. *Iowa City Citizen*, 11/12/19.
32. *Waterloo Times-Tribune*, 11/13/19.
33. *Cedar Rapids Gazette*, 10/23/51.
34. *Chicago Defender*, 1/20/40.
35. James Peterson, *Slater of Iowa*, 22–23.
36. *Chicago Tribune*, 11/12/32.
37. David M. Nelson, *The Anatomy of a Game*, 176.
38. *Waterloo Courier*, 8/16/66.
39. *Chicago Tribune*, 11/16/19.
40. *Iowa City Citizen*, 11/17/19.
41. *Iowa City Citizen*, 11/22/19.
42. *Cedar Rapids Gazette*, 11/24/19.
43. *Waterloo Times-Tribune*, 11/21/19.
44. *Des Moines Capital*, 11/23/19.
45. *Cedar Rapids Gazette*, 11/24/19.
46. *Daily Iowan*, 11/23/19.
47. *Daily Iowan*, 11/25/19.
48. *Chicago Tribune*, 11/25/19.
49. *Cedar Rapids Gazette*, 11/24/19.
50. *Chicago Tribune*, 11/25/19.
51. *Des Moines Capital*, 11/30/19.
52. *San Antonio Evening News*, 12/06/19.
53. *Iowa City Citizen*, 11/24/19.
54. *Iowa City Citizen*, 12/15/19.
55. Duke Slater Vertical File, University of Iowa Special Collections and University Archives.

Chapter 6

1. *Cedar Rapids Gazette*, 1/20/20.
2. *Iowa City Press-Citizen*, 5/10/20.
3. *Iowa City Press-Citizen*, 5/17/20.
4. *Iowa City Press-Citizen*, 5/24/20.
5. *Waterloo Times-Tribune*, 6/24/20.
6. *Cedar Rapids Gazette*, 7/3/20.
7. *Cedar Rapids Gazette*, 11/2/67.
8. *Cedar Rapids Gazette*, 11/17/99.
9. *Iowa City Press-Citizen*, 9/16/20.
10. *Cedar Rapids Gazette*, 9/17/20.
11. *Waterloo Courier*, 12/4/19.
12. *Cedar Rapids Gazette*, 9/26/21.
13. *Cedar Rapids Gazette*, 8/16/20.
14. *Waterloo Times-Tribune*, 8/18/20.
15. *Iowa City Press-Citizen*, 8/23/20.
16. *Waterloo Courier*, 9/29/20.
17. *Waterloo Courier*, 10/4/20.
18. *Iowa City Press-Citizen*, 10/19/51.
19. *Waterloo Courier*, 10/4/20.
20. *Mason City Globe-Gazette*, 9/14/36.
21. *Mason City Globe-Gazette*, 3/27/57.
22. *Waterloo Courier*, 10/11/20; *Cedar Rapids Gazette*, 10/11/20.
23. *Iowa City Press-Citizen*, 10/13/20.
24. *Waterloo Courier*, 10/18/20; *Iowa City Press-Citizen*, 10/18/20.
25. *Des Moines Capital*, 10/17/20.
26. *Waterloo Courier*, 10/18/20.
27. *Waterloo Times-Tribune*, 10/19/20.
28. Maynard Brichford, *Bob Zuppke: The Life and Football Legacy of the Illinois Coach*, 51.
29. *Cedar Rapids Gazette*, 10/25/20.
30. *Waterloo Courier*, 10/25/20.
31. *Iowa City Press-Citizen*, 10/26/20.
32. *Iowa City Press-Citizen*, 11/8/20, *Cedar Rapids Gazette*, 11/8/20.
33. *Chicago Tribune*, 12/13/34.
34. Eric C. Wilson, "Hawkeyes I Remember," Iowa-Oregon State game program, 9/23/72.
35. *Chicago Tribune*, 12/13/34.
36. *Iowa City Press-Citizen*, 11/15/20; *Cedar Rapids Gazette*, 11/15/20.
37. *Iowa City Press-Citizen*, 11/15/20.
38. *Daily Iowan*, 11/14/20.
39. *Cedar Rapids Gazette*, 11/15/20.
40. *Waterloo Times-Tribune*, 11/15/20.
41. *Iowa City Press-Citizen*, 11/17/20.
42. *Iowa City Press-Citizen*, 11/22/20; *Cedar Rapids Gazette*, 11/22/20.
43. Donald Twalm, *New Outlook*, Vol. 131, May-August 1922, 254.
44. *Iowa City Press-Citizen*, 11/22/20.
45. *Daily Iowan*, 11/21/20.
46. *Iowa City Press-Citizen*, 11/26/20.
47. *Daily Iowan*, 11/23/20.
48. *Capital Times*, 11/20/20.
49. *Chicago Tribune*, 11/28/20.
50. *Waterloo Times-Tribune*, 12/5/20.
51. *Iowa City Press-Citizen*, 12/6/20.
52. *Iowa City Press-Citizen*, 12/14/20.
53. *Iowa City Press-Citizen*, 12/16/20.
54. *Waterloo Courier*, 2/17/55.
55. *Davenport Democrat & Leader*, 5/16/27.
56. *Chicago Tribune*, reprinted in the *Fort Wayne Journal-Gazette*, 6/19/21.
57. *Waterloo Courier*, 2/17/55.

Chapter 7

1. *Iowa City Press-Citizen*, 11/23/20.
2. *Cedar Rapids Gazette*, 9/13/21.
3. *Iowa City Press-Citizen*, 9/17/21.
4. *Iowa City Press-Citizen*, 9/17/21.
5. *Cedar Rapids Republican*, 9/25/21.
6. *Iowa City Press-Citizen*, 9/26/21.

7. *Waterloo Courier*, 10/3/21; *Iowa City Press-Citizen*, 10/3/21.
8. *Cedar Rapids Gazette*, 10/3/21.
9. *Chicago Tribune*, 11/20/21.
10. *Cedar Rapids Gazette*, 10/3/21.
11. *Charleston (WV) Gazette*, 12/14/59.
12. *Charleston (WV) Gazette*, 12/14/59.
13. *Cedar Rapids Gazette*, 8/16/66.
14. *Cedar Rapids Gazette*, 11/22/58.
15. *Cedar Rapids Gazette*, 11/8/49.
16. *Cedar Rapids Gazette*, 10/9/49.
17. *Cedar Rapids Gazette*, 10/9/49.
18. Aubrey Devine, "Reminiscences of that First Game," Iowa-Notre Dame game program, 11/11/39.
19. James Peterson, *Slater of Iowa*, 28.
20. *Waterloo Courier*, 8/16/66.
21. *Charleston (WV) Gazette*, 12/14/59.
22. *Cedar Rapids Gazette*, 10/9/49.
23. *Clinton Herald*, 2/9/59.
24. *Bluefield (WV) Daily Telegraph*, 1/12/34.
25. *Charleston (WV) Gazette*, 12/14/59.
26. James Peterson, *Slater of Iowa*, 30.
27. James Peterson, *Slater of Iowa*, 28.
28. *Iowa City Press-Citizen*, 10/31/21.
29. Emil Klosinski, *Notre Dame, Chicago Bears, and Hunk Anderson*, 58.
30. Emil Klosinski, *Notre Dame, Chicago Bears, and Hunk Anderson*, 58.
31. James Peterson, *Slater of Iowa*, 30.
32. James Peterson, *Slater of Iowa*, 30.
33. *Waterloo Courier*, 8/16/66.
34. *Cedar Rapids Gazette*, 8/14/58.
35. *Chicago Tribune*, 8/14/58.
36. *Waterloo Courier*, 8/16/66.
37. James Peterson, *Slater of Iowa*, 28.
38. James Peterson, *Slater of Iowa*, 28.
39. *Cedar Rapids Gazette*, 11/22/58.
40. *Iowa City Press-Citizen*, 10/22/46.
41. *Waterloo Times-Tribune*, 10/9/21.
42. *Daily Iowan*, 10/9/21.
43. *Iowa City Press-Citizen*, 10/10/21.
44. *Mason City Globe-Gazette*, 9/14/36.
45. Mervin Hyman and Gordon White, *Big Ten Football*, 263.
46. Howard Roberts, *The Big Nine*, 118.
47. Francis Wallace, *Knute Rockne*, 94–95; Francis Wallace, *The Notre Dame Story*, 173.
48. *Cedar Rapids Gazette*, 10/12/21.
49. James Peterson, *Slater of Iowa*, 32.
50. James Peterson, *Slater of Iowa*, 32.
51. *Syracuse Herald*, 10/24/34.
52. James Peterson, *Slater of Iowa*, 32.
53. *Iowa City Press-Citizen*, 10/17/21; *Cedar Rapids Gazette*, 10/17/21.
54. *Daily Iowan*, 10/16/21.
55. *Cedar Rapids Republican*, 10/16/21.
56. *Cedar Rapids Gazette*, 10/17/21.
57. *Iowa City Press-Citizen*, 10/17/21.
58. *Waterloo Courier*, 10/24/21.
59. *Chicago Tribune*, 10/12/21.
60. *Cedar Rapids Republican*, 10/30/21; *Waterloo Times-Tribune*, 10/30/21.
61. *Cedar Rapids Republican*, 11/03/21.
62. *Iowa City Press-Citizen*, 11/05/21.
63. *Waterloo Courier*, 11/04/21.
64. *Iowa City Press-Citizen*, 9/21/51.
65. *Cedar Rapids Republican*, 11/6/21; *Waterloo Courier*, 11/07/21.
66. *Waterloo Courier*, 11/07/21.
67. *Daily Iowan*, 11/6/21.
68. *Waterloo Times-Tribune*, 11/04/21.
69. *Cedar Rapids Republican*, 11/13/21; *Iowa City Press-Citizen*, 11/14/21.
70. *Cedar Rapids Republican*, 11/13/21.
71. *Cedar Rapids Republican*, 11/13/21.
72. *Daily Iowan*, 11/13/21.
73. *Cedar Rapids Republican*, 11/15/21.
74. *Cedar Rapids Gazette*, 11/21/49.
75. *Cedar Rapids Republican*, 11/20/21; *Iowa City Press-Citizen*, 11/21/21.
76. *Waterloo Courier*, 11/21/21.
77. *Daily Iowan*, 11/20/21.
78. *Chicago Sun-Times*, reprinted in the *Clinton Herald*, 12/31/56.
79. *Mason City Globe-Gazette*, 4/1/57.
80. *Waterloo Courier*, 11/29/21.
81. *Iowa City Press-Citizen*, 12/8/21.
82. *Chicago Tribune*, 11/25/21.
83. *Iowa City Press-Citizen*, 11/29/21.
84. *Appleton (WI) Post-Crescent*, 12/6/21.
85. *Waterloo Courier*, 12/12/21.
86. *Daily Iowan*, 12/18/21.
87. *Iowa City Press-Citizen*, 12/13/21.
88. *Iowa City Press-Citizen*, 11/29/21.
89. *Olean (NY) Times*, 11/9/25.
90. *Iowa City Press-Citizen*, 12/3/21.
91. *Iowa City Press-Citizen*, 12/3/21.
92. *Iowa City Press-Citizen*, 12/12/21.
93. *Iowa City Press-Citizen*, 12/20/21.
94. *Waterloo Times-Tribune*, 12/11/21.
95. James Peterson, *Slater of Iowa*, 42.
96. *Capital Times*, 12/22/21.
97. *Capital Times*, 12/27/21.
98. Howard Roberts, *The Big Nine*, 117.
99. *Davenport Democrat & Leader*, 1/1/22.
100. *Mason City Globe-Gazette*, 4/1/57.
101. *Leslie's Weekly*, 12/24/1921.
102. *Cedar Rapids Republican*, 12/29/21.
103. *Iowa City Press-Citizen*, 12/31/21.
104. *Iowa City Press-Citizen*, 12/22/21.
105. *Gettysburg Times*, 10/23/30.
106. *Iowa City Press-Citizen*, 12/13/21.
107. *Los Angeles Times*, 1/1/98.
108. *Iowa City Press-Citizen*, 11/29/21.
109. *Iowa City Press-Citizen*, 11/19/21.
110. *Fort Wayne (IN) News-Sentinel*, 11/13/21.
111. *Iowa City Press-Citizen*, 4/13/22.

CHAPTER 8

1. *Iowa City Press-Citizen*, 9/11/22.
2. *Rock Island Argus*, 9/11/22.
3. *Waterloo Courier*, 9/11/22.
4. *Iowa City Press-Citizen*, 8/24/22.
5. *Iowa City Press-Citizen*, 8/24/22.
6. *Davenport Democrat & Leader*, 9/20/22.
7. *Davenport Democrat & Leader*, 9/21/22.
8. *Rock Island Argus*, 9/11/22.
9. *Rock Island Argus*, 9/25/22.
10. *Iowa City Press-Citizen*, 9/21/22.
11. *Davenport Democrat & Leader*, 10/1/22.
12. *Rock Island Argus*, 9/29/22.
13. *Waterloo Courier*, 8/16/66.
14. *Rock Island Argus*, 10/2/22.
15. *Rock Island Argus*, 10/7/22.
16. *Mount Pleasant News*, 3/28/53.
17. *Rock Island Argus*, 10/9/22.

18. *Rock Island Argus*, 10/9/22.
19. *Rock Island Argus*, 10/11/22.
20. *Rock Island Argus*, 10/16/22.
21. *Davenport Democrat & Leader*, 10/16/22.
22. *Davenport Democrat & Leader*, 10/18/22.
23. *Rock Island Argus*, 10/23/22.
24. *Rock Island Argus*, 10/30/22.
25. *Rock Island Argus*, 10/30/22.
26. *Rock Island Argus*, 10/30/22.
27. Sheila Tully Boyle and Andrew Bunie, *Paul Robeson: The Years of Promise and Achievement*, 108.
28. *Rock Island Argus*, 11/9/22.
29. *Rock Island Argus*, 11/10/22.
30. *Rock Island Argus*, 11/13/22.
31. *Rock Island Argus*, 11/17/22.
32. *Rock Island Argus*, 11/20/22.
33. *Davenport Democrat & Leader*, 11/20/22.
34. *Rock Island Argus*, 11/23/22.
35. *Rock Island Argus*, 11/22/22.
36. *Rock Island Argus*, 11/27/22.
37. *Chicago Defender*, 1/8/58.
38. *Hammond (IN) Times*, 12/1/22.
39. *Massillon (OH) Independent*, 12/4/22.
40. John Carroll, *Fritz Pollard: Pioneer in Racial Advancement*, 155.
41. *Iowa City Press-Citizen*, 12/8/22.
42. *Chicago Defender*, 12/16/22.
43. *Davenport Democrat & Leader*, 4/1/23.
44. *Davenport Democrat & Leader*, 4/2/23.
45. *Davenport Democrat & Leader*, 7/17/23.
46. *Davenport Democrat & Leader*, 7/17/23.
47. *Davenport Democrat & Leader*, 9/14/23.
48. *Davenport Democrat & Leader*, 9/7/23.
49. *Rock Island Argus*, 9/24/23.
50. *Mason City Globe-Gazette*, 3/30/57.
51. *Rock Island Argus*, 10/4/23.
52. *Rock Island Argus*, 10/1/23.
53. *Rock Island Argus*, 10/1/23.
54. *Rock Island Argus*, 10/1/23.
55. *Rock Island Argus*, 10/8/23.
56. *Davenport Democrat & Leader*, 10/8/23.
57. *Rock Island Argus*, 10/15/23.
58. *Rock Island Argus*, 10/15/23.
59. *Rock Island Argus*, 10/22/23.
60. *Rock Island Argus*, 10/18/23.
61. *Rock Island Argus*, 10/29/23.
62. *Rock Island Argus*, 10/30/23.
63. *Rock Island Argus*, 10/31/23.
64. *Rock Island Argus*, 10/31/23.
65. *Rock Island Argus*, 11/5/23.
66. *Rock Island Argus*, 11/12/23.
67. *Rock Island Argus*, 11/19/23.
68. *Rock Island Argus*, 11/19/23.
69. *Rock Island Argus*, 11/26/23.
70. *Rock Island Argus*, 12/3/23.
71. *Rock Island Argus*, 12/3/23.
72. *Rock Island Argus*, 12/10/23.

Chapter 9

1. *Davenport Democrat & Leader*, 4/16/24; *Davenport Democrat & Leader*, 8/18/25; *Oxford Mirror*, 8/13/25.
2. *Rock Island Argus*, 9/26/24.
3. *Rock Island Argus*, 9/22/24.
4. *Rock Island Argus*, 9/22/24.
5. For more information about Jim Thorpe, see *Native American Son: The Life and Sporting Legend of Jim Thorpe*, by Kate Buford.
6. *Rock Island Argus*, 9/29/24.
7. *Rock Island Argus*, 10/6/24.
8. *Rock Island Argus*, 10/13/24.
9. *Rock Island Argus*, 10/13/24.
10. *Rock Island Argus*, 10/20/24.
11. *Rock Island Argus*, 10/28/24.
12. *Rock Island Argus*, 10/22/24.
13. *Waterloo Courier*, 10/28/24.
14. *Rock Island Argus*, 10/25/24.
15. *Davenport Democrat & Leader*, 11/16/24.
16. *Rock Island Argus*, 10/27/24.
17. *Rock Island Argus*, 10/27/24.
18. *Rock Island Argus*, 11/5/24.
19. *Waterloo Courier*, 10/28/24.
20. *Rock Island Argus*, 10/27/24.
21. *Rock Island Argus*, 10/28/24.
22. *Rock Island Argus*, 11/3/24.
23. *Rock Island Argus*, 11/3/24.
24. *Chicago Tribune*, 10/30/24.
25. *Rock Island Argus*, 11/10/24.
26. *Rock Island Argus*, 11/10/24.
27. *Davenport Democrat & Leader*, 11/16/24.
28. *Rock Island Argus*, 11/17/24.
29. *Rock Island Argus*, 11/24/24.
30. *Rock Island Argus*, 11/28/24.
31. *Waterloo Courier*, 12/5/24; *Davenport Democrat & Leader*, 12/3/24.
32. *Rock Island Argus*, 12/7/24.
33. *Rock Island Argus*, 12/15/24.
34. *Lincoln State Journal*, 12/15/24.
35. *Rock Island Argus*, 12/20/24.
36. *Rock Island Argus*, 9/19/25.
37. *Davenport Democrat & Leader*, 9/30/25.
38. *Rock Island Argus*, 10/2/25.
39. *Rock Island Argus*, 9/21/25.
40. *Rock Island Argus*, 9/21/25.
41. *Rock Island Argus*, 9/28/25.
42. *Davenport Democrat & Leader*, 10/28/25.
43. *Rock Island Argus*, 9/28/25.
44. *Rock Island Argus*, 9/30/25.
45. *Rock Island Argus*, 10/5/25.
46. *Rock Island Argus*, 10/12/25.
47. *Rock Island Argus*, 10/19/25.
48. *Rock Island Argus*, 10/26/25.
49. *Rock Island Argus*, 10/31/25.
50. Kate Buford, *Native American Son: The Life and Sporting Legend of Jim Thorpe*, 245.
51. *Rock Island Argus*, 10/29/25.
52. *Rock Island Argus*, 11/2/25.
53. *Rock Island Argus*, 11/4/25.
54. *Rock Island Argus*, 11/4/25.
55. *Rock Island Argus*, 11/6/25.
56. *Rock Island Argus*, 11/16/25.
57. *Rock Island Argus*, 11/16/25.
58. *Rock Island Argus*, 11/16/25.
59. *Rock Island Argus*, 11/19/25.
60. *Rock Island Argus*, 11/21/25.
61. *Rock Island Argus*, 11/23/25.
62. Pro Football Researchers Association linescore.
63. *Rock Island Argus*, 11/25/25.
64. *Rock Island Argus*, 11/28/25.
65. *Rock Island Argus*, 11/30/25.
66. *Rock Island Argus*, 11/30/25.
67. *La Crosse Tribune and Leader-Press*, 9/11/36.

Chapter 10

1. John M. Carroll, *The Impact of Red Grange on Pro Football in 1925*, The Coffin Corner, Vol. 20, No. 2.

2. *Mount Pleasant News*, 3/28/53.
3. *Chicago Defender*, 3/26/62.
4. *Rock Island Argus*, 9/17/26.
5. *Rock Island Argus*, 9/16/26.
6. *Davenport Democrat & Leader*, 8/30/26.
7. *Rock Island Argus*, 9/23/26.
8. *Rock Island Argus*, 9/27/26.
9. *Rock Island Argus*, 9/27/26.
10. *Rock Island Argus*, 10/4/26.
11. Howard Roberts, *The Story of Pro Football*, 260.
12. *Rock Island Argus*, 10/8/26.
13. *Rock Island Argus*, 10/11/26.
14. *Rock Island Argus*, 10/11/26.
15. *Davenport Democrat & Leader*, 10/11/26.
16. *Davenport Democrat & Leader*, 10/11/26.
17. *Rock Island Argus*, 10/15/26.
18. *Rock Island Argus*, 10/18/26.
19. *Rock Island Argus*, 10/20/26.
20. *Rock Island Argus*, 10/22/26.
21. Pro Football Researchers Association linescore.
22. *Rock Island Argus*, 10/25/26.
23. *Rock Island Argus*, 10/25/26.
24. *Davenport Democrat & Leader*, 10/25/26.
25. John M. Carroll, *Red Grange and the Rise of Modern Football*, 136.
26. *Rock Island Argus*, 11/1/26.
27. *Rock Island Argus*, 11/3/26.
28. *Cedar Rapids Gazette*, 10/23/51.
29. Pro Football Researchers Association linescore.
30. *Rock Island Argus*, 11/11/26.
31. *Rock Island Argus*, 11/16/26; *Rock Island Argus*, 11/17/26.
32. *Rock Island Argus*, 11/22/26.
33. *Rock Island Argus*, 11/22/26.
34. For more information on the Chicago Cardinals, see the outstanding *When Football Was Football: The Chicago Cardinals and the Birth of the NFL*, by Joe Ziemba.
35. *Mason City Globe-Gazette*, 3/27/57.
36. *Davenport Democrat & Leader*, 11/16/26.
37. *Chicago Tribune*, 11/26/26.
38. *Davenport Democrat & Leader*, 11/29/26.
39. *Chicago Tribune*, 12/19/26.
40. *Oelwein Daily Register*, 12/11/26.
41. *Rock Island Argus*, 11/13/26.
42. Charles K. Ross, *Outside the Lines: African Americans and the Integration of the National Football League*, 99; John Carroll, *Fritz Pollard: Pioneer in Racial Advancement*, 215.
43. Manque Winters, *How Good Do We Have to Be? Rising Above Rejection*, North American Society for Sports History Proceedings, 2000, The Amateur Athletic Foundation, 95–96.
44. *Appleton (WI) Post-Crescent*, 10/14/27.
45. *Chicago Tribune*, 9/26/27.
46. *Chicago Tribune*, 9/26/27.
47. *Chicago Tribune*, 10/3/27.
48. *Chicago Herald-Examiner*, 10/3/27.
49. *Chicago Tribune*, 10/10/27.
50. *Chicago Tribune*, 10/10/27.
51. *Chicago Tribune*, 10/17/27.
52. *Chicago Tribune*, 10/31/27.
53. *Chicago Tribune*, 11/7/27.
54. *Chicago Tribune*, 11/14/27.
55. Pro Football Researchers Association linescore.
56. *Chicago Tribune*, 11/21/27.
57. *Chicago Tribune*, 11/25/27.
58. *Chicago Tribune*, 11/25/27.
59. *Chicago Herald-Examiner*, 11/25/27.
60. *Chicago Tribune*, 11/28/27.
61. *Chicago Tribune*, 11/28/27.

Chapter 11

1. *Oelwein Daily Register*, 8/21/28.
2. *Suburbanite Economist*, 9/14/26.
3. Andy Piascik, *Gridiron Gauntlet*, 171, 175.
4. *Wisconsin Rapids Daily Tribune*, 10/11/28.
5. *Appleton (WI) Post-Crescent*, 10/10/28.
6. *Wisconsin Rapids Daily Tribune*, 10/11/28.
7. *Chicago Tribune*, 9/24/28.
8. *Southtown Economist*, 9/26/28.
9. *Chicago Tribune*, 10/8/28.
10. *Chicago Tribune*, 10/15/28.
11. John Carroll, *Fritz Pollard: Pioneer in Racial Advancement*, 182.
12. For more information about Fait Elkins, see "The Twists of Fait," by Bil Gilbert, *Sports Illustrated*, 10/16/91.
13. Pro Football Researchers Association linescore.
14. Pro Football Researchers Association linescore.
15. *Chicago Tribune*, 11/26/28.
16. *Chicago Tribune*, 11/30/28.
17. Joe Ziemba, *When Football Was Football: The Chicago Cardinals and the Birth of the NFL*, 157.
18. *Davenport Democrat & Leader*, 3/4/28.
19. *Southtown Economist*, 8/16/29.
20. Craig R. Coenen, *From Sandlots to the Super Bowl*, 91.
21. For more information on Nevers' time with the Duluth Eskimos, see *Leatherheads of the North: The True Story of Ernie Nevers and the Duluth Eskimos*, by Chuck Frederick.
22. Joe Ziemba, *When Football Was Football: The Chicago Cardinals and the Birth of the NFL*, 162.
23. Joe Ziemba, *When Football Was Football: The Chicago Cardinals and the Birth of the NFL*, 162.
24. Joe Ziemba, *When Football Was Football: The Chicago Cardinals and the Birth of the NFL*, 162; *Chicago Defender*, 7/15/50.
25. *Chicago Tribune*, 9/30/29.
26. *Appleton (WI) Post-Crescent*, 10/5/29.
27. *Appleton (WI) Post-Crescent*, 10/2/29.
28. *Chicago Tribune*, 10/7/29.
29. *Waterloo Courier*, 10/10/29; *Appleton (WI) Post-Crescent*, 10/18/29.
30. *Chicago Herald-Examiner*, 10/14/29.
31. *Chicago Defender*, 11/9/29.
32. *Chicago Tribune*, 10/21/29.
33. *Chicago Herald-Examiner*, 10/21/29.
34. *Chicago Tribune*, 10/28/29.
35. *Chicago Tribune*, 10/28/29.
36. Pro Football Researchers Association linescore.
37. *Chicago Tribune*, 11/7/29.
38. *Chicago Tribune*, 11/7/29.
39. *Suburbanite Economist*, 11/5/29.
40. *Chicago Tribune*, 11/11/29.
41. *Chicago Tribune*, 11/18/29.
42. *Chicago Tribune*, 11/18/29.
43. *Chicago Tribune*, 11/25/29.
44. Joe Ziemba, *When Football Was Football: The Chicago Cardinals and the Birth of the NFL*, 164.
45. Paul Michael, *Professional Football's Greatest Games*, 76.
46. Joe Ziemba, *When Football Was Football: The Chicago Cardinals and the Birth of the NFL*, 164.
47. Paul Michael, *Professional Football's Greatest Games*, 76.

48. *Chicago Tribune*, 11/29/29.
49. Joe Ziemba, *When Football Was Football: The Chicago Cardinals and the Birth of the NFL*, 165.
50. *Chicago Tribune*, 11/29/29.
51. *Chicago Herald-Examiner*, 11/29/29.
52. Paul Michael, *Professional Football's Greatest Games*, v-vi.
53. *Mount Pleasant News*, 3/5/53.
54. Joe Ziemba, *When Football Was Football: The Chicago Cardinals and the Birth of the NFL*, 165.
55. *Chicago Tribune*, 12/2/29.
56. *Chicago Tribune*, 12/9/29.
57. *Chicago Tribune*, 12/22/29.

Chapter 12

1. *Southtown Economist*, 9/12/30.
2. *Chicago Tribune*, 9/15/30.
3. *Chicago Tribune*, 9/22/30.
4. *Chicago Tribune*, 9/22/30.
5. *Chicago Herald-Examiner*, 9/29/30.
6. *Portsmouth (OH) Times*, 10/2/30.
7. *Chicago Tribune*, 10/6/30.
8. *Chicago Tribune*, 10/9/30.
9. *Chicago Tribune*, 10/9/30.
10. *Wisconsin State Journal*, 11/6/30.
11. *Hammond (IN) Times*, 1/17/34; *Wisconsin State Journal*, 11/6/30.
12. *Chicago Tribune*, 10/13/30.
13. Pro Football Researchers Association linescore.
14. *Washington Times*, 2/4/2006.
15. *Chicago Tribune*, 10/20/30.
16. *Mason City Globe-Gazette*, 3/27/57.
17. *Chicago Tribune*, 10/23/30.
18. *Chicago Tribune*, 10/26/30.
19. *Dunkirk (NY) Observer*, 10/27/30.
20. *Chicago Tribune*, 10/27/30.
21. *Chicago Tribune*, 10/27/30.
22. *Chicago Tribune*, 11/3/30.
23. *Chicago Tribune*, 11/3/30.
24. *Chicago Tribune*, 11/10/30.
25. *Chicago Tribune*, 11/17/30.
26. Joe Ziemba, *When Football Was Football: The Chicago Cardinals and the Birth of the NFL*, 171.
27. *Chicago Tribune*, 11/17/30.
28. *Chicago Tribune*, 11/17/30.
29. *Milwaukee Journal*, 12/9/30.
30. *Chicago Tribune*, 11/24/30.
31. *Chicago Tribune*, 11/28/30.
32. *Chicago Tribune*, 11/28/30.
33. *Belleville (KS) Telescope*, 6/7/79.
34. *Chicago Tribune*, 11/28/30.
35. *Chicago Defender*, 1/3/31; *Chicago Tribune*, 12/8/30.
36. *Chicago Tribune*, 12/16/30.
37. *Mason City Globe-Gazette*, 12/24/30.
38. *Jet Magazine*, 9/1/66, 54.
39. *Chicago Tribune*, 9/21/31.
40. *Chicago Tribune*, 9/24/31.
41. *Chicago Tribune*, 10/12/31.
42. *Wisconsin State Journal*, 10/15/31.
43. *Chicago Tribune*, 10/19/31.
44. *Chicago Tribune*, 10/25/31.
45. *Chicago Tribune*, 10/26/31.
46. *Chicago Herald-Examiner*, 11/2/31; *Chicago Tribune*, 11/2/31.
47. *Chicago Tribune*, 11/9/31.
48. *Massillon (OH) Independent*, 11/4/31.
49. *Chicago Tribune*, 11/16/31.
50. *Portsmouth (OH) Times*, 11/20/31.
51. *Chicago Tribune*, 11/23/31.
52. *Chicago Tribune*, 11/27/31.
53. *Chicago Tribune*, 11/29/31.
54. *Olean (NY) Times*, 12/4/31.
55. *Mason City Globe-Gazette*, 9/14/36.
56. *Chicago Defender*, 11/28/31.

Chapter 13

1. John Carroll, *Fritz Pollard: Pioneer in Racial Advancement*, 183.
2. *Los Angeles Times*, 12/19/31.
3. *Chicago Defender*, 10/24/31.
4. *Van Wert (OH) Bulletin*, 12/9/31.
5. *Los Angeles Times*, 12/20/31.
6. *Chicago Defender*, 1/2/32.
7. *Chicago Defender*, 1/9/32.
8. *Chicago Defender*, 12/19/31.
9. *Chicago Defender*, 1/9/32.
10. John Carroll, *Fritz Pollard: Pioneer in Racial Advancement*, 183.
11. *Los Angeles Times*, 1/18/32.
12. *Los Angeles Times*, 1/24/32.
13. *Mason City Globe-Gazette*, 3/27/57.
14. *Oakland Tribune*, 1/27/32.
15. Personal interview with Sherman Howard, 11/14/2011.
16. John Carroll, *Fritz Pollard: Pioneer in Racial Advancement*, 171.
17. *Chicago Defender*, 11/26/32.
18. *Chicago Defender*, 10/22/32.
19. *Chicago Defender*, 10/29/32.
20. *Chicago Defender*, 10/31/31.
21. C. Robert Barnett, *The Reaction of the Popular Press to the Last Two Black National Football League Players, 1932–1934*, North American Society for Sports History Proceedings, 1982.
22. Daniel Coyle, "Invisible Men," *Sports Illustrated*, 12/15/2003.
23. Associated Press, as reported in the *Syracuse Herald*, 10/24/34.
24. *Hammond (IN) Times*, 10/18/33.
25. *Clinton Herald*, 10/29/55.
26. *Chicago Defender*, 9/22/34.
27. *Mason City Globe-Gazette*, 10/9/34; *Ogden (UT) Standard-Examiner*, 10/21/34.
28. *Oelwein Daily Register*, 10/9/34.
29. *Chicago Defender*, 11/10/34.
30. *Chicago Defender*, 12/14/35.
31. *Chicago Defender*, 11/16/35.
32. *Dunkirk (NY) Observer*, 11/15/35.
33. *Oelwein Daily Register*, 9/12/36.
34. *Chicago Defender*, 10/17/36.
35. *Chicago Defender*, 10/17/36.
36. *Chicago Defender*, 10/3/36.
37. *Mason City Globe-Gazette*, 9/14/36.
38. *Chicago Defender*, 11/21/36.
39. *Chicago Defender*, 7/24/37.
40. John Carroll, *Fritz Pollard: Pioneer in Racial Advancement*, 204.
41. *Hammond (IN) Times*, 1/20/36.
42. *Chicago Defender*, 10/2/37.
43. *Hammond (IN) Times*, 10/11/37.
44. *The Garfieldian*, 11/10/37.
45. *La Crosse Tribune and Leader-Press*, 11/4/37.
46. *La Crosse Tribune and Leader-Press*, 11/10/37.

47. *Oshkosh Northwestern*, 11/8/37.
48. *The Garfieldian*, 10/28/37.
49. *The Garfieldian*, 11/18/37.
50. *La Crosse Tribune and Leader-Press*, 11/21/37.
51. *La Crosse Tribune and Leader-Press*, 11/22/37.
52. Bob Gill and Tod Maher, *Not Only the Ball Was Brown: Black Players in Minor League Football, 1933–46*, Coffin Corner, Vol. 11, No. 5.
53. *Chicago Defender*, 12/4/37.
54. *Chicago Defender*, 6/25/38.
55. *Chicago Defender*, 12/25/37.
56. *Chicago Defender*, 8/27/38.
57. *Chicago Defender*, 9/10/38.
58. *Chicago Defender*, 10/1/38.
59. *Chicago Defender*, 10/1/38.
60. *Chicago Defender*, 10/1/38.
61. *Chicago Defender*, 10/1/38.
62. *Chicago Defender*, 10/1/38; *Chicago Heights Star*, 11/8/38.
63. *Chicago Defender*, 8/26/39.
64. *Chicago Defender*, 7/15/39.
65. *Chicago Defender*, 8/26/39.
66. *Chicago Defender*, 2/13/37.
67. *The (Baltimore) Afro-American*, 9/9/39.
68. *Chicago Defender*, 11/4/39.
69. Charles K. Ross, *Outside the Lines: African Americans and the Integration of the National Football League*, 57.
70. For more information on semi-pro football, see the terrific reference *Outsiders: Minor League and Independent Football, 1923–1950*, by Bob Gill and Tod Maher.
71. *Chicago Defender*, 11/4/39.
72. *Chicago Defender*, 12/2/39.
73. *Chicago Defender*, 6/17/39.
74. *Chicago Defender*, 3/14/42.
75. *Chicago Defender*, 11/4/39.
76. *Carroll Daily Herald*, 9/21/39.
77. D.W. Stump, *Kinnick: The Man and the Legend*, 62.
78. *Waterloo Courier*, 1/12/40.
79. *Iowa Alumni Review*, December 1972, 12.
80. *Chicago Defender*, 1/20/40.
81. *Chicago Tribune*, 8/17/66.
82. *Chicago Defender*, 6/29/40.
83. *Chicago Defender*, 8/3/40.
84. *Chicago Defender*, 8/24/40; *Oakland Tribune*, 9/8/40.
85. *Chicago Defender*, 9/21/40.
86. *Chicago Defender*, 10/19/40.
87. *Chicago Defender*, 10/12/40.
88. *Chicago Defender*, 11/2/40.
89. *Chicago Defender*, 11/16/40.
90. *Chicago Defender*, 11/6/43.
91. *Chicago Defender*, 9/15/23; *Waterloo Courier*, 9/3/28; *Chicago Defender*, 11/29/30.
92. *Chicago Defender*, 10/29/32.
93. *Chicago Defender*, 6/12/37.

Chapter 14

1. *Mason City Globe-Gazette*, 3/29/57.
2. *Mason City Globe-Gazette*, 3/30/57.
3. *Cedar Rapids Gazette*, 11/21/49.
4. *Mason City Globe-Gazette*, 3/29/57.
5. *Charleston (WV) Gazette*, 11/14/27.
6. Kenneth L. "Tug" Wilson and Jerry Brondfield, *The Big Ten*, 115.
7. *Mason City Globe-Gazette*, 3/29/57.
8. James Peterson, *Slater of Iowa*, 40.
9. *Chicago Defender*, 1/24/42.
10. *New York Daily Worker*, 12/1/41.
11. *Chicago Defender*, 12/20/41.
12. *Chicago Defender*, 1/24/42.
13. *Carroll Times-Herald*, 8/27/45.
14. *Chicago Defender*, 9/23/44; *The Garfieldian*, 11/1/45; *The Garfieldian*, 9/12/46.
15. *Southeast Economist*, 9/19/46.
16. *Mount Pleasant News*, 3/28/53.
17. *Chicago Defender*, 5/22/43.
18. *Chicago Defender*, 6/5/43.
19. *Chicago Defender*, 9/9/44.
20. *Iowa City Press-Citizen*, 9/22/71.
21. *Mason City Globe-Gazette*, 9/26/45.
22. *Chicago Defender*, 12/25/43.
23. *Hammond (IN) Times*, 12/5/45.
24. *Chicago Defender*, 10/7/44.
25. *Des Moines Register*, 3/30/75.
26. Emlen Tunnell, *Footsteps of a Giant*, 68.
27. *Des Moines Register*, 8/31/46.
28. *Iowa City Press-Citizen*, 10/26/46.
29. *Iowa City Press-Citizen*, 7/25/47.
30. *Daily Iowan*, 2/25/47.
31. *Associated Press*, as reported in the *Hagerstown (MD) Daily Mail*, 11/7/47.
32. *Chicago Defender*, 10/4/47.
33. William J. Grimshaw, *Bitter Fruit: Black Politics and the Chicago Machine*, 105–106.
34. *Chicago Defender*, 1/17/48.
35. *Chicago Defender*, 3/6/48.
36. *Waterloo Courier*, 8/4/48.
37. *Chicago Tribune*, 11/5/48.
38. *Chicago Defender*, 9/11/48.
39. *Chicago Defender*, 11/13/48.
40. *Chicago Tribune*, 1/9/55.
41. *Chicago Defender*, 11/20/48.
42. *Chicago Defender*, 12/18/48.
43. *Cedar Rapids Gazette*, 10/9/49.
44. *Cedar Rapids Gazette*, 10/9/49.
45. *Chicago Defender*, 2/19/49.
46. *Des Moines Register*, 1/10/49.
47. *Chicago Defender*, 8/27/66.
48. *Chicago Defender*, 8/13/49.
49. Francis Wallace, *The Notre Dame Story*, 173.
50. Howard Roberts, *The Big Nine*, 119.
51. *Cedar Rapids Gazette*, 8/9/49.
52. *Chicago Defender*, 7/29/50.
53. *Chicago Defender*, 7/15/50.
54. *Cedar Rapids Tribune*, 12/1/49.
55. *Chicago Defender*, 8/26/50.
56. *Chicago Defender*, 9/9/50.
57. *Chicago Defender*, 9/30/50; *Chicago Defender*, 6/9/51.
58. *Chicago Defender*, 5/20/50.
59. *Chicago Defender*, 11/18/50.
60. *Mason City Globe-Gazette*, 4/1/57.
61. Personal interview with Sherman Howard, 11/14/2011.
62. *Cedar Rapids Gazette*, 5/8/51.
63. *Mason City Globe-Gazette*, 4/1/57.
64. *Des Moines Register*, 3/18/51.
65. Mervin Hyman and Gordon White, *Big Ten Football*, 262.
66. *Cedar Rapids Tribune*, 9/6/51.

Chapter 15

1. *Chicago Defender*, 2/16/52.
2. *Mount Pleasant News*, 3/28/53.

3. *Mason City Globe-Gazette*, 11/12/54.
4. *Mount Pleasant News*, 3/28/53.
5. *Oelwein Daily Register*, 12/2/52.
6. *Cedar Rapids Gazette*, 10/9/49.
7. *Cedar Rapids Gazette*, 10/9/49.
8. *Cedar Rapids Gazette*, 10/9/49.
9. *Davenport Democrat & Leader*, 9/29/49.
10. *Davenport Democrat & Leader*, 9/29/49.
11. *Davenport Democrat & Leader*, 9/29/49.
12. *Mount Pleasant News*, 3/5/53.
13. *Jet Magazine*, 11/27/52, 50; *Daily Iowan*, 4/27/57.
14. *Mount Pleasant News*, 3/5/53.
15. *Mason City Globe-Gazette*, 11/12/54.
16. *Burlington Hawkeye*, 3/28/53.
17. *Chicago Defender*, 3/31/51.
18. *Cedar Rapids Gazette*, 2/1/65.
19. *Cedar Rapids Gazette*, 11/21/49; *Mount Pleasant News*, 3/28/53.
20. *Cedar Rapids Gazette*, 8/11/97.
21. *Cedar Rapids Gazette*, 11/21/49.
22. *Cedar Rapids Gazette*, 2/1/65.
23. *Cedar Rapids Gazette*, 11/21/49; *Cedar Rapids Gazette*, 2/1/65.
24. *Mount Pleasant News*, 3/28/53.
25. *Clinton Herald*, 12/31/56.
26. *Davenport Democrat & Leader*, 9/29/49.
27. *Clinton Herald*, 12/31/56.
28. *Oelwein Daily Register*, 12/2/52.
29. *Oelwein Daily Register*, 12/2/52.
30. *Mason City Globe-Gazette*, 3/27/57; *Des Moines Register*, 9/4/66.
31. *Davenport Democrat & Leader*, 9/29/49.
32. *Mount Pleasant News*, 3/28/53.
33. Personal interview with Sherman Howard, 11/14/2011.
34. *Burlington Hawkeye*, 3/28/53; *Mason City Globe-Gazette*, 11/12/54.
35. *Oelwein Daily Register*, 12/2/52.
36. *Cedar Rapids Gazette*, 11/24/49.
37. *Davenport Democrat & Leader*, 9/29/49.
38. *Postville Herald*, 3/28/90.
39. George W. Slater, "Negroes Becoming Socialists," *Chicago Daily Socialist*, 9/15/1908.
40. *Oelwein Daily Register*, 12/2/52.
41. *Chicago Defender*, 2/20/54.
42. *Chicago Defender*, 8/29/53.
43. *Chicago Defender*, 1/16/54.
44. *Chicago Defender*, 11/23/54.
45. *Dixon (IL) Telegraph*, 8/4/54.
46. *Chicago Defender*, 6/20/53.
47. *Mount Pleasant News*, 10/7/53.
48. *Cedar Rapids Gazette*, 11/17/54.
49. *Des Moines Register*, 11/5/55.
50. *Chicago Tribune*, 1/9/55.
51. *Clinton Herald*, 10/29/55.
52. *Chicago Tribune*, 1/9/55.
53. *Chicago Defender*, 2/7/56.
54. *Chicago Defender*, 1/21/63.
55. *Chicago Defender*, 3/26/56.
56. *Chicago Defender*, 4/28/56.
57. *Chicago Defender*, 4/28/56.
58. *Chicago Defender*, 5/19/56.
59. *Cedar Rapids Gazette*, 11/24/54.
60. Brian Chapman and Mike Chapman, *Evy and the Hawkeyes: The Glory Years*, 152.
61. *Mason City Globe-Gazette*, 12/8/56.
62. *Clinton Herald*, 12/31/56.
63. *Clinton Herald*, 12/31/56.
64. *Mason City Globe-Gazette*, 3/30/57.
65. *Mason City Globe-Gazette*, 4/4/57.
66. *Mason City Globe-Gazette*, 3/27/57.
67. *Mason City Globe-Gazette*, 3/30/57.
68. *Mason City Globe-Gazette*, 3/30/57.
69. *Hagerstown (MD) Daily Mail*, 11/7/47; *Chicago Defender*, 3/4/50; *Chicago Defender*, 3/18/61.
70. *Chicago Defender*, 3/23/57.
71. *Chicago Defender*, 5/4/57; *Chicago Defender*, 4/10/57.
72. *Chicago Defender*, 4/10/57.
73. *Chicago Defender*, 5/11/57.
74. *Chicago Defender*, 5/23/53; *Chicago Defender*, 5/15/54.
75. *Chicago Defender*, 5/1/58.
76. *Cedar Rapids Gazette*, 8/14/58.
77. *Chicago Defender*, 8/23/58.
78. *Chicago Defender*, 8/23/58.
79. *Chicago Tribune*, 8/14/58.
80. *Chicago Defender*, 8/23/58.
81. *Chicago Daily News*, 8/13/58.
82. *Chicago Defender*, 9/13/58.
83. *Chicago Defender*, 9/9/58.
84. *Chicago Defender*, 9/6/58.
85. *Chicago Defender*, 10/18/58.
86. *Chicago Defender*, 10/9/58.
87. *Cedar Rapids Gazette*, 1/11/59.
88. *Chicago Defender*, 1/13/59.
89. *Chicago Defender*, 5/4/59.
90. *Clinton Herald*, 2/9/59.
91. *Chicago Defender*, 10/10/59.
92. *Chicago Defender*, 10/27/59.
93. *Chicago Defender*, 1/20/59.
94. *Chicago Defender*, 2/21/59.
95. *Chicago Defender*, 11/2/59.
96. *Chicago Defender*, 11/5/59.
97. *Chicago Defender*, 8/26/65.

Chapter 16

1. *Mason City Globe-Gazette*, 12/10/59.
2. *Chicago Defender*, 12/8/59.
3. *Chicago Defender*, 12/8/59.
4. *Mason City Globe-Gazette*, 12/10/59.
5. *Chicago Defender*, 5/5/58.
6. *Chicago Defender*, 12/16/59.
7. *Chicago Defender*, 12/16/59.
8. *Chicago Defender*, 12/16/59.
9. *Chicago Defender*, 5/7/60.
10. *Corpus Christi (TX) Times*, 12/11/59; *Chicago Defender*, 12/17/59.
11. *Chicago Defender*, 1/28/60.
12. *Chicago Tribune*, 7/6/60.
13. *Chicago Defender*, 7/7/60.
14. *Cedar Rapids Gazette*, 7/12/60.
15. *Chicago Defender*, 7/7/60.
16. *Chicago Defender*, 7/14/60.
17. *Chicago Defender*, 7/14/60.
18. *Cedar Rapids Gazette*, 8/31/60.
19. *Jet Magazine*, 3/3/60, 30.
20. *Chicago Defender*, 12/6/60.
21. *Chicago Defender*, 12/7/60.
22. *Chicago Defender*, 12/6/60.
23. *Chicago Tribune*, 12/12/60.
24. *Chicago Defender*, 12/13/60.
25. *Chicago Defender*, 12/6/60.
26. *Chicago Defender*, 12/6/60.
27. *Chicago Defender*, 12/13/60; *Chicago Defender*, 8/16/66.

28. *Chicago Defender*, 12/15/60; *Chicago Defender*, 12/22/60.
29. *Chicago Defender*, 9/19/61.
30. *Chicago Defender*, 9/28/60.
31. *Cedar Rapids Gazette*, 9/28/60.
32. *Chicago Defender*, 9/29/60.
33. *Chicago Defender*, 3/26/62.
34. *Chicago Defender*, 3/18/61.
35. *Chicago Defender*, 3/7/63.
36. *Chicago Defender*, 4/8/63.
37. *Chicago Defender*, 2/13/60; *Chicago Defender*, 1/9/60.
38. *Chicago Defender*, 2/15/60.
39. *Chicago Defender*, 3/16/63.
40. *Capital Times*, 4/3/41; *Chicago Defender*, 4/12/41.
41. *Chicago Defender*, 1/8/58.
42. *Chicago Defender*, 6/5/63.
43. *Cedar Rapids Gazette*, 4/30/64.
44. *Des Moines Register*, 5/7/64.
45. *Des Moines Register*, 5/7/64.
46. *Cedar Rapids Gazette*, 4/30/64.
47. *Chicago Defender*, 8/27/66.
48. *Jet Magazine*, 6/1/61, 24.
49. *Chicago Defender*, 9/19/64.
50. *Chicago Defender*, 6/22/64.
51. *Chicago Defender*, 11/5/64.
52. *Black World/Negro Digest*, November 1961, 17–18.
53. *Chicago Defender*, 8/4/62.
54. *It's Sports Time with Phil Rizzuto*, 8/16/66, Duke Slater Vertical File, University of Iowa Special Collections and University Archives.
55. *Chicago Defender*, 7/15/50.
56. *Des Moines Register*, 5/7/64.
57. *Cedar Rapids Gazette*, 10/6/64.
58. *Chicago Defender*, 6/16/62.
59. *Chicago Defender*, 9/5/64.
60. *Chicago Defender*, 12/25/65.
61. *Des Moines Register*, 8/16/66.

Chapter 17

1. *Chicago Tribune*, 8/16/66.
2. *Chicago Tribune*, 8/17/66.
3. *Cedar Rapids Gazette*, 8/16/66.
4. *Des Moines Register*, 8/16/66.
5. *Waterloo Courier*, 8/16/66.
6. *Clinton Herald*, 8/17/66.
7. *Chicago Tribune*, 8/17/66.
8. *Jet Magazine*, 9/1/66, 54.
9. *Chicago Defender*, 8/16/66.
10. *Chicago Tribune*, 8/16/66.
11. *Des Moines Register*, 8/16/66.
12. *Jet Magazine*, 9/1/66, 55.
13. *Chicago Defender*, 9/10/66.
14. *Jet Magazine*, 9/1/66, 54, 55.
15. *Chicago Defender*, 8/17/66.
16. *Chicago Defender*, 8/27/66.
17. *It's Sports Time with Phil Rizzuto*, 8/16/66, Duke Slater Vertical File, University of Iowa Special Collections and University Archives.
18. *It's Sports Time with Phil Rizzuto*, 8/16/66, Duke Slater Vertical File, University of Iowa Special Collections and University Archives.
19. *Chicago Tribune*, 8/19/66.
20. *Jet Magazine*, 9/1/66, 52.
21. *Waterloo Courier*, 8/16/66.
22. *Cedar Rapids Gazette*, 8/24/66.
23. Duke Slater Vertical File, University of Iowa Special Collections and University Archives.
24. *Ames Tribune*, 8/16/66.
25. *Davenport Democrat & Leader*, 9/29/49.
26. *Cedar Rapids Gazette*, 10/26/66.
27. *Chicago Defender*, 4/8/67; *Chicago Defender*, 2/25/71.
28. *Chicago Defender*, 4/8/67.
29. *Iowa City Press-Citizen*, 9/16/69.
30. *Hayward (CO) Daily Review*, 9/10/69.
31. Associated Press, 11/23/70.
32. *Iowa City Press-Citizen*, 4/21/69.
33. *Chicago Defender*, 11/18/71.
34. *Galveston (TX) Daily News*, 8/8/72.
35. *Chicago Defender*, 9/25/71.
36. *Chicago Defender*, 9/4/71.
37. *Iowa City Press-Citizen*, 5/28/70.
38. *Cedar Rapids Gazette*, 10/4/72.
39. *Cedar Rapids Gazette*, 3/26/72.
40. *Iowa City Press-Citizen*, 6/5/72.
41. *Iowa City Press-Citizen*, 6/5/72.
42. *Cedar Rapids Gazette*, 6/6/72.
43. *Cedar Rapids Gazette*, 6/6/72.
44. *Cedar Rapids Gazette*, 6/6/72.
45. *Cedar Rapids Gazette*, 6/6/72.
46. Kenneth L. "Tug" Wilson and Jerry Brondfield, *The Big Ten*, 115.
47. *Cedar Rapids Gazette*, 6/6/72.
48. *Cedar Rapids Gazette*, 6/22/72.
49. *Cedar Rapids Gazette*, 6/9/72.
50. *Iowa City Press-Citizen*, 6/15/72.
51. *Iowa City Press-Citizen*, 10/26/72.
52. *Des Moines Register*, 6/18/72.
53. Eric C. Wilson, "Hawkeyes I Remember," Iowa-Oregon State game program, 9/23/72.
54. *Daily Iowan*, 10/30/72.

Chapter 18

1. Personal interview with Gary Herrity, 11/8/2011.
2. George Wine, *Black and Gold Memories*, 47.
3. *Chicago Defender*, 7/15/50.
4. *Daily Iowan*, 5/1/2007.
5. Joe Ziemba, *When Football Was Football: The Chicago Cardinals and the Birth of the NFL*, 395.
6. United Press International, 12/29/62.
7. Associated Press, as reported in the *Austin-American Statesman*, 12/22/63.
8. Associated Press, 1/15/71.
9. *Chicago Defender*, 10/13/65.
10. *Cedar Rapids Gazette*, 10/9/49.
11. *Appleton (WI) Post-Crescent*, 11/19/59.
12. *Los Angeles Times*, 1/26/32.
13. John Carroll, *Fritz Pollard: Pioneer in Racial Advancement*, 233.
14. *Bluefield (WV) Daily Telegraph*, 1/12/34; *Chicago Tribune*, 10/24/71.
15. Gerald Holland, "How to Take a Biscuit Apart and Put It Back Just Like It Was," *Sports Illustrated*, 9/18/61; Dan Daly and Bob O'Donnell, *The Pro Football Chronicle*, 115.
16. *Chicago Tribune*, 8/20/66.
17. Sean Lahman, *The Pro Football Historical Abstract*, 245.
18. K.C. Joyner, *Blindsided*, 170.
19. Dan Daly and Bob O'Donnell, *The Pro Football Chronicle*, 7, 39.
20. Dan Daly and Bob O'Donnell, *The Pro Football Chronicle*, 115.

21. *Washington Times*, 2/4/2006.
22. Pete Palmer, et al., *The ESPN Pro Football Encyclopedia*, 1306; John Hogrogian, Paul Klatt, and John Turney, *All-Pro Football Teams: 1920-present*, 24, 31.

APPENDIX D

1. Pete Palmer, et al., *The ESPN Pro Football Encyclopedia*; John Hogrogian, Paul Klatt, and John Turney, *All-Pro Football Teams: 1920-Present*.

APPENDIX E

1. Pete Palmer, et al., *The ESPN Pro Football Encyclopedia*; John Hogrogian, Paul Klatt, and John Turney, *All-Pro Football Teams: 1920-Present*.

APPENDIX F

1. John Hogrogian, Paul Klatt, and John Turney, *All-Pro Football Teams: 1920-Present*.
2. John Hogrogian, Paul Klatt, and John Turney, *All-Pro Football Teams: 1920-Present*.
3. John Hogrogian, Paul Klatt, and John Turney, *All-Pro Football Teams: 1920-Present*.

Bibliography

Barry, John M. *The Great Influenza: The Epic Story of the Deadliest Plague in History.* New York: Penguin, 2005.
Boyle, Sheila Tully, and Andrew Bunie. *Paul Robeson: The Years of Promise and Achievement.* Amherst: University of Massachusetts Press, 2005.
Brichford, Maynard. *Bob Zuppke: The Life and Football Legacy of the Illinois Coach.* Jefferson, NC: McFarland, 2009.
Buford, Kate. *Native American Son: The Life and Sporting Legend of Jim Thorpe.* New York: Knopf, 2010.
Carroll, John M. *Fritz Pollard: Pioneer in Racial Advancement.* Urbana: University of Illinois Press, 1998.
_____. *Red Grange and the Rise of Modern Football.* Urbana: University of Illinois Press, 2004.
Carroll, Kevin. *Dr. Eddie Anderson: Hall of Fame College Football Coach.* Jefferson, NC: McFarland, 2007.
Chalk, Ocania. *Pioneers of Black Sport: The Early Days of the Black Professional Athlete in Baseball, Basketball, Boxing, and Football.* New York: Dodd, Mead, 1975.
Chapman, Brian, and Mike Chapman. *Evy and the Hawkeyes: The Glory Years.* New York: Leisure, 1983.
Coenen, Craig R. *From Sandlots to the Super Bowl.* Knoxville: University of Tennessee Press, 2005.
Cohane, Tim. *Great College Football Coaches of the Twenties and Thirties.* New Rochelle, NY: Arlington House, 1973.
Crosby, Alfred W. *America's Forgotten Pandemic: The Influenza of 1918.* New York: Cambridge University Press, 2003.
Cummins, Tait. *Who's Who in Iowa Football.* Cedar Rapids, IA: Stamats, 1948.
Daly, Dan, and Bob O'Donnell. *The Pro Football Chronicle.* New York: Macmillan, 1990.
Dukes, Mark, and Gus Schrader. *Greatest Moments in Iowa Hawkeyes Football History.* Chicago: Triumph, 1998.
Finn, Mike. *The University of Iowa Football Vault: The History of the Hawkeyes.* Atlanta: Whitman, 2008.
_____, and Chad Leistikow. *Hawkeye Legends, Lists, and Lore: The Athletic History of the Iowa Hawkeyes.* Champaign, IL: Sports, 1998.
Fleming, David. *Breaker Boys: The NFL's Greatest Team and the Stolen 1925 Championship.* New York: ESPN, 2007.
Foner, Philip S., ed. *Black Socialist Preacher: The Teachings of Reverend George Washington Woodbey and His Disciple Reverend George W. Slater, Jr.* San Francisco: Synthesis, 1983.
Frederick, Chuck. *Leatherheads of the North: The True Story of Ernie Nevers and the Duluth Eskimos.* Duluth, MN: X-Communication, 2007.
Gerber, John C. *A Pictorial History of the University of Iowa.* Iowa City: University of Iowa Press, 2005.
Gill, Bob, and Tod Maher. *Outsiders: Minor League and Independent Football, 1923–1950.* Haworth, NJ: Saint Johann, 2006.
Grimshaw, William J. *Bitter Fruit: Black Politics and the Chicago Machine.* Chicago: University of Chicago Press, 1995.
Harty, Pat. *Game Day Iowa Football: The Greatest Games, Players, Coaches, and Teams in the Glorious Tradition of Hawkeye Football.* Chicago: Triumph/Athlon Sports, 2007.
Hogrogian, John, and the editors of the Pro Football Researchers Association. *All-Pros: The First 40 Years.* North Huntington, PA: PFRA, 1995.
Hyman, Mervin, and Gordon White. *Big Ten Football.* New York: Macmillan, 1977.
Joyner, K.C. *Blindsided: Why the Left Tackle is Overrated and Other Contrarian Football Thoughts.* New York: Wiley, 2008.
Klosinski, Emil. *Notre Dame, Chicago Bears, and Hunk Anderson.* North Hollywood, CA: Panoply, 2006.

Lahman, Sean. *The Pro Football Historical Abstract: A Hardcore Fan's Guide to All-Time Player Rankings*. Guilford, CT: Lyons, 2008.
Lamb, Dick, and Bert McGrane. *75 Years with the Fighting Hawkeyes*. Dubuque: Iowa Athletic Department, 1964.
Levy, Alan H. *Tackling Jim Crow: Racial Segregation in Professional Football*. Jefferson, NC: McFarland, 2003.
MacCambridge, Michael. *America's Game: The Epic Story of How Pro Football Captured A Nation*. New York: Anchor, 2004.
_____, ed. *ESPN College Football Encyclopedia: The Complete History of the Game*. New York: ESPN, 2005.
Maly, Ron. *Tales from the Iowa Sidelines*. Champaign, IL: Sports, 2003.
Maxwell, Michael. *The 50 Greatest Plays in Iowa Hawkeyes Football History*. Chicago: Triumph, 2008.
Maxymuk, John. *Uniform Numbers of the NFL: All-Time Rosters, Facts, and Figures*. Jefferson, NC: McFarland, 2005.
McCallum, John D. *Big Ten Football Since 1895*. Radnor, PA: Chilton, 1976.
Michael, Paul. *Professional Football's Greatest Games*. Englewood Cliffs, NJ: Prentice-Hall, 1972.
Neft, David S., Richard M. Cohen, and Rick Korch. *The Football Encyclopedia: The Complete, Year-By-Year History of Professional Football from 1892 to the Present*. New York: St. Martin's, 1991.
Nelson, David M. *The Anatomy of a Game: Football, the Rules, and the Men Who Made the Game*. Newark: University of Delaware Press, 1993.
Palmer, Pete, et al., eds. *The ESPN Pro Football Encyclopedia*. New York: Sterling, 2006.
Peterson, James Andrew. *Slater of Iowa*. Chicago: Hinckley and Schmitt, 1958.
Peterson, Robert. *Only the Ball Was White: A History of Legendary Black Players and All-Black Professional Teams*. Englewood Cliffs, NJ: Prentice-Hall, 1970.
Piascik, Andy. *Gridiron Gauntlet: The Story of the Men Who Integrated Pro Football in Their Own Words*. Lanham, MD: Taylor Trade, 2009.
Roberts, Howard. *The Big Nine: The Story of Football in the Western Conference*. New York: Van Rees, 1948.
_____. *The Story of Pro Football*. Chicago: Rand McNally, 1953.
Ross, Charles K. *Outside the Lines: African Americans and the Integration of the National Football League*. New York: New York University Press, 2001.
Silag, Bill, ed. *Outside In: African American History in Iowa, 1838–2000*. Des Moines: State Historical Society of Iowa, 2001.
Stump, D.W. *Kinnick: The Man and the Legend*. Iowa City: University of Iowa Press, 1975.
Thomas, Ron. *They Cleared the Lane: The NBA's Black Pioneers*. Lincoln: University of Nebraska Press, 2002.
Tunnell, Emlen, and Bill Gleason. *Footsteps of a Giant*. Garden City, NY: Doubleday, 1966.
Turnbull, Buck. *Stadium Stories: Iowa Hawkeyes*. Guilford, CT: Globe Pequot, 2005.
Wallace, Francis. *Knute Rockne: The Story of the Greatest Football Coach Who Ever Lived*. Garden City, NY: Doubleday, 1960.
_____. *The Notre Dame Story*. New York: Rinehart, 1949.
Whittingham, Richard. *What a Game They Played: An Inside Look at the Golden Era of Pro Football*. Lincoln: University of Nebraska Press, 2001.
Wieting, Stephen G., ed. *Sport and Memory in North America*. London: Frank Cass, 2001.
Wilson, Kenneth L., and Jerry Brondfield. *The Big Ten*. Englewood Cliffs, NJ: Prentice-Hall, 1967.
Wine, George. *Black and Gold Memories: The Hawkeyes of the 20th Century*. Iowa City: Iowa Athletic Department, 2003.
Ziemba, Joe. *When Football Was Football: The Chicago Cardinals and the Birth of the NFL*. Chicago: Triumpha, 1999.

Index

Aaron, Hank 165
Adamowski, Benjamin S. 168–170
adjusting goal line on field 96, 131
Akron Pros 96, 109, 189
Alcorn State University 179
Alderman Kells 143
Alexander, Archie 31, 32
Alexander, Joe "Doc" 79
Alford, Gene 135
All-American 1, 5, 6, 45, 46, 49, 50, 58, 68–73, 99, 103, 141, 163
All-American Football Conference 151
All-Big Ten *see* Big Ten Conference
all-pro 3, 6, 7, 88, 93, 95, 99, 101, 108–110, 114, 117, 124, 131, 136, 151, 186–189
all-time All-American 132, 144, 147, 152, 155
Almond, Governor J. Lindsay, Jr. 166
Ambassador A.A. 139, 194
American Association 143
American Football League 102–109, 188, 189
American Giants 139, 142, 143
American Negro Exposition 147
Ames College 18, 20, 22, 25, 38, 39, 48, 49, 51, 57
Anderson (Brown Bombers player) 143
Anderson, Eddie 63, 64, 100, 101, 104
Anderson, Heartley "Hunk" 61, 62, 64, 78, 84, 87, 85, 95, 160, 165; respect for Slater 1, 63, 72, 187
Andrews, Roy 97, 132
Anthony, "Bugs" 84
Arizona Cardinals *see* Chicago Cardinals
Armstrong, Johnny 83–93, 95, 96, 98, 100, 101, 103–106
Army football 40
Arnston, Neal 56
assistant corporation counsel 141, 146
assistant Illinois commerce commissioner 146, 147
Atkins, Clyde 165

Bachman, Charlie 34
Baker, Gene 162
Baker, Roy "Bullet" 113
Banks, Earl 161, 178
Banks, Ernie 8, 162, 164, 165, 172, 173
Barnes, George S. 166
Barnett, Jim 68, 69
barnstorming trip 94, 102, 138, 139
Barragar, Nate 139
Barrett, Edward 168
Barrett, Johnny 17, 20, 21, 29
Barron, Irving "Stub" 33, 165
Barry, Sam 61
baseball 83, 89, 103, 153
Basing, Myrt 97
basketball 42, 44
Beattie, Bob 124, 188
Becker, Fred 46, 48
Behman, "Bull" 121
Belden, Charles "Bunny" 128, 129, 133, 135
Belding, Lester 36, 39, 45, 49, 52, 53, 57, 63, 66–68, 70, 71, 75, 159, 165
Bell, Horace 145
benched 16, 91, 130, 131; *see also* Kansas City Blues/Cowboys
Benjamin, Wendell 146
Berrien, "Nanny" 16, 21, 25, 26
Berwanger, Jay 156, 158
Bethel AME Church (Chicago) 168, 174, 178, 180
Bethel AME Church (Clinton) 11, 12
Bidwell, William 123
Big Ten Conference 6, 13, 30, 33–35, 37, 42–44, 50, 57–60, 69, 70, 74, 92, 140, 141, 146, 147, 164, 176, 181; All-Big Ten 5, 41, 49, 57, 58, 70, 178; Big Ten title 5, 35, 39, 41, 49, 69, 70, 73, 159
Blair, Jimmy 179
Blinkinsop, Ray 21
Block, Lawrence 23, 52, 55
blocked kicks 27, 37, 43, 48, 78, 119, 129
Bloodgood, Al 98
Blueitt, Napoleon 82
Blueitt, Virgil 23, 82
Blumer, Herb 130
Bolton, Judge John F. 154, 168
Bowen High School 17, 18
Bowlby, Arch H. 83, 84, 87–89, 93, 95–99, 102–104
boxing 33, 59, 75, 83

Boyd, Bill 125, 129, 130, 133
Boyd, Marshall 48
Boyd, Willard L. 181, 182
Boyle, Judge Samuel 177
Boyle, Sarah Patton 172
Bradley, Harold, Jr. 115, 161
Bradley, Harold, Sr. 115, 116, 146
Bradley, Omar Nelson 39–41
Bradshaw, Wes 103, 105, 106
Branch, Foster 139
Brands, E.G. 88
Brandt Florals 143
Brigham, Leon 49
Bright, Johnny 158
Brightmire, Willis 46
Brindley, Walt 79
Brooklyn Dodgers 133
Brooklyn Horsemen 106, 107
Brooks, Rick 179
Brown, Paul 1
Browning Field 103, 104
Brumbaugh, Carl 131, 136
Buck, Cub 46
Bud Billiken parade 155
Buffalo Bisons 119
Burch (referee) 39
Burley, Dan 166
Butler, Sol 1, 82, 84, 86, 87, 89, 90, 105, 109, 110, 116, 138, 143
Byers, Bill 57
Byrer, Lew 137

Cain, Carl 161
Calumet Stars 142, 143
Camp, Walter 50; 1921 snub 72, 73, 182, 184; trophy 180
Camp Dodge 39–41
Campbell, Kenneth 145
Canton Bulldogs 80–82, 86, 105, 109, 118
Carideo, Frank 139
Carideo All-Stars 139
Carlisle Indian School 20, 21, 89
Carney, Charley 54
Carroll, John 142
Carver, Roy J. 185
Carver-Hawkeye Arena 185
Carver Scholarship/Slater Award 185
Casteel, Mike 81
Cedar Rapids High School 18
Central College 36
Centre College 74

211

Index

Chamberlain, Wilt 173
Chamberlin, Guy 111, 160
Champaign (IL) High School 24
Chandler, Albert "Happy" 164
Chicago (South Side) 1, 7, 108, 118, 120, 133, 153–156, 162, 169, 171, 172, 175, 178; return to 6, 47, 100, 108–110, 139, 141; rough neighborhood 9, 10, 147, 156, 162, 171; youth 5, 9, 10, 108; *see also* law practice
Chicago Alumni Club (Hawkeyes) 156
Chicago Bar Association 170, 173
Chicago Bears 77, 78, 80–82, 84, 86–89, 91–98, 100, 102, 104, 108, 109, 111, 112, 114–117, 120, 123, 124, 127, 130–133, 136, 144, 145, 147, 148, 151, 152, 187
Chicago Blackhawks 116, 138, 139
Chicago Boy Scout Council 166
Chicago Brown Bombers 142, 143, 145
Chicago Bulls (AFL) 104, 105, 107, 108
Chicago Cardinals 4, 6, 9, 81, 85, 100, 101, 138–140, 142, 143, 151, 152, 161, 172, 186, 188; Slater as member 107–136
Chicago Coliseum 147
Chicago Comets 145, 146
Chicago Cubs 108, 173
Chicago (Harley-)Mills 116, 132
Chicago League of Negro Voters 166
Chicago Negro All-Stars 140; alternate name of the Chicago Comets 145
Chicago Panthers 147, 148
Chicago Sports Association 151
Chicago Stadium 131
Chicago Varsity Club 162, 178, 179, 185
Chicago White Sox 108
Choi-Settes Golf Tourney 172
Circuit Court judge *see* Cook County Circuit Court
City of Hope Medical Center 164; Sportsman's Award Dinner 171, 172
Civil War/slavery 9, 11
Claassen, Spike 152
Clark, Dutch 135
Clark, Kenneth 70
Claypool, Ralph 116
Cleveland Browns 1, 151
Cleveland Bulldogs 90, 92–94, 114
Cleveland Indians 133, 136
Cleveland Panthers 76, 105
Clinton County Bar Association 166
Clinton High School 4, 5, 76, 91, 121, 165, 184; Slater as member 13–31
Clinton Kiwanis 71
Clinton Legion 94
Cobb, Tom 132
Coe (Clinton player) 28–30
Coe College 35–37
Coffey, Helen 182

Coffey, Letha 182
College All-Star game 142, 145, 147, 148, 151, 164
College Football Hall of Fame 24, 26, 43, 156–158, 163, 176, 183
color ban/color line (NFL) 1, 6, 7, 110, 111, 116, 125, 140, 142, 144, 145, 147, 148, 151, 152
Columbus Park youth club 151
Comiskey, Charles 164
Comiskey Park 100, 107, 108, 118, 120, 122, 123, 127–130, 133, 165, 173
Commercial Hotel 160
Committee of One Hundred 172
Comstock, Rudy 113, 121
Condon, David 147, 176
Conzelman, Jim 77–80, 82, 86, 87, 100, 123, 126, 186, 187
Cook County Bar Association 160, 166, 172
Cook County Circuit Court 160, 173
Cook County Municipal Court 7, 153, 154, 156, 159, 161, 166
Cook County Superior Court 7, 31, 154, 166–169, 171, 173, 177
Corgan, Chuck 91, 98
Cornell College 18, 36, 37, 53
Cornell University 74, 145
Coughlin, "Roundy" 71–73
Craig (Clinton coach) 27, 28
Crane High School 30
Crangle, Jack 65
Creighton, Milan 133, 136
Crisler, Fritz 47, 48
Crusinberry, James 74
Cubs Park *see* Wrigley Field
Cuff, Ward 186
Cummins, Tait 4, 155, 156
Curtis, Joe 46

Daley, Mayor Richard M. 164, 165, 168–171, 177, 178
Daly, Dan 8, 188
Daniels, Arlington 146
Dartmouth College 81
Davenport High School 19, 22, 23, 28, 29, 80
Davis, Corneal A. 164, 168
Davis, Edward L. 177
Davis, Frederick Slater 182
Davis, Parke 74
Davis, Walter S. 161
Davis, William McKinley "Deacon" 161
Dawson, William L. 164
Dayton Triangles 80, 81, 90, 91, 95, 112, 116, 117, 122, 187
Debs, Eugene 11
DeClerk, Frank 87
DeKalb High School 16
Del Prado Hotel 150
Democratic Party 145, 147, 153, 154, 156, 170, 171
Dempsey, Jack 73, 142
Denfield, Gilbert 48, 49
Des Moines Comets 143, 145, 147, 148
Detroit Lions 100, 135, 142

Detroit Panthers 96, 100
Detroit Pioneers 147
Devine, Aubrey 15, 24–26, 43, 45–49, 53–57, 60, 62–75, 77, 93, 150, 156, 159, 165, 181
Devine, Glenn 24, 26, 43, 47, 49, 53, 69, 71, 75, 159, 165
Dewey, Thomas 154
DeWitz, Rufe 109
Diehl, Wally 121
Dilweg, LaVern "Lavvie" 122, 125, 129, 134
Dixie Classic 74
Dobson, Paul 43
Doby, Larry 8, 164
Doherty, Bill 179
Donaldson, W.A. 147
Donnelly (Clinton player, 1915) 28, 29
Donnelly, Bill 18, 38
Donoho, Jack 131
Douglas, Sen. Paul 156
Douglas Park 77–81, 87, 89, 90, 92, 93, 95, 96, 99
Douglass High School 140
Drake Relays 59
Drake Stadium 25
Drake University 158
Driscoll, John "Paddy" 33, 34, 45, 46, 101, 109, 111, 115, 120, 131, 136, 154, 186
Dubuque College 28
Dubuque High School 23, 24
Duffield, Marshall 138
Duffield Coast Stars 138
Duke Slater Award (University of Iowa) 179, 185
Duke Slater exhibit 184
Duke Slater Scholarships (University of Iowa) 179, 185
Duluth Eskimos 118, 128
Duluth Kelleys 90, 93, 96
Dunn, Charles 25
Dunn, Joseph "Red" 113, 119
Dunn Field 93
Durant Stars 87, 88

Earp, Francis "Jug" 77–79
East Chicago Gophers 140
East Des Moines High School 24
Ebbets Field 133
Eby, Moray 35
Eckersall, Walter 25, 34, 35, 41, 43, 44, 46, 50, 58, 70, 72, 164
Edgewater Beach Hotel 166
Edison Park 148
education, emphasis on 13, 30, 31, 149, 158, 160
Edwards, "Big Bill" 106
Eglan (Iowa City player) 28
Elkins, Fait "Chief" 117, 119
emancipation 9, 11, 153
Englewood High School 16, 20, 23, 24, 26, 27
Erickson, Hal 100, 111, 115, 116
ESPN 187, 188
Evans, Bill 58, 71, 72, 164, 168
Evansville Crimson Giants 78, 100, 123

Evashevski, Forest 163, 166, 176

"Famous All-American trio" 95
fan favorite 8, 17, 71, 73, 81, 110, 138, 140, 142
Farmer, Lee 146
feet and shoes, size of 5, 15, 36, 55, 61, 118, 132, 147, 156, 165, 184
Fenner, Harold 122
Ferguson, Judge Henry C. 156
Ferlic, Frank 169, 170
first African-American all-star team 82
first African-American all-star team to visit West Coast 138
first indoor NFL football game 131
first NFL night game 121
first NFL preseason camp 118
Fisher, Robert 21
Fitzgibbon, Paul 134
Flaherty, Ray 124
Flanigan, Walter 76, 78, 82, 83
Fleckenstein, "Wild" Bill 117, 144
Fleischer, Bob 176, 177
Flenniken, Mack 127
Fletcher, Ralph 44, 53, 54
Fletcher, Robert 53, 54
Folwell, Bob 106
Ford, Adrian 106
Ford, Henry II 172
Fordham University 187
Fort Madison Prison 148
Foster, Leonard 177
Foster, Rube 164
Franck, Sonny 158
Frankford Yellow Jackets 105, 113, 114, 116, 117, 119–121, 128, 129
Franklin College 53
Franta, Herbert "Chief" 120
Fred "Duke" Slater Award (Chicago Varsity Club) 178, 185
Fred Duke Slater Trophy 179
Fredericksen (Clinton player) 17
Friedman, Benny 114, 124, 127, 129, 144, 151, 186
Fritz Pollard All-Stars 82, 83
Frost, Wilson 177
Fry, Wesley 104, 112

Galloway, Ledrue 146
Garvey, Hector 62, 78
Gavin, Buck 78, 79, 89, 90, 92, 95
gentlemanly nature *see* sportmanship
Georgia Tech 20
Giaver, Bill 85, 86, 88–90
Gilbert, Wally 93, 96
Gillespie, Dizzy 165
Gillies, Fred 108, 109, 111, 115, 143, 172
Gipp, George 61, 164
Glanton, Luther 162
Glatts (Clinton player) 17
Good American Awards 172
Gordon, Ed 141
Gordon, Lou 125
Gordon, Walter 141
Grady, Al 4, 179, 184
Graham, Percy "Red" 47

Grambling College 163, 179
Grand Rapids Maroons 133
Grange, Garland 123
Grange, Harold "Red" 85, 102, 104–106, 109, 112, 113, 123, 127, 130, 132, 136, 152, 164; respect for Slater 106, 130, 131, 165, 187
Grant, Chet 64
Gray, Edward 50
Great Depression 140
Great Lakes Naval Station 33–35, 41, 45, 152
Green, Judge Wendell E. 153–156
Green Bay Packers 77–79, 96, 97, 112, 113, 116, 119, 120, 122, 124, 125, 129, 130, 132–136, 189
Greenwood, Glen 36
Grid Grad game 93
Grinnell College 37
Grouwinkel, Gary 165
Grubbs, Frank 48
Guyon, Joe 20, 21, 29, 91, 165

Hagerty, Jack 129
Halas, George 1, 34, 77, 84, 87, 88, 95, 144, 145, 147, 148, 178, 187
Hamilton, Milo 166
Hammond Pros 90, 93, 98, 109, 111
Harding, Hallie 138
Harlem Globetrotters 164
Harmon, Pat 155, 160
Harper, Lucius C. 153
Harris, Dud 126
Harris, Homer 141, 144, 146
Harvard University 21, 31, 73, 74
Hathaway, Russell 81
Haugsrud, Ole 118
Hawkins, Max 174
Hawley, Jesse 25, 32
Haycraft, Ken 120, 129, 130
Healey, Ed 77, 81, 82, 84, 87, 89, 95, 111, 188
Heisman, John 20
Heldt, John 71, 75
helmet, use of 1, 5, 14, 15, 30, 33, 55, 63, 64, 77; helmet toss 33, 63, 65, 68, 69
Hendrian, Dutch 95
Heneage (referee) 17
Henry, Pete 188
Herrity, Gary 4, 15, 26, 30, 66, 71, 161, 184
Heston, Willie 152
Hewitt, Bill 160, 186
Hibbing Miners 85
Higgins, Charles 47
Highland Park College 20
Hill, Charley 91, 98
Hill, Don 119
Hinkle, Paul 47
Hogan, Paul 111
Holbrook, Frank "Kinney" 31, 32
Holden, Albon 48
Holland, Jerome "Brud" 145
Holm, Tony 132
Homan, Henry "Two-Bits" 113
Hoover, Pres. Herbert 115
Horner, Gov. Henry 146, 147
Hornsby, Rogers 162

Hotel Des Moines 162
Howard, Sherman 1, 2, 4, 5, 139, 156, 160, 161, 178
Howe, David Ward 145
Howell, Ralph P. 31
Hubbard, Cal 125, 129, 188, 189
Hudson, Dick 82, 87, 109, 110, 138, 143, 162
Hughes, James L. 76, 79
Hughes, Langston 164
hunger strike 14
Hunter, Judge Robert L. 177
Hutson, Don 152, 159, 160
Hyman, Mervin 13, 157

Illinois Colored All-Stars 83
Illinois Rally for Civil Rights 173
Illinois State Training School for Boys at St. Charles 151
Indiana University 53–55, 57, 68, 74
Indianapolis Clowns 173
Ingwersen, Burt 15, 17, 18, 20, 22, 24–27, 30, 37, 38, 43, 44, 53, 54, 78, 157, 165, 172, 177
Iowa Athletic Association 19
Iowa City Blackhawks 103, 153
Iowa City High School 22, 23, 28
Iowa City Lions Club 71
Iowa Field 33, 35, 37, 39, 48, 55, 59, 60, 68, 75, 80
Iowa Field House 52
Iowa Hawkeyes 1, 3–6, 18, 25, 85, 104, 115, 140–142, 150, 152, 153, 156, 158, 161, 163–165, 174, 176, 178–18; Slater as member of 31–75
The Iowa Room 164
Iowa Stadium/Kinnick Stadium 180–182, 184
Iowa Tigers 89
Ironmen Memorial Scholarship *see* 1939 Ironmen
It's Sports Time with Phil Rizzuto *see* Rizzuto, Phil

Jackson, Levi 166
Jefferson, Bernie 145
Jefferson Hotel 33
Jefferson Jubilee 156
Jefferson Park Bulldogs 148
Jesse Owens Education Foundation *see* Owens, Jesse
Jeter, Bob 165, 166
Jetter, Margaret Culbertson 178
Jim Thorpe's Rock Island national champions *see* Rock Island Independents
jobs, part-time 13, 33, 52, 60, 103, 115, 139, 156, 177
Joesting, Herb "The Owatonna Thunderbolt" 120, 136, 159
Johnson, Dale 105, 109
Johnson, Fate 144
Johnson, George H. 95, 97
Johnson, Jack 70, 166
Johnston, Wayne A. 166
Joint Negro Appeal 170, 171
Joliet Devils 145

Index

Jones, Ben 111, 113
Jones, Calvin "Cal" 73, 161, 162, 178
Jones, Dr. David 118, 120, 122, 125, 126, 132, 133, 137
Jones, Elizabeth Stewart 178
Jones, Howard 32, 33, 35–40, 42, 43, 45, 50, 64, 68, 70, 76, 138, 141, 142, 152, 157, 159, 160; praise of Slater 6, 64, 71, 72, 150; psychology 61, 69, 150
Jones, Shag 143
Jordan (Keewatin player) 21
Joyner, K.C. 187
Judge Slater Apartments 179, 180

Kadesky, Max 71, 85–88, 168
Kansas City Blues/Cowboys 91, 92, 97, 98, 109; 1924 benching 91, 93, 94, 103, 129, 189
Kaplan, Ave 87, 105
Kappa Alpha Psi 60, 185
Kassell, Chuck 120, 121, 133, 134
Kaufmann, Robert 23
Keewatin Academy 19–21, 29, 30
Kelly, Bill 113, 117
Kelly, "Wild Bill" 36, 39, 40, 43, 52–54, 165
Kemp, Ray 140, 144
Kendsigdon (Keewatin headmaster) 20, 21
Kennedy, Pres. John F. 171
Kennedy, Robert F. 172
Kennelly, Mayor Martin 155
Kenosha-Hammond All-Stars 93
Kent, F.W. 62, 63
Kezar Stadium 139
kickoffs 81, 85, 90, 93, 95–97, 116, 117
Kiesling, Walt 187
Kiley, Roger 62, 64, 155, 165, 168
Killinger, Glenn 107
Kinderdine, George "Hobby" 122, 187
King, Dick 82, 83
King, Dr. Martin Luther, Jr. 172, 173
King's All-Stars 82, 83
Kinney, Leroy 52, 55, 59, 60, 75
Kinnick, Nile 3, 4, 146, 156, 157, 162, 176, 178, 180, 182, 186
Kinnick-Slater Stadium 181, 184
Kinsley Park Stadium 121
Kipke, Harry 164
Kirkpatrick, Jesse 37
Kline, Merv 15–17, 20, 22–27
Knight, "Whitey" 28, 29
Knop, Oscar 87, 88
Knox College 60, 61
Kohler, Robert 45
Kolls, Louis 83
Kotal, Eddie 116
Kraker, Joe 91
Kriz, Leo 71, 107
Kuehl, Waddy 85, 88

La Crosse Lagers 143
Lafayette College 74
LaFleur, Joe 78
Lahman, Sean 187
Lamb, Roddy 96–98, 100, 108, 113
Lambeau, Curly 77, 79, 96, 97
Lambert, B.J. 52
Lane, George H. 165
Lane Tech High School 23, 24
Langston University 171
law practice 118, 140, 141
law school classes 7, 31, 58, 70, 76, 95, 99, 103, 110, 115, 151, 158, 177
Lawson, Jim 103
Layden, Elmer 103, 156, 158, 165, 187
Leemans, Alphonse "Tuffy" 186
"A Legend in His Lifetime" 8, 178, 189
Lenox College 31
Lewellen, Verne 96, 112, 113, 116, 119, 120, 125, 132
Lewis, Loren Leland "Tiny" 128
Lewis, William Henry 50, 73
Lillard, Joe 138, 140, 144, 148, 151
"limbo of antiquity" 163, 189
Lincoln University 106, 139, 162; convocation speech 162, 163
Lintzenich, Joe 131
Little Twig, Joe 91, 92, 98
Locke, Gordon 52–57, 62–69, 71, 72, 74, 165
Lohman, Fred 34–36, 38, 39, 43, 45, 47, 49, 52
Los Angeles City Council 172
Los Angeles Rams 152
Los Angeles Wildcats 102, 103, 107, 108
Louis, Dutch 36
Louis, Joe 8, 55, 142, 143, 147, 151, 156, 164, 166, 172, 179
Louisiana State University 163
Lyman, William "Link" 34, 43, 82, 111, 127, 132
Lynch, Lorin 179
Lyon, George "Babe" 133
Lyon, Herb 178

MacDonnell, Mickey 113, 114, 119
Mack, Jerry 23
Macomb Eagles 145
Mahoney, Ike 100
Major League Baseball 73, 92, 108, 118, 135, 165, 173, 189; color barrier 6, 110, 149, 153, 165, 176, 187
Makeever, Carl 29
Malloy, Les 136
Marshall, Bobby 50, 73, 77, 85, 96
Marshall, Thurgood 164
Martin, Senator Thomas Ellsworth 59
Martineau, Earl 159
Mathys, Charlie 53, 97
Mavrias, Jim 52
Mays, Willie 8, 179
McBride, Jack 133
McCarthy, Vince 98
McClellan (Great Lakes player) 34
McCrary, Herdis 130
McGinnis, Ralph 22
McGrane, Bert 4, 156
McGuire, Charles 47, 48, 72, 165
McKalip, Bill 135
McKinley, Judge Mike 31, 58, 156, 160
McLain, Mayes 128
McMillen, Jim 65, 95, 165
McMullen, Dan 131
McNally, Johnny "Blood" 132
Memphis Tigers 130, 131
mentor, Slater as 1, 2, 52, 141, 146, 148, 152, 158, 161, 177, 178
Merrill Foxes 147
Metcalfe, Ralph 2, 155, 156, 162, 164, 166
Meter, Van 28
Michael, Paul 123
Michalske, Mike 112, 113, 117, 122, 125, 129, 187
Michigan State University 163, 183
Miller, Al 176
Miller, Glenn 71
Mills Stadium 147
Milwaukee Badgers 79, 80, 87, 94, 99, 100; Slater as member of 82, 86
Milwaukee Braves 165
Milwaukee Night Hawks 128
Minick, Paul 71, 104, 116
Minneapolis Marines 82, 87, 93
Minneapolis Red Jackets 119, 120, 122, 125
Minnesota Shift 38, 55
Misiewicz, Bill 184
Missouri Valley Conference 34, 73
Mr. and Mrs. John V. Synhorst Athletic Scholarship see Synhorst, John
Mohardt, Johnny 62, 92, 104
Mohr, Albert 43, 44
Molenda, Bo 122
Moline Indians 76, 84, 89
Mollison, Judge Irvin 155
Mooney, Cyril J. 15–18, 20
Moore, Judge Herman 155
Moran, Francis "Hap" 112, 129
Morgan Park mayor 145
Morrison, Harry 23, 25
Morrison, Richard 169, 170
Morrison Hotel 153
motivated by candy 24
Motley, Marion 173
Mount Glenwood Cemetery 172, 178, 179
Mount Morris College 22, 23
Mumford, Arnett "Ace" 162
Municipal Court judge see Cook County Municipal Court
Murphy, Edward "Nips" 18, 21, 23, 26, 28
Myers, David 125, 133, 140
mythical Iowa high school state championship 13, 14, 18–20, 22–28, 30

NAACP 151, 153, 166
Nagurski, Bronislau "Bronko" 127, 130, 132, 136, 152, 159, 187, 188
Nash, Tom 134
Nashville Silver Streaks 143
National Collegians/Nevers' All-Stars 139

Index

National Colored Democratic Convention 147
National Football League 1, 3, 6, 7, 9, 17, 24, 72, 75–78, 80–82, 84–86, 88, 90–96, 99–104, 107–127, 129–140, 142, 144, 145, 148, 151, 152, 161, 171, 176, 185–189
NCAA 6, 13, 58, 59, 74, 75, 159, 164
Negro Leagues 165, 173
Nevers, Ernie 1, 118–136, 139, 159, 178, 186, 187
New York Giants 97, 102, 113, 114, 124, 127, 129, 132, 152, 189
New York Stars 173
New York Yankees (AFL/NFL) 104, 106, 107, 109, 112, 113, 117, 151
New York Yankees (MLB) 95, 162, 165, 173
Newark Bears 106, 107
Newark Tornadoes 126
Nichols, Sid 24–26
nickname "Duke" 10, 150
Nile Kinnick Memorial Scholarship *see* Kinnick, Nile
1900 Iowa Hawkeyes football team 35, 36, 41, 69
1920 Olympic Games 51, 52, 84
1920s NFL All-Decade team 188, 189
1921 NCAA Track and Field Championships 6, 58, 59
1925 NFL championship dispute 101, 108, 111
1931 USC-Notre Dame game 64
1938 Negro All-Stars 144, 145, 151, 194
1939 Ironmen 3, 146, 147, 174, 181, 185
1941 Negro All-Stars 151
1942 Big Ten track and field championships 146
Nixon (Davenport coach) 23, 29
Nixon, President Richard 172
Noble, Dave 105
Nocera, John 165
Normal Field 9, 80, 108, 112, 113, 116, 118, 161
Northrop Field 45
Northwest Professional Football League 143
Northwestern (IL) College 20
Northwestern University 34, 35, 39, 41, 45, 46, 51, 55, 57, 69, 70, 74, 140, 141, 145, 150
Norton, Marty 97
Notre Dame University 1, 34, 61–65, 72–74, 78, 83, 92, 100, 103, 130, 139, 146, 150, 152, 155, 162, 165, 184
Novak, Eddie 95, 98, 105

Oak Park High School 17–20
O'Brien, Chris 108, 111, 112, 114, 116–118
O'Brien, Willis "Fat" 18
O'Dea, Pat 68
O'Dell, Bob 158
O'Donnell, John 160
Oelwein High School 160
official, Slater as football 139, 142, 145
Ohio State University 69, 70, 163
Omaha Olympics 85, 86
on-field play calling 47, 55
One-Man-Line 160, 187
onside punt 44, 49, 53, 55; execution of 43, 44
Orange Tornadoes 124
Order of Eastern Star 172
Oregon State University 164
Osborne, Clinton M. 15–21, 25, 165, 168
Osborne Shift 15, 20, 22
Ottley, Roi 162
overlooked legacy 3–5, 8, 70, 152, 155, 184–189
Owen, Steve 97, 98, 113, 124, 127, 129, 188, 189
Owens, Jesse 2, 8, 155, 156, 162, 164, 166, 172, 173, 179; Jesse Owens Education Foundation 171

Pacific Coast Conference 70, 74
Page, Harry 58
Paige, Satchel 179
Paine, Norman 57
Palmer House 9
Palmer School Arena 83
Panic of 1907 10
Pape, Oran "Nanny" 125
Parker, Clarence "Ace" 186
Parsons, Judge James B. 171
Paterson Panthers 143
Payne (Lane Tech coach) 24
Penn State University 74
Petcoff, Boni 188
Peters, Frosty 126
Petersen (Clinton coach) 20, 21, 24, 25, 27
Peterson, James A. 4, 11, 14, 17, 164, 165; tribute banquet for Slater 164, 165
Phelan, Robert 83, 86, 87
Philadelphia Quakers 105–107
Philbrook (Rock Island player) 16
Pittsburgh Pirates (MLB) 92
Pittsburgh Pirates (NFL) 140
Plansky, Tony 124
playing against multiple opponents 6, 46–49, 56–58, 62, 71, 72, 74, 78, 79, 104, 106
Pollard, Frank 82
Pollard, Fritz 1, 3, 4, 23, 50, 73, 77, 80, 82, 83, 85, 109, 110, 116, 138, 139, 141, 155, 162, 186, 187, 189
Polo Grounds 113, 124, 127, 151
poor/poverty/"rags-to-riches" 4, 7, 9, 14, 151, 161, 178
"Portias" 160
Portlock, Reverend J.A. 168
Portsmouth Spartans 122, 126, 128, 131, 132, 135, 136
Postville High School 160
Pottsville Maroons 101, 108, 111, 117
Powell, Adam Clayton 172
Prasse, Erwin 168
Presentation Day 112
Presnell, Glenn 132, 135
Princeton University 74
Professional Football Hall of Fame 4, 121, 125, 157, 186–189
Professional Football Researchers Association 4, 188
Progressive Party (Chicago) 153
Providence Steam Roller 121, 126, 127
Provident Hospital 172
Proviso High School 146
Pullman Panthers 132
Purdue University 6, 67, 69, 74
Pyle, Charles C. 102

quarantine games 36, 37
quitting high school 13, 151

Raby, Al 173
racial incidents 22, 25, 40, 48, 49, 55, 72, 73, 91, 94, 107, 130, 131, 139
Racine Legion 82, 89, 90, 92
Racis, Frank 127
receiving 85
recruiter, Slater as 2, 7, 141, 146, 152, 156, 158, 161, 176, 178, 181
Reed, Ronald 35, 36
Regnier, Pete 45
Rice, Grantland 71, 74, 103, 118
Rickey, Branch 164
Rienow, Robert 182
Rienow Hall II *see* Slater Hall
Riley, Mike 158, 161
Ringwood Park 16, 17, 29, 30, 80
Ritt, Bill 133
Rizzuto, Phil 173, 178; *It's Sports Time with Phil Rizzuto* 177
Roach, Rollin 111
Robert S. Abbott Awards 164
Robertson, Oscar 173
Robeson, Paul 1, 50, 73, 77, 80, 82, 83, 139, 166
Robinson, Eddie 163, 179
Robinson, Frank 164
Robinson, Jackie 6, 8, 153, 164–166, 172, 173, 179, 187
Roby, Doug 85
Rochelle High School 16
Rochester Jeffersons 79, 85, 100
Rock Island Football Club Northland bus 102, 105, 107
Rock Island Green Bush 133
Rock Island High School 16, 17, 27, 28, 84
Rock Island Independents 4, 6, 24, 129, 133, 165; Slater as member of 76–109
Rock of Gibraltar 187
Rockne, Knute 1, 6, 61–64, 72, 73, 157
Rodriguez, Kelly 129
Rogge, George 134
Rooney, Bill 93
Rooney, Cobb 93, 122, 128
Rooney, Joe 93
Roos, Babe 67, 68
Roosevelt, Pres. Theodore 13

Roosevelt Field 140
Rose, Gene 124, 126, 128, 129, 134
Rose Bowl game 41, 70, 74, 163–165, 172
Rosenfield, Walter 98
rushing 21, 23, 24, 27–30, 33–35, 92
Russell, Bill 8, 162
Ruth, George Herman "Babe," Jr. 73

Sabo, John 38
Saggau, Bob 158
St. Charles School 151
San Francisco Dons 162
San Pedro Longshoremen 138
Saperstein, Abe 164
Savoldi, Joe 130, 131
Scanlon, Dewey 118
Schmeling, Max 143
Schorling Park 82
Schrader, Gus 4, 180–182, 184
Schulte, Henry 43
scoring plays 23, 24, 27–30, 85, 124, 133
Searcy, V.A. 102, 103, 168
Second Baptist Church 11
Sengstacke, John 155
sense of humor 7, 15, 17, 18, 22, 34, 55, 63, 65, 118, 126, 140, 163, 164, 170
Seven Blocks of Granite 187
Shaw, Ed 86
Shelburne, John 82
Sheraton Hotel 172
Sherman Hotel 164, 170
Shevlin, Tom 150
shoes see feet and shoes, size of
Shuler (Davenport player) 29
Shuttleworth, Craven 69, 71
Sies, Herb 80, 81, 83–87, 90, 93
Simmons, Don 141, 143–147
Simmons, Oze E. "Ozzie" 140–142, 144, 146–148, 152, 162, 166, 177, 178
Simons, Obern 152
Sioux City High School 24, 26, 27
Sioux City Olympics 147
Slater, Annabelle (Phillips) 11, 182
Slater, Aurora (Hoskins) 11, 182
Slater, Etta J. (Searcy) 102, 103, 109, 145, 147, 149, 154, 156, 164, 168, 171–173, 178
Slater, "Big George" W., Sr. 9, 108
Slater, George W., Jr. 9, 13–15, 17, 110, 148–150, 154; ministry 5, 7, 9–12, 102, 149, 153, 160, 174; support of education 13, 30, 31, 115, 149, 158
Slater, Jennie (Graham) 11, 147
Slater, Letha C. (Jones) 9, 11, 151
Slater, Missouri 14, 149
Slater, Pauline 11, 172
Slater, Sarah (Venable) 9, 108
Slater Hall/Rienow Hall II 3, 182–185
Smith, Alfred E. 127
Smith, Fred 147
Smith, Ray 179
Smith, Richard "Red" 117
Smith, Russ 176

Smith, Wilfrid 109, 114
Snider, Art 154, 155
Soldier Field 112, 114, 144, 145, 173, 179
Solem, Ossie 141, 142
Sonnenberg, Gus 100
South Side Boys Foundation 156
Southeastern Conference 163
Southern California All-Stars 139
Southern University 162
Spanish influenza 35–39, 41, 51
speeches 7, 145, 151, 153, 154, 158–163, 165, 166, 168, 171
sportsmanship 2, 7, 61, 64, 65, 73, 84, 107, 110, 118, 127, 140, 147, 153, 165, 171, 177, 182, 183, 187
Spring Valley Wildcats 112
Springsteen, Bill 111
Stagg, Amos Alonzo 157
Stagg Field 51, 59
Stahlman, Dick 105
Stanford University 118
Stanley, Ivor W. 182
State of Iowa Sports Hall of Fame 156
Staten Island Stapletons 125
Stein, Bill 122
Stein, Russ 72
Sterling High School 28, 29
Sternaman, Edward "Dutch" 77, 78, 81, 84, 87, 89, 92, 95
Sternaman, Joe 77, 88, 94, 98, 104, 105, 107, 115–117
Stevenson, Adlai 155, 156
Stevenson, Ben 106
Stewart, Walter "Stub" 24
Stiehm, Ewald "Jumbo" 74
Stinchcomb, Pete 78, 81
Strader, Norman "Red" 112
Stratton, Governor William 164
Strode, Woody 151, 152
Strong, Ken 159
Student Army Training Corps (S.A.T.C.) 36–39
Sturgis Wildcats 125
Stuydahar, Joe 159
Sullivan, Ed 172
Superior Court judge see Cook County Superior Court
Sutton, L.F. 31
Swanson, Clarence 43
Swanson, Evar 94, 97, 114
Sykes, Joe 36
Synhorst, John 36, 39, 42–44, 185

tackles 16, 17, 24, 25, 29, 37, 39, 43, 48, 54, 64, 67, 78, 83, 95–98, 106, 109, 130
tackling, affection for 6, 10, 58, 64, 144
Tatge, Lou 54
Tatum, Reece "Goose" 179
Taylor, Marshall "Major" 178
Taylor, Sec 152
teammates, respected by 7, 25, 30, 49, 53, 60, 101, 104, 110, 118, 140, 165, 177
Templeton (Oak Park player) 17
Texas A&M University 74

Thanksgiving Day games 19, 24, 25, 30, 82, 93, 100, 108, 114, 117, 123, 130
third African-American college football assistant 141
Thomason, John "Stumpy" 133
Thompson, George 70, 71, 85, 101
Thorpe, Jim 20, 73, 89–94, 97, 99, 117, 152, 159, 164
Three League Park 23
timeout, calling for 36, 77, 104
Tinsley, Jess 128
Toledo Grills 147
Toledo Maroons 83
track career 6, 42, 44, 51, 52, 58, 59, 68, 75
Trafton, George 87, 95, 111, 160
Tri-Cities (Moline, IL, Rock Island, IL, and Davenport, IA) 16, 81, 83, 89, 90, 96, 98, 99, 102, 105, 107, 109
Trickey, Jim 46, 50
Trona Field 138
Truman, Pres. Harry 153, 154, 156
Trumbull, Walter 70, 71
Tryon, Eddie 106, 112, 113
Tucker, B. Fain 160
Tunnell, Emlen 152, 178, 186
Tunney, Gene 142
Turner, Clyde "Bulldog" 160
turnovers 17, 20, 24, 36, 54, 56, 57, 64, 92, 93, 95, 124
Tuskegee University 106
typhoid epidemic 21

Underhill, Marshall 39
Universal Stadium 132
University of California 70, 74, 141
University of Chicago 9, 25, 47, 48, 54, 182
University of Illinois 17, 37, 38, 41, 43–45, 47, 49, 53–55, 65, 66, 69, 72, 74, 78, 85, 152, 165, 172
University of Iowa College of Engineering 32
University of Iowa College of Law 31, 58, 115
University of Iowa College of Liberal Arts 58
University of Iowa College of Medicine 185
University of Minnesota 38, 42, 45, 46, 51, 55–57, 67, 68, 72–74, 141, 145, 159
University of Missouri 32
University of Nebraska 34–36, 43, 72, 73
University of Nebraska–Omaha 149
University of Nevada 1
University of Phoenix Stadium 186
University of Pittsburgh 80
University of South Dakota 45
University of Southern California 64, 138, 150
University of Washington 172, 174
Urban League of Chicago 179
Uriell, Frank H. 171
Ursella, Rube 85, 89–94, 96–98

Index

Valley Junction Independents 109
Vandever, Bobby 147, 148
Vaughan, Sarah 165
Vorwick, Billy 22, 23, 25, 26
Voss, Tillie 79, 83

Wabash Avenue court 162
Walker, Battling 83
Walker, James C. 46
Walker, James J. 146, 152
Wallace, Francis 64
Wallace, Henry A. 147
Walquist, Laurie 37, 43, 44, 53, 54, 98, 116, 165
Ward, Willis 166
Warner, Glenn Scobey "Pop" 132
Washington, Kenny 147, 148, 151, 152
Washington & Jefferson College 72, 74
Washington Park youth club 151
Waterloo Rotary Club 71
Watson, Jack 51
Waukegan Collegians 147
Weir, Ed 188
Weisensee, John 75
Weller, Raymond "Bub" 108, 109, 112, 113
Welsh, Bud 28
Wesley Memorial Hospital 174, 175
West, Emerson "Pony" 36, 37
West Aurora High School 21–24
West Des Moines High School 19, 24–26
Whisler (Rock Island player) 16, 17
Whitaker, John 142
White, Byron "Whizzer" 2
White, Stewart 48
White Sox Park (Los Angeles) 138
white teammates, restrictions on living or eating with 25, 32, 60, 149, 182
Whiteside, Larry 173
Whitfield, Mel 179
Widerquist, Chet 95, 100, 107, 122
Wilberforce University 139, 162
Wilkins, Eliza 182
Williams, Clyde 25, 46, 50
Williams, Henry L. "Doc" 38, 55, 56, 157
Williams, Jay Mayo "Ink" 77, 82, 90, 93, 109, 110, 116, 138, 139, 162
Williams, Russell 53
Willis, Bill 151
Willis, Ernest 18
Wills, Harry 166
Wilson, Eric 59, 182, 183
Wilson, George "Wildcat" 103
Wilson, Kenneth "Tug" 6, 164, 181
Wilson, Mike 92
Wilson, Nancy 173
Wilson Wildcats see Los Angeles Wildcats
Windy City Football League 143
Winkleman, Ben 86
Winkler A.C. 145
Winters, Manque 110
Woodbey, George 10
Woolpert, Phil 162
World Series 153, 162, 165
World War I 11, 33, 35, 38, 41, 48
World War II 41, 151, 180
Wright, Pat 33
Wrigley Field (Los Angeles) 139
Wrigley Field/Cubs Park 81, 87, 88, 108, 120, 132, 133, 135, 136, 152, 173, 177
Wroblewski, Sigmund 169, 170
Wynne, Chester 64

Yale University 32, 74, 150
Young, A.S. "Doc" 186
Young, Claude "Buddy" 152, 155
Young, Fay 146, 147, 161
Young, Lafe 57
Youth Foundation Program 162

Ziemba, Joe 4, 117, 130, 186
Zion Tabernacle Church 10
Zuppke, Robert 17, 37, 44, 53–55, 65, 66, 72, 157